★ BEST ★
LITTLE
STORIES
★ FROM ★
WORLD
WAR II

★ BY ★
C. BRIAN
KELLY
WITH
INGRID SMYER

CUMBERLAND HOUSE™

Published by Cumberland House, an imprint of Sourcebooks, Inc.
P.O. Box 4410, Naperville, Illinois 60567-4410
(630) 961-3900
Fax: (630) 961-2168
www.sourcebooks.com

Library of Congress Cataloging-in-Publication Data

Kelly, C. Brian.
  Best little stories from world war ii / by C. Brian Kelly.
      p. cm.
  1. World War, 1939-1945. 2. World War, 1939-1945--Anecdotes. I. Title.
  D743.K4 2010
  940.53--dc22
                                2010035660

Printed and bound in the United States of America.
VP 10 9 8 7 6 5 4 3 2 1

Other Books by C. Brian Kelly
And Ingrid Smyer

BEST LITTLE STORIES
FROM THE AMERICAN REVOLUTION
with "Select Founding Mothers" by Ingrid Smyer

BEST LITTLE STORIES
FROM THE CIVIL WAR
with "The Civil War's Two First Ladies" by Ingrid Smyer

BEST LITTLE IRONIES, ODDITIES & MYSTERIES
OF THE CIVIL WAR
with "Mary Todd Lincoln: Troubled First Lady" by Ingrid Smyer

BEST LITTLE STORIES
FROM VIRGINIA
with "The Women Who Counted" by Ingrid Smyer

BEST LITTLE STORIES
FROM THE WHITE HOUSE
with "First Ladies in Review" by Ingrid Smyer

BEST LITTLE STORIES
FROM THE WILD WEST
with "Fascinating Women of the West" by Ingrid Smyer

BEST LITTLE STORIES
OF THE BLUE AND THE GRAY
with "Generals' Wives" by Ingrid Smyer

BEST LITTLE STORIES FROM THE LIFE
AND TIMES OF WINSTON CHURCHILL
with "His American Mother Jennie" by Ingrid Smyer

*To the children—yours, ours, everybody's,
with the hope that they'll never have
to experience such a war.
But let us revere and never forget those who,
for the right reasons, did.*

CONTENTS

Introduction

Many among us today have forgotten. Too many simply don't know...don't really understand.

It may be a cliché to say so, but truly, World War II produced a million and one heroes. Beyond such figurative language, of course, it was a searing experience for millions upon millions of people, worldwide. It produced statistics on such gross and massive scale that they lose their humanity. They become mere numbers—20,000,000 Russians killed; 6,000,000 Holocaust victims; 326,166 Americans among the millions of Allied and Axis military personnel killed. The horrific figures roll off the tongue, pass by the eye, all too easily. How often do we visualize the people, real people, they represent? Each of the dead, each of the living caught up in the global storm—man, woman, or child—had his or her own place in this cataclysmic event we call World War II.

Many among us today have forgotten. Too many simply don't know...don't really understand.

Whether soldier or civilian, victor, villain, or victim, nobody who was there will ever forget it. For many—let's be honest about it now—it was the most exciting, the most gratifying thing that happened in their entire lives. But for so many more others, the most tragic. For millions, it was the end of life itself. For millions of others, it brought a change in lifestyle, outlook, occupation or location never to be undone. In this country for one, life simply would not be as before. The farm boy had seen the world. The women had zeroed in on their equality. Racial segregation was on its way out, albeit not there yet. The mobile society had arrived. Technology had triumphed.

Good had conquered evil...for the time being.

But at what cost! Far more, worldwide, than the twenty million, more than the other six million, far more than those two figures added together, but instead a total, both soldier and civilian, by any measure unprecedented in world history, a number now calculated at fifty or sixty million, but even then totally inadequate as an expression of the toll in pure human misery.

xiv ★ Best Little Stories from World War II

Among the changes, though, the once-isolationist, Depression-stricken United States of America suddenly had become the ranking world power. A savior to the civilized world from modern barbarism too!

It is amazing to look back now, going on a century later…and to remember how different we were. Among military men, majors and colonels in their twenties! Teenagers flying fighter planes against fellow young people on the opposing side. Innocent civilians of all ages, all sides, both genders, under the gun, the bomb, the artillery barrage.

As a kid, lucky for me, but wide-eyed with wonder anyway, my closest brush with it all was looking out to sea from Palm Beach, Florida, and seeing the sudden, lightninglike blink of distant naval guns or torpedo hits just off the coast. Or finding the oil-covered debris on the beach a day or so later. In New England a year later, alternatively, it was collecting for the scrapmetal drives or gathering milkweed pods for the life jackets our sailors and merchantmen needed to survive even more torpedo hits somewhere out there in a still-teetering world.

Later, not quite at war's end, I began to peck out newspaper stories from the front on my mother's typewriter, recopying the news of the war.

One April afternoon, I went to the movies. I came out to unusually quiet, subdued streets. It was FDR…dead. FDR, president since 1933…because I was born after that, he was the only president I had ever known. Then, more happily, just weeks later, came V-E Day, followed in late summer by V-J Day!

Suddenly, it was all over. Life moved on. For the still-living, that is. Home folk and veterans picked up their pieces and went their many ways.

But…what a generation! Just consider: among the veterans, Dwight D. Eisenhower, John F. Kennedy, Richard M. Nixon, Gerald Ford, Ronald Reagan, George H.W. Bush…each of whom became president of the United States. And so many others who contributed to society in myriad ways…and more who led quiet, more mundane lives.

In time, I became a newspaper reporter. And later than that, editor of *World War II* and *Military History* magazines.

Vicariously speaking, the war wasn't behind me after all. In my magazine role, not too surprisingly, I kept running into amazing, moving, LITTLE stories from World War II. Odd things, terrible things, brave things that happened to people in the war, people great and "small."

In 1989, rather than see these stories simply disappear, I thought: Why not gather them all together between two covers as a more lasting record, as a book? My mother, Claire Burke, my future wife (and collaborator on future books) Ingrid Smyer, and I took a chance on that dream. We self-published the first edition of *Best Little Stories from World War II*, a collection of 101 short narratives based upon a variety of sources.

Imagine our gratification as our "little" book, just over two hundred pages, kept selling...and selling! First thing we knew, we had gone through eight editions and sold more than thirty-five thousand copies!

All the time, though, I kept finding more and more stories I wanted to add to the original, many of them additional pieces I had written for the two magazines, often as Best Little Stories columnist (and editor emeritus) for *Military History* alone.

At this stage, I owe the Cowles History Group in Leesburg, Virginia, former publisher of *World War II* and *Military History* magazines, a vote of thanks for later allowing fresh publication between these covers of my additional stories that first appeared in one magazine or the other. Both the new stories and the old ones are part of this new, greatly expanded version of *Best Little Stories from World War II*, now consisting of more than 160 stories and a biographical sketch of Eleanor Roosevelt by my wife and fellow author, Ingrid Smyer.

Just as important, we owe another vote of thanks to Ron Pitkin, president of Cumberland House Publishing in Nashville, Tennessee, (now an imprint of Sourcebooks, Inc: Naperville, Illinois), for agreeing back in 1998 to publish my *World War II* book in its expanded form.

At this stage, too, as I review, edit, and ponder the stories before me...as I think back to those days of Palm Beach hotels populated by Army Air Corps trainees, rather than tourists, of those nighttime explosions out to sea, one thought keeps coming back to me, back to me again and again...that what this book effort amounts to, in my own small but thankful way, is tribute to a passing generation...to those often-incredible men and women who either fought or endured, sometimes both, through that terrible conflict we call World War II.

Don't we all...still owe them all?

★★★

Charlottesville, Virginia
C. Brian Kelly
January 1998
and summer 2010

Prologue

WHAT IF? YOU MAY ASK. And indeed you should, we should. What if this man, beyond all others, had not repeatedly escaped death on the western front during World War I? This messenger man.

Such dedication! Such sacrifice! Such selfless heroics!

Lowly in rank, self-effacing, he was a runner for his regiment. That meant trotting, sometimes sprinting, or crawling, through shot and shell while carrying dispatches from headquarters behind the lines—sometimes a mile or so—up to the very front trenches. In one battle, the regiment began with a full complement of three thousand men. It departed the battlefield with five hundred still able to fight another day.

Once again, our hero emerged without a scratch, despite duty so dangerous that two men would go on a message errand at a time—the assumption being that one would be killed on the way.

"By all accounts he was a good soldier: cautious, sensible, quite fearless. He won every medal and decoration available...but never rose above the rank of corporal and never applied for a promotion," noted biographer Robert Payne.

He once wrote a friend about his job as a dispatch runner: "In Wytschaete during the first day of the attack three of us eight dispatch runners were killed, and one was badly wounded."

There are those same odds again—one of every two runners eliminated! Not always true, not in every battle, one could say, but then, what is the equation for any one man when the number of battles goes up, up...and up?

In any case, in the same action at Wytschaete, the officers were debating how to reward their brave dispatch runners. Four company commanders were summoned to the headquarters dugout. "That meant that the four of us [messengers] had to step out. We were standing some distance away about five minutes later when a shell slammed into the dugout..."

What if! Just five minutes', or just a few yards' difference. The world will never know.

The shell wounded the regiment's Lieutenant Colonel Englehardt while also killing or wounding all of his staff. Years later, our hero's same Colonel Englehardt would recall that the young dispatch runner and another enlisted man, an orderly, had positioned themselves in such a way as "to protect me with their bodies from the machine-gun fire to which I was exposed."

Another time, the dispatch runner was asked to cross ground so heavily covered by machine-gun fire that he was promised another medal for valor simply for undertaking such a suicidal-appearing mission! He did it, and he did add the latest decoration to his list of awards and medals.

Always running, darting, dashing.

He would not pass through four years on the front totally unscathed, it must be acknowledged. At the Somme in 1916, he was sitting in a dugout with eleven or twelve fellow soldiers. A shell fell among them. Four men killed outright, six "hideously wounded." Our man? A shrapnel injury to the face. It was minor enough to allow him to stay at the front. The war, after all, was his life.

Just days later he volunteered for an especially risky-looking message run during an enemy artillery barrage. Typically, two men were sent…our man this time was not the lucky runner who got through.

But he wasn't killed, either. *What if?* Downed by a shell fragment that struck his upper left leg, he was sent home for recuperation.

Just a few months later he was back at the front—and disturbing the sleep of his friends in the trenches by stabbing the hated, pervasive rats with his bayonet.

The war proceeded.

In March of 1918, his unit starving for supplies of all kinds in a heavily shelled sector, he and a companion crawled out from the trenches one night in search of food and water. The friend cut a chunk of meat from the hindquarters of a dead horse, and our hero filled a gasoline can with water he found in a shell hole. They carried both treasures back to their comrades in the trenches.

Then, in October of 1918, came the great gas attack, not far from Ypres, Belgium. It was chlorine sent wafting among the trenches in artillery shells that landed from eventide until midnight. The men in the trenches wore gas masks, but they were primitive devices at best.

Our man, eyes burning, set off with a dispatch the next morning, about seven o'clock. It was to be his last run…the gas had gotten him, and two days later, he lay, spent, in a hospital bed—"totally blind."

Fortunately for him, the doctors had dealt with chlorine before. It was the war's "most deadly gas," and its victims could convulse and die within minutes. They also could suffer permanent blindness. Our man, an aspiring artist of sorts before the war, "was one of the lucky few who survived without much lasting damage."

His life did change, though. "The pain in the eyeballs passed away, and within a week he was able to distinguish dim shapes. As he lay in the hospital bed, it occurred to him that he would never be able to paint again, and in fact, except for a few sketches, he never did."

He suffered depression, sometimes turning his face to the wall and speaking to no one. He appeared to recover, but at first it was to resume the same old aimless existence that had characterized his life before the war. Home again, he acted as an informer for his defeated country's army, first infiltrating and reporting on Bolsheviks, then on a small, grassroots workers party.

And who knows what might have developed if he hadn't been sent to inform for the army about that same tiny political splinter? As it was, some unpredictable demon at last came to the fore in our "selfless hero"…as he took over the party himself, as it then grew under his ruthless direction and took over his country, as his ruthless country then re-armed and took over much of adjoining Europe.

What if? What if our deeply disturbed "messenger" had not escaped so many close calls and repeated dangers during World War I? What if this man, beyond all others of his day and age, had *not* survived? This man, Adolf Hitler.

★★★

Based upon The Life and Death of Adolf Hitler *by Robert Payne (Praeger, New York, 1973).*

★ WAR AND PEACE ★
AT ODDS

Ambassador's Briefcase Purloined

ONCE UPON A TIME, IN a slow and seemingly peaceful era for America, a coastal steamer regularly plied the docile waters between Washington, D.C., and Norfolk, Virginia. Old-timers still say the overnight voyage was a delight. For young U.S. Navy Ensign John D. Bulkeley, though, it would be the beginning of his own personal war with Japan. Neither the Japanese—nor even the U.S. Navy, it seems—ever quite knew what hit them.

The twenty-four-year-old Bulkeley went aboard the Wilson Lines coastal steamer in July 1936. His ship, the cruiser *Indianapolis*, was tied up at the huge U.S. Navy base in Norfolk, and he was looking forward to an off-duty weekend in Washington and Baltimore.

Entering the dining salon that evening in his white dress uniform, Bulkeley was struck by the sight of four Japanese, all well dressed, sitting at one of the tables. A steward told the curious young officer that one of them was the Japanese ambassador to the United States. To Bulkeley, the other three looked very much like military officers in mufti, or civilian clothes.

The steward also told Bulkeley the foursome often made the same round trip—Washington to Norfolk and back.

The young American's suspicions were aroused. Why would an ambassador spend so much time traveling to Norfolk? Didn't he have enough to occupy him in the diplomatic world of Washington? And why those three men of obvious military bearing as his frequent companions?

To Bulkeley, the answer seemed obvious enough. The naval base at Norfolk! They must be spying on the base and all the American warships that docked there. In fact, the briefcase so carefully kept by the ambassador's feet, even during dinner, must contain the most recent fruit of their labors.

Never one to waffle in the toils of indecision, Bulkeley made up his mind on the spot. He must get his hands on that briefcase!

He formed his plan as he watched the foursome through dinner, which for the Japanese meant the consumption, the copious consumption, of tea. Enough, Bulkeley said later, "to float a battleship."

Surely they would have to awaken during the night and use the common head—there were no such facilities in the steamer's small, individual cabins.

No one in official Washington was aware of the high drama that unfolded later that night as the young ensign from the *Indianapolis* posted himself at a vantage point on the deck near the ambassador's cabin and waited in the darkness.

For four or five hours, nothing happened. The coastal steamer by now had entered the Potomac River, her passengers peacefully bedded down—except for the waiting Bulkeley. Finally, about 4 A.M., the ambassador emerged from his cabin. Exactly as anticipated, he "walked down the deck toward the sandbox to heed the call of nature."

Exactly as planned, also, Ensign Bulkeley swung into action. "Moments later, I scrambled through the hatch of the Jap's cabin, grabbed his briefcase, and barreled back through the hatch."

Bulkeley slipped out of sight, toward the stern of the small ship. What next? Would the ambassador return, sleepily crawl back into bed without noticing the briefcase was gone? Or—? Unfortunately for Bulkeley, it was or. He did notice the theft. "He began screaming and hollering and raising holy hell. Then the other Japs joined in the screaming. The racket was so loud, they no doubt heard it in Tokyo."

Bulkeley again wasted no time. With the river shoreline dimly in sight on both sides, and still in his dress whites, he went over the rail and into the water. Sidestroking and holding the briefcase above the water, he plugged for the Maryland shore while the Wilson "liner" pulled steadily away, in the direction of Washington.

Minutes later, soaked shoes squishy from their bath, Annapolis grad Bulkeley was trudging along a dirt road with his precious cargo, the Japanese briefcase. Reaching a larger road, he managed to hitch a ride into the Federal City, which in those prewar days was well shut down for the weekend.

Bulkeley hid himself in a seedy hotel until Monday morning, the briefcase still his constant companion. And on Monday morning, he took a taxi to the U.S. Navy headquarters on Constitution Avenue. Safe inside, he found his way to an unmarked door that was Navy Intelligence. He knocked.

"Some old gent—he must have been 106 years old and going down for the third time—cautiously opened the door. He was stone-faced, and wearing civilian clothes. I found out later that he was a captain in Naval intelligence. He never invited me inside. Merely said, 'Yes?' and stood there while I told him of the events on the Norfolk-Washington steamer. Then I proudly held up the Jap ambassador's briefcase. The old bastard turned ashen—I thought he was going to faint. Finally, he asked my name, rank, and duty station, then slammed the door shut in my face."

Bulkeley was stunned. Before he could react, however, the door suddenly reopened, "and the same gent snatched the briefcase out of my hand, told me to report back to the *Indianapolis* immediately and again slammed the door."

Back in Norfolk, Bulkeley discovered that word of his adventure had traveled ahead of him. Boarding his ship, he was hauled before its skipper. The skipper said he didn't want to know any details and informed Bulkeley he was being transferred, right then, to the transport *Chaumont*. In twenty-four hours, the *Chaumont* cast loose its lines at Norfolk and sailed for Shanghai, China. Bulkeley was gone from sight of official Washington and the outraged Japanese.

The Japanese, though, would feel his sting again. Regaining a naval state of grace in Shanghai, he conducted intelligence against them there. Then, with war openly underway after Pearl Harbor, he commanded the tiny PT-boat "fleet" that harassed the invading Japanese in the Philippines—that also carried Douglas MacArthur to safety in his dramatic escape from embattled Corregidor.

He earned the Medal of Honor for his unrelenting gallantry and leadership in those waters; he continued his wartime commands in the landings in the Tobriand Islands of the Pacific (1943); at Normandy and on the French Riviera (June and August 1944). In all, the future admiral finished the war as one of the U.S. Navy's most highly decorated combat commanders. But he never did find out what was in the Japanese ambassador's purloined briefcase.

★★★

Based upon Sea Wolf: A Biography of John D. Bulkeley, USN *by William B. Breuer (Presidio Press, Novato, Calif., 1989).*

Inches from Death

"FROM THE BEGINNING HE AND I got along famously," wrote the one about the other. "Both of us were students of current military doctrine. Part of our passion was our belief in tanks—a belief derided at the time by others."

The man who wrote this statement commanded a battalion of America's new Mark VIII Liberty tanks, but the machines came out of the factory just too late to reach Europe before the end of the war—World War I.

A 1915 graduate of West Point, he was understandably unhappy at missing the big show. "I suppose we'll spend the rest of our lives explaining why we didn't get into this war," he complained. He also vowed, "By God, from now on I am cutting myself a swath and will make up for this."

He would, he did, but at that time, it was his colorful pal, a fellow U.S. Army officer based at Camp Meade, Maryland, who caught everybody's attention. Five years older, he was a twentieth-century swashbuckler famous for leading America's first tank corps at Saint-Mihiel and in the Meuse-Argonne campaign. He now, between wars, commanded the 304th Brigade's light tanks at Camp Meade.

These two had such a passion for their tanks in those interwar days, they themselves "stripped a tank down to its last nut and bolt and managed to put it back together—and to make it run," according to military historian Carlo D'Este.

Despite such familiarity with their charges, the two officers were almost killed by their peacetime tanks—not once but twice.

In the first such incident, a cable stretched tight from one tank to another abruptly parted with the two officers standing close by. The metal snake whipped past them at incredible speed…but fortunately didn't take their heads off.

Shaken? Absolutely. Wrote the quiet, younger officer of the pair: "We were too startled at the moment to realize what had happened but then we looked at each other." They *looked* and, said the younger, he was sure he was "just as pale" as his stunned compatriot.

Old friend Dwight D. Eisenhower pins a decoration on George S. Patton in North Africa, March 1943. (U.S. Army)

After dinner that evening, the older of the two asked, "...were you as scared as I was?"

Absolutely. "I was afraid to bring the subject up," the so-far untested younger officer told his companion. As the younger man also wrote many years later, "We were certainly not more than five or six inches from sudden death."

But there would be a second brush with death as they experimented with tanks in their small corner of the peacetime army. This time the older officer of the two, the flamboyant one, was firing a .30 caliber machine gun when it overheated, seized up, and sent its live rounds flying in all directions. Fortunately again, it was only another near-miss for the U.S. Army's two early tank experts—its leading apostles and advocates of the tank in that era too.

One, of course, was well known as the officer who had led the American tank corps in France during World War I. The other, his early role in the development of tank tactics largely forgotten today, was the man, wrote D'Este, who "established and ran the largest tank training center in the United States." That had been at Camp Colt in Pennsylvania during the last months of the Great War.

At Camp Meade in the years right after WWI, the younger of the two and the combat veteran, five years older (West Point, 1909), trained and experimented with their tanks on a daily basis. They played poker together twice a week, they were neighbors in base housing (old barracks turned into homes by dint of great wifely effort), they entertained each other and their respective family members...armed with pistols, they even drove up and down the highway leading to their base in hopes of encountering robbers who had been preying upon unwary drivers.

They never did run into the bandits, but they managed to develop—and protect—a core of expertise in tank tactics, despite explicit discouragement from an undermanned peacetime army strictly interested in infantry tactics. Both considered the tank to be far more useful than the doubtful auxiliary role the infantrymen had in mind. They and just a few other young officers "thought this was wrong," the less experienced of the pair later wrote. "Tanks could have a more valuable and more spectacular role. We believed... that they should attack by surprise and mass....We wanted speed, reliability and firepower."

During World War II, of course, the tank indeed would find such a role, most spectacularly as lead element in the German *blitzkrieg*, but also for the

Allies…especially for America's chief apostle of armor tactics, the combat veteran of WWI days.

While he in this new war became known as the American general the Germans feared most, it was the younger West Point graduate—and early tank advocate—who emerged as commander of all Allied forces in Europe, as mastermind of the Normandy invasion.

His old friend, the swashbuckler with ivory-handled pistols, for his part, achieved glory as commander of the armor-laden Third Army in its dash across continental Europe after Normandy, its rescue of American forces trapped at Bastogne during the Battle of the Bulge.

He also, almost as famously, was chastised by his younger pal for slapping not one but two hospitalized soldiers in Sicily, neither one of them wounded or physically ill.

Unhappily, he would die young, at the end of 1945, from injuries suffered in a traffic accident in Germany. "This is a helluva way to die," he said moments after the impact on December 9—paralyzed by his spinal injury, he lingered near death until December 21.

His old friend, fellow tanker and bandit-hunter of the interwar years, soon would become president of the United States.

George and Ike. Ike and George.

★★★

Based upon Patton: A Genius for War *by Carlo D'Este (HarperCollins, New York, 1995).*

Underground War

"ANYONE WHO STILL WORKS AGAINST Germany today is shoveling his own grave." The speaker, behind a cluttered desk at the Gestapo headquarters in Hamburg, was Inspector Paul Kraus. As a petty tyrant in the Gestapo's Foreign Division, he ran a "worldwide network of agents and man-hunters." He held life-and-death power over thousands who fell into Gestapo hands during the mid to late 1930s.

As Jan Valtin sat before him, routine calls would interrupt. Business calls… *Gestapo business.* A female aide, Hertha Jens, would take the calls and tell him.

Someone from a distant prison or bureaucratic cranny. Convict Meier has finished serving his sentence. What to do with him now?

Kraus would think and mumble aloud. Meier…Meier? What had been his alleged crime against the state? Oh, yes. That. How did he behave in prison? He "behaved" fine, it seems. "All right, let him go, he seems to have become sensible."

But not a man named Schultz. "Schultz?…He was a stubborn customer. We'll send him to Sachsenhausen. Put him on ice for another year or so." And so, "an anti-Nazi's fate was decided."

The fact was that Valtin himself had been a prisoner for four years, since 1933. He was both an anti-Nazi and a victim of the Gestapo; he was, in fact, an agent of the Communist Comintern headquartered in Moscow, and his apparent defection to the Gestapo in 1937 was only a ruse ordered by his Comintern superiors through a worldwide network of their own that reached even into the Gestapo's most tightly secured prisons.

Valtin, Kraus, the woman Jens, and thousands more, both inside and outside Nazi Germany…all, the cruel, the cynical, and the still-idealistic, were warriors in an underground, little-known war that raged between the rival Comintern and Gestapo for years before the outbreak of World War II.

For his own lifelong commitment to the apparently glowing panacea of exported communism, Valtin had been tortured, imprisoned, vilified, cut off from his family, threatened with death countless times, and forced to witness unspeakable brutality and the deaths of many others.

The cynicism and brutality, he was coming to realize by 1937, were on both sides in this unrelenting war. But Valtin kept such thoughts to himself even as he was released by the Gestapo and allowed to rejoin his *comrades* in Denmark, ostensibly as an agent for the Nazis but in reality still working for the Comintern and "feeding" the Gestapo harmless bits of information.

Valtin's disillusionment was still burrowing into his soul, undermining years of resolve, when, by chance, a key Comintern agent was captured in Germany by the Gestapo, a genuine Russian named Popoff. It was only a matter of time before he would give in to torture and talk. Valtin's communist colleagues laid plans to kidnap a key Gestapo agent and later propose a swap of the respective prisoners.

Valtin's role in the snatch could endanger his wife, still in Germany and under surveillance as a guarantee of his loyalty to the Gestapo. When Valtin mentioned this, one of the *comrades* said: "The Party comes first. We must rescue Popoff before he goes to the dogs."

The Party comes first! wrote Valtin later. *Mountains of wrecked lives are buried beneath that epitaph!*

The plan went forward. With Valtin's help, a Gestapo man called "Oskar" was lured to Copenhagen for a meeting. He was attacked in a side street, knocked unconscious, and carried off in a taxi driven by a Party member. A few days later, again knocked unconscious, he was carried aboard a Soviet steamer in Copenhagen harbor, the *Kama*. He was still aboard when it set sail the next morning for Archangel, final fate unknown.

Soon, Valtin broke with his comrades, was himself taken prisoner and held in a cottage outside of Copenhagen, his own final fate precarious in the extreme. ("I knew too much and had to be destroyed.")

After three weeks under guard in the seaside cottage, and about to be placed aboard another USSR-bound ship, he escaped one morning by setting the small house on fire and mingling with the crowd of onlookers who gathered outside. He hitched a ride to Copenhagen, where he dropped out of sight—a fugitive from both the Gestapo and the worldwide agents of Moscow.

In Germany, his hostage wife was thrown into prison, where she died. "Did she, herself, put an end to her life? Was she murdered in cold blood? 'The Gestapo never jokes!' Neither does it give explanations. Our son, Jan, became a ward of the Third Reich. I have not heard of him again."

★★★

Based upon Out of the Night *by Jan Valtin (Alliance Book Corporation, New York, 1941).*

Movie Show in Shanghai

AUGUST 21, 1937, WOULD BE American sailor Freddie John Falgout's twenty-first birthday. Stationed aboard the cruiser *Augusta*, flagship of the U.S. Asiatic Fleet, he would be spending that special day far from his hometown of Raceland on the Louisiana Bayou.

He and his ship were at exotic Shanghai, on Central China's Whangpoo River…but in the midst of fierce battle. Shanghai's celebrated Bund commercial center by the docks, its strip of prestige shops along Nanking Road, and its other allurements were not merely exotic, they were dangerous. Although the international sectors of the teeming Chinese city, sixth largest in the world, supposedly were exempt from the struggle between attacking Japanese forces and Chinese defenders, the frequent stray round did take its toll.

A stray Japanese shell killed three hundred civilians on Nanking Road shortly after the fighting began August 13, and another five hundred died in the Great World Amusement Palace when it was struck by an errant Chinese bomb.

The *Augusta* had arrived August 14, "Bloody Saturday," at Shanghai, as part of a flotilla dispatched to protect Americans and others in the city's international settlements. With Japanese warships deployed nearby on the Whangpoo, the *Augusta* and her men more or less saw the shells of the opposing sides whistle by, but with no harm done, for several days.

On the evening of August 20, the off-duty men of the American cruiser gathered on the well deck, protected by smokestacks and seaplane catapults, for the showing of a movie. Freddie John Falgout, on mess duty that day, was among the men who carried benches topside from the galley. The movie-showing was routine, a morale-boosting measure ordered by the skipper, Captain Harold V. McKittrick.

Freddie Falgout, however, had brought along a book to read until darkness fell in earnest and the movie began to roll. "Not far away, a Japanese gun crew fired 36-millimeter 'pom-pom' shells at low-flying Chinese planes."

One of the shells, its trajectory spent without a target found, fell at 6:38 P.M. among the American sailors, almost at Freddie Falgout's feet. The flying shrapnel struck nineteen men in all, but only one was killed—Freddie Falgout. And he by a fragment only the size of a dime—it struck him in the heart.

His widowed father heard about it in Louisiana the next day, from a neighbor who had heard on the radio about the American sailor killed in Shanghai. An official telegram then confirmed the news.

After Freddie Falgout's body came home six weeks later, more than ten thousand persons attended his small-town funeral on the Bayou—full military honors. How could they know? Later, another three hundred thousand American service personnel would die in World War II, but Freddie…Freddie Falgout, on the eve of his 21st birthday, apparently was the first American casualty of the entire war.

★★★

Based upon Douglas and Jan Baldwin in Military: The Press of Freedom, *Vol. IV No. 7, December, 1987.*

Monster Created

THE ONETIME CORPORAL WHO COMMANDED the generals of Germany during World War II, who very nearly "owned" them, body and soul, was in an odd and ironic way a creature of the military establishment's own making. As is well known, the Austrian-born Hitler served the German army in World War I as a lowly corporal. Living in Munich at the outbreak of war, he was allowed to join the sixteenth Bavarian *Landwehr* (Infantry) Regiment after petitioning the King of Bavaria for permission to enlist.

He was decorated for bravery in combat, earning nearly every available medal up to and including the Iron Cross First Class. He was wounded and, in October of 1918, was blinded by gas. At war's end, still assigned to his regiment, he found Bavaria in political upheaval, as was all of defeated Germany. In Bavaria's case, a socialist regime had taken over the provincial government, and Hitler's regimental barracks had fallen under the sway of a revolutionary soldiers' council.

Hitler himself wore the red markings of the revolutionaries.

Still a soldier, he voluntarily took on duties as a guard at a prisoner-of-war camp, but the POWs soon were gone, sent home. He stayed on in his barracks as Bavaria went from a socialist regime to a communist one, as a "soviet republic." Such a state of affairs was intolerable to both the shrunken, postwar German army and to closely allied private armies that had sprung up all over the politically unstable country. Often composed of embittered war veterans, mixed with street toughs, these Free Corps *(Freikorps)* tended to be right-wing in their ideology and of like mind with the tightly restricted military establishment. Awaiting them in Munich, entirely unknown, was their man of destiny.

At the moment, though, he was still a mere corporal and housed in a barracks controlled by members of a so-called Red Army. In May 1919, a combined *Reichwehr* (German army) and *Freikorps* force stormed Munich—and Hitler's own regimental barracks. Hitler was among those marched off as prisoners. He then turned informer, and on his word ten men were executed for their left-wing activities.

Still housed in the regimental barracks, Hitler now became a confidential agent for the *Reichwehr's* Munich Command, Political Department. His job was to monitor and infiltrate radical political groups. The assignment one night (September 12, 1919) was to listen in on a public meeting of a little-known rightist group, the German Workers' Party (DAP).

The meeting in a beer hall only attracted about forty persons and Hitler, unimpressed so far, was about to leave quietly when another onlooker rose to propose that Bavaria realign itself with Austria as part of a Catholic union. That stopped Hitler, a rabid pan-Germanist, in his tracks.

The impromptu rejoinder that he then heatedly delivered was a fateful one—the DAP fell all over itself in its haste to enlist Hitler as a member, while his *Reichwehr* superiors also hastened to insert "their" man in a potentially supportive right-wing workers' group. Even the WWI luminary General Erich Ludendorff was involved in the plans for the undistinguished corporal. He, the same man responsible for "inserting" the exiled Lenin into czarist Russia, proposed not only that Hitler should join the DAP, but also that he should strive to strengthen it.

Hitler, of course, carried out both "assignments" remarkably well. He gained control of the small DAP, which in time became the much more potent National Socialist German Workers' Party (NSDAP) which then vaulted him to command of Nazi Germany, with the generals then at the feet of their onetime corporal and political informer.

★★★

Based upon David T. Zabecki in World War II *magazine, July 1987.*

Street Fights and Bombs

BORN IN THE GERMAN PALATINATE on the west side of the Rhine, Gertrud Breier was about ten years old when she saw the first visible sign of the evils soon to visit her homeland. Her family and their close friends, the von Bassmanns, had walked to a fair in Ludwigshafen-Rhine, a pleasant two-hour trek from their own town of Frankenthal.

In their verdant province of vegetable fields and vineyards, such walks—or long strolls in the forest—were a common family activity. This one, in the early 1930s, would always stand out in Gertrud's memory.

"On the way home, on the outskirts of the city, some motorcycles appeared suddenly out of nowhere. The men asked everyone to step back....The men were in uniforms and their arm bands each had a swastika. I had never seen that symbol before, and I didn't know what it meant."

Moments later, a Mercedes convertible appeared, "and a lot of people on the street started to exclaim '*Heil! Heil! Heil!*'"

Dark-haired and dressed in a brown uniform, a man in the car "raised his hand to salute and the people cheered."

Gertrud's father turned to von Bassmann: "That is Adolf Hitler, the leader of the new National Socialist Party. What is he doing on the left [west] side of the Rhine River?" Von Bassmann, a Jew, said that was a bad sign, and the two men fell to whispering with one another.

At home that night, Gertrud's mother told her to forget the incident and described Hitler as a mixed-up man and troublemaker who had been in jail and liked to show off. At school the next day, Gertrud's teacher said not to talk about such a person, who belonged on the other side of the Rhine anyway. (By terms of the Versailles Treaty, the French had occupied the Palatinate after World War I; in the early 1930s, the French troops had left.)

Life in the Palatinate remained fairly tranquil for another two years or so, but momentous events were brewing. Gertrud's "politician" father was an advisor to German Chancellor Heinrich Bruening, and in 1932 Bruening was forced out of office, due in large part to pressures from the politically powerful National Socialists. Thereafter, Gertrud's father was a restless, "deeply worried" man.

Then, in January 1933, Hitler was named Chancellor. The effects, even in tiny Frankenthal of the Palatinate, were immediate.

"Street fights between members of different parties and violence in some of the factories disturbed our once quiet and peaceful old town."

With Gertrud's father now in hiding, Nazi thugs descended on the family home at bedtime, January 31. They ransacked the place, yelled at Gertrud's mother, shoved her around, and even kicked her. In February, the family was forced to move to a smaller house in Ludwigshafen, where Gertrud's father found a court job as an executor of wills. At her new school, Gertrud had a member of the Nazi women's league for a teacher. "She divided the class into two groups. One group she favored: the children of her fellow Nazi party members. The other group was very small: children like me from the good and silent anti-Nazi families. We were about eight girls; we sat at the right front side of the classroom. Since there were two Jews among us, we called ourselves the 'chosen elite.'"

Life in the Palatinate no longer was so tranquil: The von Bassmanns, being Jewish, emigrated to America. Most of the schoolchildren joined the Hitler Youth (but not Gertrud and her friends). Books were burned. Children had to attend Saturday classes on "nationalism." Parents became afraid of their own children as potential informers. "More and more people disappeared—presumably arrested just for being 'politically unreliable,' without any concrete proof."

Austria was annexed. Next door to Gertrud's family home, Jewish neighbors had their house burned and they themselves were taken away in a green police wagon (to be cremated at Dachau).

With the invasion of Poland on September 1, 1939, came, finally, The War. Soon after: "One small French aircraft dropped a few bombs on Frankenthal, my hometown and birthplace. The house that belonged to my mother's family for 300 years was destroyed."

With the war came a vigorous—and expensive—black market for food and other necessities. And, as time passed, more and more air raids. Finding shelter was a major concern—school children went to bed at night dressed and with a few key belongings beside them. "When the first alarm sounded, we would jump out of bed, run out of the house, and get to the shelter as fast as we could. Many a night's sleep was interrupted."

One time, Gertrud, a teenage girl by now, was caught in the country by an air raid. "I couldn't get to a shelter. I just didn't know where to run. It was during the day and I found a hole—maybe it was an empty water hole or a hole left by an uprooted tree. I threw myself in that hole as the earth shook and bombs fell and exploded all around me. People were screaming. When it was all over, there were wounded and dead people all around me—a horrible sight. I asked myself, 'Is that the promise the Third Reich made—the great victory?'"

Another time, Gertrud and her father were in a bomb shelter shaken as never before with explosion after explosion close by. It seemed endless, and near them in the shelter was a young woman with a newborn baby in her arms. She screamed hysterically. "The bombs kept exploding, and the mother squeezed her baby so hard that it died in her arms."

★★★

Based upon The Governess *by Gertrud Breier (Vantage Press, New York, 1988).*

War of Nerves

EARLY ONE AFTERNOON IN 1936, Werner von Blomberg, a tall, broad man in his early fifties, obviously was consumed with nervous tension as he walked his two dogs in Berlin's Tiergarten. An American correspondent who came across the German war minister noticed that Blomberg's face was white, "his cheeks twitching."

The same correspondent had seen Blomberg just a few hours earlier on March 7, 1936—at a historic meeting of the German Reichstag in the city's Kroll Opera House. Blomberg had been one of the men on the stage, and he had been nervous then, too, his fingers drumming in silent agitation.

Seated on the stage with War Minister Blomberg had been the rest of Adolf Hitler's cabinet; ranged in rows before them had been the six hundred deputies of the Reichstag, or national legislature.

Addressing them all was Hitler himself. At times speaking in a low, hoarse voice, and at others rising to a shrill, hysterical scream, Hitler announced the German occupation of the demilitarized Rhineland—his first military adventure as head of the new Nazi state.

It wasn't much of an adventure—only three German battalions actually crossed the Rhine in violation of the Versailles Treaty of 1919. But it was enough, quite possibly, to provoke a strong French reaction; enough, by Hitler's own confession later, to provoke the most nerve-wracking forty-eight hours of his life.

The *Führer* had no need to worry about the reaction of his rubber-stamp parliamentary body, for at the news of German troops on the march, the deputies sprang to their feet with wild cries of delight. "Their hands are raised in slavish salute," wrote William L. Shirer in his *Berlin Diary*, "their faces now contorted with hysteria, their mouths wide open, shouting, shouting, their eyes burning with fanaticism, glued on the new God, the Messiah."

Overnight, France did *not* mobilize in response. The crisis appeared safely passed—Hitler's first external coup. And at the State Opera on March 8, as the "New Germany's" leadership gathered anew for Heroes Memorial Day, a braver-looking General Blomberg delivered the main address in honor of the country's dead from World War I, twenty years earlier.

"We do not want an offensive war," he told his audience (and the world), "but we do not fear a defensive war." He dismissed "whispers" of the German army's poor rapport with Hitler's Nazi Party. "We in the army are National Socialists," Blomberg proclaimed. "The party and the army are now closer together."

According to the politically naive war minister, the Nazi revolution in Germany differed from history's earlier revolutions by "re-creating" the army, rather than destroying it. More than that, "the National Socialist state places at our disposal its entire economic strength, its people, its entire male youth."

In all, quite a responsibility had been placed on the army's shoulders. And the burden was likely to grow heavier, "because we may be placed before new tasks."

The last, as onetime Corporal Adolf Hitler led his nation and his generals into war with nations on either side of Germany, was certainly true, but Blomberg would not be on hand to take part. He had dragged his feet over the proposed Rhineland adventure. As it unfolded, he visibly blinked in fear. By chance, he recently had married a typist from his office. At first, Hitler had welcomed such a "democratic" romance. After the Rhineland affair, by odd coincidence, reports suddenly circulated that she had a past as a prostitute. Blomberg, for whatever reason, then became the first of many professional officers serving Hitler to be forced out of his entourage.

★★★

Based upon Berlin Diary *by William L. Shirer (Alfred A. Knopf, New York, 1941).*

"Inspection" Interrupted

OFFERED A THREE-MONTH CONTRACT to "inspect" China's fledgling air force in the spring of 1937, aviator Claire Chennault accepted retirement for deafness from a United States Army that was, itself, deaf to his theories of air combat. He was a longtime advocate of coordinated fighter tactics, but winners for the moment were the believers in the "invincible bomber."

Japan already was nibbling at China following the outright occupation of Manchuria in late 1931 and establishment of the puppet Manchuko regime in early 1932.

Retired Major Chennault boldly sailed into Kobe, Japan, aboard the *President Garfield*. He was greeted at dockside by a fellow American and former flying colleague, Billy MacDonald, who had arrived in China the year before as a volunteer instructor for the Chinese Air Force flying school at Hangchow.

"How is it an instructor in the Chinese Air Force can move about freely in Japan?" asked Chennault.

MacDonald had an obviously rehearsed answer—ready not so much for Chennault, but for the Japanese. "You're mistaken, Major. I'm an assistant manager of a troupe of acrobats. See, it says so right here in my passport!"

It seems that "assistant manager" MacDonald had left the "troupe" in Osaka and gone ahead to meet Chennault. "For the next few days you and I are going to be 'tourists'—like the Japanese tourists that wander around the U.S. Ever noticed them?"

Chennault nodded. Since he already expected real war between China and Japan, and then the same between the United States and Japan, he, of course, had noticed the Japanese "tourists" MacDonald referred to. "Especially around harbors and airfields," he now rejoined.

"We'll return the compliment."

And they did. For the next few days they traveled about Japan in a rented car, visiting construction sites, industrial centers, shipping facilities, and anything else that could be a potential bombing target. More than simply visiting, they also shot reels of photographs with cameras hidden under their coats.

If they were noticed officially, no one stopped them.

Four years later, with full-scale war raging, Claire Chennault found his own photos and notes on potential Japanese targets more informative and useful than like material supplied by the U.S. War Department.

His inspection trip in China shortly afterward revealed a woefully inadequate and unprepared air arm, but Chennault was unable to finish his three-month tour. He was at the Italian Flying School (for the Chinese) at Loyang in July when the Japanese used an incident near the Marco Polo Bridge outside of Peking as their reason for open assault upon China—with no declaration of war.

From Loyang, Chennault immediately dispatched a telegram to China's Generalissimo Chiang Kai-shek offering his services in any capacity the Chinese might like.

In two days, Chiang wired back: "Your voluntary offer of services grate-fully accepted. Proceed to Nanchang. Direct final combat trainer fighter groups there."

Chennault, for a time placed in charge of the Chinese air force, was thrilled at the opportunity to test his theories of air warfare in actual combat. More important, though: "I was convinced that the Sino-Japanese War would be a prelude to a great Pacific war involving the United States. I felt that the more I could learn about the Japanese and the more damage I could inflict in the early stages of the conflict, the better I would be able to serve my country eventually."

★★★

Based upon Chennault and the Flying Tigers *by Anna Chennault (Paul S. Eriksson, Inc., New York, 1963).*

Diplomacy Under Physical Stress

EMIL HACHA, SIXTY-SIX AND suffering from a heart condition, was not exactly a prisoner undergoing relentless interrogation, but he might as well have been.

He was, instead, the head of one state conferring with the head of a neighboring state—a conference in the wee hours of the morning that was more like a Gestapo interrogation.

In November 1938, as chief justice of Czechoslovakia's Supreme Court, he led a relatively quiet life outside the turbulent mainstream of prewar European politics. His safe isolation ended when his country's National Assembly named him to replace Eduard Benes as president.

That change, brought about by Benes's post-Munich resignation, meant that the failing Hacha would be the man to stand up to Hitler on behalf of a nation.

He was not up to it, but it could be said that he tried.

With German troops massing along the borders of Bohemia in early March 1939, he sought an audience with Hitler and was indeed "invited" to Berlin. He and his foreign minister, Frantisek Chvalkovsky, arrived in the evening of March 14, and were received with military honors.

The visitors then were summoned before Hitler at the unusual hour of 1:15 A.M., March 15. In the *Führer's* study at the newly built Chancellery, the two Czechs next were subjected to one of the most extraordinary browbeatings in the history of diplomacy.

Hitler; his own foreign minister, Joachim von Ribbentrop; Herman Goering; and General Wilhelm Keitel all were present for the merciless hounding, which went on for the next three hours. The two Czechs were told that their country was to be "introduced" into Nazi Germany's Third Reich, and they must sign documents of surrender or see Prague pulverized by bombing at daybreak... just hours off.

Hacha pleaded with Hitler that his people "have a right to live a national life." But Hitler and his henchmen were not to be appeased. In and out of the room at different times, Hitler himself warned them that for every Czech battalion attempting to stem an invasion, there would be a German division ready to overcome it.

By one informed account, the Germans pressed their two visitors brutally. "They literally hounded Dr. Hacha and Mr. Chvalkovsky round the table on which the documents were lying, thrusting them continually before them, pushing pens into their hands, incessantly repeating that if they continued in their refusal half of Prague would be in ruins from bombing within two hours."

The pressure, obviously, was unbearable. Hacha, resisting for hours, passed out. Revived by Hitler's personal physician, Dr. Theodore Morell, the Czech leader fainted a second time a few minutes later. Morell stabbed him again with a reviving injection of some kind.

In the meantime, a Hitler-dictated document had been hurriedly translated into Czech. At 4 A.M., Hacha finally signed, agreeing, for the sake of "calm, order, and peace in Central Europe," to place his country "under the protection of the German Reich."

Hitler was exultant at his first "conquest" of a non-German country (he already had taken over Austria and the Sudentenland).

Rushing into his nearby office, he exclaimed to the secretaries present: "Children! This is the greatest day of my life! I shall go down in history as the greatest German."

That evening, as his forces occupied Czechoslovakia, Hitler publicly announced: "Czechoslovakia has ceased to exist!"

Hacha, for his part, returned home as state president of the Reich Protectorate of Bohemia and Moravia, a puppet's role he would hold until his country was overrun by the Red Army at war's end. He was in a Prague prison when he died on June 27, 1945, his country soon to become a "protectorate" again, this time under Soviet dictate.

★★★

Based upon various sources.

War's First Battle

THE WAR IN EUROPE BEGAN with the German invasion of Poland on September 1, 1939. True? Not entirely. The first "battle" of World War II was fought—in Poland, to be sure—six days earlier. Moreover, the ultimate commander of the German combat team that fought the little-known Battle of Mosty in Polish Silesia on August 26, 1939, was a displaced admiral of the German navy, one Wilhelm Franz Canaris.

As any history buff knows, Canaris was chief of Nazi Germany's *Abwehr*, or military secret service. With the attack on Poland originally scheduled for 4:15 A.M., August 26, a Saturday, the admiral's *Abwehr* was supposed to send sixteen *Kampigruppen* (combat teams) into Poland twelve hours ahead of the German armies for a series of raids on Polish communication and transportation facilities, such as telephone lines or bridges. In other cases, the special K-teams were to seize and hold certain facilities intact for their own *Wehrmacht's* use.

Late on August 25, the teams were assembled and ready at their jump-off points—Canaris and his staff had done their homework and followed their orders explicitly. But an agitated aide from the chief of staff's office called to report that Hitler had postponed the invasion because of political developments. "You must do everything humanly possible to halt your combat teams," said the aide.

Fifteen of the K-teams were halted in time, but one, headed by Lieutenant Albrecht Herzner, already, irrevocably, was on its way. Herzner, striking out from a German base at Zilina in Slovakia, had been ordered to seize the railroad station at Mosty and secure the Jablunkov Pass in the Beskids. The rail line here ran from Slovakia, past Mosty, and on deeper into Polish Silesia. Following his original orders, Herzner positioned his team and gave the signal to attack. Opening fire at 1 A.M. on August 26, his K-group overwhelmed the Poles guarding Mosty, capturing the rail station and securing the pass as planned. The Germans then settled down to await the expected arrival of an entire invading division.

When no division appeared after a time, the young German commander approached the Polish colonel he and the K-team had taken prisoner. What's going on, Herzner asked, weren't the two countries at war? "I told you they aren't," the Polish officer replied. He suggested that Herzner call his home base on the telephone in the station house and find out the facts. Herzner did—and was told to return to Zilina immediately. The war had not started after all!

It was a ludicrous situation, but no joke. In the war that did start six days later, Herzner was among the millions of casualties. So was Poland, which collapsed in just twenty-seven days of assault by the new German *blitzkrieg*.

★★★

Based upon The Game of the Foxes *by Ladislas Farago (David McKay Company, Inc., New York, 1971).*

Eagle's Brief Flight

LIKE FIVE ORPHANS, THE SUBMARINES *Vulture, Wild Cat, Lynx, Wolf,* and *Eagle* had been cast into a hostile world, entirely on their own, with nowhere to go—not even home.

For them, home was Poland, and under the crushing weight of the German *blitzkrieg,* Poland was sinking from sight. All five boats of the Polish navy had been able to escape their base at Gdynia in the Gulf of Gdansk after it was struck by German dive-bombers at the onset of Hitler's Poland campaign (September 1, 1939).

While Poland's land forces reeled before the German steamroller, the five submarines roamed the nearby sectors of the Baltic Sea to do what they could in defense of their homeland, even if confined to their own watery environment.

Since the Germans sent few ships eastward into the Baltic, the Polish underwater flotilla found little action in its guard duty—specifically in Puck's Bay, which controlled the sea approach to Gdansk. The real action was provided by the wide-ranging *Luftwaffe,* whose deadly aircraft had to be avoided at all costs.

In only a few days, the home waters were swept clear of Polish surface ships, and on September 12 Gdynia itself was abandoned. "Only the five submarines remained to continue the war at sea," reported Edwyn Gray in *Submarine Warriors.*

For the orphaned submarines, however, continuing the war meant merely surviving, and one by one they each were confronted by a final moment of truth. For the *Sep (Vulture),* it came on September 15. Badly damaged by *Luftwaffe* bombing, *Sep* had only one choice. She must turn for Stockholm in neutral Sweden and accept internment for the duration of the war.

Likewise, a bomb-damaged *Rys (Lynx)* limped into Swedish waters on September 17 for safe haven and internment. *Zbik (Wild Cat)* managed to stay on the loose until September 25, but by then she, too, was forced to give up the fight as, at home, Warsaw was about to surrender.

That left just two of the orphans roaming the seas, both unaccounted for and neither aware of the other's whereabouts or activities. *Wilk (Wolf),* in fact, had set out for England in hopes of joining up with the Free Polish Navy there. Thus, *Orzel (Eagle)* would be the last of the five still in home waters.

Like her sisters of the sea, *Orzel* had left her berth at Gdynia in the first hours of the war. On station in Puck's Bay, she had found no targets, but she managed to elude the roaming *Luftwaffe* for days. She spent part of the time laying mines and once barely avoided a German trap featuring false calls for help from another "submarine."

She then cruised the Baltic beyond Puck's Bay until all communication with Gdynia ceased as of September 12. From then on, *Orzel* would be on her own.

Double disaster struck the same day. Her hydraulic system collapsed, and so did her skipper, a Commander Kloczkowski. As the boat's executive officer, Lt. Comdr. Jan Grudzinski, took over the helm, the *Orzel* headed for Tallinn in ostensibly neutral Estonia, both to make repairs and to place Kloczkowski in a hospital for treatment of his serious illness. Under prevailing international law, the Poles expected they would be allowed a belligerent ship's right to remain in port twenty-four hours, make their repairs, and sail again.

At first, their Estonian hosts appeared to agree. The skipper was hospitalized and repairs to the hydraulic system were completed in just a few hours. Refueled and her stores replenished, Orzel was ready to depart long before the twenty-four hours expired.

But now the Estonians said she must wait for six hours after a German freighter cleared the harbor waters. After a long—and it seemed deliberate—delay, the freighter finally turned her back to Tallinn and headed to sea. In theory, *Orzel* could follow in just six hours.

But no, the Estonians now said, a new accord binding upon the three Baltic states required disarmament and internment of any belligerent's warship appearing in their waters. (Estonia, Latvia, and Lithuania, it should be recalled, were tiny countries pressed on one side by Nazi Germany and on the other by the Soviet behemoth; in the end, they were occupied by the Soviets, next by the Germans, then "liberated" again by the Soviets.)

The latest edict was enforced by armed guards placed on board the Polish *Orzel*. The Estonians removed Captain Grudzinski's charts, navigational instruments, and vital components of the boat's deck guns. Next, her torpedoes would be removed, but that couldn't be done until the following day.

The Poles made use of the respite to plan their own next move—more exactly, to plot an escape. They were heartened the next morning by a message written on the back of a visiting card from the capital city's British naval attaché. "Good luck and God bless you," it said.

As dockyard workers struggled at removing the boat's twenty torpedoes, the *Orzel's* Polish crew was busy too. One crewman, apparently fishing from a dinghy in the harbor waters, was instead plotting an escape channel to the boat's rear. Another, unobserved, sabotaged the hawsers holding the sub in place—a strong pull would snap the last uncut strands.

A British signalman (left) and a Polish warrant officer (right) look out of the bridge of the Orzel. (U.S. Navy Historical Center)

The boat's radio was dismantled before watching Estonians, but a contrived short circuit and small electrical fire persuaded them it must be reassembled in order to trace the short circuit. Grudzinski himself, meanwhile, sabotaged the torpedo hoist after fourteen of the deadly "fish" had been lifted out of his boat, leaving six. He blamed the Estonian workers, whose foreman then agreed to call off the job for the day—a Sunday—and return the next morning to remove the final six "fish."

By such ruses, the friendly and cooperative Poles made their preparations for the coming night. By then, the Estonians were so lulled that they left only two armed guards on board the submarine.

They were easily disarmed, with no harm to either one, and after a crewman cut the dockyard's main electricity cable with an axe, the boat simply backed away from her berth in the suddenly prevailing darkness. Under quiet electrical power, she scraped over a mud bank for one tense moment before she could turn, bow on, for the open sea.

As her diesels then roared to life, the harbor guns responded loudly, but *Orzel* cleared a gauntlet of shells and machine-gun and rifle fire until reaching deep water and plunging into a dive that put her beyond reach.

The orphan still remained in an entirely hostile environment, however, and she was bereft of charts, navigational equipment, and usable deck guns.

She sailed first for the Swedish coast, where she dropped off her two Estonian prisoners in a collapsible rubber boat. She then headed back to sea—and a war patrol.

The officers, in the meantime, got together and drew up a set of homemade charts based upon each man's best memory. The salvaged radio told the crew of Warsaw's surrender and their country's sad fate.

Soon, the *Orzel* had spent sixteen days patrolling the Baltic without encountering a single enemy target (she still had her six unsullied torpedoes aboard). And now a BBC broadcast informed the crew of sister-boat *Wilk's* successful flight to England. Why shouldn't *Orzel* attempt the same, despite her navigational shortcomings and short supply of remaining fuel?

The proposal meant traversing heavily patrolled waters, threading a navigational needle between Sweden and Danish territory to escape the Baltic, then crossing the danger-filled North Sea to enter English waters—it would not be easy even in a fully equipped submarine.

Nonetheless, by mid-October, the *Orzel* had run that gauntlet safely too. Her skipper Grudzinski was awarded Poland's highest military decoration, the Virtuti Militari, for his remarkable feat in guiding her to safety—and to a renewed chance to fight the common German enemy.

Orzel had her opportunity to fight, as part of the Royal Navy's Second Submarine Flotilla, when Germany launched her lightning invasion of Norway the following April. On station off the Norwegian coast the morning of April 8, *Orzel* launched her torpedoes against a German troop transport and thus became the first Allied sub to sink a German ship taking part in the invasion of Norway.

That campaign lasted until well after Nazi Germany's next move, the invasion of France and the Low Countries on May 10. The Norwegian campaign was marked by various naval engagements and significant ship losses on both sides. One, her exact fate never known, was the *Orzel*. Long overdue, reported the Polish Admiralty-in-exile on June 11, the orphaned *Orzel* and all her crew were "presumed lost." The *Eagle*, after a brief flight, was gone.

★★★

Based upon Submarine Warriors *by Edwyn Gray (Presidio Press, Novato, Calif., 1988).*

Revolting Visit to Poland

WITH THE SMOKE OF WARSAW barely clearing, a German colonel leading a tour of stunned foreign correspondents explained that such total, unprecedented military success could be attributed not only to "our irresistible arms" but also "to our superior intelligence service."

Here was a public plaudit for Admiral Wilhelm Canaris, whose *Abwehr* indeed had done its homework well and contributed materially to the outcome in Poland.

Canaris, a mysterious and enigmatic figure whose true loyalties are hotly debated by historians even today, was in fact typical of the schizophrenic impulses that marked so many of Hitler's commanders.

At 9:15 the morning of the Poland invasion, Canaris, obviously excited, even elated, called his staff officers into a Berlin auditorium for a briefing in which he fervently told them, "I demand unquestioning and unconditionally positive loyalty to the *Führer*." He ended with the familiar refrain, "Heil Hitler."

Minutes afterward, on his way back to his office, he was told that Britain had ordered total mobilization. "My God," said Canaris. "If England comes into this, it will be the end of our poor Germany."

Ten days later, touring the field of battle in Poland, Canaris found himself questioning his own demands for loyalty to Hitler. In the field, his men reported massacres of Poles by the SS and the Gestapo. Canaris was shown a directive from SS Chief Heinrich Himmler calling for the systematic extermination of Polish civilians, especially the aristocracy and the Roman Catholic clergy. The same directive cited an order from Hitler as its authority. Canaris couldn't believe it.

He hurried to Chief of Staff Wilhelm Keitel's office in Hitler's personal train, parked at Ilnau, to "report" his information about "these unheard-of atrocities." But Keitel, who obviously knew all about them, was unreceptive. "If I were you, *Herr* Canaris," said the Hitler lackey, "I would not get mixed up in this business. This 'thing' has been decided upon by the *Führer* himself."

Keitel went on to explain that since the *Wehrmacht* had no stomach for "this 'thing,'" Hitler had ordered the SS and the Gestapo to handle it. "As a matter of fact, every military command in Poland will from now on have a civilian chief besides its military head, the former to be in charge of the 'racial extermination' program."

Stunned, Canaris was about to protest when Hitler himself entered the railroad car. Here was the intelligence chief's chance to take his complaint to the very top—but, as Keitel put his finger to his lips to signal silence, Canaris's nerve failed him. Numb, he replied to Hitler's questions about French intentions to the west without really thinking. When he returned to Berlin four days later, Canaris was physically sick.

★★★

Based upon The Game of the Foxes *by Ladislas Farago (David McKay Company, Inc., New York, 1971).*

Incredible, Ubiquitous Samaritan

THE LAST THING ON WILLIAM M. Miller's mind the night of February 21, 1940, was the stalled Phony War in Europe. "I had just purchased my first car, a Lincoln Zephyr V 12," recalled the Pennsylvania native.

On the way home from an evening in the state capital of Harrisburg, the exuberant young American decided to see how fast his new car would go. Three feet of snow covered the ground, but during the day the roads had been clear. He forgot that melting snow would have seeped onto the roadways and frozen into sheets of ice by the 2 A.M. hour.

"The last time I looked down at the speedometer, I was going 110." The predictable happened.

"I slowed down for a curve, and my brakes locked because I was on a sheet of ice and had no control of the car. I hit a concrete culvert head-on and flew through the windshield as if I had been shot out of a cannon. I eventually sold the car for $85 junk value with a 24-inch circular hole in the windshield."

In a coma for four days, Miller later learned that a passing stranger, Warren Felty, had found him lodged in a snowbank, unconscious. Accompanied by a friend, Felty hurriedly placed Miller in their car and rushed him to a Harrisburg hospital.

But that's not the end of the story.

Five years later, the war in Europe now very much on captured B-17 pilot Miller's mind, he was one of the half-starved Allied POWs forced to undertake a "death march" of seventy-five miles to Spremberg, Germany, to avoid liberation by the advancing Red Army. This time (January 1945), two feet of snow covered the ground; the temperatures were "zero or below," and the "worst blizzard in that part of Germany in eighty years" struck at the shuffling column.

"Prisoners were falling to the ground, unable to continue. Our German guards were older men and just could not keep up. I actually saw American officers carrying the German guards' rifles, as well as supporting them along the line of march."

By the second day, conditions only worsened. "It seemed as if we had been on the road for a week. Everyone seemed to be in a daze. Friends whom you had made in camp didn't recognize you and wouldn't even talk to you. It was every man for himself, and later our senior officers admitted they had lost all control over the situation. At this point, no one could help anyone. You were on your own."

With a promised stopping point five miles ahead, Miller was on his very last legs. "I had discarded everything that I was carrying except a small amount of food. I just could not go any farther. I couldn't put one foot in front of the other. My hands and feet were numb."

Predictably, the exhausted Miller collapsed—into a snowbank. "I had fallen behind my camp unit, and the last thing I remembered was the sight of all the prisoners passing by and none stopping to help. Either I passed out or went off to sleep, both certain death in the snow."

But no, Bill Miller was to escape certain death a second time. Call it a miracle. "Someone was kicking and shaking me and pulling me to my feet. Incredible as it may be, it was Warren Felty of Middletown, Pennsylvania, the same person who had saved my life five years and 4,000 miles away, under just about identical circumstances."

How could it be? Well, as a B-17 pilot with the Ninety-fourth U.S. Bomb Group at Bury St. Edmonds, England, Miller had been shot down October 20, 1943, while flying his first mission over Germany. Captured after bailing out of his stricken plane, he spent the rest of the war at Stalag Luft III at Sagan, Germany, the same POW camp that produced the "Great Escape."

Felty, in the meantime, also had become a B-17 pilot—with the Ninety-sixth Bomb Group in England—and he also had been shot down and taken prisoner. Both men were held at Stalag Luft III, but in different compounds. Only on the death march to Spremberg had they been reunited.

Felty, of course, helped Miller finish the second day's journey to the stopping place five miles ahead. While there were many more difficult moments before the POWs were liberated at the end of April, the stop enabled Miller to regain his strength for the rest of the ordeal—to survive.

After the war, he accidentally ran into Felty once more—back home in Pennsylvania. On the verge of losing a job for lack of a local distributor for his company's products, Miller was having breakfast in a roadside restaurant at Harrisburg and wondering what to do about his job situation. Outside, a passing motorist who had never before been to the restaurant decided to stop and go in.

It was Felty, and in just two hours he had made arrangements with his own company to be the distributor that Miller needed. Miller's job had been salvaged.

"He was just driving by and something compelled him to stop," said Miller.

★★★

First published in World War II *magazine, May 1988.*

Jockeying for Position

ERWIN ROMMEL WAS FURIOUS. ONLY three days after German forces invaded Poland, Hitler, arriving aboard his special train, was visiting the front. He wanted a tour of the battlefields, so he, his staff, and various official escorts, Rommel included, packed into seven heavy-duty Mercedes automobiles (equipped with not four, but six wheels).

The small motorcade was led into the danger zones by two armored scout cars. Following close behind was a huge column of seventy additional vehicles carrying the *Führer's* entourage of Nazi Party hacks and governmental "dignitaries," all anxious to have lead positions. At stopping points, they rushed from their cars for photographs at Hitler's side if at all possible, then ran pell-mell back to their autos for the next lap in the journey to Fourth Army headquarters—and for further jockeying for position in the convoy.

Since the rough and primitive back roads of Poland were not built for such traffic, clouds of dust roiled up in protest.

Rommel was Hitler's headquarters commandant at the time, and when Hitler's infamous secretary Martin Bormann complained about the unruly motorcade activities, Rommel shot back: "I'm not a kindergarten teacher. You sort them out if you want!"

That was on September 4, 1939, three days after the war's start, but by September 20, the same sort of fawning behavior was still going on. By then, Hitler had moved from his train to the Casino Hotel in Zoppot.

Watching in considerable astonishment was the German General Walter Warlimont, a visitor to the Hitler headquarters. As he looked on one morning, twenty to thirty cars were assembled "two abreast" in the hotel driveway for a trip to a battle area north of Gdingen. "It was the job of General Rommel, the Headquarters Commandant, to get this cortege moving, with Hitler at its head," wrote Warlimont.

When Warlimont asked Rommel why two abreast, "Rommel replied that, after many unhappy experiences, he had laid on this 'order of march' because it offered the best hope of satisfying the precedence and protocol requirements of the large number of non-military visitors who had meanwhile flowed into the headquarters."

Erwin Rommel, "The Desert Fox." (National Archives)

Thus, with cars two abreast, six or eight exalted personages could travel "level with each other and at the same distance from Hitler, and for them that was more important than anything."

But Rommel's best-laid plans went awry that very day. "The cortege went down a narrow track where the two-abreast formation was no longer possible and the majority of the cars were held up at a barrier while Hitler and the leaders drove on."

Even though word was passed among those left behind that the tour had been interrupted for a quick Hitlerian visit to a field hospital, Bormann, for one, was again outraged. "Nevertheless, although they were almost on the battlefield, Martin Bormann, the Head of the Party Chancellery, made a fearful scene and cursed General Rommel in outrageous language because of the supposed slight inflicted on him."

Once again, the future "Desert Fox" was fuming. But he had to hold his tongue. "There was nothing Rommel could do in answer to such insolence. When I straightaway gave vent to my indignation...Rommel merely asked me to tell Schumndt, the senior military aide, equally forcibly what I thought about it."

★★★

Based upon Inside Hitler's Headquarters, 1939–45 *by Walter Warlimont (Weidenfeld and Nicolson, London, 1964) and* Hitler's War *by David Irving (Hodder and Stoughton, London, 1977).*

Plans Gone Astray

LUFTWAFFE MAJOR HELMUT REINBERGER would have preferred completing his journey to a staff conference in Cologne by train, but with Germany on a war footing the trains were packed. His travel plans still unresolved, Reinberger took refuge the evening of January 9 in the officers' club at Munster. There had to be some other way for him to reach Cologne the next day, January 10, 1940. But how?

Fortune appeared to smile when he happened to meet Major Eric Honmanns, a reserve officer of the *Luftwaffe* who needed to build up his flying time and could stand, at the same moment, to work in a visit with his wife in Cologne. It was a made-to-order encounter. Reinberger happily accepted Honmanns's offer to fly them both to Cologne the next morning.

The secret plans that Reinberger was carrying for discussion at the conference made it all the more vital that he reach his destination in a timely fashion.

There was, to be sure, a security edict against carrying such papers by air, but what could be more secure against enemy eyes than a fast flight by military aircraft over German home territory with a fellow *Luftwaffe* officer at the controls?

The two men had some common ground to share beyond their air force affiliation. Honmanns, a World War I veteran of the air, was the commandant of an airfield at Loddenheide, near Munster. Reinberger was a commander too—of the paratroop school at Stendal. At the moment, however, Reinberger was serving as a liaison officer to *Luftflotte 2* at Munster as part of the team planning the airborne role in Nazi Germany's pending assault upon the Low Countries and France. The top-secret plans in his yellow briefcase detailed *Luftflotte 2's* part in the coming campaign, while also revealing that Germany's basic strategy of 1940 was very much the same as its strategy of 1914, a looping sweep north into Belgium and then down into France.

Hardly inspired and even widely expected, that was the plan as Hitler and his foot-dragging generals argued and debated the next step after rustic Poland's collapse before the shiny new *Blitzkrieg* machine the previous September. Both Britain and France had declared war on Germany as a result of Hitler's aggression against their treaty-partner Poland, but in the long weeks since his war machine raced across Poland, not much else had happened.

This was the period of the Phony War, when all Europe waited for the other shoe to drop, and did little else—except, on Britain's part, to bottle up the German pocket battleship *Graf Spee* at Montevideo and, on Soviet Russia's part, to grab a slice of Poland and to launch a war against tiny Finland.

For Hitler during these months of relative inactivity, there was nothing phony about his war plans. He would have, he said—he might have—dallied with certain peace proposals, but more immediate, more strengthening to his hand in the long run, were the plans to turn west after Poland and deal with his enemies there. To wage *real* war against them.

Only the reluctance of his generals to move so fast, the complaints that the *Wehrmacht* was not fully ready, and the weather—one of the worst winters in memory—had held him back.

There were doubts, too, as to the efficacy of repeating Germany's basic strategy of World War I. The new Germany of Nazi guise was disposed to strike quickly and hard with its shiny war machine, and not to fight a protracted war of attrition. Hitler saw the risks of any stalemate remotely approaching the standoff of the western front during World War I.

On the very morning that Majors Reinberger and Honmanns prepared to fly off to Cologne, their own *Luftwaffe's* meteorological experts were forwarding good news to the *Führer*. They predicted nearly two weeks of "clear winter weather" over Western Europe beginning January 15. Wasting no time, Hitler picked January 17 for his long-awaited attack on the West. Always meticulous, he included in his orders the very moment of assault, fifteen minutes before sunrise.

The *Luftwaffe*, in the meantime, would begin its attacks three days earlier, January 14, but only in France, in order to mask the true intent of wheeling north through neutral Belgium and Holland once more. Thus, the conference that Major Reinberger hoped to find in Cologne this morning of January 10 had acquired all the more urgency.

As he and his fellow *Luftwaffe* major climbed into their Me-108 "Typhoon" for the flight to Cologne, they had no idea of the momentous decisions about to be made at the highest levels of their government. Likewise, their government was, at high level, totally—even blissfully—unaware of their friendly arrangement.

In contrast to the long-range prediction, the weather the morning of January 10 was hardly auspicious. It was a chill day of ice and fog. From Lodenheide, Honmann's Typhoon floated up into an atmospheric soup. He turned southeast, and the soup only thickened. They wafted across the broad Rhine without noticing that historic landmark. Caught in a strong wind, they wandered farther west.

Now a river did appear below them, but it obviously could not be the Rhine—too narrow. In fact, it was the river Meuse.

The two men didn't have time to ponder the possibilities of the phenomenon below, for now the wings of the Me-108 were icing up. Major Honmanns had flown the Typhoon only once before. Now, in his excitement, he shut off the fuel flow to the engine, which promptly stopped. The Me-108 headed downward in silence.

Honmanns managed to keep their plane more or less intact in the forced landing that followed. By some accounts, it really was a crash landing—and a pair of trees sheared off the wings before the errant Typhoon skittered into a hedge at the end of a field. Shaken, the two *Luftwaffe* men emerged from their damaged craft with the obvious question uppermost in their minds. Where were they?

The answer, in just a few weeks, would seal the fate of France and, over the longer haul, set the course of World War II. More immediately, though, the *Führer* would fly into one of his famous rages—"foaming at the mouth," said his chief of staff, Wilhelm Keitel—at learning of the mishap that landed Majors Reinberger and Honmanns in *Belgian* territory.

For that's where they had come down, near the Belgian village of

Mechelen-sur-Meuse—on the wrong side of the frontier. As Reinberger knew, it was no place to be with a briefcase full of war plans calling for a march across neutral Belgium (and adjoining Holland). Specifically, the plans said: "The German army in the West will take the offensive between the North Sea and the Moselle, with very heavy support from the air forces, across the territory of Belgium and Luxembourg...."

Feverishly, Reinberger prepared to burn his papers...but since neither he nor Honmanns was a smoker, neither had a match on him. An onlooking Belgian farmer, who had told them where they were, now supplied a lighter. Crouching by a hedge, Reinberger set the papers afire...in moments, the potential damage could be undone.

But no, Belgian soldiers from the frontier guard arrived just in time to see what Reinberger was doing and to stamp out the flames.

The two Germans next were taken to a military command post heated by a stove. The vital—and singed—papers lay on a tabletop as the initial formalities were observed. The two fliers identified themselves and explained they had become lost, then their aircraft lost power and came down.

Any further events awaited the arrival of an officer in command of the frontier detachment, and Reinberger pretended to doze off. About the time the officer arrived, Reinberger came to life—he grabbed the papers from the tabletop and stuffed them into the stove. Once again, the incriminating evidence almost went up in smoke.

But the Belgian officer moved just as quickly—he reached into the flames and pulled out the German plans, which already had started to burn. Turning angrily on Reinberger, he shouted: "Always the same, the Germans. Treat them correctly, and they do dirty on you."

Desperate by now, Reinberger lunged for the officer's revolver. But the Belgian pushed him aside so violently that he hit the floor.

Rising unsteadily, Reinberger said he only wanted the handgun to kill himself. "I'm finished," he wailed. "I'll never be forgiven for what I've done." Honmanns attempted to intercede. "What do you expect?" he asked. "He is a serving officer. What will become of him?"

That was a question of some interest, actually, to both Germans. In view of the storm about to engulf Western Europe, one answer is that they were a lucky pair. Initially held in Belgium, then sent to England and finally to Canada, they safely sat out the entire conflict as prisoners of war.

First, though, the Belgians took the papers for close study and Reinberger was allowed to inform his embassy in Brussels of the mishap. In a room containing hidden microphones, he then quite falsely assured a visiting German military attaché that the offending papers had been burned down to mere fragments "no bigger than the palm of one's hand."

The report made its way to *Luftwaffe* headquarters in Berlin and eventually—on January 12—to Hitler. "I was present," said his chief of staff, Keitel, after the war, "during the greatest storm I ever saw in my life. The *Führer* was possessed, foaming at the mouth, pounding the wall with his fists and hurling the lowest insults at the 'incompetents and traitors of the General Staff,' whom he threatened with the death penalty. Even Goering [the Hitler favorite who was the titular head of the *Luftwaffe*] came in for a terrible scene."

On January 17, the Belgians having studied the matter and reached the proper conclusions, their foreign minister, Paul-Henri Spaak, called in the German ambassador to complain that the captured material obviously was an attack order with every detail worked out, except for the time factors to be inserted later.

Ironically, it cannot be said that the Allies were immediately enlightened by the plans that fell into their hands—only partially burned, at that. They at first wondered if the apparent intelligence coup were not the intended fruits of an elaborate German "disinformation" scheme.

On the other side of the fence, Hitler and his General Staff did not immediately shift gears, either. Adjustments to the plan were made, but it, in essence, still proposed to send the weight of Germany's armed might through the Low Countries. To be sure, the assault scheduled for January 17 was called off. The weather then set in again. One delay led to another, and soon spring appeared to be the window of opportunity.

By then, another plan had come to the *Führer's* attention. Radically different, it had been sent up the ladder of command in written form, many times, only to be ignored by the author's superiors.

But…as events fatefully turned out, not forever.

★★★

First published in World War II *magazine, November 1988.*

Dinner Guest

THE MAN WHO CAME TO dinner one night was General Erich von Manstein, Prussian to the core and easily one of the most brilliant military strategists Hitler had fallen heir to as the master of Nazi Germany. The dinner host was Hitler himself.

It was February 1940, and after many delays the plan for the invasion of France was still on, but the exact date was uncertain. Despite its premature disclosure to the Allies as a result of the errant plane's crash in Belgium January 10, the plan still was an imitation of Germany's World War I *Schlieffen* strategy of looping into northern France by way of neutral Belgium.

Manstein, however, carried with him the seeds of another plan, *Sichelschnitt*, or "cut of the sickle." For months now, Manstein had been pushing his alternative scheme to plunge into the eastern rib cage of France by way of the Ardennes, while feinting in the direction of Belgium.

The blade thus plunging into France from an unexpected quarter would be German armor.

It so happened that few in Nazi Germany's military hierarchy, Hitler included, were all that happy with their variation of the old *Schlieffen* plan, especially after it was revealed by the plane crash. Still, it was *the* plan, and for months now Manstein's efforts to sell the High Command on his scheme had been thwarted. No less than seven Manstein memos sent up the chain of command had been pigeonholed.

There the matter might have ended, there the Nazi conquest of France *might* have been averted, and there World War II might have fallen into the same sort of frozen stalemate that characterized the western front of World War I. Except that Hitler got wind of the Manstein scheme. The *Führer* then invited the general to dinner one night and afterward took him into the study to hear the details.

The apparent fallacy of Manstein's vision was the rough, heavily forested terrain of the Ardennes. How could German tanks operate on its few roads leading into French territory?

In November, however, Manstein already had posed that question to the key man in development of Germany's *panzer* forces, General Heinz Guderian. "Manstein asked me if tank movements would be possible through the Ardennes in the direction of Sedan," Guderian recalled after the war. "He explained his plan of breaking through the extension of the Maginot Line near Sedan, in order to avoid the old-fashioned *Schlieffen* plan, familiar to the enemy and likely to be expected once more. I knew the terrain from World War I, and, after studying the map, confirmed his view."

So, in effect, did Hitler following the dinner tête-à-tête. By February 24, 1940, the plan for subduing France had been changed—the strategy would be Manstein's own *Sichelschnitt*. As history since has recorded, it was indeed the plunge of the dagger that brought France to her knees.

Hitler was so pleased that he gladly took full credit for himself. As for Manstein's contribution, Hitler disdainfully explained: "Among all the generals I talked to about the new plan in the West, Manstein was the only one who understood me."

★★★

Based upon various sources.

Bold Gamble Supported?

THE ACTION IN EARLY APRIL of 1940 was in Norway and Denmark, along with their adjacent waters, and that's where the world's attention was focused. Beating the British to the punch, Nazi Germany had launched its *blitzkrieg* of Norway. In London, as is well known, the Chamberlain government was soon to topple, but what about Berlin? What was going on there, in the rapacious aggressor's nerve center?

As early as April 2, American radio correspondent William L. Shirer had reported from his base in Berlin: "Germany is now waiting to see what the Allies intend to do in stopping shipments of Swedish iron ore down the coast to the Reich. It's accepted here as a foregone conclusion that the British will go into Scandinavian territorial waters in order to halt this traffic. It's also accepted as a foregone conclusion here that the Germans will react."

As Shirer added in his entry for April 2 in his famous *Berlin Diary*, it all still was a puzzle. "S. whispers about Nazi troops being concentrated at the Baltic ports. But what can Germany do against the British navy?"

It was a question that still lingered on April 8. The British had announced their mining of Norwegian waters to stop the traffic in iron ore essential to the

German war effort. Spokesmen in Berlin said, "Germany will know how to react." In his diary entry, Shirer once again asked, "But how?"

He had a partial answer the next morning. "Hitler this spring day has occupied a couple more countries. At dawn Nazi forces invaded the two neutral states of Denmark and Norway in order, as an official statement piously puts it, 'to protect their freedom and independence.'"

The news, Shirer added, was stupefying. "Copenhagen occupied this morning, Oslo this afternoon, Kristiansand this evening. All the great Norwegian ports, Narvik, Trondheim, Bergen, Stavanger, captured. How the Nazis got there—under the teeth of the British navy—is a complete mystery."

In Berlin on April 9, meanwhile, correspondents such as Shirer were treated to a boastful press conference featuring German Foreign Minister Joachim von Ribbentrop.

"We waited a half-hour. At eleven A.M. Ribbentrop strutted in, dressed in his flashy field-gray Foreign Office uniform and looking as if he owned the earth."

After a few preliminaries by his press chief, Ribbentrop "sprang up, snake-like," to accuse the Allies of plans to invade and create a threatening base in Scandinavia. He declared that Germany had occupied Denmark and Norway to protect them and "defend their true neutrality until the end of the war."

At the broadcast center for foreign correspondents, Shirer encountered "for the first time a swarm of censors." They warned him to be "careful" in what he reported. So far, it appeared the German operation had been a huge success. No resistance by the Danes, and in Norway a mere sputter expected to end by nightfall.

Later in the day, though, the picture began to change. "Apparently something has gone wrong with the Norwegian part of the affair," noted the Shirer diary. "The Norwegians were not supposed to fight, but apparently did—at least at one or two places. There are reports of German naval losses, but the Admiralty keeps mum. All the Danish and Norwegian correspondents were fished out of their beds at dawn this morning and locked up at the Kaiserhof. It was the first they knew that their countries had been protected."

Later, of course, it turned out that German naval losses had been significant. The fighting in Norway would last an entire two months, only ending with full German control a month after the invasion of France and the Low Countries.

On April 18, meanwhile, Shirer heard an account, from another American correspondent, of Copenhagen's capitulation on April 9. German coal ships with troops hidden under the hatches had tied up in the neutral harbor two days before.

"At dawn (April 9) up came the hatches and the German soldiers piled out.

The Royal Palace is but a short distance from the docks. Up the streets toward the palace marched the Nazi troops. The amazed Danes, going to work on their bicycles, could not believe their eyes. Many said afterwards they thought it was some film being shot."

When some of the Danes didn't understand German orders to detour on side streets, "The Germans fired, killing a dozen or so."

In his April 19 entry, Shirer noted it was the eve of Hitler's fifty-first birthday. Propaganda chief Josef Goebbels was in full flower on the radio. But when Shirer passed the Hitlerian Chancellery that night, he noticed all of seventy-five persons "waiting outside for a glimpse of the leader."

"In other years on the eve of his birthday there were ten thousand." As Hitler again plunged into war, where were the German people?

★★★

Based upon Berlin Diary *by William L. Shirer (Alfred A. Knopf, New York, 1941).*

"Intend to Fire Torpedo"

OFF NORWAY THE MORNING OF April 8, 1940, an Allied submarine and a disguised German transport played a deadly cat and mouse game that went on for hours—and could have upset an invasion.

The Polish *Orzel (Eagle)*, assigned to the Royal Navy's Second Submarine Flotilla since escaping occupied Poland, opened the game as the "cat" in the affair. Submerged off Kristiansand, *Orzel* spotted an odd-looking passenger ship with no discernible flag showing and the name *Rio de Janeiro* emblazoned on her bows.

It was about 10:30 A.M., and she was pointed north, plowing toward Bergen, Norway.

The British had noted a spurt of German air and naval activity in recent days, with Norway as the obvious target for fresh German aggression. But the British, in their compelling need to contain German expansionism, were willing themselves to violate Norway's neutrality. Just the night before they had laid three minefields off the Norwegian coast.

What the British didn't know in any great detail was the fact that six small task forces of German fighting ships and troop transports already were on their way to Norway under an overall plan calling for their arrival at various objectives at 4:30 the next morning, April 8.

Orzel had come across one of the German ships taking part in the surprise attack on Norway, although her identity was not immediately apparent. What *was* apparent upon a closer look from *Orzel's* periscope was the poorly painted-out port of registration: Hamburg, Germany.

A search of the Polish submarine's reference materials disclosed the disguised ship was a passenger liner of 9,800 tons normally sailing to South America. *Orzel's* skipper, Jan Grudzinski, thought it all too suspicious to ignore—he surfaced nearby and messaged the *Rio*: "Stop engines. The Master with ship's papers is to report on board immediately."

The stranger, instead of replying, increased speed and turned toward Norway's territorial waters. *Orzel* quickly followed and let loose a burst of machine-gun fire that sent paint chips fluttering from the strange ship's sides.

She slowed and lowered a boat after displaying a signal of acknowledgment. But the boat didn't really approach the Allied submarine. As the Poles realized the Germans were merely stalling, two Norwegian gunboats could be seen approaching the scene.

Undeterred, Grudzinski signaled anew: "Abandon ship immediately. Intend to fire torpedo in five minutes' time."

By now it was 12:00. No response came from the German ship. No one could be seen on her decks. The boat lowered earlier still was making no attempt to reach the submarine.

At 12:05, true to his word, Grudzinski fired from his Number Two tube. Seconds later, the "fish" struck the *Rio* halfway down the hull from the bow.

As if on signal, "hundreds of soldiers in field-gray uniforms suddenly appeared on deck." Obviously, they had been cooped belowdecks, in hiding, to keep the co-opted passenger ship's true role as a troop transport secret. Now they burst into view in pathetic panic, some leaping into the deadly cold water, others running about the decks aimlessly. The ship's lifeboats, unaccountably, remained unattended in their davits.

The *Orzel*, meanwhile, submerged to avoid an oncoming airplane, then stood watch for a short while by periscope. The gunboats from neutral Norway had reached the stricken ship and were taking on survivors "unaware that the soldiers were on their way to invade their homeland," wrote Edwyn Gray in *Submarine Warriors*.

When Grudzinski realized that the *Rio* was not about to sink after all, he circled to the other side and sent another torpedo into her. This one completed the submarine's task; the onetime passenger liner went down almost immediately.

What was left in the chill seas was a horror scene, despite the best efforts of the Norwegian gunboat crews. Hundreds of bodies spotted the water, which was cold enough to kill in minutes. "They keep together with folds of uniform clutched tightly in a last spasmodic grasp," recalled one onlooker. "The one on the right is face downwards in the water...the faces of the two others, livid red and screwed up in a contortion of dread and fatigue, leaving a pitiful impression. Those two I shall never forget. They were both boys: capless, with yellow hair."

Now, as *Orzel* departed, a Norwegian destroyer joined the scene. All told, 122 survivors were plucked from the water and taken ashore. There they provided the Norwegian government clear warning of the German attack—Hitler, they said, had sent them to protect Norway from a pending British invasion.

In Oslo, the Norwegian cabinet didn't know what to do, although it ordered the coastal batteries on alert and imposed a blackout that night. In Berlin, the German General Staff was afraid the vital surprise element of its invasion plan had been blown sky-high. The next morning, Norway was invaded anyway, the Scandinavian country's resistance brave in places but overall spotty and uncoordinated. Despite fierce battles on land and sea over the next few weeks, Norway fell into German hands for the next five years.

★★★

Based upon Submarine Warriors *by Edwyn Gray (Presidio Press, Novato, Calif., 1988).*

"Never Such a Fleet"

PICTURE THE "PARADE"—STUMPY COASTAL *schuits* from Holland and various other coasters and paddle steamers; tugs towing barges and even mud scows; sloops, yachts, and fishing boats; Belgian drifters and little white boats—even speedboats soon lost to sight among the whitecaps. And trawlers, ferryboats, and minesweepers—and more than a few lifeboats without their ship. Often crashing through the mob, too, destroyers looking big as a house. And still more. "There was the old *Brighton Belle* that carried holiday crowds in the days before the Boer War. She swept mines in the Great War, and she swept mines in this war through all the fury of the last winter."

Crossing the Channel in the middle of this odd armada, our speaker was in the company of motorboats, of rescue launches, shrimp boats—even a flat-bottomed lighter used in the evacuation of another British army twenty-five years before at a place called Gallipoli.

And this place? This place was Dunkirk, unforgettable Dunkirk, now and forevermore known for the rescue of an entire army by a fleet of small boats operating night and day, May 29 to June 4, 1940, under the guns of the enemy. Angry guns too!

Crossing the Channel on his way *over* to the crowded beaches, Arthur Durham Divine was only halfway there on that first night when "we began to meet the first of the returning stream." And so it was, hour after hour, an assembly line of bobbing containers full of men—all size containers and all numbers of men—that endlessly repeated the cycle, over and back, over and back. Buckets on a chain.

"The little boats that ferried from the beach to the big ships in deep water listed drunkenly with the weight of men," wrote Divine later. "The big ships slowly took on lists of their own with the enormous numbers crowded aboard. And always down the dunes [at Dunkirk] and across the beach came new hordes of men, new columns, new lines."

Journalist Divine (for Britain's Kemsley newspapers) saw the moving, *fantastical*, and absolutely vital Dunkirk evacuation from a perspective that was unique. As a boating enthusiast, he was among the hundreds who answered the Admiralty's call for boats of all kinds. He then was assigned to a motorboat thirty feet long—one cabin forward and the rest open to the elements; twin engines to give her speed…and one admiral aboard with him—*the* admiral, in fact, who was in charge of small boats. And so, Divine saw it all, start to end.

In the Channel itself, the dangers could be collision among so many craft heading both ways at once or attack from the air or from the enemy's own speedy boats. Close up to Dunkirk, the danger was of another kind and all the more tangible and constant. "The breakwaters and lighthouse were magnificently silhouetted against the flames of burning oil tanks—enormous flames that licked high above the town."

For days, as the men lined up, Dunkirk remained under relentless, pounding German fire—"The din was infernal." Related one rescued soldier: "When we were hit by bombs we swam ashore, but when the ship didn't go down, we swam back to her again to take her out of the harbor. Then she turned turtle and we had to swim again. Some of us were in the water for hours before we were picked up by a British warship."

Divine, for his part, reckoned that perhaps eight hundred boats of all kinds took part in the evacuation of the British, French, Polish, and Belgian troops (but mostly British) who had been pushed backs-to-the-sea by the Nazi juggernaut in May 1940. With Dunkirk's docks destroyed by German bombs, all those thousands had to flee from raw beaches and a single mole just wide enough for three men at a time.

The boats were captained by as motley an assortment as were the boats themselves—bankers, lawyers, dentists, Sea Scouts, taxi drivers, boys, and old men. "Many were poor; they had no coats but made out with old jerseys and sweaters. They wore cracked rubber boots."

This was the odd navy, Divine wrote, that sailed "toward the pillars of smoke and fire and the thunder of guns, into waters already slick with oil of sunken boats, knowing perfectly well the special kind of hell ahead." Still, he added, "They went, plugging gamely along."

In his admiral's command boat, nearing the fiery beaches, Divine witnessed a *Luftwaffe* air attack on British destroyers standing off and guarding the evacuation zone—"the night was brilliant with bursting bombs and the fountain sprays of tracer bullets." He saw the crowded beaches, "black with men." He saw how, with near-perfect discipline, the weary, defeated, harried men stepped into the water, rank upon rank, to climb aboard the boats (or to be dragged aboard), men who in ranks advanced from water ankle-deep to knee-deep, then to hip-deep and even to shoulder-deep to take their turn.

Despite the "infernal" din that made shouting necessary for any conversation, "I will always remember the voices of the young subalterns as they sent their men aboard, and I will remember, too, the astonishing discipline of the men."

Being with the admiral meant "We stayed there until everybody else had been sent back, and then went pottering about looking for stragglers." During that final exercise: "A salvo of shells got one of our troopships alongside the mole. She was hit clean in the boilers and exploded in one terrific crash." At the moment, perhaps one thousand French troops were waiting on the mole to go aboard the ship. Now they had to turn back—they had filed out under shellfire, and they turned back under shellfire, their ship gone. "It was quite the most tragic thing I ever have seen in my life. We could do nothing with our little park dinghy."

But so many had escaped in the dramatic hours and days just before. According to Divine, in fact, the pier that allowed thousands upon thousands to go aboard the rescue flotilla never was itself hit, yet it was always a target of German bombers and artillery.

Overall, said Divine afterward, "it was the queerest, most nondescript flotilla that ever was, and it was manned by every kind of Englishman, never more than two men, often only one, to each small boat." Who would deny his conclusion that "there was never such a fleet went to war before."

Moreover, as miracle of miracles, "where the government and the Board of Admiralty had hoped to bring away 30,000 men, we brought away 335,000." Britain in just a few weeks' time would be engaged in battle for the country's very survival—the Battle of Britain. And when that battle of the skies was done, itself another miracle, Winston Churchill himself would note that so many owed so much to so few.

And true...but at Dunkirk just weeks earlier, the same sentiment applied, exactly.

★★★

Based upon A Treasury of Great Reporting: "Literature Under Pressure" *from the Sixteenth Century to Our Time, edited by Louis L. Snyder and Richard B. Morris (Simon and Schuster, Inc., New York, 1949–1962).*

Titanic Connection

DURING THE EVACUATION OF DUNKIRK, it is said that a British soldier aboard one of the "small ships" taking part in the historic rescue mission threatened to jump overboard when told the skipper had been on the *Titanic* the night it sank in April 1912.

To the contrary, a fellow member of the British Expeditionary Force (BEF) told him, anybody who could survive the sinking of the *Titanic* ought to be just the right man to get them through the hazards of the Dunkirk evacuation.

Little did either man know that their skipper, Charles Herbert Lightoller, was not only aboard the *Titanic* as Second Officer the night she sank in the North Atlantic, but he had momentarily had gone down with the ship and yet miraculously survived.

His story truly the stuff of legends, the same Lightoller, now 66 years of age, voluntarily took his converted Admiralty pinnace *Sundowner* across the

English Channel from Ramsgate to the embattled port of Dunkirk on June 1, 1940—almost 30 years after his escape from the sinking *Titanic* as her senior surviving officer.

Just one in the ramshackle fleet of hundreds, his 58-foot harbor launch was hardly noticed among the "small ships" responding to the Royal Navy's call for help in rescuing the 400,000-man BEF from the fire-swept beaches of the French port.

Later, though, onlookers could hardly believe the number of rescued soldiers who unfolded, like pages in a book, from Lightoller's converted harbor taxi when it landed, safe and sound, in England after a dramatic dash across the Channel. To squeeze aboard and yet stabilize their rescue vehicle, many of the soldiers had to lie down, both below deck and above, for the hours-long trip. When the soldiers began to shift and move upon arrival at Ramsgate, they nearly capsized the overloaded craft.

"Stacked like sardines, one on top of the other," is how then–Private Reginald King described the arrangement on board. The journey across the English Channel in the waning hours of the Dunkirk evacuation was memorable for its misery. "The boat appeared to be swerving this way and that, and most of us men were being sick," he recalled. "As we were on top of the other, you can imagine the mess." (www.historylearningsite.co.uk/dunkirk_memories.htm)

But almost any discomfort was better than the situation the soldiers left behind. As members of the rear guard leaving France as the great evacuation played out, King and his mates at first were thrilled to find the destroyer HMS *Worcester* waiting at the end of a mole, but quite a bit less thrilled when they were turned away at gunpoint. "We were 'volunteered' over the side because of overcrowding and had to climb down to take our place in a tiny boat. We were constantly under attack at this point and it was with relief that we reached the little boat and managed to secure some spaces."

Attacked and strafed three times in their new quarters, King and his fellow infantrymen were relieved to see the German aircraft suddenly turn on bigger game, the *Worcester* herself. "We suddenly realized that getting off the *Worcester* was perhaps a blessing in disguise, not the death sentence that we thought had been handed down. They gave the *Worcester* a hammering, almost sinking her, and it was only later that we heard she had managed to limp back to port."

But now came the sickening, hours-long journey across the English Channel to Ramsgate.

For *Titanic* survivor Charles Lightoller, his son Roger, and 18-year-old Gerald Ashcroft, serving as additional crew, this was the second leg of a 12-hour round trip. Despite all the strafing and bombing runs by the *Luftwaffe* they would rescue two crewmen from a burning motor cruiser, pull three Royal Navymen out of the seas off Dunkirk, and take 122 soldiers on board from the beleaguered HMS *Worcester*. All told, Lightoller helped an amazing 130 souls escape the onrushing German *blitzkrieg* in the refurbished steam launch, usually capable of carrying perhaps 21 persons.

An adventurous Englishman to the core, he was born in Chorley, Lancashire, on March 30, 1874—the same year as Winston Churchill. At all of thirteen, young Lightoller first went to sea in 1888 for an apprenticeship period of four years aboard the sailing ships of the day. Still a teen and only on his second voyage, he was shipwrecked in the Indian Ocean and briefly stranded on an uninhabited island. Once rescued, he then won quick promotion to Second Mate on another voyage for his efforts in fighting a fire that broke out in the sailing ship's cargo of coal.

Soon he was serving aboard steamships as a full Mate, but nearly died from malaria after spending three years on the West African coast. In 1898, he thought he would have a go at the Klondike Gold Rush in the Yukon, and when that didn't prove highly successful, he also had a brief fling as a cowboy in Canada. That, too, wasn't quite for him, so he worked passage back to England as a wrangler aboard a lowly cattle boat.

His next move indeed was a fateful one. For he now, in 1900, not only qualified for his Master's Certificate, he joined the White Star line, future owner-operators of the *Titanic*, as an officer aboard passenger liners sailing to Australia and the United States. After serving the *Majestic* on its New York run, he moved to White Star's *Oceanic*, pride of the fleet, and in time became *Oceanic's* First Officer.

During this period, he made two fateful "acquaintances": One was his Australian-born future wife, Sylvia Hawley-Wilson; the other, on board the *Majestic*, was her captain, Edward J. Smith…later to be the captain of the *Titanic* the night she sank on her maiden voyage.

And for Lightoller, what a crazy, unbelievable night that was, even for a survivor of the storied ship's final hours.

On watch as Second Officer in the early evening of April 14, 1912, Lightoller had turned in and was just falling asleep at 11:40 P.M. when he felt the "grinding vibration" of her encounter with an iceberg, notes the online *Encyclopedia Titanica* (www.encyclopedia-titanica.org). Obviously, the ship had hit something, but going out on deck in his pajamas, he saw no indications of trouble, no signs of alarm.

Just ten minutes later, though, he was throwing on his clothes. Water was rising in the mail room far below, he had been told.

Out on the boat deck soon after, he took charge of loading the port-side, or even-numbered, lifeboats. Strictly enforcing the rule of women and children first, he saw off the famous Margaret "Molly" Brown and John Jacob Astor's young wife Madeleine, among others. When a group of men took over Lifeboat 2, "Lightoller jumped into the boat and threatened them with his empty gun, driving them all out." His quick response allowed another 36 women and children to get off safely.

That was at 1:55 A.M., and by 2 A.M., all the lifeboats were gone, except for four collapsible crafts with canvas sides. Ordered by the ship's First Officer to join the passengers in one of them, Lightoller said, "not damn likely." Just minutes later, the great ship's bow was pointing downward and the upper decks were awash with rising waters. People were jumping, leaping, overboard. For his part, Lightoller was busy atop the officers' quarters cutting free a second, desperately needed collapsible.

At this moment, the *Titanic* "took a great plunge forward."

Lightoller turned to face the oncoming sea and dived straight into the icy water. For seconds, it appeared he might somehow swim clear, but then he was sucked up against the grating at the mouth of a large ventilator shaft and momentarily held there, helpless.

And, notes the *Encyclopedia Titanica*, "he was taken down with the ship."

Not far of course, not for good by any means. Instead, he was about to be spat out. "As the water hit the hot boilers, the blast blew him back to the surface, where he found himself alongside the capsized Collapsible B," the very collapsible craft he had been trying to free just minutes before.

But this seeming good fortune still offered its own perils. For one, the collapsible was upside-down and barely afloat as 30 or so men crawled aboard from the deadly-cold waters of the North Atlantic.

For another, they had to stand unsteadily to make room for all through the long night hours still remaining—three or four of the survivors aboard the collapsible died before dawn. "She was packed [with people] standing from stem to stem," Lightoller later said.

Shortly after daylight the survivors transferred to two nearby lifeboats, and Lightoller found himself aboard a woefully overcrowded craft that was close to foundering by the time it reached the side of the freshly arrived liner *Carpathia* that morning. It was the last lifeboat to reach the rescue ship, and he was the last to leave the lifeboat. Thus, Lightoller not only became senior surviving officer, but the last *Titanic* survivor to achieve rescue by the *Carpathia*. Captain Smith, the Chief Officer and the First Officer all either went down with the ship or died in the waters alongside.

Just two years later, of course, Lightoller's native England was at war with Germany—World War I. As First Officer aboard the White Star line's *Oceanic* just before the war, he remained in that post as the ship was converted to armed merchantman and sent on war patrol off the Shetland Islands. Unfortunately, she ran aground one night and again he supervised the lowering of lifeboats for a fatally stricken ship. Working his way up from the torpedo boat skipper and lieutenant's rank, he eventually commanded a Royal Navy destroyer that, typical now for Lightoller, rammed and sank a German U-boat, then had to back up all the way into port, more than 100 miles, because of the damages to its bow section.

It was after WWI, between the war years, that he found, purchased and re-outfitted the admiralty pinnace (with a diesel motor, among other changes), which then was re-christened the *Sundowner* (wanderer in Australian parlance) by his Australian wife Sylvia. For several years, the couple and their children enjoyed many a cruise around England and other European waters in their 58-foot boat.

One long-lasting "cruise," though, taken in mid-summer 1939 at the Royal Navy's request, was in fact an intelligence-gathering survey of the Germany's northern coastline.

Then came the great drama of Dunkirk in May of 1940. The Royal Navy called on Lightoller again. Would he mind lending his launch for use in evacuating some of the Dunkirk troops? The Navy had the personnel standing by, able and ready to do the job…

Absolutely not, he said—he would take her across the Channel himself!

And so he did, to the great relief of Private King and so many of his mates, even if the voyage home to England had been a wee bit uncomfortable.

Additional Note: Not yet ready to rest on his laurels, notes the online *Titanic* encyclopedia site, "Commander Lightoller joined the Home Guard, but the Royal Navy engaged him to work with the Small Vessel Pool until the end of World War II," By then, sadly, Lightoller and his wife had lost both their youngest son, Brian, and their eldest son, Roger, to the war. Brian, an RAF pilot, was killed even before Dunkirk and Roger, a commander of motor gunboats, died in a German Commando raid on Granville, France, late in the war. Lightoller himself survived until late 1952, when he died of natural causes at the age of 78. The *Sundowner*, though, still serves as a museum piece in Ramsgate Harbor.

★★★

Based on the online Encyclopedia Titanica (www.encyclopedia-titanica.org); *the online* nationalhistoricships.org.uk *website, and the* Memories of Dunkirk (www.historylearningsire.co.uk), *maintained by British history teacher Chris Trueman.*

Treasure Ships En Route

Tough to say which might be the greater danger. The two German U-boats reported to be prowling the North Atlantic waters ahead...or the vicious gale buffeting the ship, a British cruiser secretly loaded with modern-day treasure.

For the HMS *Emerald's* skipper, Francis Cyril Flynn, the weather would be the more immediate problem as his cruiser slipped her moorings at Greenock, Scotland, on June 24, 1940, for its high-speed dash across the ocean for Canada.

"We left the Clyde that night with reports of bad weather," he said later. "The reports were correct. The seas whipped up as we rounded the north coast of Ireland next morning. When we turned out into the Atlantic we were punching into a rising gale."

Then, too, there was the Admiralty's warning that a pair of German submarines were lying in wait beneath the stormy seas. And the gale only worsened. Soon, the cruiser's escorting destroyers couldn't maintain speed in the heavy seas...they plowed straight on while *Emerald* zigzagged side to side behind them at higher speed.

As the seas grew even heavier, the destroyers simply couldn't keep up the pace. Flynn decided he and the cruiser must make the crossing alone, on their own. "I put my ship up to 22 knots. The first three days the going was such that many of our crew became seasick."

But no thought of turning back or, with U-boats to avoid, of slowing down. Not with the vital treasure aboard—a half billion dollars of Britain's gold and securities being sent for safekeeping to Canada.

This was at a time, please understand, when England's wartime fortunes were at their lowest, a moment when Nazi Germany might invade Shakespeare's "scepter'd isle" itself. Thus it was that *Emerald* carried in her holds and ammunition magazines 2,229 boxes of gold bullion (four bars to a box) and 488 boxes of securities...with even more of England's vital holdings scheduled to come in additional dashes across the submarine-infested North Atlantic.

Ahead, in Canada, certain preparations were underway to receive and house Great Britain's liquid assets safely and in secret. And who knew? Perhaps Canada would be asked to provide a new home for a British government-in-exile attempting to continue the fight against Hitler's Germany. Could happen, if events along the far-off English Channel began to go even more badly in the summer weeks ahead.

As it was, Alexander S. Craig, an official from the Bank of England who arrived with the *Emerald* and her treasure on July 1, told two of his Canadian contacts: "We're cleaning out our vaults. In case of invasion, you know. Rest of the stuff will be coming over shortly."

Naturally, the Canadians were more than willing to help out. In fact, Canada "helped out" as one of the Allies of World War II in many, many ways, and often at high cost in materiel and personnel. Among Canada's fighting forces, for example, the Canadian Second Division was the major Allied element committed to the costly raid on the French port city of Dieppe in August 1942, with three thousand of the five thousand participating Canadians (a staggering 60 percent) listed as casualties. Overall, Canada contributed one million military personnel to the war effort—and counted 41,992 killed as a result.

The record of Canadian participation included a division and armored brigade that took part in the invasion of Sicily, then moved up the boot of Italy in that long, tough campaign. Another Canadian division and armored brigade took part in the Normandy landings and played a key role in taking the French city of Caen. The First Canadian Army (eight divisions, five of them Canadian) made up the left flank of the Allied drive across Europe and into Germany after Normandy.

In addition, an expanded Canadian fleet helped guard the Allied convoys crossing the North Atlantic, while Canada's air force sent abroad forty-eight squadrons, among them an entire bomber group, while also providing domestic training facilities for the RAF, safe and far removed from enemy action.

Also vital to the Allied cause, but a role undertaken entirely in secret, Canada became the repository of Britain's financial assets. Thus, the cross-Atlantic dash of the *Emerald* in late June of 1940—while carrying the greatest treasure ever committed to one ship. Thus, too, a succession of additional Atlantic dashes during the same summer…ships packed with gold and securities worth a total of $7 billion. And small change.

The largest single consignment, stuffed aboard a Royal Navy battleship, a cruiser, and three onetime luxury liners, or five ships in all, began its hazardous voyage from Britain July 8, a $1.75 billion consignment that may have amounted to the greatest single treasure ever transported anywhere, by air, land, or sea, to that date.

"We had the usual Admiralty reports of submarines active in the vicinity," said Admiral Sir Ernest Russell Archer, commander of the treasure convoy—escorted by four destroyers, incidentally. "We managed to dodge their U-boats. Enemy raiders were also active, but none showed up. Were we nervous? We knew what we had on board. You took the ships and did what you could."

Even so, there was immediate concern when one of the converted liners, the Polish *Batory*, developed engine trouble and couldn't keep up with her partners in the high-finance shipment. The cruiser *Bonaventure* was ordered to stay with her while the others dashed ahead.

Then came another disquieting setback. "We hit a most frightful fog, with floating ice at the same time," said the *Bonaventure's* skipper, Vice Admiral Jack Egerton. "For nearly 12 hours it stopped us dead. I had to stick close to the *Batory* in the fog. Between us we carried some 60 million sterling in bullion [or $250 million]—and you couldn't see an iceberg until it was practically on top of you."

In the end, though, both ships completed the crossing, unscathed by iceberg or torpedo.

In Canada, meanwhile, the securities from Britain were placed in hastily prepared underground quarters in Montreal, while the gold bullion went to the central Bank of Canada in the capital city of Ottawa. Both facilities—and the special trains ordered to carry the treasure to its final resting places—were heavily guarded, to be sure.

In Montreal, nearly two thousand boxes were required to hold the stocks and bonds shipped from England. The securities belonging to this individual or that were bundled together, a process eating up more than seventy miles of tape.

Fortunately, there were records of ownership to consult. The British government at the start of the war had required its citizens to register their foreign securities—then, with the danger of actual invasion looming after the fall of France, the government simply gathered up securities held in British banks, crated them, and shipped them off to the sub-basement in Montreal's twenty-four-story Sun Life Assurance Company building.

There, the Canadians created a giant vault, 60 feet square, 11 feet high, by cannibalizing two miles of track (providing 870 rails) from an unused rail line to provide the steel supports. The vault created for the newly named United Kingdom Security Deposit was so tightly secured, it took two bank officials, each one armed with a single combination, to unlock it. Neither, of course, knew the other's combination—neither could open the vault alone.

Others then spent weeks going through the securities, identifying them, classifying them, confirming their ownership…and finally, bundling them. At the end, the Bank of England's Alexander Craig was able to boast, "Not a certificate was missing. In view of the pressures under which they were assembled and shipped, it was quite extraordinary."

The gold bullion, meanwhile, flowed into a 60-by-100-foot vault in the Bank of Canada on Wellington Street in Ottawa—again under tight security.

The transfer of Britain's gold bullion continued until August—a three-month period during which the Germans sank 134 ships in the North Atlantic but, miraculously, never did sink one of the gold-bearing ships.

Oh, well, we might be tempted to say today, aside from the cost in human lives, insurance would have covered the monetary loss, right? Not quite. No insurance company in its right mind would have covered such a risk in wartime… even if it *could* dredge up the funds matching the loss from the sinking of just one of the treasure ships.

★★★

Based upon "Britain's Treasure Goes West" by Leland Stowe, Secrets & Spies: Behind-the-Scenes Stories of World War II *(Reader's Digest, Pleasantville, N.Y., 1964).*

Landing with Piggyback Rider

SO MUCH DURING THE BATTLE of Britain in the summer and early fall of 1940 was new, untested, as yet unrefined. Pilots of today, even of the later war years, would find some of the tales of baling wire and seat-of-the-pants flying nearly unbelievable. Ken Haviland, an American-born RAF night-fighter pilot, was there for those incredible days, as one of Churchill's famous "few."

Night-flying had its problems. "There was…the matter of lighting a runway on a grass field so you could see where to land. At first, in 1940, we were given lights that were self-contained in cans, battery operated. You laid them out and had to turn on each one, individually. The problem was that when there was an enemy intruder in the area, you had to go out and turn them off, and then when it was all clear, turn them on again. But in the dark you couldn't see to find them to turn on again! Finally, an engineer at our airfield laid out permanent runway lights, just like you see today. It was quite a stroke of genius."

Even in daylight, the improvised airfields of grass provided an occasional unsought thrill. "Originally, Fighter Command used ordinary grass fields that were mowed down for us. At one place, we had an auxiliary field about a mile or so from the main one, and there was a taxi-way mowed to connect the two—over a mile. At Digby, we operated with a Spitfire squadron at one end of the field and our squadron at the other. We had a scramble one day, and the Spitfires passed over us going in the other direction! In those days, we took off in formation, so things really got dangerous."

Radar was not yet perfected. And at night it was all too easy to visually misidentify other planes in the air. "It was especially bad when we flew the Mosquito, because it was a twin-engine fighter, and the Germans had the Messerschmitt 110, which was also twin-engined."

Even radar, however, could not always prove an identity case. "I was on the tail of an intruder once, and the radar operator on the ground told me it was friendly. I was ordered not to attack it. The German was able to get away. This was annoying because if I had shot him down, it would have been the first kill with a Mosquito."

Before obtaining the more advanced Mosquito, Haviland had to fly the Defiant, equipped with guns in a turret behind the pilot's seat. "That meant you had to shoot at the enemy when he was broadside of you. You had to pull up side-by-side, practically."

Such a maneuver obviously wasn't very practical. "I [once] managed to get alongside a Dornier, and my gunner started firing away at him, but he simply rolled over and slipped away. There was nothing I could do to catch him in the right position for a kill."

Overall, Haviland put in 1,600 hours of combat flying time by war's end and earned the Distinguished Flying Cross. It was after the Battle of Britain, of course, that he flew the Mosquito, often as a night-fighter pilot accompanying the big bombers in their raids on Germany. He later became a professor of aerospace engineering at the University of Virginia.

There, he might have had some difficulty explaining one more adventure from his "seat-of-the-pants" days in the air…explaining in aerodynamics terms the time he accomplished a piggyback landing of two airplanes at once!

Haviland and his trusty Mosquito had been "out" one night checking on German radar frequencies. Returning to base in the English countryside in the dark, he was alerted that there was an enemy intruder in the area.

"So we had to keep our lights off. I landed the airplane, but down on the runway, I found I couldn't control it. It wanted to swerve off to the side. Also,

I couldn't throttle back, couldn't even cut the ignition on the port engine. Finally, the navigator turned the fuel shut-off and the engine stopped. I looked up above my head, and I thought it seemed unusually dark out. There was this strange object sticking into the canopy, too. Turns out it was the exhaust pipe of a Halifax bomber that had landed right on top of us!"

How could it happen?

"Well, he had no radio and had come in to land, too. He made a steeper approach than I had, and that was how we landed together. There he was, right on top of us! By the time we all stopped, his gear had collapsed, so we were bearing *his* weight, too."

And no one hurt? "We had trouble getting out of the Mosquito. The people outside on the runway thought we must be all dead, but we were arguing with the people from the Halifax. There was aviation gasoline showing in our tanks, which had been ripped open, and it's a wonder we didn't all get blown to pieces. The Mosquito was a total loss, as you might expect."

Haviland's entry for his logbook that day was somewhat understated: "Halifax landed on top of us. Bit of a mess."

★★★

Based upon interview by Luther Y. Gore, Military History *magazine, October 1985.*

Parachutist Draped on Wing

THE BLITZ WAS ON, AND in London, Sunday, September 15, 1940, was a bright and clear day. Anyone on the ground could look up and see the British fighters—their fighters—as they engaged waves of *Luftwaffe* bombers above.

For the German air force, it was a major effort, a peak in the storied Battle of Britain that contributed heavily to Hitler's ultimate decision against invasion of England. The bombing raids this Sunday morning were aimed at London, Portland, and the Spitfire production facilities near Southampton.

Rising to defend London against Hermann Goering's Dorniers were fourteen RAF fighter squadrons, and among all those pilots was a young man flying into his first combat, Sergeant R. T. Holmes of the 504th Hurricane Squadron based at Hendon.

He and his fellow Hurricane pilots first encountered cumulus clouds at eight thousand feet. "This was quite dicey," he later explained, "for we had only practiced formation flying in clouds in pairs, and to suddenly find twelve of us climbing through this bumpy stuff was quite a rare experience."

In short order, there would be even more dicey maneuvers. Directed by radar, Holmes and his gang met the oncoming Dorniers at seventeen thousand feet. "I was tail-end Charlie, weaving above and consequently the last to attack."

In minutes, both the Dornier and the Hurricane formations had broken up, the Germans—most of them—turning for home, and the 504th Squadron re-forming itself. "I spotted three Dorniers blazing a lone trail toward London. No one seemed to have noticed them, so I decided to give them a little attention."

As his idea of "a little attention," the intrepid Briton first attacked the two outside bombers, on each one's flank. "The first man belched oil all over my windscreen, blotting my vision entirely; but when the oil cleared, due to my overtaking speed, I saw his tail very close to my nose, and one of his airscrews stopped."

As related in the book *1940* by Laurence Thompson, Holmes "just grazed under his belly" and shot past below.

He now had a go at No. 2. "It was the second plane which caught fire at his wing root and from which came a parachutist who momentarily draped himself so artistically over my wing. I didn't give much for the chances of either of these machines getting home, but could not claim them destroyed, as I had not seen them crash." Mark them down as "probables."

But there still was the leader, who continued to press on for London. "One stern attack, without much apparent effect, left me low in ammo for we only had a total of 15 secs' firing. I thought a head-on attack might cool his ardor, and climbed up and past him to his left from my last breakaway."

At this point, Holmes became aware that his own engine sounded rough, his oil pressure had dropped, and "there was oil bubbling up the inside of my windscreen—my own oil." Undaunted, he bore in for his head-on attack, using up the last of his ammunition in the process.

"I knew the engine had had it anyway, so more in frustration than in hate I kept on and clipped one side of his fragile-looking twin tail with my port wing."

It seemed only a slight bump as the Dornier's tail "snapped off." In seconds, though, the Hurricane's own port wing dipped; the end of the wing tore away, and the British fighter spun out of control.

As Holmes struggled to free himself from the cockpit and bail out, the spinning fighter passed through the cloud layer—"and I knew I was halfway down already."

Finally extricating himself and dropping into the slip-stream, Holmes was hurled against his own aircraft's tail assembly; his right arm was rendered numb and useless. Plummeting earthward, he worked his left hand under his left armpit and pulled the ring. "There was a jerk so sickening that both my boots flew off my feet and then complete silence, and I said to myself in awe: 'It worked!'"

An instant later, wafting downward upon London, Holmes saw, just above the city's Victoria Station, "the front half of the Dornier floating lazily like an autumn leaf onto the station roof."

He himself landed safely enough, but with one more painful bump. "I hit a Chelsea rooftop myself, missed my grip, and rolled off into the dustbin."

About the time of the same *Luftwaffe* "peak," Hitler and Goering had a violent argument. *Luftwaffe* tactics changed (fewer daytime raids). The invasion of England was off—Russia, instead, would be "on." Intrepid young men like Sergeant R. T. Holmes, Churchill's famous "few," had saved their country from invasion.

★★★

Based upon 1940 by Laurence Thompson (William Morrow and Company, New York, 1966).

Stricken Pilot's Pivotal Decision

IT WAS THE LONG ARM of a mother, his own mother, that first plucked this intrepid airman from the sky. He had been flying combat missions since January of 1940. But his brother was killed, and their mother went all the way to the top, to the head of the air force, to have the younger of her sons pulled out of the line.

It wasn't until July 1940, the air Battle of Britain just heating up, that he could rejoin his old squadron. By now, France was kaput...and he had missed a lot of time in the air. Others were becoming aces while he had yet to score his first aerial victory.

The Battle of Britain, a question of basic survival for England, soon assumed its epic proportions, with many men flying, downed, and killed every day. Our man, a fighter pilot, flew and flew...many missions, no victories. But no mishaps, either. Not until October 29, 1940, anyway—and this time it was not his mother but the enemy who would pluck him from the sky.

Our man and his squadron mates began the day in slow, somnolent routine—with breakfast and coffee, newspapers, and music on the radio, wrote Edward H. Sims in his 1987 book *Aces over the Oceans*. Finally, the orders came down: Fighter escort…fighter escort for an afternoon strike planned against the large city just across the Channel.

Over the target a couple of hours later, in a sky churning with fighting aircraft, our man is hit from behind—*"thump! thump! thump!"* Seconds later, he is trailing both black smoke and the white "flag" of lost engine coolant. He turns for the English Channel and home.

He still has six thousand meters of altitude between him and Mother Earth; his nimble fighter will glide a good distance in fairly slight decline even after the engine goes rough, slows…and dies in final seizure.

With luck, he might come close to the friendly shoreline on the far side of the "great ditch." *With luck*, and already he has ducked out of the churning melee over the target city and struck out alone, for home. Just ahead he sees his first glimmer of hope, the enemy shoreline, with Channel waters just beyond, and he is now down to about five thousand meters in that slow descent.

Relatively speaking, all is going well enough. But the needle keeps on moving…now near the four thousand mark. His "cushion" steadily loses air. Ahead the Channel. And behind him now, what is this? Behind now, "a speck in the sky." As his own fighter crawls, the speck looms "larger and larger" and could it be, and yes,…it is! The enemy!

Our man cannot turn and fight. At the enemy's own coastline now, he still needs every possible foot of altitude. The other fighter is upon him, and as the first cannon shells reach out for the crippled plane, there is only one chance—he dives. He drops headfirst vertically for 1,500 meters. He pulls level, fighting off a blackout due to lack of blood in the brain—the "G Force" effect.

As full vision returns, he's lost the lone attacker—he's over the chill Channel waters. But he's also down to only a thousand meters, not nearly enough to carry him to his side of the Channel. He has a basic choice—turn back to the enemy meadows so temptingly close and become a prisoner of war for the duration…or press on and take his chances while ditching into the Channel.

Smoke in the cockpit hastened our man's decision. He would bail out and hope somehow for friendly rescue.

He turned his ship upside down for fast departure but forgot to trim for inverted flight. The plane, an anvil strapped to the back of a fly, was falling with him!

He emerged safely, however, and soon was tossing alone in his inflatable dinghy in the icy Channel waters. Late in the day, a speedy rescue craft scooped him up close to the enemy coast and scooted for home under enemy shellfire.

That evening, he celebrated his birthday. *Luftwaffe* fighter pilot Gerhard Barkhorn would comment years later: "The decision to bail out over the sea so close to England turned out to be a pivotal one in my combat flying career."

Pivotal is right…Barkhorn would "fly more than 100 missions before scoring a victory," adds author Sims, himself once a WWII fighter pilot. Before Barkhorn was finished, however, he flew 1,104 combat missions in all, he scored more than 300 aerial victories, and he became one of the two highest-scoring aces in history.

And all because he refused at a crucial moment in his life to give up and take the easy, even a seemingly honorable, way out.

★★★

First published in World War II *magazine, September 1990.*

Pet Spy in England

THE GERMAN *ABWEHR*, OR MILITARY intelligence apparatus, was happy with the slim young man known as "Schmidt-Hansen," a native of the Danish Jutland. His face, wrote one of the *Abwehr*'s interviewers, was "fine and energetic, all his features and manners testifying to a good upbringing."

As further qualification, so far as the *Abwehr* was concerned, he had a good record as a prewar Nazi in his native land. Finally, he spoke English.

In no time flat, Hansen was paired with a pro-Nazi Swede named Goesta Caroli, and on the night of September 3, 1940—at the height of the Battle of Britain—they stepped out of a black-painted Heinkel above the thirteenth-century cathedral of Salisbury, England.

Their parachutes floated them down into a grove outside of town, but young Hansen landed in a tree. Cutting himself loose from the chute's rigging, he then fell to the ground and broke an ankle.

They stuck together, found a doctor, and had Hansen's ankle set in a cast. In three days, still apparently making his way to London to set up his spying base,

Hansen radioed to his German superiors: "Roads blocked with refugees. Most of them look Jewish."

That pandering signal was the first of more than one thousand that Hansen would be sending his superiors for nearly five wartime years spent as the elated *Abwehr*'s hottest spy in all England. As far as the *Abwehr* was concerned, "he was their pet, their pride, their miracle man," wrote Ladislas Farago in his 1971 bestseller *The Game of the Foxes*.

The broken ankle soon forgotten (and Caroli soon faded from view too), Hansen may also have been the *Abwehr*'s most irreverent, wheedling, sulky, or sentimental spy.

He thought nothing of filling the wartime airwaves with four-letter expletives when angered by his masters in Germany and their demands for specific information.

He complained quite freely: "You never let me know what you think of my work. An occasional pat on the back would be welcome. After all, I am only human."

He told the *Abwehr* he had struck up a relationship with a young woman who worked as a secretary at the Allied invasion headquarters in Norfolk house. Along with the tidbits of inside information he had gleaned from her, he once signaled his German headquarters: "Well, what do you think of Mary? Isn't she quite a gal?"

So outstanding was his work in the *Abwehr*'s eyes that in the sixth week he was awarded the Iron Cross First Class—"the first spy in the field to be awarded the coveted decoration," wrote Farago. Months later, an apparently sentimental Hansen came to his thousandth signal to the *Abwehr*. "On the occasion of this, my one thousandth message," he radioed, "I beg you to convey to our *Führer* my humble greetings and ardent wishes for a speedy victorious termination of the war."

The intelligence service had, in the meantime, performed handsprings in response to the mercenary Hansen's demands for money.

In 1941 (before Britain was at war with Japan), Hansen met a Japanese military attaché on a bus in London one evening and was given his fellow "passenger's" copy of the *London Times* as the attaché rose to leave the bus. Pasted to the inside pages were eighty £50 notes.

"Won't be reporting for a couple of days," radioed Hansen later that day. "I'm getting drunk tonight."

As it turns out, the *Abwehr* should have wished he got drunk more often, fell under a bus, or otherwise incapacitated himself. For Hansen, nearly from the moment he set broken foot on English soil, had been deftly "turned."

When Hansen broke his ankle landing in England by parachute, the *Abwehr* had contacted one of its other "best spies" in England to lead Hansen to a "safe" doctor. The go-between, though, had been suborned earlier by Britain's counterespionage agency, MI 5, and when the *Abwehr* radioed *him*, it was really "talking" to MI 5.

Hansen soon agreed to cooperate with his British captors, whereas the uncooperative Caroli spent the war under lock and key (hence his fading from *Abwehr* view). Hansen—and many other double agents like him—represented a major intelligence coup—not for the *Abwehr*, but rather for MI 5.

★★★

Based upon The Game of the Foxes *by Ladislas Farago (David McKay Company, Inc., New York, 1971).*

Penalty Exacted for Coventry

"THE TRUTH IS THAT WE were not so ready, nor organized, for anything so terrific as this."

So wrote a clergyman after the *Luftwaffe's* infamous raid on Coventry, England, on November 14, 1940, and terrific it was.

For eleven hours, from dusk to dawn, the bombers came, four hundred to five hundred of them in waves. It was perfect flying weather.

To make matters worse for those on the ground, beneath the continuing cascade of incendiaries and high-explosive bombs, the city's water mains were knocked out by the first bomber waves. Coventry's firemen had little means for fighting the multitude of blazes springing up all around them.

The result, by morning, was devastation of an estimated 100 acres, with 1,000 homes destroyed and 32,000 damaged. In addition, 554 persons were reported killed.

"The German attack on Coventry has been described as probably the most concentrated and destructive on any British objective outside London throughout the war," said British journalist Laurence Thompson in his postwar book *1940*.

The best-known victim of the Coventry raid was its cathedral, reduced during the "terrific" night to mere shards of its walls—and to its fifteenth-century spire.

The target at Coventry, said *Luftwaffe* General Albert Kesselring later, had been its arms factories. "Fire and smoke clouds made it impossible to aim accurately. The dispersion inevitable in any bombing is thus considerably increased and punishes adjacent areas in no wise intended as objectives."

Certainly, Coventry had been punished. "The situation seemed to justify German claims that Coventry had been knocked out of the war," added Thompson in his book. But not so. The city's armament production resumed at one-third capacity the day after the raid and in two months, it further seems, "it was back to normal."

The real punishment, though, was to be suffered by Germany itself. The "final lesson" of Coventry, wrote Thompson, "was learned not by the *Luftwaffe*, but by a British observer, the Deputy Chief of Air Staff, Air Vice-marshal A.T. Harris, who as Commander-in-Chief of Bomber Command did to Hamburg nearly three years later what the *Luftwaffe* had tried to do to Coventry."

The horrendous fire storm loosed at Hamburg took a staggering toll of 43,000 lives.

Even at that, production in Hamburg's factories and shipyards in a few months' time "was back to 80 percent normal."

In the interim, the British public and the country's wartime leadership debated the issue of bomb-raid reprisals against German cities. Winning out as official policy was retaliation, even though polls indicated that a sizable segment of the British public was against it.

★★★

Based upon 1940 *by Laurence Thompson (William Morrow and Company, New York, 1966).*

Blues vs. Reds

NOT YET WELL KNOWN TO the Western world, one Georgi Zhukov found himself in command of a so-called "blue" army engaged against a "red" army along the western borders of the vast Soviet state. Nazi Germany and the USSR were friends, allies in the recent rape of Poland.

The "reds" in reality were the USSR's western front troops, and "blue" was considered interchangeable with "German" for purposes of the military exercise. It was only December of 1940. Nazi Germany had not yet turned on its all too willing partner in the subjugation of Poland that followed their Non-Aggression Pact of August 1939.

Zhukov, commander of the Kiev Military District, played for real in the eight-day exercise, and the "winner" at the end was *not* the "red" army, despite help from the referees. The winner was Zhukov, and seven months later, the "winner," employing much the same strategy, was the real German army.

So goes the Zhukov account given in a document released by the Soviet news agency Novosti in the 1980s, with the explanation that the first-person rendition consisted of "notes based on Zhukov's words."

By those notes based on words, Zhukov began his "blue" force operations "in areas where the Germans carried out their operations later." Further: "I delivered the main blows where the Germans later delivered their main blows. The situation developed roughly the same way it developed during the war. The configuration of our border, the terrain and the situation prompted me to take the decisions which the Germans took later."

Not everyone in the Soviet military hierarchy was too pleased. "The people in charge deliberately held up the advance of 'blue.'" Even so, "on the eighth day, 'blue' advanced as far as Baranovichi, though, I repeat, their progress was deliberately impeded."

In a strategy council following the war game, Zhukov took the risk of criticizing the location of Soviet fortifications along the border. "I knew the idea would cause displeasure because the system of fortifications I criticized was approved by the Labour and Defense Council, that is by Stalin." But the much-feared Soviet dictator merely listened and asked a few questions.

"He asked, for instance, why 'blue' were so strong and why we engaged so many German forces at the beginning of the game. I told him that that corresponded to the Germans' capabilities and that we were guided by a real estimate of the forces which the Germans could throw against us, creating a great advantage in the area of the main strike. That was why 'blue' advanced so fast in the game."

Stalin must not have been too perturbed with Zhukov himself, for shortly afterward Zhukov was appointed chief of the General Staff.

How, then, were the Soviets so stunned when the real German forces invaded on June 21, 1941, just a few months later?

The Novosti account offered a few insights on behalf of the Red Army's most famous field commander. For one, when Hitler assured Stalin that German troops were filling up conquered Poland merely to avoid British bombing,

"I think Stalin believed Hitler." For another, Stalin didn't always share the intelligence reports reaching his desk. And he suspected British information as part of a ploy to draw the Soviet Union into the war as an ally.

Red tape, a slow-moving bureaucracy, and half-measures of various kinds also contributed to the lack of preparation. Stalin himself made "mistakes," but he also hoped to forestall war with Germany if at all possible.

"Stalin believed—correctly—that we needed at least two more years to prepare for war," said the Georgi Zhukov account.

In all, "one should not explain everything only by Stalin's mistakes," and while there were mistakes made by any number in the Soviet hierarchy, "we must remember how far ahead of us Germany was in terms of military capability, industrial level, economic efficiency and preparedness for war."

Indeed, "It must not be forgotten that we entered the war as still an industrially backward state in comparison with Germany."

On a related point, Zhukov was—for the often-difficult Russian ally even in World War II days—very nearly effusive in grateful praise for the American supplies that helped the Soviets to hold out and get back on their feet after the initial German onslaught.

The real surprise when Hitler launched his Operation BARBAROSSA, Zhukov also said, was not "that the Germans crossed the border," but Nazi Germany's "six-fold and eight-fold superiority in forces in decisive areas…the scale of their troop amassment and the force of their strike."

Thus, for the first six months, the "blue" Germans were the winners. In time, and at terrible cost, the real "reds" eventually prevailed, as everybody knows—and often, as at Leningrad, Stalingrad, and, ultimately, even Berlin, with Marshal Zhukov himself at the military lead.

★★★

First published in World War II *magazine, May 1988.*

Patterns on a Dining Room Table

OUT OF CHINA IN THE spring of 1941 came the startling intelligence that the Japanese had a fighter plane that could outrace, outclimb, and out-turn any aircraft in somnolent America's military arsenal. For some who were not so somnolent, even before Pearl Harbor, this was grim news indeed. One such man was U.S. Navy aviator John ("Jimmy") Smith Thach.

Apprised of the Zero's performance capabilities, Jimmy Thach hastily repaired, of all places, to his dining room table with a box of ordinary kitchen matches.

"I decided that we had better do something about this airplane," he would later explain, "and I drew on my days on the football field and the basketball court. I knew there that if you come up against somebody who is faster than you are, you have to trap him somehow so that he can't use his superiority, whatever that may be."

For nights on end in the months before his country was drawn into World War II, navy pilot Thach spread out his matches on the dining room table to simulate aircraft formations. The next day, he and his squadron mates would try out his newly learned wrinkles.

He already thought the three-plane formation favored in Europe and the United States was unwieldy. In tight turning maneuvers, one wingman was likely to "slide" into the other. Thach experimented instead with a combat unit of four aircraft, divided into two pairs flying a wide formation. And from that arrangement of kitchen matches came the U.S. Navy's "Thach Weave," whereby each split pair keeps an eye on the other's tail and turns in toward the oncoming enemy's path the moment he appears.

The idea was "if any enemy came after one (pair), from above, ahead or astern, you might be able to confuse him by doing something he didn't expect." Further, the two aircraft "turning in" would have a quick shot at the oncoming Zeros. The turn itself, at the same time, would alert the second pair that they were under attack.

Thach and his squadron mates tried it out. His Lt. Comdr. Edward ("Butch") O'Hare was to take four navy fighters flying at full speed and attack Thach's own formation of planes flying at only half-speed. "So he made all sorts of attacks, quite a few of them from overhead, coming down this way and that. It looked like a pretty good thing to me. Every time he came in to shoot—you can tell when an airplane is in position to shoot—we just kept weaving back and forth."

When the navy pilots landed, O'Hare (for whom Chicago's O'Hare Airport is named) was obviously excited. "Skipper," he said, "it really worked. It really worked. I couldn't make any attack without seeing the nose of one of your half-throttle planes pointed at me."

Explained Thach further: "You needed no communication. You were flying along watching the other two planes of your combat unit. They suddenly made a turn. You knew there was somebody on your tail and you had to turn in a hurry."

Then, a year later and six months after Pearl Harbor, came the Battle of Midway. Thach and his pitiful handful of fighters from the *Yorktown* accompanied the carrier's twelve torpedo planes for their near-suicidal attack on Japanese Admiral Chuichi Nagumo's Carrier Strike Force. As the Americans bore in for the attack, swarms of Zeros met them.

Thach radioed the leader of his unit's other two-plane section to spread out and weave. But his section leader's radio was out. With no reaction from that source, Thach then ordered his own wingman, Ram Dibb: "Pretend you are a section leader and move out far enough to weave."

The Zeros by this time had swooped in. "The air was just like a beehive and I wasn't sure at that moment that anything would work." But then…"my weave began to work! I got a good shot at two Zeros and burned them."

Thach, later a full admiral, didn't expect to come back from the landmark U.S. victory at Midway. But he did. So did his aerial maneuver, the Weave, soon to be passed on to U.S. fighter pilots worldwide. Fortunately for them and the country, Thach had been one of those individuals who was wide awake and prepared for war before the war.

★★★

Based upon The Pacific War Remembered, *edited by John T. Mason, Jr. (Naval Institute Press, Annapolis, Md., 1986).*

Generals from the Eighties

ONE PROVIDES THE PLAN FOR conquering France. Another walks into a Polish field of fire. A third comes closest to Moscow, then, later, is executed as a Resistance member. Still another is the genius behind the *Panzer* divisions. A fifth is the *Luftwaffe* general whose claim to fame is his holding action against Allied land armies in Italy.

And so on goes the list. Not all of Hitler's generals, but a startling array of his not-always-so-eager stalwarts hailed from a single historical bracket, from the decade of the 1880s. For that minuscule window of time is when they were born, so many of them that one has to wonder what impact an infantile epidemic in the 1880s might have wrought upon the course of World War II six decades later. Among the best known of Hitler's military hierarchy, only two would have escaped such a purge—Gerd von Rundstedt (too old) and Erwin Rommel (a year too young).

Hitler himself would have missed World War II with a wipeout of the 1880s, since he was born in 1889. Without him, one may wonder also if there would have been a Second World War at all...and yet, how long would Germany have remained discomfited and sorely rankled by the more stringent provisions of the Versailles Treaty? Or lived peaceably with the knowledge of defeat in World War I? The crystal ball does not say.

Without her generals of the 1880s, meanwhile, Germany would have gone to war in 1939 minus the moving force behind her tank-led *blitzkrieg*, Heinz Guderian (born in 1888).

Then, too, without Erich von Manstein's "Sickle Plan" for the invasion of France by way of the allegedly impassable Ardennes, Germany might have fallen into the same stalemate that greeted her loop through neutral Belgium in World War I. Manstein, it may be recalled, was born in 1887.

Who else? Well, Albert Kesselring, the *Luftwaffe* field marshal who learned to fly when in his late forties, was born in 1885. Nearly sixty years later, he stubbornly held to every foot of Italy possible until the war's eleventh hour, as a ground commander *par excellence*.

Among the ranking commanders taking part in Hitler's invasion of the Soviet Union in 1941 was nearly the entire "Class of the 1880s." For here were Guderian, Manstein, Fedor von Bock (1880); Paul von Kleist (1881); Walter von Reichenau (1884); Guenther von Kluge (1882); and Wilhelm List (1880), to say nothing of various lesser lights. At the same time, pulling strings from headquarters back home were Franz Halder (1884), chief of the Army General Staff, and Walter von Brauchitsch (1881), commander in chief.

In the USSR, the ranking general coming closest to Moscow (together with Hermann Hoth) was Erich Hoepner (1886), whose Fourth Armored Corps had Moscow in its sights late in 1941, until the Russians (and their wintry clime) stopped the advance, then threw it back. A conspirator against Hitler even before the war, Hoepner was accused, tortured, and hanged after the July 20, 1944, bomb plot against Hitler had failed.

Hoepner went to his death refusing to oblige by committing suicide. Kluge, on the other hand, aware of the anti-Hitler conspiracy but a fence-straddler and no activist, did commit suicide when summoned to Hitler's side from the Normandy front in the summer of 1944.

Many in that generation of the 1880s, in fact, met terrifying ends. Werner von Fritsch (1880), chief of the army's High Command and an opponent of Hitler's war plans, was "eased" out of high position in the late 1930s , charged that he was a homosexual. He later was cleared of that cloud and a related charge of submitting to blackmail, but too late, of course, to regain his former post. Recalled to active duty for the invasion of Poland in 1939, as a "Colonel-in-Chief," he walked into the stream of fire from a Polish machine gun.

If Fritsch deliberately sought death, as many surmise, that was not the case with Fedor von Bock, who commanded Army Group Center for the abortive drive on Moscow. Among the many generals dismissed for their alleged "failures" in battle, the former field marshal enjoyed a quiet retirement of sorts in war-torn Germany—until he was killed in an Allied air raid on Schleswig-Holstein May 4, 1945, four days before war's end.

Perhaps the worst fate of all from the generation of the 1880s, though, was that suffered by Karl Heinrich von Stuelpnagel (1886), military governor of occupied France from 1942 to 1944. Noted for his harsh measures against the French Resistance, Stuelpnagel nonetheless was up to his neck in the conspiracy against Hitler that hatched the bomb plot of July 1944.

Before word of Hitler's survival reached Paris, Stuelpnagel exposed his role by ordering the arrest of Gestapo and SS men under his command. Called back to Berlin, he stopped his car at Verdun, walked off a ways, and then shot himself in the head with a pistol.

The suicide attempt failed—he succeeded only in blinding himself. A month later, led by hand to the gallows that he couldn't see, he was hanged in Plötzensee Prison…one more of Hitler's generals from the generation of the 1880s.

★★★

Based upon World War II *magazine, July 1988.*

Memorable Utterances

HARDLY EVER AT A LOSS for words, Winston Churchill certainly had a language and imagery all his own. He had during World War II, for instance, a great many things to say beyond his more famous lines such as the pledge that the British would fight on the beaches, in the fields, in the hills, and in the streets.

Lesser-known but just as pithy is his remark in 1943 on the merits of a proposed campaign in Burma: "Going into the swampy jungle to fight the Japanese is like going into the water to fight a shark."

Then there was his entertaining thought in reaction to an early war meeting in Berlin of Soviet Foreign Minister Vyacheslav Molotov and his German counterpart, Joachim von Ribbentrop. As C. L. Sulzberger recounted the episode in his post-war book, *World War II*, "On that night [November 13, 1940], Molotov had been bargaining with Ribbentrop for spheres of influence in a conquered world." A raid by the British RAF, however, forced the two ministers to seek cover. "But Ribbentrop assured his guest that Britain was finished."

Molotov himself had a memorable reply, "If that is so, why are we in this shelter, and whose are these bombs which fall?"

The irrepressible Churchill, however, had the last word, it seems here, with his remark: "We had heard about the conference beforehand and, though not invited to join in the discussion, did not wish to be entirely left out of the proceedings."

Churchill could also give vent to controlled wrath. "This wicked man," he labeled Hitler upon the sudden bombing of English cities in 1940. And further: "This monstrous product of former wrongs and shame has now resolved to break our famous island race by a process of indiscriminate slaughter and destruction."

Did the prime minister, a savvy politician as well as a national leader and symbol of his nation's bulldog determination, always feel what he had to say? When it came to the defense of his "famous island race," there would seem to be little doubt that he spoke with real, deeply held feeling. But how about those Bolshevik Russians once allied with the monstrous Hitler himself? The story is that as Churchill dictated a speech to the Russian people in response to Hitler's invasion of their country, real tears coursed down his cheeks.

Churchill in his long lifetime naturally had quite a bit to say about many things, many of those utterances still memorable. Although his finest hour as image-maker was in World War II, it may sometimes be forgotten that he once was a newspaper correspondent covering the adventures of a nineteenth-century British Empire in places such as South Africa, India, and the Sudan. Sometime early in the twentieth century, though, he made his choice when it came to attendance at news-making events. "It is better to be making news than taking it," he decided, "to be an actor rather than a critic."

By the time of World War II and all its tragedy, ordeal, and responsive heroism—including that of the unbowed spirit who led the British—he certainly had become a maker of news rather than a "taker."

Even in private company his were utterances that mesmerized his listeners. "I marvelled how he could appear so carefree with the enormous load of anxieties on his shoulders," wrote a British corps commander after a dinner party at Chequers in the summer of 1940, Britain's most difficult hour, "and I wish I could remember some of the splendid sentences that rolled off his tongue."

There was one moment during World War II, however, when even the ebullient Churchill apparently was rendered speechless. As was his wont, recalled Max Hastings in his *Oxford Book of Military Anecdotes*, he had spontaneously called a section of the War Office, this one dealing with the Middle East, to confer with its chief officer. Simply asking if he had the right office on the line, Churchill then began a round of questions.

"How do you think the operations are going in Syria?" he asked.

"Oh," came the answer, "I think everything is going all right."

Churchill probed further. How about the turning movement being executed by the French?

Again the answer: "Oh, that seems to be all right."

Finally Churchill asked to whom he was speaking.

"Corporal Jones, Duty Clerk," came the answer.

End of conversation.

★★★

First published in World War II *magazine, July 1990.*

Saga Piled upon Saga

NOT ONLY TRIUMPH FOR ONE side, tragedy for the other, but often the totally unexpected attends so many wartime sagas of the sea. In the *Graf Spee* fight of December 1939, who, first of all, would have expected the lighter-gunned British cruisers *Ajax, Exeter,* and *Achilles* to contain the monster that was before them—a modern, fully armed pocket battleship?

And then, secondly, who expected the famous scuttling of the great German Goliath? Certainly not the crowds watching as the *Graf Spee* made ready, it seemed, to leave the neutral port of Montevideo for the wide seas—and the waiting British, with who knew how many warships. But in midstream, as it were, the pocket battleship stopped full. "The great crowd immediately below us, denied their sight of a battle, was quite hushed. What was going to happen? Time passed in considerable speculation and suspense, but the truth, unlikely though it appeared, was beginning to dawn on some of us."

Thus went the recollection of the British naval attaché based in nearby Buenos Aires. "Exactly as the sun set behind her, a great volume of smoke billowed up—and an enormous flash was followed in due course by the boom of a large explosion. So the *Graf Spee* met her end." Scuttled, rather than go forth and meet the awaiting Royal Navy flotilla.

Still, the unexpected here was caused by man, when often at sea, it is not. Take, for instance, the double saga of the *Jervis Bay* and the *San Demetrio.* The initial action belonged to the armed British merchantman *Jervis Bay,* whose six-inch guns were the prime protection for an entire convoy of thirty-seven homebound ships when they were accosted in the North Atlantic by the powerful German pocket battleship *Scheer* in the autumn of 1940.

As the convoy's sole escort, *Jervis Bay* bravely charged forward, her smaller guns merely popping in vain. The sleek German wolfhound blinked in surprise at this seagoing mutt's effrontery, then savaged the pest with big eleven-inch guns. The saving grace for the Allies was that *Jervis Bay's* suicidal attack allowed the convoy to scatter while *Scheer* was momentarily busy at her kill. By the time *Jervis Bay* was dealt with, the *Scheer* could only catch up to and pummel five of the original thirty-seven. Those five did become victims of the raider, but thirty-two others did not. For his willing sacrifice, the *Jervis Bay's* captain, E. S. F. Fegen, received the Victoria Cross—posthumous, since he went down with his ship.

But the double saga was not yet over, since one of the five *Scheer* victims was to reappear—like a ghost, but a very solid ghost. After the tanker *San Demetrio* had been smashed and holed by the *Scheer's* big shells, it seems, a handful of surviving crew abandoned their burning ship and its cargo of high-octane aviation fuel for the uncertainties of a lifeboat. As told by Richard Hough in his book *The Longest Battle: The War at Sea, 1939–1945*, they survived their first night in the freezing North Atlantic latitudes and passed most of the next day without real incident—that is, unfortunately, without discovery or rescue.

Late in the afternoon, they came upon a drifting, burning ship. Rowing closer, they soon saw that it was their own, the *San Demetrio*, still afloat!

With nightfall upon them and the seas running high, they didn't quite dare to attempt reboarding, but moved to the "weather side" for protection against the nasty elements and tried to stay close. By next morning, however, she was gone, practically—on the horizon and still blazing away. It would be a long haul to catch up to her again.

The night on the open water, though, had been so sapping, the survivors determined the very ship they had abandoned would be their only hope of salvation. "She was the only thing we could see in all the wide circle of ocean and she looked good," wrote Able Seaman Calum MacNeil later. "At least very warm. She might blow up at any time, but that was quick and painless death compared with this slow freezing and sickness, this forced labour of failing muscles."

Just as important, perhaps more, also noted MacNeil later, the *San Demetrio* was their own ship, "still floating in spite of what she had suffered." Not only was she home to the woebegone band in the lifeboat, but: "She was ours and had not failed us. She had looked for us and by some miracle had found us. We could not fail her."

The survivors did catch up and they did creep back aboard. The ship that they found upon reboarding was a wreck—smashed and burned, flames still flaring, provisions destroyed, engine room partially flooded, the dead—or their ashes—all about. But the survivors from the lifeboat somehow got the fire out. They got the engines going "after a superhuman effort of salvage." They turned (somehow again) for home. They did all this, plus took the tanker all the way to Glasgow, Scotland, "without charts, compass or steering," says Hough, all in a manner "typical of the gallantry, determination and endurance of those who fought the Battle of the Atlantic."

Graf Spee had only been a start. *Jervis Bay* and *San Demetrio* were only continuation. The Atlantic, North and South, but mostly North, would remain a long, grueling saga of the war.

★★★

Based upon The Longest Battle: The War At Sea, 1939–1945, *by Richard Hough (William Morrow and Company, New York, 1986).*

Early Martyr at Auschwitz

"IN AUSCHWITZ," REPORTED A PROTESTANT doctor later, "I knew of no other similar case of such heroic love of neighbor, though I was indeed there from 1941 to 1945."

Father Maximilian Kolbe had arrived in May of 1941, before Nazi Germany invaded the Soviet Union, before Pearl Harbor, but after the subjugation of France and the Low countries.

Polish born, he was forty-seven, but not terribly well. Twice in his life he had been in a TB sanitorium. There he had a name. At Auschwitz he had a number: 16670.

Commandant Fritsch told a subordinate named Krott what to do with Father Kolbe and other priests with him. "Take these useless creatures and parasites of society and show them what work means." It didn't matter that Father Kolbe was the founder of the Knights of the Immaculata, a worldwide organization dedicated to the Virgin Mary.

The priest's fellow prisoners included Miecislaus Koscielniak, an artist. Koscielniak remembered the Feast of Corpus Christi that June of 1941. "[Father Kolbe] spoke of the great and almighty God, of the suffering by which God prepared us for a better life. He exhorted us to manly forbearance, for even these trials pass. Since there is a divine justice and providence, we need not lose heart."

Father Kolbe also told his fellow prisoners: "No, no, they will not kill our souls....We will not give up. And when we die, then we die pure and peaceful, resigned to God in our hearts."

Thus he preached. But this was no restorative religious retreat. It still was Auschwitz. His wardens gave him the dirtiest jobs because he was so openly a priest. They set dogs on him to make him work faster. They beat him and left him for dead under some brush.

He wound up in the camp infirmary. There, said a fellow priest, Father Conrad Szweda, "Father Kolbe's face was lined with scars, his eyes lifeless, the fever burned in his body so that his mouth dried out; he could no longer speak."

But his condition did improve somewhat. And when it did, said Father Szweda, "With manliness and with full resignation he bore his sufferings. Often he replied, 'For Jesus Christ I am prepared to suffer still more.'"

One day, Krott had loaded up the Franciscan priest with more wood than he could possibly carry, then ordered him to run. Father Kolbe tried. He tried to run with all the wood, but he tripped and fell heavily. He was then kicked in the face and stomach and hit with a club.

His illness didn't really go away. He was placed in the typhus ward at the infirmary. Here, said Father Szweda, "It was easier for me to speak with him. His bed was at the chief entrance to the hall. He gave conditional absolution to each dead person who passed him. Often he heard confessions, prayed with the others...."

One time, Szweda brought him tea, but Father Kolbe turned it down. "Why should I be the exception?" he said. "The others don't have it."

June passed, July came on. "At the end of July 1941, we were together in Block 20, the infirmary," wrote a fellow prisoner. "Like many others I crawled at night on the bare floor to the bed of Father Maximilian. The greeting was moving. We exchanged some impressions on the frightening crematorium. He encouraged me, then I confessed.

"Discouragement and doubt overwhelmed me; I still wanted to live. He helped me strengthen my belief in the victory of good. 'Hate is not creative; love is creative,' he whispered to me."

Soon, his fever not yet fully abated, he was transferred to Block 12, with the infirm and the fatally ill as companions. They were considered good for nothing as workers.

Here, the Protestant doctor came to know "the Servant of God as a man of unusual ways and extraordinary character."

While spiritually "healthy," Father Kolbe "had much to suffer bodily," said the doctor. "Tuberculosis consumed him." Even so, he was "calm," always waiting for the doctor to treat others before stepping forward himself. He repeatedly sacrificed himself for others.

His health again improving a bit, the Franciscan priest next was moved to Block 14, to join prisoners assigned to farm labor. Only one more move remained ahead for Father Kolbe.

The final drama of his life began one morning as the prisoners from Block 14 shuffled off to their day's harvesting work. That day one of the farm-working prisoners ran off, escaped.

His fellows could have rejoiced for him, and perhaps did...but what would befall them as a consequence? At Auschwitz, the rule was, ten prisoners executed for every escapee who stayed at large. Father Kolbe certainly knew that by chance, by God's will, he was in the eye of such a storm.

That night, the inmates of Block 14 were not allowed to go to supper. The next morning, they were called out, ordered to stand in formation but told to remain there as the prisoners from other blocks went off to work. The storm was gathering.

They stood in their formation under the hot sun until given a half-hour lunch break about three o'clock. They were then forced to remain in their ranks until evening. By then several of the prisoners had collapsed.

Now there would be a roll call, and the missing man would still be missing. It was a moment demanding the personal attention of Commandant Fritsch. After a subordinate named Palitsch announced that ten from Block 14 must die, Fritsch personally moved through the ranks pointing his finger at one man here, another there, until all of the doomed ten had been chosen.

Only human, many of those spared the random choice were relieved. Even so, the separation of the ten from the ranks was an ordeal to witness. One choice especially. A Polish army sergeant, Francis Gajowniczek. "My poor wife!" he wailed. "My poor children! What will happen to my family?"

That was when Father Kolbe acted.

"After the selection of the ten prisoners," said Dr. Nicetus Wlodarski, an onlooking fellow prisoner, "Father Maximilian slipped out of line, took off his cap, and placed himself before the commandant. Astounded, Fritsch asked him, 'What does this Polish pig want?"

Pointing to Gajowniczek, Father Kolbe in effect condemned himself. "I am a Catholic priest from Poland," he said. "I would like to take his place, because he has a wife and children."

Obviously startled, Fritsch hesitated a moment, then with a wave of his hand gave his assent. "Away," he said.

Thus, a saint was created.

As the sergeant with a family returned to the ranks of Block 14, Father Kolbe joined the condemned men now transferred to the underground cells of Block 11, where, naked, all ten would be held under the sentence of starvation to death.

As was his established pattern, Father Kolbe to the end offered his fellows physical and spiritual comfort. Bruno Borgowiec, by his own description, was the appointed "secretary and interpreter in this subterranean bunker." Thus he often was with the guards in visits to the death cells—when a prisoner died, "I had to record the identity number of the deceased or translate questions and answers in conversations with the prisoners."

Over the next two weeks, denied both food and drink, "one after the other" of the doomed ten died, Borgowiec said.

All this time, Father Kolbe "did not whine, neither did he murmur." Those still surviving were so weak they could only whisper their prayers with him. But he "was still standing or kneeling in the middle of the cell and looking calmly at those entering, while the others were already lying on the ground."

Three weeks passed, and now the cells were in demand for new victims. Father Kolbe and three of his original companions still lived. That apparently wouldn't do. On August 14, all four were injected in the left arm with a lethal dose of carbolic acid.

It is not a date often mentioned in histories or chronologies of World War II, but on October 10, 1982, Polish-born Pope John Paul II of the Roman Catholic Church completed a long preparatory process by declaring his fellow Pole, Father Maximilian Kolbe, a saint.

★★★

Based upon The Hero of Auschwitz: The Story of Saint Maximilian Kolbe, OFM CONV., *The Knight of the Immaculata (Prow Books/Franciscan Marytown Press, Libertyville, IL, undated).*

Whose Planes These?

CALL IT THE SOVIET UNION's Pearl Harbor. At the tip of a storied peninsula stands a storied city where, in 1854, a young artillery officer named Leo Tolstoy once watched war and battle unfold before his eyes: the Russian port city of Sevastopol on the Black Sea, at the tip of the Crimean Peninsula.

But now, years later, came the night of June 21–22, 1941. No war yet between the two tyrannical giants, Nazi Germany and Soviet Russia, but many, many rumors…and almost as many denials.

A full alert throughout the Soviet navy had been ordered from Moscow. Sevastopol and units of the Black Sea Fleet had been blacked out as a precaution. City officials objected but were told to obey and mind their own business as the main power station was shut down at navy orders.

In short order, the city and its military and harbor installations were dark. *Almost*, that is. Two lighthouse beams, self-generated, shone forth bravely. By mundane chance, they had been turned on earlier to guide an outgoing garbage scow, and now the telephone line to each was—for reasons unknown—out of commission. A messenger on motorcycle was sent roaring off to give the lighthouse keepers the word.

By two o'clock the morning of June 22, a Sunday, the fleet units, the city, were battened down, ready for an attack that might or might not actually materialize. Who could be sure? Shortly after three o'clock, Captain N. G. Rybalko, officer of the day at fleet headquarters that historic night, received word from watchers (acoustical-instrument *listeners*, actually) at two coastal points to the west that they had "picked up" the sound of approaching aircraft.

Could they be Soviet planes? Should they be fired upon? *Whose planes were they?* The word was—no Soviet planes were in the air.

Going up his chain of command to the very top of the fleet hierarchy, Rybalko asked permission to fire upon the apparent intruders. If it turned out he was wrong, if there were Soviet aircraft in the air, he was told, he would be shot the next day.

And he was left with no clear answer.

But Rybalko bravely persisted until he did obtain explicit permission from Vice Adm. I. D. Eliseyev, chief of staff for the Black Sea Fleet. And even then there was a further snag. Lieutenant I. S. Zhilin, on night duty with elements of the regional antiaircraft command, had called earlier, requesting that same permission to shoot down the intruding aircraft.

Now that Rybalko could say yes, go ahead, Zhilin balked.

The story is told in Harrison Salisbury's book *The 900 Days: The Siege of Leningrad*. The story is that Lieutenant Zhilin was very careful with his bureaucratic P's and Q's.

"Bear in mind," he warned Rybalko, "that you are taking full responsibility for this order. I am putting this note into my operations journal."

Exasperated by this time, Rybalko shouted in reply, "Write what you want, but open fire on those planes!"

Seconds later, the Soviet "triple A" guns were firing into the night sky above Sevastopol and the lower Crimea. But seconds later also, the bombs were falling. German bombs.

All up and down the USSR's western borders, too, Hitler's Operation BARBAROSSA, his invasion of the Soviet Union, would be erupting that early summer morning.

By now, it was perhaps 3:15 A.M. in Sevastopol, and more time was wasted trying to convince Moscow. Naval Commissar Nikolai G. Kuznetsov tried to call Stalin, but could only reach *Politburo* member Georgi Malenkov, who growled, "Do you understand what you have reported?"

"I understand," replied Kuznetsov, "and I report on my own responsibility. War has started."

Even when finally alerted in person, Stalin, for hours to come, would call the frenzied military activity at the borders merely a provocation by the "German generals."

In the Baltic Sea, far to the north and west, meanwhile, the clock had barely reached 3:20 A.M. when four German cutters torpedoed a Latvian steamer loaded with wood off the Swedish island of Gotland.

Surviving Soviet sailors were machine-gunned in the water. The several killed in this encounter may have been the first casualties suffered by the Soviet Union in its "Great Patriotic War" against Nazi Germany.

There would be 20 million more—20,000,000—before that war within a world war would come to a stop four years later.

★★★

First published in World War II *magazine, July 1991.*

Warnings Repeatedly Ignored

FROM THE TIME OF HIS appointment as commander of the Soviet Fifteenth Infantry Corps in April of 1941, General I. I. Fedyuninsky had no doubt that *something* was developing on the German side of the USSR's western border, just thirty miles from his new headquarters at Kovel in the Special Kiev Military District (West Ukraine). "From a great variety of sources and from our army and frontier-guard reconnaissance, we knew that since February German troops had begun to concentrate along our borders," he later wrote.

In addition, there were overflights by German aircraft, even sporadic cross-border commando raids.

Meanwhile, the Soviet frontier fortifications were developing slowly. New equipage—tanks and airplanes—was sporadic in its arrival along the USSR's truly vast western frontier. And the soldiers...the soldiers stationed along the border areas simply were complacent. "Many of them thought that our army could win an easy victory, and that the soldiers of any capitalist country, including Nazi Germany, would not fight actively against the Red Army," wrote Fedyuninsky. "They also underrated the military experience and the enormous technical equipment of the German army."

The one consolation for commanders in the field such as Fedyuninsky was the thought that at least *Stalin* knew.

And he did, apparently. But rather than speed up his country's defensive efforts, sound the alarm, or pull some rabbit out of the hat, Stalin was doing very little. "At that time, we did not yet know that Stalin, disregarding the reports of our intelligence and of the commanders of our frontier districts, had badly misjudged the international situation and particularly the timing of the Nazi aggression," said Fedyuninsky.

As late as June 14, the government-controlled press agency TASS put out a statement saying rumors of pending German aggression were "completely groundless." Many Russians never forgot that bit of false assurance.

Out in the field, at his station close to the border, Fedyuninsky four days later was told of a German deserter who had "come over" to the Reds. The German had fled his own side for fear of punishment for striking an officer while drunk. The deserter said Nazi Germany would invade the Soviet Union precisely at 4 A.M. on June 22. (Different histories give this story in conflicting detail.)

Fedyuninsky's warnings based upon the deserter's very precise statement were ignored by the Russian chain of command—and early on the morning of June 22, of course, the Germans *did* invade Russia. The "accepted" hour historically indeed is 4 A.M., but there were sporadic probes and clashes even earlier that Sunday morning.

Rushing his Fifteenth Infantry Corps forward, Fedyuninsky found the frontier forces "fighting to the last man," even though they were overwhelmed. And not only to the last *man*! "Even the wives of the frontier guards were in the firing line, carrying water and ammunition, and taking care of the wounded. Some of the women were firing at the advancing Nazis."

Not only the guards but also the Red Army forces were overwhelmed in those first hours...in those early days, weeks, even months. Even Stalin seemed to be overwhelmed by such catastrophe—he was mysteriously gone from public sight...and silent. It was to be late fall before the Nazi juggernaut could be halted anywhere, its momentum even then merely stopped and many months to go before it discernibly was being rolled back, and back, with gathering momentum again...in reverse of its direction in 1941.

In the meantime, though, while disaster still stalked, there at last came Stalin's famous and, by all accounts, stirring speech of July 3, a rallying cry that reached beyond communist ideology, deep into the Russian soul. "It is hard to describe the enormous enthusiasm and patriotic uplift with which this appeal was met," said Fedyuninsky. "We suddenly seemed to feel much stronger."

The war, however, was far from over, and in the moments and years ahead, Fedyuninsky was to distinguish himself as a commander with a key role in breaking the nine-hundred-day siege of Leningrad.

★★★

First published in World War II *magazine, July 1991.*

War "Half as Bad as It Sounds"

GERMAN TANK GUNNER KARL FUCHS, a callow youth, was in on the big show—Hitler's invasion of the Soviet Union, June 1941. "He was born in 1917 and as a youth grew up with the teachings of National Socialism," wrote his widow, Helene Fuchs-Richardson, many years later. "He was an impressionable young man and, like many of his contemporaries, was overwhelmed by the preaching of the party."

They had met as students at the University of Wurzburg, both studying education and planning to be teachers. "Karl's happy disposition, his sense of humor, his idealism, and his talent in music, especially in singing, made him a truly special person."

But the war came along, and soon Karl was writing home from the front, the later-to-be dreaded eastern front. At first, things went swimmingly for the young Hitlerites and their middle-aged generals plunging into Soviet territory by storm and surprise.

To Helene, June 17, 1941, while on the move to the East—

> *Our status at present here at this temporary base is still uncertain. No one knows what is going to happen to us but we feel that some kind of decision will be forthcoming in a matter of days—if not in a matter of hours. We all sense that something is about to happen. Don't worry about me…*

To his wife again, June 25, 1941, from Lithuania—

> *We marched into Vilnius [Vilna], cheered on by the jubilant citizens. Yesterday*

I knocked off a Russian tank, as I had done two days ago! If I get in another attack, I'll receive my first battle stripes. War is half as bad as it sounds...

Karl and his Seventh *Panzer* Division were attached to the Thirty-ninth *Panzer* Corps, itself a part of *Panzergruppe* 3 on the left wing of Army Group Center. His division forced its way into Vilna, Lithuania, on June 24 before turning toward Minsk in Russia proper.

To his wife from Russian territory, June 28, 1941—

Up to now, all of the troops have had to accomplish quite a bit. The same goes for our machines and tanks. But, nevertheless, we're going to show those Bolshevik bums who's who around here! They fight like hired hands—not like soldiers, no matter if they are men, women, or children on the front lines. They're all no better than a bunch of scoundrels....

The impressions that the battles have left on me will be with me forever. Believe me, dearest, when you see me again, you will face quite a different person, a person who has learned the harsh command: "I will survive!" You can't afford to be soft in war; otherwise you will die. No, you must be tough—indeed, you have to be pitiless and relentless. Don't I sound like a different person to you? Deep down in my heart, I remain a good person and my love for you and our son will never diminish. Never! This love will increase as will my longing for you. I kiss you and remain forever.

Your Korri

★★★

Based upon Sieg Heil! War Letters of Tank Gunner Karl Fuchs, 1937–1941, *compiled, edited, and translated by Horst Fuchs Richardson (his son); historical commentary by Dennis Showalter (Archon Books, Shoe String Press, Hamden, Conn., 1987).*

Countdown

As the fateful year began in America, the federal budget was a mere $17.5 billion. Dick and Pat were six-month newlyweds. The Nixons.

In Washington, FDR assumed the throne for his third term. In Washington also, American and British military leaders held secret talks, deciding by their

ABC-1 plan that Nazi Germany would be first priority for both in the event
that the United States should enter the war against Germany and Japan.

In March 1941, the Congress agreed to FDR's Lend-Lease Plan, which
allowed him to "lend" material help to any nation considered vital to U.S.
interests. Read: Britain as the intended recipient.

In April, FDR extended America's sea frontier zone far into Atlantic waters
in an effort to stop German submarines from operating close to U.S. shores…
largely against the British. In May, a German U-boat sank the American merchant ship *Robin Moor* inside the line. In Singapore, U.S. military men met with
British and Dutch counterparts and formulated *what-if* plans for joint strategy
against Japan in the event it attacked the United States.

Soon FDR denounced the collaborative Vichy French and seized the luxury
liner *Normandie*. And so, the pace quickened. In May 1941, FDR declared a
state of national emergency. In June, he froze German and Italian assets in the
United States.

FDR was not being entirely arbitrary in all his actions. Highhanded, some
will still say, but he, of course, was reacting to events elsewhere, outside of
"Fortress America." Hitler by now had overrun all of Western Europe except
Portugal, Spain, Sweden, Switzerland, and England, and he was at war with
England. He had made war on Yugoslavia and Greece, and with his ally Italy
was fighting in North Africa. In the Far East, the Japanese were flexing muscle
and pummeling the helpless China giant.

Communists everywhere were in shock, since their ideal, the Soviet Union,
had joined the German dismemberment of Poland back in 1939.

In June 1941, Hitler resolved their dilemma by attacking the USSR on a
broad front.

Days before, FDR had closed down the German and Italian consulates in
America. Now, he promised aid of all kinds to the beleaguered Soviet Union. In
July, by reciprocal agreement, U.S. Marines landed in Iceland as a protective force.

The buildup of events continued. Relentlessly. FDR in July seized Japanese
assets, in response to Japan's incursions in French Indochina (the future
Vietnam). In July, too, the Philippines' armed forces were nationalized under
U.S. command, with Douglas MacArthur named commander in chief of all
American forces in the Far East.

In August, FDR and Winston Churchill met in Newfoundland, to issue their
Atlantic Charter (a basis for the postwar United Nations, as events turned out).

The pace again quickened. The draft in America meant eighteen months'
service instead of a mere year. FDR issued his "shoot on sight" order (against

Axis ships or planes) for the sea frontier zone. The U.S. Navy took on shepherding duty for all ship convoys east to Iceland.

And so it went. In October, the U.S. destroyer *Kearney* was torpedoed off Iceland. Later that month, the U.S. destroyer *Reuben James* was sunk off Iceland. And the United States was not even at war.

★★★

First published in World War II *magazine, March 1991.*

Farewell from Stalin

THE NEOPHYTE ARTILLERY OFFICER who briefly spoke on the telephone with his father the day the Germans invaded their Soviet Union had been rated only "fair" in the fundamentals of Marxism-Leninism.

That rating, occurring a short while before, had been at the Red Army's Artillery Academy. He earned a "fair" in tactics, as well. In shooting, artillery equipment, and English, however, he earned a better grade: "good."

Yakov Dzhugashvili, in his late thirties, emerged a senior lieutenant. The commander of his 151st Training Section, according to the Soviet press agency Novosti, gave the aspiring officer a higher rating in an efficiency report— "showed himself well prepared during probationary period for the post of battery commander. Coped with his work well. Can be recommended for the next rank—captain."

But the commander's higher-ups decided that Yakov Dzhugashvili would need a year's experience commanding an artillery battery before he could be made a captain.

That was in March 1941, and fate—in the form of Nazi Germany's invasion June 22—would not grant him that added year of preparation.

On June 27, Yakov was in action for the first time, his battery a part of the Fourteenth Armored Division's Fourteenth Howitzer Artillery Regiment. On July 4, the German Third Panzer Division cut off Yakov's division. By July 16, among thousands like him, the fledgling officer had been captured near Vitebsk.

Interrogated by his captors, he allegedly explained details of his capture this way: "On July 12, our unit was surrounded and a heavy air bombardment followed. I decided to fight my way to our troops, but was hit and stunned. I would have shot myself if I had been able to."

In the same interrogation, he allegedly told his German captors they never could take Moscow—a prediction in which he was proved correct.

He and his famous father never had an easy relationship, it seems. Yakov's own autobiographical statement, written for an official Soviet dossier in 1939, had explained that he was born in Baku in 1903, "into the family of a professional revolutionary."

The Bolshevik Revolution of 1917, of course, then came along, and by 1939, Yakov could add, "Father is now at Party work in Moscow."

Somehow, in the alarm and confusion of June 22, 1941, the day of the German invasion, they managed a telephone connection and had a last conversation with each other. Allegedly, that is also what Yakov told his German interrogators.

What might Stalin have told his son on that day, in their last conversation? "As he learned that I was leaving for the front, he said, 'Go and fight.'"

Yakov, son of Stalin, did not survive his captivity. In fact, his fate surely ranks among the more tragic of the entire war.

According to Soviet historian Alexander Kolesnik's account for Novosti, it is not clear whether Yakov ever learned that his wife, Yulia Meltser, was thrown into prison for nearly two years after his capture.

But Yakov did hear, was stunned to hear, was "hardest hit" to hear, his father Stalin's statements that in the Red Army, "there are no prisoners of war, there are traitors."

Yakov consistently refused to cooperate in German attempts to use him for propaganda aimed at undermining the determination of Soviet troops to fight on against the Germans.

He survived a starvation camp where prisoners resorted to cannibalism. He joined an escape plot but was betrayed. Always, among POWs, he was a marked man—*Stalin's son*. He first was cajoled, then pressured, then threatened, in German efforts to "turn" him, Stalin's son, to use him for propaganda.

It was an added burden few could ever appreciate—*Stalin's son*.

A former POW once housed with him said: "His attitude to the Nazis was uncompromising. During checks he did not stand to attention, and in general [he] behaved defiantly and never saluted the German officers, for which he was often sent to the punishment cell."

Finally, he was transferred to the Sachsenhausen death camp. On April 14, 1943, said another POW incarcerated with him, "Yakov refused to enter the barrack and ran instead to the no man's land."

The sentry who then shot him is quoted as saying that Yakov, *Stalin's son*, gripped the wires at the perimeter and shouted: "Hey, you are a soldier, so don't be a coward. Shoot me!"

With the report of the sentry's pistol, Yakov Dzhugashvili's last wish was granted. His death was instantaneous.

★★★

Based upon Military Bulletin, *July 1988, distributed by Novosti, Soviet Press Agency.*

Ally in the White House

A FORMER U.S. SECRETARY OF Commerce and architect of the Roosevelt administration's New Deal domestic policies, he was an already-exhausted and, indeed, sickly man as he took up residence in the White House itself for three and a half wartime years. And not for any rest period, either. On the contrary, he would be traveling abroad repeatedly on behalf of his president and commander in chief, Franklin Delano Roosevelt.

Politically, he was not the most popular of FDR's lieutenants, true, but he now played a crucial role for the Allies during the war.

He held no military rank, no further cabinet post, no ambassadorship, but FDR's longtime confidant and political ally now turned from New Deal strategies to join the key Allied policymakers of World War II. Bouncing across the Atlantic again and again, he soon was a familiar face in London, even a visitor to wartime Moscow. It goes almost without saying that he was wined and dined by Churchill and Stalin.

And yet, his stomach shrunken by cancer surgery at age fifty, he was an unlikely and frail warrior at best. Long before Pearl Harbor, long before the FDR confidant embarked upon his high-risk wartime missions, FDR himself told others, "The doctors have given Harry up for dead."

On the contrary, FDR aide Harry L. Hopkins somehow survived the four war years still to come—he even outlived Roosevelt himself, albeit by less than a year.

He first met Churchill when he spent the better part of a month visiting England early in 1941, a time when the Roosevelt administration unofficially was doing its best to shore up sagging British fortunes in the face of the Nazi behemoth chewing up Western Europe.

Hopkins then—shortly after Nazi Germany's invasion of its own ally the Soviet Union in late June 1941—traveled thousands of dangerous miles east to Moscow and the Kremlin. The trip required two stages, we are reminded by Matthew B. Wills in his 1996 book, *Wartime Missions of Harry L. Hopkins*.

On the first leg, Hopkins crossed the Atlantic from Washington, D.C., to England by air, but he then had to endure a risky two-thousand-mile flight from the British Isles to Archangel—twenty hours non-stop aboard a lumbering American-made Consolidated PBY Catalina. "The responsibility for getting Hopkins to Russia fell squarely on the shoulders of twenty-eight-year-old RAF Flight Lieutenant David McKinley," wrote Wills. "Although McKinley had experience with long-range patrols over the North Atlantic, he never had flown around the North Cape of Norway to Archangel."

Harry Hopkins (third from right) poses with Winston Churchill (third from left) and various U.S. and British dignitaries in July 1942. (U.S. Navy Historical Center)

The greatest risk, obviously enough, would be possible attack by German fighters based in occupied Norway. What to do in that event?

McKinley had a plan, a tenuous one, but a plan nonetheless. "I was attacked many times by German and Italian fighters in the Mediterranean," McKinley, by now a retired airvice-marshal, told author Wills. "And each time I dived to sea level where the fighters seemed unable to pull out and so, plunged into the water. I would have tried like tactics had I been attacked on the Archangel route."

Fortunately, they were not attacked, but Hopkins, already exhausted, still faced a four-hour flight from Archangel to Moscow. Before taking off on that added hop, he had enjoyed only two hours of sleep and then had gone through a sumptuous, vodka-laced welcoming dinner aboard a Soviet admiral's yacht.

Awaiting FDR's frail emissary at the end of this taxing itinerary was the Soviet dictator Joseph Stalin, one of the most feared men in the world, one of history's bloodiest tyrants. As the exhausted traveler extended FDR's promises of material help for the USSR in its hour of greatest need, Stalin—unsurprisingly—was more than cordial. He furnished Hopkins a monster list of Soviet war needs while also offering various claims and assurances that later turned out to be less than entirely truthful.

They would meet again, naturally, at the international conferences that both FDR and his successor, Harry S. Truman, would attend, at Yalta in the Crimea and Potsdam, Germany.

But Hopkins carried the policy ball for FDR—and American interests in general—at another key conference, this one held in London much earlier, in the summer of 1942. That was when the American and British military chiefs met to hammer out a joint Allied strategy for defeating Nazi Germany's formidable forces in Africa, Europe, and the Soviet Union. With conflicting plans on the table, the most urgent question was when and where to go on the offensive.

The summertime conference resulted in the decisions to invade North Africa that fall and to postpone any cross-Channel assault on occupied Europe until the Allies were strong enough to land and stay, as they did at Normandy two years later.

Hopkins survived the strain of such tough conferences, his repeated travels, and the war itself before finally succumbing to his health problems in early 1946. He had lived long enough, though, to receive a grateful nation's Distinguished Service Medal after the formal surrender of Japan in September 1945. As might be expected, the citation cited his "exceptional ability to weld our Allies to the common purpose of victory over aggression" while also noting his "selfless, courageous and objective contribution to the war effort."

Indeed, during his residency in the presidential quarters themselves, America's allies knew that in addition to the crippled—also ailing—FDR, they could turn to another sympathetic and helpful man in the White House, Harry Hopkins.

★★★

Based upon Wartime Missions of Harry L. Hopkins *by Matthew B. Wills (Pentland Press, Raleigh, N.C., 1996).*

Fleet of Moles

NELLIE WAS HER NAME, THIS dragonlike, earth-gobbling machine that was Winston Churchill's pet both in World War I and in World War II. Never mind that in the first of those wars she never was built, and in the second, her day already had passed. The fact is that for a time there really was a 77½ foot, 140-ton machine that slid through the earth like a giant slug and left a deep trench in her wake.

After pushing development of the tank in WWI with considerable foresight, Churchill next conceived of a fleet of mechanical "moles" like Nellie that would burrow trenches up to fixed defenses during the night. At that point, the infantry following the mechanical monster's track would spring to the attack against a thoroughly startled enemy.

In the stalemated trench warfare of WWI, such a fleet would have been very useful indeed. But the mechanical state of the art was not yet on-line.

When World War II came along, with the long "Phony War" following the German invasion of Poland in September 1939, Churchill again proposed his mole concept, in case of another trench stalemate on the great continent lying across the English Channel.

But the German *blitzkrieg* unleashed against France and the Low Countries in May 1940 forever dashed the concept of static defenses withstanding the new, highly mechanized weapons of war. Nonetheless, while assuming the post of prime minister, Churchill insisted that England would have her Nellie.

Apparently for the first time, the full and detailed story of the Churchillian project, a well-kept secret during the war, appeared in a booklike "paper" published in 1988 by the Society for Lincolnshire (England) History and Archaeology as *"Nellie": The History of Churchill's Lincoln-Built Trenching Machine,* by John T. Turner.

A press release from the historical group underscored Churchill's initial hope to avoid "the trench warfare and horrific casualties of the First World War." Despite the highly mobile tank warfare that Nazi Germany introduced in Poland, and then employed to perfection in the conquest of France, a handful of "mole machines" was built anyway. And "Nellie was a masterpiece of heavy engineering, the biggest machine of its kind ever built, and it worked."

As might be imagined, creation of such a huge self-propelled, trench-digging machine at a time of national emergency and carefully husbanded resources was a mind-boggling feat—"a tale of a challenge accepted, wrestled with, and overcome against terrific odds."

Flinging away the loose dirt as it traveled, the fantastic machine "was to travel at .5 mph through no man's land at night, cutting a trench six feet wide and six feet deep for infantry to follow and penetrate enemy lines."

Fairly successful in field trials, the original Nellie carried a three-man crew. They were the pilot, seated in a topside conning tower with a slit window for visibility; a driver seated below, facing the rear and driving totally blind; and the unfortunate engineer, trapped in a mechanical cubicle full of oil fumes and deafening engine noise (from two 600-horsepower engines).

The machine, visited by Churchill in person during its field trials, consisted of a plow-and-cutting section in front and the "propel" section in the back. Like a very slow-moving submarine, it could dig into the earth, nose first, find its proper level, and then proceed on the chosen course (more or less). Steering, though, was a major problem, and tree roots tended to stop Nellie in her self-made tracks.

In the end, Nellie never was sent to the Continent, and she died a dinosaur's unlamented death. Only six of the giant machines were completed.

"On Churchill's instructions," writes author Turner, "they were to be kept serviced and ready in case a need for them arose." It never did, and "all but one were reduced to scrap shortly after the end of the war." The one remaining machine, apparently the original, was consigned to like fate in the 1950s—once Churchill was out of office.

And so vanished the last of Churchill's once farsighted mole-machines— "and much that might have been learnt has been lost forever."

★★★

Based upon "Nellie": The History of Churchill's Lincoln-Built Trenching Machine *by John T. Turner (Society for Lincolnshire History and Archaeology, 1988).*

Mount Your Tanks!

BY JULY 9, 1941, NAZI GERMANY's power-laden Army Group Center had sealed the Minsk Pocket, having overrun 21 Soviet rifle divisions and 14 tank brigades, taken 300,000 prisoners, and accounted for 2,600 tanks and 1,500 guns of the Red Army. By now, too, would-be school teacher Karl Fuchs was both a tank commander and a platoon leader in his Twenty-fifth *Panzer* Regiment, Seventh *Panzer* Division.

To his wife on July 5, 1941—

My darling wife! My dear boy (their infant son)

We have fought in battle many days now and we have defeated the enemy wherever we have encountered him. Let me tell you that Russia is nothing but misery, poverty and depravity! This is Bolshevism!

It is late in the evening now and quite dark already. We only wait for our expected orders: Mount your tanks! Start your engines! Move out! Mandi (a nickname), if you were only here and could see me—tanned by the sun, dusty, dirty, with eyes as clear as a falcon!

Our losses have been minimal and our success is great. This war will be over soon, because we are fighting against only fragmented opposition....

As time went on, so did the letters from the eastern front. On September 22 Karl wrote that the countryside, like its people, "seems eternally gray and monotonous." Everywhere, nothing but poverty and "wretched misfortune."

Terrible conditions for the fighting men of the Reich, too. Mud, rain, with "time and space...suspended." But, once the battle is over, peace will reign for Germany and all Europe. The men at the front are convinced, and so should be the people back home. Children in school should be so taught.

As October began, Karl's tank outfit was a part of the German drive on Moscow itself.

The foolish Russians hadn't expected the Germans to risk the on-coming Russian winter! The Last Hour of Bolshevism is near and that means that Old England's destruction is imminent.

By October 15, snow, pure and white, on the ground. Now, in fact, there is a grudging respect for the Russian winter:

What all of us fear most now is the snow and the accompanying cold temperatures, but we'll get used to it.

His friend Roland had just died of wounds. Why did he have to die now, the end seemingly in sight? But…no time to "bemoan his fate." Rather, it's time for the invading Germans to think of revenge for their dead comrades. They can expect to "roll on," since after the great victories thus far, the Russians can hardly offer major opposition.

In early November—yes, it would be nice to buy and send him some woolen clothing items. Can't wait to get home, naturally. By November 11, temperatures in his area of operations reflected a "gripping cold" unlike anything Germany itself would experience.

On November 12, he wrote his mother that he and his comrades might not be able to return by the end of the year, or even early in the next year, 1942. He would be thinking of home and family when Christmas came. Still, disappointment must be endured, sacrifices must be made. It is a struggle for the future of the German people.

You at home must always keep in mind what would have happened if these hordes had overrun our Fatherland. The horror of this is unthinkable!

On December 2 came the first official letter: Karl had been killed on the field of battle—"his heroic death occurred when he was fighting bravely for a greater Germany in the frontlines during a heavy battle with Russian tanks."

Karl's company commander, a Lieutenant Reinhardt, said he had been buried in "a dignified resting place." It was near Kiln, north of Moscow, which the Germans at the very peak of their invasion never quite reached. And so, Karl Fuchs, absorbed, swallowed up, and forever a part of the same eternally gray and monotonous countryside he held in such obvious contempt.

★★★

Based upon Sieg Heil! War Letters of Tank Gunner Karl Fuchs,1937–1941, *compiled, edited, and translated by Horst Fuchs Richardson (his son); historical commentary by Dennis Showalter (Archon Books, Shoe String Press, Hamden, Conn., 1987).*

Faith, Hope, and Charity

"THIS MORNING," WROTE ITALIAN FOREIGN Minister Galeazzo Ciano on November 9, 1941, "Mussolini was depressed and indignant." And well he might have been, since the night before an Italian convoy bound for embattled Libya had been roughly accosted by the Royal Navy.

The composition of the convoy had been seven merchantmen under the protection of no less than two cruisers and ten destroyers. The ration of nearly two warships for each supply-laden merchant ship was planned with the expectation that otherwise British "wolves" would appear among the Italian "sheep."

As Count Ciano noted, the wolves appeared anyway. "An engagement occurred, the results of which are inexplicable. All, I mean all, our ships were sunk [the merchantmen, that is] and one or maybe two or three destroyers. The British returned to base having slaughtered us."

The "lair" of the wolves so upsetting to Mussolini that morning was a mere island in the Mediterranean no bigger, overall, than Greater London. An island only sixty miles from Sicily and half-an-hour's flight time from Italian airfields. An island lying nearly athwart the vital supply line to Italian and German armies in North Africa—a beleaguered outpost that soon would prove most depressing not only to Mussolini, but also to Hitler and his "Desert Fox," Erwin Rommel.

The island was Malta, a fulcrum of war and battle for many centuries even before the advent of World War II. Once allied with Rome against Carthage, it also had sustained capture by the ancient Byzantines, the Arabs, and the Normans. As refuge for the Knights of St. John in 1565, it withstood a famous siege by vastly superior Turkish forces. Next to come along was Napoleon, who seized the island base while on his way to invade Egypt in 1798. The British then blockaded Malta, landed their troops, and eventually gained control of the island.

By the time of World War II, Malta was a British Crown colony. Its seventy-five square miles of land held a population of about 280,000. It boasted its old fortifications of the Turkish siege, an undeveloped British fleet base, and not much else in the way of defenses or war-making capability. Its chief defense at first consisted of three old Gladiator biplanes that were called, appropriately, *Faith, Hope*, and *Charity*.

And in the days ahead, Malta would undergo one of the most furious sieges by air ever unloosed upon a single territory. First, it was the Italian air force, and then the mighty German *Luftwaffe*. With Malta's key position recognized by all the warring parties, the RAF moved in many more aircraft (including Spitfires), while the Royal Navy staged subs and surface ships from the island.

The result was crucial interdiction of the supply line to the Axis forces in North Africa—their eventual disintegration was due in large part to Malta's denial of vital supplies. But Malta, too, had to be supplied. It had to survive under the fury of just about daily air strikes.

With its population living what one writer called "a troglodytic existence in caves," Malta by May of 1942 had endured 2,470 air raids. Its RAF fighters and bombers flew from six airfields constantly holed with bomb craters—fighter pilots might fly four or five sorties a day for weeks at a time.

By the time the war moved up the map into southern Europe in 1943, the RAF had lost nearly 1,000 aircraft staged from Malta—but the Germans and Italians combined had lost an estimated 1,400 in related combat.

British convoys to the gallant island also took a terrible beating. Launched from both Gibraltar and Alexandria, Egypt, one double convoy of seventeen ships succeeded in docking just two of them at Malta. Another convoy, the fourteen-ship Operation Pedestal, landed five at Malta.

There was a moment, probably an inspired moment, when Hitler and Mussolini seriously considered seizing Malta. As Tobruk fell to Rommel in June 1942, however, they gave up the idea—Malta remained a thorn in the side to the end of the *Afrika Korps'* days in Africa.

In the meantime, Malta had earned Britain's George Cross, the highest British award for heroism of civilians. The award always went to individuals, but in Malta's case, a unique one, it was bestowed collectively to the entire island population.

★★★

First published in Military History *magazine, October 1988.*

No Action Taken

ODD TO THINK NOW, BUT in the spring of 1933, a former assistant secretary of the U.S. Navy, now the newly inaugurated president, Franklin D. Roosevelt, had warned in his first cabinet meeting of possible war with an expansionist nation in the Far East—Japan.

The exchange of fire at the Marco Polo Bridge near Peking, China, soon led to overt, full-scale invasion of China by Japan in the summer of 1937. By year's end, Peking, Shanghai, and Nanking had fallen. Japan sent troops into French Indochina (Vietnam now) in 1940, and joined Nazi Germany and Fascist Italy in the Tripartite Pact, linking the three Axis powers in an unholy alliance.

In September 1941, with U.S.-Japanese relations steadily worsening, Japan's governmental and military chiefs agreed—in the presence of Emperor Hirohito—that war was inevitable. They next would accept Admiral Isoruku Yamamoto's advice that the only chance of holding off the American industrial giant in outright war would be to strike a crippling blow first.

On November 3, 1941, the American ambassador to Japan, Joseph Grew, warned his diplomatic superiors of a possible surprise Japanese attack on U.S. facilities.

Admiral Chuichi Nagumo's carrier strike force (six flattops, 350 to 360 aircraft) secretly set sail from northeastern Japan's Kuril Islands on November 26, 1941. Destination: Pearl Harbor in the Hawaiian Islands. In late November, U.S. intelligence personnel noted the departure—and subsequent disappearance—of the carriers. In Washington, Japanese envoys continued negotiations with U.S. diplomats.

U.S. battleships under Japanese attack at Pearl Harbor. (National Archives)

Also in late November, a Hawaii-bound American liner, the *Lurline*, and intelligence personnel in San Francisco picked up low-frequency radio signals northwest of Hawaii. The reason was obvious to anyone paying attention to a report from Dutch intelligence that Tokyo had sent word to its Bangkok embassy to expect attacks on Malaya, the Philippines, and Hawaii.

As Japanese diplomats in consulates across America began to destroy their secret documents on December 3, leaders of the Japanese strike force faced up to the disappointing news from Honolulu-based spies: the U.S. carriers *Enterprise* and *Lexington* were at sea and not in port.

At dawn on December 7, Pearl time, the U.S. destroyer *Ward* spotted a midget submarine at the mouth of Pearl Harbor's main entrance channel and fired upon it. Soon, too, the American freighter *Cynthia Olsen* reported being attacked by a submarine one thousand miles northeast of Hawaii.

Just minutes after seven o'clock the same morning, U.S. Army Privates Joe Lockhard and George Elliott saw a large, inexplicable "blip" on their new-fangled radar device at a northern point of Oahu Island. After ascertaining that it really was a large formation of approaching aircraft, they called in a report to a duty officer at Pearl.

No action taken.

★★★

First published in World War II *magazine, November 1991.*

Tough Farewell for FDR

TAKE YOU BACK, TAKE YOU BACK...to a scene in 1922. A crowd has gathered in the lobby of an office building at 120 Broadway, New York, New York. Why the crowd? A man has fallen down on the highly polished floor. People are embarrassed for him, wondering what to do. Struggle as he will, he cannot get up by himself.

It took two men, FDR's chauffeur and a helpful stranger with strong shoulders, to help the future president back to his feet.

After a year of rehabilitation, Franklin Delano Roosevelt, recent polio victim, needed to go back to work. He needed the money...he needed the creative, positive outlet that work affords.

The man arriving for work those mornings in the fall of 1922 wore braces of leather and metal from ankle to hip, seven pounds to a leg. A lock behind the knee joint kept his legs from bending. He was able to walk only when supported on either side by his crutches. Instead of his legs, his torso and arms did the walking. If he lost his balance, as often did happen at first, he toppled.

Normally, his chauffeur—he had to have a driver—helped him into the office building at 120 Broadway. Usually, they used a wheelchair for FDR's entrance. In bad weather, they always used the chair. In *really* bad weather, FDR simply didn't go to work.

He worked—as partner in a law firm—short hours, short weeks…and after a while, every other week, until resigning with the explanation that his health required him to spend too much time out of town, in search of the sun, a beach and warm, buoyant waters allowing him to stand on his own.

Now, *fast-forward*. He found the year-round, warm (88 degrees) bubbling waters of Warm Springs, Georgia, central feature of a somewhat run-down spa resort in 1924. Loved it at first sight. Loved it so much, he bought the entire resort complex at the base of Pine Mountain for $195,000—$25,000 down and the rest to be paid over a ten-year period.

The water here was no real cure, but in the pool he and other polio victims could walk, swim…play water polo. He even thought he felt a tingle in one foot for the first time since he had been stricken with the crippling disease. Suddenly, it was a good-natured, fun-loving "Doctor" Roosevelt greeting fellow victims, sharing the restorative waters with them, helping them, creating their muscle charts, working closely with their real doctors.

Fast-forward again, please. In 1928, politics would call upon the reluctant but once politically active FDR. He had been on the Democratic ticket of 1920, after all, as candidate for vice president…but that was before being struck with polio. Now, in 1928, a peculiar situation was unfolding for his fellow Democrats.

New York Governor Al Smith would be running for president. Party stalwarts felt they needed FDR running for governor to assure New York's 45 electoral votes for the national ticket in '28. By this time, the always-popular FDR not only had regained his old confidence and ebullient personality, but his activities at Warm Springs had attracted renewed, sympathetic public attention.

Supported by friends and family, however, he at first refused. Explained biographer Nathan Miller in *FDR: An Intimate History*: "He was convinced that his recovery from polio was so far advanced that he was on the verge of learning to walk with only a single leg brace and a cane, and wished to continue his treatment. Warm Springs was also financially shaky and needed his full support before it could be firmly established."

When New York's Democrats nominated FDR anyway, then quickly adjourned their 1928 state convention, he finally gave in. "Well," he said, "I've got to run for governor. There's no use in all of us getting sick about it."

The rest is history. Al Smith lost and FDR won. Roosevelt successfully ran again in 1930. And in 1932, he ran for president and won the first of his four terms, a record unprecedented in American history. As early as his 1928 gubernatorial campaign, meanwhile, he dealt openly with his disabled status. "A governor does not have to be an acrobat," he told a press conference. "The work of the governor is brainwork."

By implication, the same could be said—and would prove to be true—of the presidency, even a wartime presidency.

All this time, FDR had been staying at various cottages dotted around the resort town of Warm Springs. As governor, he still came and visited often. Then, in 1932, the year he first ran for president, he built his own rustic two-bedroom hideaway on the side of Pine Mountain—soon to be known as FDR's "Little White House."

To develop some idea of his lasting affection for Warm Springs—and soon, his cottage there—one must consider that he visited the resort area forty-one times in all, eighteen of them after he was elected president in 1932. His time spent there comes to a total of 102 weeks, or two entire years out of the last twenty-one years of his life. As president, he made Thanksgiving visits to Warm Springs a real tradition—six of them during his presidential years.

Keep in mind, too, the onetime resort now had become a permanent treatment center for polio victims—FDR, in fact, had founded the National Foundation for Infantile Paralysis, or March of Dimes, which in time would fund the development of both the Salk and Sabin vaccines and then, after the eradication of polio, become the March of Dimes Birth Defects Foundation.

As for FDR's traditional Thanksgiving visit and dinner with the Warm Springs patients and Foundation supporters...*fast-forward*, please...to 1941, war on the way, and FDR was late. So late, he didn't arrive until Saturday morning of the Thanksgiving weekend. "We finally got away on Friday, November 28, with the 'Thanksgiving' dinner at the Foundation set back to Saturday night," wrote his longtime secretary Grace Tully in her book *FDR: My Boss*.

The traditional FDR get-together with his fellow "polios" and friends did take place that Saturday evening, but it lacked the convivial atmosphere of previous occasions. "He had hardly arrived," wrote Grace Tully, "when Secretary [of State Cordell] Hull called from Washington to say that the Far East picture was darkening and that the talks in Washington [with envoys from Japan] were in such brittle state that they might be broken at any time."

The news "threw him [FDR] out of his normal mood of gaiety at Warm Springs," reported Tully as well. "It was evident to the few of us who were aware of what happened that there would be little genuine relaxation unless Mr. Hull came up with a brighter report later in the day."

As was customary at these gatherings, FDR spoke off-the-cuff at dinner that Saturday night. That afternoon he had listened to the radio broadcast of the traditional Thanksgiving weekend Army-Navy football game, and with that as his key, he somberly noted "the contrast of a nation at peace and at play with a world torn by the destruction and unhappiness of war." As Miss Tully also would recall, "There was a quiet chill in the great room when he earnestly remarked near the end of his talk: 'It may be that next Thanksgiving these boys of the Military Academy and of the Naval Academy will be actually fighting for the defense of these American institutions of ours.'"

Barely two weeks later, of course, on Sunday, December 7, the Japanese struck at Pearl Harbor.

President Roosevelt and party, in the meantime, spent just the one night at Warm Springs that last weekend of November 1941. Secretary of State Cordell Hull had called back after dinner Saturday with nothing but continued bad news. "Mr. Hull was deeply worried and felt that anything might happen," wrote Miss Tully. "He advised the President's return."

FDR decided he had better leave the very next morning if he was to be back in Washington by Monday morning. As Miss Tully also explained, "The train was ordered back from Atlanta, where it had gone to await the President's need." What about public awareness of these grim developments on the eve of Pearl Harbor? "The press was informed and the very fact of this hasty turnabout injected an alarming note into all the stories of the next morning."

In the meantime, FDR had to make his good-byes. One especially difficult farewell was to another longtime secretary, Missy Leland, a surprisingly young stroke victim and now herself a semi-invalid undergoing rehabilitation at Warm Springs. ". . . [Missy] was nearly in tears at losing us so soon and in her understanding of the tremendous pressure then bearing down upon her beloved Boss," wrote Miss Tully later. (Missy Leland in fact soon would return to her family home and die, still in her forties.)

Almost as heart-tugging would be FDR's farewell to the "polios" assembled minutes later at the front of their health center's Georgia Hall. This was an unusually solemn leave-taking, with FDR telling the patients—*his* patients, in a way, "This may be the last time I talk to you for a long time."

Indeed, with a war on just days later, he did not come back for nearly a year and a half...not until April of 1943. As Grace Tully noted, "He did talk to them again but not until we were deep in war, and never again was he to return to Warm Springs in a carefree and holiday mood."

★★★

Based upon various sources, including those cited in text.

★ WAR, WAR, ★ EVERYWHERE WAR

No Place for a Visitor

HERE'S THE NIGHTMARE. YOU'RE A fifteen-year-old kid, and one fine Sunday morning in December you're standing on something called the aft boat well deck of the mighty United States battleship *Arizona*. Off in the distance, you and your pal, Seaman First Class William Stafford, hear something that sounds like thunder.

You and Stafford, an older friend from home who happens to be a sailor assigned to *Arizona*, are standing there talking…wondering. Across the shipping channel columns of smoke suddenly billow.

What the h___ is going on? More to the point, what's a fifteen-year-old sailor, strictly a visitor on board the battleship, to do? (You had lied of course, to join the peacetime navy—girls, you know, just loved that uniform!)

Those nearby explosions—not exactly routine. Could it be some kind of gunnery practice? And those planes in the sky, black line after line, coming your way?

Oops! Out there, across the water, there goes a smaller ship, maybe a destroyer or minelayer. A bomb hits and breaks her in half. And that does it! Aboard *Arizona*, general quarters is sounded. Everybody on board, hundreds of sailors, now run, racing pell-mell, to their battle stations.

Stafford too. "I've got to go," he says. "I'll see you later." And so he's gone. Well, sure, friend or no friend, he's got a battle station to go to like everybody else. *Duty!*

And so, with the Japanese bombing Pearl Harbor, with the devastating surprise attack on the U.S. Pacific Fleet, with all that death and destruction that brought the United States into World War II, with sheer pandemonium around you—an explosion rends the ship, then a second one; the crew runs, screams; guns begin to fire back into the sky; your friend has gone to his duty station—with all that, you're now standing there at the stern of the mighty ship, all alone. Alone and wondering…can't this, please, just be a nightmare?

But for young Martin Matthews, born in Shelbyville, Kentucky, it was no nightmare. He really was there at Pearl Harbor. He really was only fifteen years old at the time. And he really was in the U.S. Navy…but this was not his normal duty station. No, he was stationed at nearby Ford Island Naval Air Station—also under attack, by the way.

As the last hours of peacetime dribbled away, he had been visiting his pal Stafford aboard *Arizona* the night of December 6. After breakfast on that morning of December 7, 1941, they had planned to go sightseeing ashore. But first they took a tour of the mighty battlewagon.

And what was one of the last things the 15-year-old said to his pal? Wasn't it something like, "I wish I could get duty aboard a battleship?"

It was one of the last things Matthews ever said to his friend, who was among the crewmen killed as *Arizona* was broken and sunk on that "date which will live in infamy," as President Franklin D. Roosevelt termed it so well when he went before Congress the next day in Washington, D.C., to demand—and get—a declaration of war.

The fact that the day would "live in infamy" would be no solace to Martin Matthews as he watched the devastating attack unfurl before him…watched as a boy none too happy to be there, to be witness to such terrible sights. "I think the second bomb that hit was close to the aft deck that I was on, and needless to say, I was petrified," Matthews later recalled. "To put it in plain English, it scared the living hell out of me."

The concussions knocked him down "a couple of times," and he sought cover. "This was not what I went into the Navy for," said Matthews, "and it was not what I wanted. Besides, I had no place to go. I didn't have a general quarters station."

As chance would have it, if he had to be at Pearl Harbor, he was in the worst place of all—*Arizona's* death toll of 1,103 was more than half the total number of men in the Pacific Fleet to die at Pearl Harbor that day. Matthews, however, didn't stay aboard the stricken ship all that long. He never could be sure later if he jumped or was blown overboard, but he found himself in the water at the stern of the battleship, still fully clothed in his dress whites for sightseeing.

Matthews swam to a mooring buoy twenty to thirty yards away, as he explained years later in an interview for the book *Remembering Pearl Harbor: Eyewitness Accounts by U.S. Military Men and Women*, edited by Roberts S. LaForte and Ronald E. Marcello. And there he clung for the remainder of the attack, unharmed despite the chunks of metal and timber flying through the air. Pieces of bodies too. "It's far too much for a young boy of fifteen years old to have seen," said Matthews.

While the Japanese planes came, wave after wave, for nearly two hours in all, he couldn't very well swim for nearby Ford Island, since its naval air facility was also under attack. Most of the American aircraft over there, he could see, "had been bombed and set afire or blown apart." The attacking Japanese, meanwhile, seemed to be "completely uncontested, unmolested."

Closer at hand, the ill-fated *Arizona* soon was in her final moments of agony. "There was ammunition, gun lockers, shells, steel fragments and pyrotechnics coming from all parts of the ship," Matthews recalled. "It was like a fireworks display. There was a series of explosions; it wasn't just one deafening roar."

But there was one decisive moment. "Things came to a final one where she seemed like the middle part just raised up in the water and kind of half buckled and then settled back down," remembered Matthews. That was the end. The battleship couldn't sink out of sight because the water wasn't that deep, but that was the end anyway. "Her bridge and masthead were above water, I remember that after…she finally settled."

About that time, the attack waned. Young Martin swam to the beach at Ford Island, where for days after he helped clean up the incredible mess the Japanese had left behind—so incredible, he subsequently said, that three whole days later he and his buddies found an American pilot still trapped in his wrecked airplane at the end of the runway.

Matthews remained a U.S. Navy sailor for the duration of the war. He served aboard eight ships and earned a Navy Commendation Medal. He went to college after the war and then went to work to make a living, just like most other people. Like most, except that he goes down in history as a Pearl Harbor survivor—as one of the youngest survivors at that.

And…what else, perhaps? Oh yes, those eight ships he served on later in the war? Three of them were sunk as well. Talk about a survivor!

★★★

First published in Military History *magazine, December 1997.*

Date to Mark

Yesterday, December 7, 1941, a date which will live in world history, the United States of America was simultaneously and deliberately attacked by naval and air forces of…

★★★

CRIPPLED MAN, CRIPPLED FLEET.

At Pearl Harbor in Hawaii, rescue and repair parties were just beginning their grim work. Farther around the globe, Japanese forces now were assaulting Malaya, Hong Kong, Guam, the Philippines, Wake Island, Midway…

In Washington, the polio-crippled commander in chief thought the better of the opening line in his draft speech. "Simultaneously," at the stroke of a pen, became the more suitable "suddenly."

U.S. Navy petty officers listen to President Roosevelt's speech to Congress December 8, 1941. (National Archives)

Emphatic dashes took the place of the two midsentence commas. The prosaic "in world history" was changed too. Set off by the helpful dashes, President Franklin D. Roosevelt's war message to the Congress of the United States now would open with its famous, ringing reference point for posterity: "a date which will live in infamy."

Thirty-three minutes after FDR delivered his "Day of Infamy" speech, Congress with but one dissenting vote approved a resolution declaring war on Japan.

The Senate vote was 82 to 0, and the House count 388 to 1, the single nay on December 8, 1941, being that of Rep. Jeannette Rankin, D-Montana, who had been one of the few members of Congress voting against war with Germany in 1917. While she had had some support in those World War I days, her no vote this time stirred boos and hisses. There was no debate over this war resolution.

America this time was angry. The country was unified in shock and outrage.

"I ask the Congress to declare that since the unprovoked and dastardly attack by Japan on Sunday, December 7, a state of war has existed between the United States and the Japanese empire." Roosevelt had hardly to ask.

His speech broadcast live by radio, he appeared at a joint session of the House and Senate. The cabinet and the Supreme Court were on attentive hand, as well. Millions listened at home, office, factory, or military post.

And so on a Sunday morning of 1941, the separate, even somewhat limited wars that had been raging in Europe and Asia became one.

With the attack on Pearl Harbor, a hesitant, still somewhat isolationist United States at last was pulled, headlong, into the vortex of violence and destruction. And not only America—in a week's time after Pearl Harbor, three dozen nations populated by one-half of the planet's inhabitants were officially at war.

They call it World War II. In its scope, in its impact on very nearly all peoples of the earth, it really was the first world war. No conflict like it had ever taken place before, and none since.

Its worldwide spread might soon have happened anyway—some other way—but in fact the way it did happen was with the attack on Pearl Harbor.

"There were loud cheers as each plane rose into the air," recalled Mitsuo Fuchida, commander of the carrier-based air armada that struck Pearl Harbor. "After circling the fleet formation, we set course due south for Pearl Harbor."

Under Fuchida's command, he later said, were 49 level bombers, 40 torpedo planes, 51 dive-bombers, and 43 fighters. That was only the first wave, though. Soon, "our second wave of 171 planes swept in." (Fuchida's numbers are at slight variance with those of U.S. sources.)

And sweep they did.

Surprised, caught barely awake that Sunday morning, was an American fleet of seventy combat vessels (ninety-four to ninety-six ships in all). Eight battleships were in port, seven of them neatly lined up as the famous "Battleship Row." Fortunately, for America, the Pacific Fleet's carriers were gone…at sea.

It took less than two hours for the Japanese to sink or to cripple seven of the battleships, three cruisers and three destroyers, while also destroying 188 aircraft at nearby fields like Wheeler, Hickam, Bellows…and leaving 2,403 Americans dead, another 1,178 wounded.

"But there are still many targets which should be hit," Fuchida argued when he returned to his carrier. His urging of another attack on Pearl Harbor was overruled.

"Immediately, flag signals were hoisted, and our ships headed northwest at high speed."

The Japanese lost only twenty-nine aircraft and fifty-five men at Pearl Harbor. But they also, in time, lost the war.

At one point during the two Pearl Harbor air attacks, Admiral Husband Kimmel, commander of the U.S. Pacific Fleet, was struck, with little injury, by a spent bullet that flew in his office window. Aware of the tragedy unfolding around him and the blame that would be his, he put the bullet in a pocket and said: "It would have been merciful had it killed me." Kimmel, along with the local U.S. Army commander, General Walter Short, was, indeed relieved from his post.

Fuchida, meanwhile, survived severe injury in the later Battle of Midway (a significant U.S. victory) and after the war became a Christian convert, a Protestant minister—and a U.S. citizen!

★★★

Based upon Military History *magazine, December 1986, and* World War II *magazine, November 1991.*

Footnote to Pearl

NOT EVERYONE GETS TO BE a historical footnote, and for young Japanese Ensign Kasuo Sakamaki on Pearl Harbor Day, that distinction came the hard way. Sakamaki in fact began the day in footnote status. He began the day in the water, and not in the air.

Not *swimming* in the water, exactly, but piloting one of the five midget submarines the Japanese launched against the U.S. Pacific Fleet on December 7, 1941, in concert with their surprise air attack on the American naval base in the Hawaiian Islands.

The midget subs did not have quite the success of the air armada for which the surprise attack chiefly is known. All five of the two-man craft were lost, and none struck a target with the three torpedoes thought to have been fired.

As a second, but grim footnote reference for Sakamaki, he apparently was the only one of the ten Japanese crewmen to survive the attack by the flotilla of midget subs.

It was, naturally, an experience he never would forget.

His "mother" submarine, the *1.24*, had surfaced off the harbor entrance to

Pearl the evening of December 6. "We could see the stars twinkling," said Sakamaki many years later. "There were so many lights visible from the shore. I listened to music from a Honolulu radio station."

Strapped onto the deck of his mother boat was a seventy-five-foot metal tube packing two eighteen-inch torpedoes. Sakamaki and his crewman, Petty Officer Kiyoshi Inagaki, were supposed to climb into it shortly after midnight, make for Pearl Harbor—seven miles away—and sink the battleship *Pennsylvania* at her moorings.

The plan was foiled from the start—Sakamaki's midget sub wouldn't steer properly and bucked the running seas "like a wild horse," he recalled. "Every time I started the engines, the nose popped up to the surface. So for three hours Inagaki and I carried heavy lead ballast from the stern to the bow. This exhausted us."

Finally on course and running beneath the water's surface, Sakamaki raised his periscope for a quick glimpse of his surroundings, only to see two American patrol boats so close, "I could see the seamen running on the deck." In the depth-charging that followed, the midget's torpedo-launching gear was wrecked and both crewmen suffered minor injuries.

But they escaped. "I made up my mind to enter the harbor and dash into a battleship and explode the torpedoes that way."

Sakamaki's midget banged into a coral reef instead, popped to the surface in full view of an American destroyer, and then—at his direction—backed into deeper waters. They would wait for dark that night—December 7—and try again to enter the harbor. "By this time, the bad air and gas in the sub and the tension had almost killed us."

They did not, after repeated attempts, manage to penetrate the harbor that night. They decided to save their tiny boat for future attacks against Japan's new enemies by keeping a planned rendezvous with their mother boat off Lanai Island, southeast of Pearl. "At dawn on December 8, we surfaced off what we thought was Lanai," recalled Sakamaki later, "but it turned out we were near the northeast coast of Oahu Island—way off course."

They then became grounded on another coral reef, firmly stuck this time. "We set the sub on fire and jumped overboard. I was so exhausted I was unable to swim, so I just floated on my back. Inagaki tried to swim to shore and I learned later that he drowned."

The exhausted Sakamaki, meanwhile, fell unconscious, even while he was floating in the water. "And the next thing I remember was being picked up on the beach by an American Army sergeant."

That would have been near Bellows Field, and the American sergeant was

David Abuki. Both men then became footnotes, since Sakamaki instantly qualified as the first Japanese combatant taken prisoner by the Americans in World War II, and Abuki as his captor.

"Pretty short war," said Sakamaki years later, by then the chief of exports for Toyota Motor Co., Ltd., Japan's largest automaker. "The Pearl Harbor attack started World War II for me—and ended it."

★★★

Based upon an undated Associated Press story.

"Too Damned Old"

THE WEATHER IN WASHINGTON ON that historic day was "gray and gloomy," Margaret Truman later was to recall. Her father, a U.S. senator in 1941, was out of town, staying at a hotel in distant Columbia, Missouri.

As the news of the Japanese attack on Pearl Harbor struck and outraged the American nation, the president in place was Franklin D. Roosevelt. He would be the commander in chief who was there for the beginning of the war, but fate had decreed that another would be in place to finish the war. On December 7, 1941, however, that was an eventuality few Americans had on their mind.

For Harry S. Truman and for many similarly scattered members of Congress, one immediate and galvanizing thought that Sunday was to return to Washington. It was an era before jet-powered aircraft.

Out in the Pennant Hotel in Columbia, Missouri, Dad put on his clothes and raced across the road to a private airport, where he begged the owner to get him to St. Louis as fast as possible. They flew in a small plane, and he arrived just in time to catch a night flight to Washington. It was quite a trip. Every time the plane landed, another congressman or senator got on. Ordinary citizens were ruthlessly ejected, and pretty soon the plane was a congressional special. They arrived in Washington around dawn. With no sleep, Dad rushed to the Capitol.

As daughter Margaret also noted in her biography, *Harry S. Truman,* the assembled senators and House members jointly heard Roosevelt's "Day of

Infamy" speech, on December 8, then retired to their respective chambers to declare war on Japan.

For the next three years, Truman remained a U.S. senator. Apparently, though, he would rather have been more directly involved in the war effort as a field artillery officer. In 1940, he had asked army Chief of Staff George C. Marshall to allow him to go on active duty (World War I artillery veteran Truman was still an Army Reserve colonel).

General Marshall pulled down his spectacles, eyed my gray-haired father, and said, "Senator, how old are you?"

"Well," said Dad lamely, "I'm fifty-six."

"You're too damned old. You'd better stay home and work in the Senate."

Truman did, and when a failing FDR prepared in 1944 to run for an unprecedented fourth term as president, the burning question became that of a vice presidential running mate. Not me, said Truman as the choice narrowed. But, in a tumultuous Democratic National Convention held in Chicago, Truman finally agreed, then beat out New Dealer Henry Wallace for the nomination.

In the November elections that followed, FDR was reelected and Truman was elected vice president. While other Democrats—including his daughter—celebrated on that election night in 1944, Vice President-elect Harry S. Truman lay awake, worrying.

Not really close to the strangely reclusive president, the worried Truman nonetheless had seen what few outside of the immediate White House circle knew that autumn. Left nearly alone for a moment on election night, Truman had unburdened himself to an old friend from southwest Missouri, Harry Easley.

For the first time the full reality of what he was facing struck Dad. "He told me that the last time he saw Mr. Roosevelt he had the pallor of death on his face and he knew that he would be president before the term was out." And so it was. Roosevelt died in April 1945—Harry Truman thus would be the man, the president, called upon to finish the war as commander in chief. By the time of FDR's death, the tide of course was running strong for the Allies. The Normandy invasion was history, Hitler's own days were numbered, and in the Pacific the American-led Allied forces were gathered for a final, all-out assault upon the Japanese home islands themselves.

Still, many decisions were left to the new Truman White House. Among them would be the decision to use the newly developed atomic bomb against Japan, in place of a far more costly (to both sides) invasion of a fiercely defended homeland.

How would that epochal decision (and others) have turned out if George Marshall had said yes to the reserve colonel of field artillery? If Truman had refused to seek nomination as FDR's running mate? If Henry Wallace or someone else (any one of several dark horses) had won the nomination? If the 1944 general election had turned out differently?

But none of these things happened. It was Truman who finished out the war as President, and he who made the war's most momentous single decision, an emotion-charged subject of debate ever since. "It was not an easy decision to make," Truman later said. "I did not like the weapon. But I had no qualms if in the long run millions of lives could be saved."

Whatever the what-ifs or the direction of the moral debate, the so-called buck had stopped at Harry Truman's desk. And he dealt with it.

★★★

First published in World War II *magazine, November 1986.*

Bird Named Swoose

As Boeing's No. 40-3097, she may not be all that well remembered. Under the name combining concept of both swan and goose, however, she still is a legend—the indestructible, ubiquitous, and amazing *Swoose.*

Her story begins in a production lot of forty-two Boeing B-17Ds turned out before the war began. It continues as No. 40-3097 crosses the Pacific in original form and alights in the Philippines. Eight hours after Pearl Harbor, as is well known, the Japanese wiped out the B-17s that were parked at Clark Field.

Only airplane rubble was left behind, with not a single one of the vaunted Flying Forts left in flyable shape, but from such rubble—and the determined genius of their ground-crew keepers—emerged patched-together, Phoenix-like creatures of the air that again *would* fly.

Was the *Swoose* one of those creations from the Clark Field rubble?

Writer-historian John H. Mitchell of Springfield, Missouri, says no, the Nineteenth Bombardment Group's No. 3097 was *not* one of the planes rebuilt from scrap parts at Clark Field—"She wasn't even at Clark when the attack occurred." Luckier than her mates at Clark, she had been flown to the U.S. airfield at Del Monte on Mindanao Island just before the Japanese attack, he says.

But…another view. Back to Clark Field: "None of our bombers was left flyable, but by heroic efforts, finding a wing of one and a rudder from another, a sailplane from a ruined fuselage, and such engines as remained whole, and putting these odd parts together on fuselages less damaged than others, our men assembled a very few bombers," notes a Smithsonian publication. "It was from such Phoenix-like resurrections that the *Swoose* came into being."

For all these new creations, of course, the war had only begun—none was to fly home into safe retirement. Not by any means, not yet, anyway. In the days and weeks to follow the Clark Field attack, they flew against the invading Japanese in the Philippines, in the Dutch East Indies, in the respective nearby islands. And one by one, they fell to the enemy until one day in Australia, along about March 1942, the body of a badly damaged No. 3097 was married to the tail ("only a stabilizer" and perhaps a few more spare parts, says Mitchell) of a previously wounded Flying Fort, with not only a hybrid resulting but its christening as the *Swoose*!

"Even with this new tail, the other parts were so pieced together and battle-scarred that the airplane little resembled the beautiful Flying Fortress that had landed in the Philippines a few months before," says the Smithsonian account.

An amateur artist went to work and placed a strange-looking bird as insignia on the creation's fuselage, helpfully adding the guarantee: "It flies."

And, actually, she did…continually and consistently. Not only in her time based in Australia, but also for months—even years!—afterward. The *Swoose* in fact became the command plane for Lt. Gen. George H. Brett, for a time commander of Douglas MacArthur's air forces (Brett's own plane had been shot up in a Japanese strafing attack).

Not only did the *Swoose* carry Brett about the southwest Pacific, but she carried him all the way back to Washington when he was reassigned; she later flew him up and down the Western Hemisphere on flights to Central and South America. She flew on, in fact, throughout all of World War II and finished her career with a total of four thousand hours of in-air time.

On the way to Washington from Australia, incidentally, the patched-together *Swoose* "established new speed records between Australia and Hawaii, and from there to San Francisco." Later, the *Swoose* was headed for a postwar meltdown into scrap, but Mayor Fletcher Bowron of Los Angeles managed to save her for display as a war memorial. His city then, in 1949, turned her over to the

Smithsonian's National Air Museum for permanent safekeeping. As befitting the Swoose, she flew all the way east under her own power. Indeed, with her wartime pilot Frank Kurtz at the controls and many of her crew aboard, she was greeted by crowds of onlookers at various stops along the way—her final flight one of proud acclaim.

★★★

Based upon John H. Mitchell and The National Aeronautical Collections *by Paul E. Garber, head curator and historian, National Air Museum, Smithsonian Institution (The Smithsonian Institution, Washington, D.C., 10th edition, 1965).*

Chennault Strikes Back

IN WASHINGTON, LATE IN 1941, the skeptics were many. Chinese Ambassador T. V. Soong sent Claire Chennault a cable citing unsettling reports to the U.S. War Department that "your group cannot be ready before February 1942 and will not last two weeks in combat."

Back in Burma, where he was training his American Volunteer Group (AVG), Chennault did his usual slow burn at thoughts of untutored bureaucratic meddling. Still, he merely replied that his fighter pilots would be ready by the end of November and continued his unorthodox training methods. The setting was Toungoo, 170 miles north of Rangoon, a damp, sweltering place. The methodology, all Chennault, was loose, relaxed discipline on the ground (open shirts, weekly "gripe" sessions) and tight discipline in the air (meaning, learn to fight the Japanese Chennault's way).

In China, the Japanese still were rampaging. It was only a matter of time before they turned south for Burma—after Thailand surrendered October 8, the Japanese placed bombers and fighters on Thai airfields along three hundred miles of the Burmese border. Hanoi, Indochina, occupied since 1940, was another staging base for Japanese airpower. The target surely would be the long Burma Road, beginning at Rangoon and ending at Kunming, China, as the only overland supply route for the hard-pressed Chinese.

Chennault's American volunteers, most of them from a military background, were not all fighter pilots by training. More than half instead had flown bombers, torpedo planes, even commercial airliners. Those with fighter training, in fact, had to unlearn their standard American lessons and adhere to Chennault's insistence upon teamwork and hit-and-run tactics. They had to realize that, on the one hand, the Japanese were no second-raters in the air, but on the other hand they tended to fly by the book, undeviating from predetermined tactics.

"The object of our tactics is to break up their formation and make them fight according to our style," Chennault told his flyers. "Once the Japanese are forced to deviate from their plan they are in trouble. Their rigid air discipline can be used as a powerful weapon against them."

Chennault acknowledged that the AVG's P-40B had a better top speed than Japanese fighters such as the Zero, a faster dive and heavier firepower, but he stressed the more unhappy points that the Japanese aircraft boasted a higher rate of climb, a higher ceiling, and a superior maneuverability. "They can turn on a dime and climb almost straight up. If they can get you into a turning combat, they are deadly."

Most difficult for the naturally combative pilots to accept was Chennault's radical precept of dive, make a pass, shoot, and break away—it smacked of running away, a court-martial offense for the British RAF stationed in nearby Rangoon and a firing-squad offense in the Chinese air force, despite Chennault's influence there. But Chennault had too few planes and qualified pilots to squander in dogfight heroics reminiscent of the Lafayette Escadrille or the Flying Circus of World War I days. Chennault wanted his men to live and fight another day.

With patience maddening to some of his men, he insisted upon training, training, and more training, while across the border Chinese cities and military targets absorbed almost daily pastings by the Japanese air force.

By the time of Pearl Harbor, however, he was just about ready. And in the days immediately after December 7, 1941, he posted one AVG squadron outside of Rangoon under RAF operational control, while moving his other two squadrons to Kunming with himself in command. The second move came right after the Japanese bombed Kunming on December 18—at dawn the next day, his P-40s were on patrol over the key city.

Chennault's other "secret weapon" now came into play, the early warning network he had developed in China—"people, telephone and telegraph lines and many hundreds of portable radio sets." At the sight of Japanese aircraft, they were to pass along instant warning, and as the alerts built up, the path of the enemy could be calculated in advance.

On the morning of December 20, Chennault was alerted by telephone that watchers in Yunnan Province had spotted ten twin-engine bombers crossing the provincial border at Laokay, headed northwest. "Their probable objective is Kunming."

In response, Chennault called forth twenty-four of his AVG's P-40s, all emblazoned with sharklike teeth painted on either side of their sleek nose. Four of them were to make the actual intercept; another four would fly a combat air patrol at high altitude over Kunming, and the remaining sixteen would stand by on the ground at an auxiliary strip west of the city.

Soon, sixty miles to the southeast, Jack Newkirk's four-plane intercept flight found the bombers. So confident were the Japanese of air superiority that they hadn't even provided their bombers with a fighter escort. The American volunteers came down on the bombers from above, their .50 calibers and .30 calibers spitting.

The bombers immediately jettisoned their deadly loads and turned for home. Newkirk, his guns jammed, did likewise after one diving pass, along with two of his fellow pilots. A fourth, Ed Rector, came out of his power drive, recovered, and went after the bombers. From the auxiliary field to the west of Kunming, meanwhile, the P-40s on standby took to the air, also in pursuit of the Japanese Mitsubishis. The swarming P-40s soon caught up and, before the raiders could reach the Indochina border, six of the original ten had gone down. Of the four still in the air, only one managed to reach home base. Chennault's AVG had lost one plane—Rector's gas gave out and he had to crash-land in a rice paddy.

The jubilant Chinese press responded to the aerial victory with banner headlines throughout the country—and a nickname for the American volunteers, the "Flying Tigers!" The Japanese, in the meantime, didn't attempt to bomb Kunming for another sixteen months, "and when they did, they brought along a 30-fighter escort."

Meanwhile, Rangoon and Burma finally had come under the Japanese gun, and here again the AVG fliers distinguished themselves. On December 23, for instance, fifty-four Mitsubishis, twelve Nakakima type-97 fighters and eight Zeros struck at Rangoon. Fifteen AVG P-40s joined the RAF in defending the city, with the Americans split into two freewheeling groups. Two AVG pilots bagged five enemy aircraft each as the Flying Tigers accounted for a confirmed total of twenty-five Japanese bombers and fighters (while losing two men and three planes). The RAF, with eighteen Brewsters in the air, claimed seven enemy downed (while losing five pilots and eleven planes).

Christmas Day at Rangoon was a repeat performance, as the Japanese struck with eighty-one bombers and forty-two fighters as escort. In battle lasting an hour and a half, the twelve serviceable P-40s flown by the Flying

Tigers accounted for another fifteen bombers and nine fighters. With bravado typical of the AVG volunteers, Squadron Leader Arvid Olson radioed Chennault in Kunming: "Could put entire Jap force out of commission with whole group here."

In the ten weeks before Rangoon finally fell, "the AVG with never more than twenty planes that could fly and sometimes as few as five, met the Imperial Japanese Air Force on thirty-one occasions and chalked up the incredible score of 217 confirmed victories and 43 probables." The cost to the "Tigers" was five men killed, one taken prisoner, sixteen P-40s lost in combat.

Winston Churchill weighed in with the message: "The victories of these Americans over the rice paddies of Burma are comparable in character if not in scope with those won by the RAF over the hop fields of Kent in the Battle of Britain."

Overall, before its absorption into the U.S. Army Air Forces in China in July 1942 (also under Chennault's command), the AVG in seven months of almost constant combat knocked down 299 Japanese aircraft, to thirty-two AVG planes downed, ten pilots lost in action, nine in accidents. Clearly, Chennault's painstaking and unorthodox training, coupled with his vital knowledge of the enemy, had paid off.

★★★

Based upon Chennault and the Flying Tigers *by Anna Chennault (Paul S. Eriksson, Inc., New York, 1963).*

Disorderly Ran the Two Ships

CECIL BROWN WAS STANDING ON the flag deck of the mighty battle cruiser *Repulse* when the first of the Japanese bombers approached. "Strung in a line," they were "clearly visible in the brilliant sunlit sky."

They flew the length of the British warship with no apparent harm done. Their estimated altitude was ten thousand feet. But around Brown, "our anti-aircraft guns were screaming constantly."

And actually, *the harm had been done.* Their bombs had been on the way. "Just when the planes were passing over, one bomb hit the water beside where I was standing, so close to the ship that we were drenched from the waterspout." Worse, though, and simultaneously, a second bomb struck the catapult deck, "penetrating the ship and exploding below in a marine's mess and hangar."

Half a mile away, the *Prince of Wales*, as a battleship a warship even more mighty than the *Repulse*, also was under attack from the air. Both capital ships and their escorting destroyers were "throwing everything they had into the air."

Until this moment in time, in history, two notions had prevailed among the leading Western military circles. First, that airpower would wilt before ship power. The second, a contradiction, that somehow there was not all that much to fear from the steadily rampaging Japanese of the Far East.

The scene that CBS newsman Cecil Brown witnessed aboard the *Repulse* on December 10, 1941, three days after Pearl Harbor, erased both impressions so dramatically that Prime Minister Winston Churchill reported to the House of Commons, "In my whole experience I do not remember any naval blow so heavy and painful."

The revolution in naval warfare was especially evident to those aboard the two stricken ships. Within twenty-four hours—his report delayed only by the necessity of rescue from the sea—Brown was explaining in his cable to CBS in New York that the Japanese attack succeeded "because of, first, a determined air torpedo attack and, second, the skill and efficiency of the Japanese bomber operations."

For Brown and others aboard the *Repulse*, the key word, the really devastating blow, had been *torpedo*. By his account, the bomb-wounded *Repulse* managed to elude any further hits during two torpedo-bomber runs. At 12:20 P.M., however, a third wave was approaching. "Stand by for barrage," barked the ship's public address system.

Brown watched as a plane circled, then approached the port side at three hundred or four hundred yards. "It's coming closer, head on, and I see a torpedo drop. It's streaking for us. A watcher shouts, 'Stand by for torpedo,' and the tin fish is streaking directly for us. Someone says, 'This one got us.'"

It had. It struck Brown's side of the ship twenty yards astern of where he was standing. "It felt like the ship had crashed into a well-rooted dock. It threw me four feet across the deck, but I did not feel any explosion. Just a very great jar."

The ship listed and took a second torpedo hit on its starboard side. "That the *Repulse* was doomed was immediately apparent."

It still seemed unbelievable. "It was most difficult to realize I must leave the ship. It seemed so incredible that the *Repulse* could or should go down."

But she did, and Brown found himself in the water along with the hundreds of surviving British seamen.

From that uncertain vantage point, he not only saw the cruiser's end, but also that of the *Prince of Wales*. "Swimming about a mile away, lying on top of a small stool, I saw the bow of the *Wales*." When the battleship gasped her last, the suction was so great, "it ripped off the life belt of one officer more than fifty feet away."

A Japanese airman's eyewitness report was blunt and short: "Our formations of bombers fell on the two capital ships amidst antiaircraft fire from the enemy. Our torpedoes hit their mark with incandescent glow flashing and dark smoke columns. In disorderly wakes ran the *Prince of Wales* and the *Repulse*, and in a moment they turned into columns of fire, going to the bottom."

Two views, same revolution in naval warfare.

★★★

First published in World War II *magazine, January 1989.*

Going around FDR's Secrecy

WHAT DID PRESIDENT FRANKLIN D. Roosevelt tell Winston Churchill in his messages to the British prime minister? The fact is, not many people really knew. Not even the intimates of FDR's official family. Not even, in the case of military matters, his own U.S. Army chief of staff, General George C. Marshall. "He didn't want a record of cabinet meetings," the chief of staff explained later. "He didn't give us the messages he was sending half the time."

Roosevelt's bent for secrecy extended to the all-important messages he was exchanging through much of World War II with Churchill, who liked to sign off as "Former Naval Person" in reference to his World War I days as First Lord of the British Admiralty. Himself a onetime assistant secretary of the U.S. Navy, FDR liked to address his transatlantic messages to "My Naval Friend."

Cute, but that left Chief of Staff Marshall, among others, out of the loop. And Marshall, as head of the U.S. armed forces, had a discernible need to know.

"He [FDR] would communicate with Churchill, he would receive a message from Churchill, and I would be wholly unaware of it, though it directly affected the affairs of the army and the air and maybe the navy," Marshall told his biographer, Forrest C. Pogue, many years later.

But Marshall found a way to circumvent FDR's predilection for secrecy without directly challenging his commander in chief. Going around the president took some doing. He did it by utilizing the good offices of highly placed contacts in a foreign government—he used the British themselves to find out what FDR and Prime Minister Churchill might be planning.

Marshall realized that Roosevelt's messages to Naval Friend would be distributed to very senior personnel in the British government, including its own chiefs of staff. They, in turn would notify the head of the British Joint Staff Mission to the United States, Field Marshal Sir John Dill, a good friend of Marshall's, it so happened.

The circuitous route of the secret FDR messages thus went like this: from FDR to Churchill and staff, on to the British chiefs of staff. "Then Dill should know it in Washington, so Dill would get a copy of it," Marshall explained in an interview with biographer Pogue on February 11, 1957. "Then Dill would come over to my office, and I would get Mr. Roosevelt's message through Field Marshal Sir John Dill. Otherwise, I wouldn't know what it was."

Quite naturally, Marshall was forced to keep his personal conduit of high-level war messages a deep, dark secret. "I had to be very careful that nobody knew this—no one in the [U.S.] War Department—and certainly not the [British] chiefs of staff, because Dill would be destroyed in a minute if this was discovered. But he knew I had to have it, and he just brought it to me and read it to me. He sat opposite me at my desk and went over this."

For Dill, it was high risk to share such top-secret information from his own government, but he was sympathetic to Marshall's predicament. "Why should the British chief of staff have it—it was from our President—and the American chiefs of staff not have it?" was Marshall's still-valid question years after World War II. "But it was just Mr. Roosevelt's desire for secrecy. But it went to everybody else, so I would get it through Dill, which is a rather unusual circumstance."

Roosevelt's secrecy was a two-way street, of course. Not only did FDR decline to share the messages he *sent* to Naval Friend, he also did not share those communications he *received* from Former Naval Person. And once again, it was Dill to the rescue of his American "cousins." He again kept the future secretary of state and proponent of the postwar Marshall Plan *au courant*. Marshall, for his part, never told his own fellow chiefs of staff, never told FDR, never told anyone at all, until his interview with biographer Pogue in 1957.

Marshall also revealed that he and his fellow wartime "conspirator" had taken an additional cooperative step that suited their very special situation: "I will go even further to say—you [Pogue] will have to guard this pretty carefully—that

Dill would frequently get messages from Mr. Churchill…[asking] him to ascertain General Marshall's possible view of this. Dill would come over and read me Mr. Churchill's communication. Then he and I would make up the reply. And very often, when I wouldn't agree with it at all, very decidedly wouldn't agree to it, I would comment very forcibly and very freely to Dill in a way I wouldn't possibly comment to the Prime Minister. Then Dill would report that to Mr. Churchill. That's what I said to Dill, and that way my own feeling got across to Mr. Churchill."

And so, there we have it. Fully acknowledged (albeit long after the fact), a prime example of conspiracy in high places…a benign, well-meant conspiracy in this case, however, that did the world a world of good.

★★★

First published in Military History *magazine, March 1997.*

Tale of a Stowaway

FEW HAD IT AS TOUGH during the war as Charlie Mott, who went to war before the war (for the United States), as a gung-ho pilot with Claire Chennault's Flying Tigers in China and Burma.

Mott had been a fighter pilot in the U.S. Navy, but he resigned his commission and risked his future navy opportunities to join Chennault's volunteers.

He then was shot down over Japanese-held territory in Burma. He had been strafing a Japanese airstrip.

He bailed out, but his luck was tough. "Hitting the silk" at low altitude, he broke an arm, a leg, and his pelvis when he hit the ground with battering impact. The Japanese who then captured him were totally unsympathetic.

"The Japs threw him into a truck that had no suspension and slammed him around for four days over rutted tracks. The Japs did not set his fractured bones."

He was thrown into a dungeonlike prison cell in Bangkok, Thailand, where he mustered the strength and fortitude to set his own arm and leg. He simply had to live with the pelvis.

Eventually recovered, he was placed "in charge of trucks supplying food to British POWs working on the infamous Burma-Siam railroad." In all, he was a POW until 1945.

But now came unexpected problems—the bureaucracy of the war's victorious Allies! "At the end of the war, Charlie was a civilian. He was not eligible for repatriation by any government. He borrowed enough money to get from Bangkok to India."

Even back home in America shortly after the war, Charlie was a veteran without real veteran status. "As a civilian, Charlie got no POW pay, no demobilization benefits, no medical benefits, no GI Bill of Rights, and no credit on his Navy time for more than three years in the CBI (China-Burma-India Theater) as a Flying Tiger and POW."

Undeterred (though many would have been), he subsequently rejoined the navy, still as a fighter pilot. He put in his years qualifying him for retirement with full benefits, after serving with distinction, and that, *almost*, is the end of the story.

Almost, since we haven't yet said how he got home from India in his statelesslike, postwar status. And that was by further demonstration of the fortitude and resourcefulness that had carried him through his wartime ordeal.

When even the *American* repatriation authorities in India clung to their red tape and refused to allow him to sail home on an officially sanctioned ship, Charlie Mott simply "stowed away on a U.S. troop transport."

★★★

Based upon Hugh Crumpler's "How's Your CBI IQ" column in Ex-CBI Roundup, *April 1989.*

MacArthur's Extended Escape

IF HE GOT THROUGH TO Australia, Douglas MacArthur had promised General Jonathan Wainwright back at embattled Corregidor, he would "come back as soon as I can with as much as I can." With a Japanese cruiser cutting ahead of the MacArthur party's PT boats in Philippine waters just a day later, however, no one could be sure that MacArthur would be going anyplace.

In the Japanese homeland, Tokyo Rose had been talking of a public execution of the sixty-two-year-old American general once he was captured. That implied chilling personal grief too—with MacArthur on Navy Lieutenant John Bulkeley's PT Boat 41 were the general's wife, Jean, their four-year-old son Arthur, and a Cantonese nanny named Ah Cheu.

The party that had left Corregidor and the Bataan Peninsula the evening before—aboard four PT boats of Bulkeley's Motor Torpedo Boat Squadron 3—also included twelve army officers, a master sergeant familiar with secure radio codes, and two ranking navy officers.

Left behind to harsh fate at the hands of the invading Japanese were twenty or so generals and thousands of fighting men, both American and Filipino. President Franklin D. Roosevelt had ordered MacArthur to leave "The Rock," as Corregidor was called. Uncomfortable with the idea of abandoning his men, MacArthur briefly considered resigning from the U.S. Army and joining the defenders of Bataan as a "volunteer" private.

But reason prevailed—if he could get out, his experience, his expertise, and his prestige in the Far East would be needed when America was ready to fight back in strength. Then, too, and unlike most of the U.S. Military personnel still in the Philippines, he had his family with him.

The projected escape from certain capture, likely torture, and possible death would not be easily accomplished in waters or skies so dominated by the Japanese.

Their engine noise covered by artillery barrages from the Corregidor fortress, the PT boats had shoved off at dusk the evening of March 11, 1942. Speedy, but small and frail, they headed into unusually rough seas that rattled and shook the passengers all night—the MacArthurs were deathly ill with seasickness until the party stopped the next day for quick rest at a midpoint in the dash for Mindanao Island, territory still held by American and Filipino forces. Signal fires on the way had indicated their run for freedom was known to the enemy.

Now, after the voyage was resumed in broad daylight (in just two PT boats), a sailor aboard Bulkeley's 41 Boat called out: "Sail ho!"

It was a Japanese cruiser cutting westward across their path. Bulkeley called for stop-engines, and for more than ten suspense-filled minutes the low-slung boat wallowed among the whitecaps at a dead stop.

The cruiser, to everyone's great relief, passed on without noticing the two small boats in the whitecapped seas. Later in the afternoon, the party repeated the hair-raising performance upon encountering a Japanese destroyer. That night, passing off occupied Negros Island, the rumble of the PT-boat engines stirred up fresh trouble—a searchlight that stabbed the inky blackness. But it was pointed upward, into the sky. The Japanese manning a coastal battery apparently thought it was aircraft they had heard. The PTs crept on by.

The seas this night were rough again, and aboard both boats the landlubbers once more were deathly ill.

Toward morning, MacArthur left his mattress, unable to sleep, and awoke his aide Sidney L. Huff. "I just want to talk," he said. For the next couple of hours, as Bulkeley's boat hurtled through the night, "the General was sitting on the mattress talking about what he had gone through in the last four years or so." He "choked up as he expressed his chagrin at being ordered to leave Corregidor." And he vowed to recapture the Philippines in such terms that Huff could see "he meant it, and he was already planning how he would do it."

At 6:30 A.M., dawn, Cagayan Point's light appeared on the horizon—Bulkeley had hit his navigational nail on the head, on time. He and his equally nerveless crewmen had run the rough seas for thirty-five hours since leaving Corregidor two days before.

For MacArthur and family, however, the escape from Corregidor and the Philippines was not yet over—they were still in the Philippines.

As it turned out, too, the B-17s that would be their next conveyance were not yet "in" from Australia. Guarded by elements of the twenty-five thousand Americans and Filipinos still fighting the invading Japanese on Mindanao, the MacArthurs spent the night at the Del Monte plantation at Cagayan, despite reports that the Japanese were rushing from Davao to Del Monte—the news of MacArthur's arrival having quickly spread across the embattled island.

MacArthur's wait for the rescue planes lasted, in fact, for four days, during which the Americans often had to "dodge" raiding Japanese planes. In Australia, American commanders were having trouble finding three airworthy Flying Forts.

By MacArthur's own account years later, four B-17s had been dispatched for the pickup, but one crashed, two others never reached their destination, and a fourth had been sent back to Australia, rejected for being "dangerously decrepit." An angered MacArthur, says biographer William Manchester, then radioed his demand for the "three best planes in the United States or Hawaii."

In Washington, Henry Stimson, Secretary of War, called MacArthur's "rather imperative command" to FDR's attention, but the message did produce results. Two newer B-17s finally appeared at Del Monte on the Monday night following the Wednesday evening leave-taking from Corregidor. A third plane had turned back due to engine trouble.

Overloaded, the two B-17s took off the same night, their passengers packed in like sardines, even over the bomb bays. As MacArthur's lead plane roared down the torchlit runway, one engine faltered, but it caught again at the last moment. The Flying Fortress struggled aloft for the five-hour flight to Darwin on Australia's lightly defended northern rim.

The two bombers had to fly over newly occupied Japanese territory—the East Indies, Timor, northern New Guinea—but they evaded searching Japanese fighters. Air turbulence over the Celebes Sea made some of the passengers sick all over again. Then, approaching Darwin, the Flying Forts were shunted away—it seems the Japanese were hitting Darwin from the air.

The B-17s landed at Batchelor Field, fifty miles away, and as the party stiffly climbed from their aircraft, MacArthur said: "It was close, but that's the way it is in war. You win or lose, live or die—and the difference is just an eyelash."

If MacArthur was relieved to have reached Australia, his wife and son also safe from the fiery end awaiting Corregidor, he was shocked to find few forces and no immediate buildup under way in Australia to mount a counteroffensive against the Japanese. His first inkling came at remote Batchelor Field, where he hailed an American officer and asked about the "buildup."

The other man didn't know what MacArthur was talking about. "So far as I know, Sir, there are very few troops here."

Startled, MacArthur told his chief of staff, Richard Sutherland, "Surely, he is wrong."

And for the moment, the MacArthurs still were a long way from safety. They were, in fact, in a remote, hardly defended war zone under intermittent attack by the rampaging Japanese.

The MacArthurs didn't want to fly again, but the nearest train station, Alice Springs, was one thousand miles away. MacArthur would have driven there, rather than fly, but young Arthur was ill and was being fed intravenously—he had to be moved much more quickly.

As a result, they flew to Alice Springs, an air raid starting behind them just as they left Batchelor Field. At Alice Springs, they landed one day after the weekly train had pulled out. A "special train" ordered up for the visitors in this "Wild West" town consisted of a locomotive with a huge cowcatcher up front, two wooden coaches, and a red caboose. It took seventy hours to make the one thousand added miles to Adelaide, from which a modern, well-appointed train finally would whisk the MacArthurs on to Melbourne.

On the dinkum Alice Springs train's long wooden benches, however, MacArthur did sink into his first deep sleep in weeks.

At Adelaide, MacArthur encountered his first welcoming crowd, replete with reporters. By now more fully apprised that no avenging army awaited him in Melbourne, that America's first focus would be the war in Europe, the outraged MacArthur scratched a few words on the back of an envelope. He then made his appearance and spoke those few words, explaining that he had been ordered to leave Corregidor for the purpose of organizing the American offensive against Japan, against the occupiers of the Philippines.

General Douglas MacArthur returns to the Philippines, fulfilling his famous promise; October 1944. (U.S. Army photo)

His last words were deliberate and all MacArthur: "I came through and I shall return."

The American Office of War Information subsequently asked him to change the last three words to read "we" instead of "I." But MacArthur refused. To him, it was his sacred pledge to the Philippines he had left behind. It was a personal thing: *I shall return!*

★★★

Based upon Sea Wolf: A Biography of John D. Bulkeley, USN *by William B. Breuer (Presidio Press, Novato, Calif., 1989) and* American Caesar: Douglas MacArthur, 1880–1964 *by William Manchester (Little, Brown and Company, Boston, Mass., 1978).*

Japanese-American vs. Japan

IT WAS APRIL 1941 WHEN American intelligence agent Richard S. sailed for the Philippines in the guise of a deckhand. He and a young companion jumped ship upon arrival and made their way to Manila, with instructions to worm their way into the city's Japanese community and report any signs of undercover Japanese military activities.

Their little-known mission came before Pearl Harbor—someone in the U.S. government this time was thinking ahead...thinking there might be war with Japan in the near future.

When war did come, Richard S. served with the U.S. Army, fighting the hopeless battles of Bataan and Corregidor. He was a member of the American party that finally ventured out of Corregidor to arrange the terms of surrender to the victorious Japanese. A Japanese sergeant singled him out and, as Richard S. recalled, "slapped me to the ground, breaking my glasses and causing cuts on my face."

When the surrender took place, Richard S. posed as a civilian unconnected with the military. He countered reports of being seen in uniform by saying he had been forced once in a while to borrow military garb while his own civilian clothing was being laundered. Repeatedly tortured, he refused to recant his cover story that he was a deckhand who had jumped ship to escape the American draft.

Grudgingly, the Japanese began to accept his story and assigned him a job as an interpreter in their occupying army's chief judge advocate's office.

Of course, Richard S. could speak and read their language with no difficulty whatsoever. Richard Sakakida was Japanese himself—Japanese-American, that is, Hawaiian-born. Like so many thousands of other Japanese-Americans, he in fact was a loyal American serving his country with skill, determination, and considerable bravery during World War II, as former Associated Press reporter and war correspondent Lyn Crost reported in her 1994 book, *Honor by Fire*.

Hers was not simply the story of the remarkable combat record compiled by the Nisei fighting the Germans in Europe, coupled with the ironic and unfortunate treatment of Japanese-Americans caught up in the wave of rage, intolerance, and suspicion that swept the country after Pearl Harbor...although Crost did tell that part of the Nisei story very well too.

No, the surprising story in her book is that of the thousands of Japanese-Americans who, in secret for the most part, took part in the war against their ancestral homeland of Japan.

True, there certainly is the inspiring story of the 100th Infantry Battalion at Monte Cassino in Italy, and of its follow-up outfit, the 100th's 442nd Regimental Combat Team, which "for its size and length of service…was the most decorated military unit in American history."

But Crost also wrote, "I want to tell you about the 6,000 Japanese-American linguists of the Military Intelligence Service, who were on every embattled island of the Pacific, fought with Merrill's Marauders through the jungles of Burma, assisted the opposing forces of Mao Tse-Tung and Chiang Kaishek in China, worked in Pentagon offices to track changes in Japan's naval and army forces, and interpreted top-secret decoded messages between Germany and Japan."

For all the vital part these Americans played in the war effort, however, their dramatic story has remained largely unknown. "The U.S. government pledged these Japanese-Americans of the Military Intelligence Service to secrecy, which endured for more than a quarter century after World War II ended, so that few know of their contributions," explained Crost.

As a prisoner of the Japanese, for instance, Richard Sakakida became the ultimate spy, spiriting out from his headquarters domain incredibly vital information until General MacArthur at last returned to the Philippines in 1944.

Forced to accompany the retreating Japanese, Richard Sakakida escaped in early 1945 but then was wounded when he was caught in an artillery crossfire. Sakakida finally came across a group of American soldiers and emerged from hiding, shouting, "Don't shoot, I'm an American!"

"Naturally," he recounted later, "it was difficult for them to believe I was an American."

But he was…and so were a lot of other Japanese-speaking—and *looking*—soldiers who bravely served the United States in the Pacific War against their ethnic homeland of Japan.

★★★

First published in Military History *magazine, June 1995.*

Bombed by Oranges

FOR NEWLY ARRIVING AMERICAN TROOPS and officers back in the early 1940s, Australia's coastal cities were recognizable as urban centers, as veritable fonts of civilized thought and activity. But the sprawling remainder of wartime Australia, especially the northern rim closest to the Japanese threat, was a different matter altogether. Here, life—even without the pressures of war—had been wild and woolly for some time.

"The whole continent of Australia is as undeveloped as the central United States was before the Civil War," wrote an American general to uninitiated colleagues confined to desks in Washington, D.C. Truly, it took on-site inspection to quite get the picture of this high-spirited, still-emerging, war-beleaguered nation way down under.

With transportation to the lightly populated and highly vulnerable Northern Territory always a problem anyway, the Americans who arrived on the scene early in World War II immediately dispatched engineer outfits to build roads and trucking units to do the driving.

These were not your American interstates of today. Even a hardened Australian of the '40s era was struck by the dust pouring into cabs and by the drivers "[who] would stand out on the running board, with the door closed, and reach in to steer the truck through the window."

Hand throttles kept the vehicles careening along at a steady 40-miles-per-hour.

Australia in the war years was a place where "scrounging" was far more than a joke or even an art form. For many, it was a way of life. The story is told, quite seriously, of the Aussie officer on leave who returned to his five-room house near Darwin one day in August of 1942...only to find it was gone!

Two months previous, in an epic of scrounging by parties unknown, an entire military camp—operations room, kitchens, showers, sleeping quarters, latrines—disappeared between a Saturday and a Monday. Seriously! "No trace of the vanished camp was ever found," said Professor Alan Howell of the University College of the Northwestern Territory in his book, *The Shadow's Edge: Australia's Northern War.*

Consider, too, the "fat cat" supply runs by air. Here the prevailing question was: Why waste empty space on aircraft returning to home base from training, administrative, or supply flights? The useful answer was: If they must go home anyway, fill 'em up! Fill 'em up with beer, food, or other luxury items that didn't seem likely to reach the camps in the great, so very distant Outback.

Thus came about "the bombing of Adelaide," an episode attributed to a Liberator bomber carrying various items in its bomb bays—oranges, booze, Coca Cola, and so on. As luck would have it, the bomb bay doors "peeled off" shortly after takeoff—and gravity took care of the rest. "Quite a sight it was to see case after case tumbling down, plus crates of oranges flying apart," recalled American Charles Edward of the 380th Bombardment Group.

Below, a crate of beer landed in Mrs. L. F. MacDonald's backyard and a Coke carton "demolished" the roof of her washhouse, said Powell's book. Oranges "showered down over the entire neighborhood." Amazingly, no one was hurt.

At the time, not all such events seemed too humorous. This was, after all, war...real war. American P-40 fighter pilot Robert Oestreicher, apparently the first Allied pilot to down a Japanese plane over Australia, is a case in point. His Forty-ninth Fighter Group won a Presidential Unit Citation, with Oestreicher one of the few Forty-ninth "originals" to survive. In those early war days, too, he helped uncrate and assemble the P-40s as they arrived by ship; then, he and a fellow pilot performed the test flights. "We made quite a few forced landings... because various things had not been hooked up," he wryly acknowledged later.

Also earning a Presidential Unit Citation was the 380th, which customarily flew lengthy missions over the Dutch East Indies, including the war's longest bombing raid before the advent of the B-29 "Super Fortress." Operating the B-24 Liberator, the 380th lost 49 of its bombers in one year, and more than 260 men overall, before decamping from the Northern Territory...no longer the vulnerable Northern Territory, exactly because of such sacrifices by Americans, Australians, and their various allies *down under.*

★★★

First published in World War II *magazine, January 1991.*

Long Odyssey into War

FOR RAF PILOT ARTHUR MURLAND Gill and members of his Number 84 Squadron in Egypt, simply reaching the war's new theater of operations against the Japanese in the Far East was a storybook odyssey of survival. This was early in 1942, with the Japanese swarming into Malaya and soon to threaten Singapore and its great British naval base.

Gill and his aircrews flew out of Egypt January 13, 1942, aboard twenty-four three-seater Blenheim medium bombers—"of which three fell by the wayside on the way out." The ground crews and other support personnel were to be shipped east aboard an old transport ship named the *Yoma*.

The squadron made its way across Palestine, Iraq, and the Persian Gulf, then to Karachi, Bombay, and Calcutta on the great subcontinent of India, across the Bay of Bengal and into Burma. The next stop would be Sumatra, Indonesia, just south of the besieged Malay Peninsula.

"We did Burma to Sumatra in one hop," explained war veteran Gill, "and we were running out of fuel by the time we got there." Worse, the RAF pilots didn't know where to land. "It was getting dusk when we arrived at the latitude and the longitude marked on the map, and there was no airfield! And so we flew on down the coast of Sumatra, one aircraft ran out of fuel and ditched in a paddy field, and the rest of us turned back."

The hope now was to reach Sabang Island, known to have a tiny three-hundred-yard strip. "Then suddenly one of the rear-gunners shouted 'Windsock!' and we did a circle 'round and there was the airfield, which was nowhere near where we had been told it was."

Moving on to Medan for operations against the Japanese, Gill and his men spent the next three weeks striking at targets in Thailand, Malaya, and Sumatra for the most part.

"On one occasion," noted Gill, "my aircraft was out of service and so I borrowed a short-nose Blenheim from Number 97 Squadron and dropped my bombs and flew back to Singapore that night—and found no lights to mark the runway! No lights there at all to get us down. We only knew it was the airfield because it was dark compared with the rest of the town, which was brilliantly lit. So eventually we landed over the palm trees and in complete darkness."

In the process, Gill ran his plane into a gaping bomb crater "and bent it badly."

He caught a ride back to Sumatra and resumed the war.

Shortly, though, the Japanese were threatening the base at Medan, and the squadron was ordered to transfer out of Java.

Since Gill didn't have a plane to call his own, he was ordered to remain behind, destroy ammunition and supplies, and find a way out on his own.

"I was in charge of the rearguard and 'Good Luck!'"

He and his ground personnel commandeered a Dutch truck for a thirteen-hour land journey to the coast through mountains, valleys, and torrential rains. "We arrived the next morning about 0800 at the extreme southern tip of Sumatra just about as the last ship out was casting off."

That last ship, it turned out, was the familiar old *Yoma*, the same ship that had carried Gill's ground crews east from distant Egypt.

★★★

Based upon interview by Peter Smith, Military History *magazine, June 1988.*

Blind Leading the Blind

AFTER PEARL HARBOR, MANY WERE the lame and the halt who felt America's patriotic fervor and tried to "join up."

Nearly everybody has heard tales of the youngsters and oldsters who bamboozled the system and sneaked their way into the nation's fighting forces by hook or by crook.

It took a young ophthalmologist, however, himself a volunteer, to run across a nearly blind man who had "conned" the system and made it into the U.S. Army.

Dr. Albert E. Meisenbach Jr. was stationed at the base hospital at Sheppard Field, Wichita Falls, Texas, before his deployment in midsummer 1942 as flight surgeon for a photo reconnaissance outfit stationed in the Southwest Pacific combat zone. In the army, the eye specialist had more general medical duties, of course. He was sent to Sheppard to equip the new Eye, Ear, Nose, and Throat (EENT) Department and for a time was Chief of the EENT and of Orthopedic and Genito-Urinary Services (plus Athletic Officer). Various kinds of surgery became a part of his routine.

He was on more familiar ground one day when he spotted a soldier groping his way down a hospital hallway. "I observed a GI holding on to the guide rail as he made his way down the hall."

His curiosity aroused, Meisenbach stopped the young man to ask why he was feeling his way along like that. "Imagine my amazement when he told me he was nearly blind!"

And it was no joke. "I took him to the clinic to confirm this and was shocked to find that he had less than 20/20 vision in both eyes." Nor was the young man's condition anything sudden—he was a practiced reader in Braille.

How could such an obvious 4-F slip into uniform? Meisenbach, naturally, asked the question.

The answer was that the otherwise fit man before him had memorized all the various eye charts used in the U.S. Army physical tests at the time. "All I had to do was get the officer to name the top letter and I would recite the entire chart to him."

And why? What could a nearly blind man accomplish in the Army? "I knew that many men would be blinded as a result of the conflict, and because of my knowledge of Braille, I know that I can help."

★★★

Based upon Memoirs of a Flight Surgeon Serving in the South Pacific During World War II *by A. E. Meisenbach, Jr., M.D., Dallas, Texas, 1988.*

Hands of Steel

THE TARGET WOULD BE ENEMY port facilities seemingly impregnable to attack—a dangerous thorn in the British lion's side.

But…how to get to it? How to pluck it out?

This well-protected complex held by the all-conquering Germans offered the only dry dock on the Atlantic seaboard large enough to accommodate the large and powerful German battleship currently tucked into harbor in occupied Norway, the *Tirpitz*.

The British would prefer to have the battleship stay there, rather than see it roam the sea lanes. They would rather keep an eye on it up there in Norway and deny it access to the only feasible repair base available to it outside of Germany.

The direct approach, of course, would be to destroy the ship itself. And… well, they *were* working on that, yes. But, in the meantime, there also were the extensive U-boat pens…the massive dry dock…the attendant supply and arming facilities, and all at Saint-Nazaire, six miles up the Loire River from its mouth in southern Brittany…also 250 miles from Falmouth, the closest British port.

And so, early in 1942, the planners at Combined Operations, headed by Lord Louis Mountbatten, developed their scheme for knocking out the *Forme Escluse*, as the dry dock was called (another name for it was the *Forme Louis Jourbet*). A Commando raid would be one element of the attack, but a raiding party alone would not be enough. The situation called for an added dimension.

And no, not even a mix of motor launches, gunboats, and Commando-type raiders would suffice.

What was needed here was a real warship, a sizable vessel to be sacrificed in order to deliver the raid's crowning blow. Not simply a blockship, nor merely a ramming ship, but a block and ramming ship.

An old American destroyer, *Buchanan*, delivered to the beleaguered British under the Lend-Lease Program and now renamed HMS *Campbelltown*, would race into the harbor basin with the speedy small craft and blunder on—quite deliberately, of course—into the dry dock. There, after ramming the facility, the old *Buchanan* would block it, presumably for weeks or months. As a result, the mighty *Tirpitz* up in Norway would hardly dare cruise the Atlantic and risk unrepairable damage (*Tirpitz's* sister, *Bismarck*, on her way to St. Nazaire, already had been sunk by this time).

That was the plan; that—almost—was the outcome. The British hastened across the English Channel and up the Loire with *Campbelltown's* silhouette altered to resemble a German destroyer and all craft flying German flags.

When discovered and fired upon just outside of the dry dock basin, the British column simply sped up—and fired back, wreaking considerable damage. Most of the small craft and many of the Commandos quickly became casualties, but not so *Campbelltown*. She smashed into the lock gates at 19 knots. "There was a staggering shock as her bows cleaved into the great caissons," wrote military historian (and former British Commando officer) Peter Young. "The main object of the raid had been achieved before a single Commando soldier had set foot ashore."

Those still surviving did step ashore, visit their demolition targets, and fight a desperate losing battle against the aroused German defenders. With few boats left unscathed, many of the men had no way to return home. They fought on, and some did their best to escape on foot. (Five did make it home by way of neutral Spain.) In all, however, the Royal Navy lost 182 officers and men killed or taken prisoner, the Commandos, 212.

German losses were great as well, but undoubtedly the most bitter moment for the defenders came the next day, when, with dozens of officers examining the rammed dry-dock facility and the British ship lodged therein, with hundreds of soldiers looking on nearby, as well, the old destroyer suddenly blew up—the five tons of explosives in her bow set off by timing devices.

As Winston Churchill once proudly said of the Commandos, "There comes from the sea a hand of steel which plucks the German sentries from their posts." *Campbelltown* and the Saint-Nazaire raiders did a bit more than just that, in ringing, even shattering, echo of Churchill's words.

★★★

First published in Military History *magazine, February 1993.*

Early Tokyo Run

"WE SETTLED IN FOR THE five hour flight. Tokyo, here we come!"

United States Army Lieutenant Edgar McElroy had already taken a firm grip on the controls of his twin-engine Mitchell B-25 as the formation—soon to be known as "Doolittle's Raiders"—turned westward over the Pacific Ocean for the long flight to Japan.

It was April 18, 1942, just four months after Pearl Harbor, and here they were—going for the enemy's jugular—striking the Japanese hard, right where they lived.

As McElroy and his crew of four knew, however, it was likely going to be a one-way trip! Their aircraft carrier, the *Hornet*, and her escorts had been spotted mid-ocean by a Japanese trawler that was able to transmit their location via radio before being sunk.

"We had been found out!" as McElroy recalled in a first-person account published posthumously in the California-based monthly *Military* (April and May 2010).

Indeed, the Japanese rightfully would be alarmed to hear that a U. S. naval task force was approaching their home waters, but only somewhat alarmed. After all, what significant harm could such a small flotilla pose? And further, why were so many U. S. Army medium bombers lined up so tightly on the U. S. Navy carrier's flight deck? Surely, they wouldn't be any use in the middle of the ocean, because if sent aloft, how could they ever be recovered by their carrier?

Even aboard the *Hornet*, there were doubts that morning. "The weather was crummy, the seas were running heavy, and the ship was pitching up and down like I had never seen before," McElroy wrote. "Great waves were crashing against the bow and washing over the front of the deck. This wasn't going to be easy."

By "this," of course, he meant taking off from the pitching carrier's short flight deck into the teeth of a near-gale force wind and water spray corning straight over the deck. Even if the 16 bombers managed their take-offs under such harsh conditions, the long five-hour flight to a forewarned Tokyo still lay ahead. The original hope had been to creep much closer before launching the bold blow against the Japanese homeland. The plan never anticipated recovery of the bombers by their sea-going home base, the *Hornet*, but rather called for an after-raid escape to Allied-held areas on the China mainland.

But now, still seven hundred miles out from Japan proper and with all advantage of surprise gone, the flight to Japan and then to friendly territory in China looked will-nigh impossible.

Indeed, McElroy recalled, Lt. Col. James Doolittle's air crews were told to drop their bomb loads on Tokyo and then "to fly as far west as possible…land on the water and launch our rubber rafts."

Added McElroy in his first-person account of the historic raid: "We were still much too far out [from Japan] and we all knew that our chances of making land were somewhere between slim and none. At the last minute, each plane loaded an extra 10 five-gallon gas cans to give us a fighting chance of reaching China."

As the pilots began the dangerous take-off attempts from the tightly packed deck of the *Hornet*. Doolittle would be going first, and then eleven others before McElroy, pilot of plane No. 13, would face his turn. For all, the deck officer's timing would be crucial if they were even going to have a chance at setting out for Japan.

"Then I saw him wave Doolittle to go, and we watched breathlessly to see what happened." related McElroy.

Doolittle's plane clawed its way into the air without incident, but the second B-25 attempting take-off "appeared to stall with its nose up and began falling toward the waves." Luckily, the pilot was able to stabilize the plane and it then "staggered back up into the air."

And so it went, one after the other. "There was [a] sense of relief with each one that made it." Another nerve-racking take-off occurred when one of the bombers did momentarily disappear completely below the end of the flight deck, but then popped back into sight and flew on.

Meanwhile, aboard plane No. 13, the adrenaline was pumping as the moment for McElroy's own attempt approached.

Indeed, it suddenly was time to gun the engines and edge forward—careful all the time to keep the left main wheel and the nose wheel on the white guidelines painted on the deck. "If I got off a little bit too far left," McElroy recalled, "We'd go off the edge of the deck; too far to the right and our wingtip would smack the ship's island."

At last, No. 12 was taking off and McElroy taxied up to the start line. Now, he really saw how short a runway the pitching flight deck afforded all the pilots.

Running up his two engines, he turned full attention to the deck officer with the signal paddles. "Now my adrenalin was really pumping! We went to full power, and the noise and vibration inside the plane went way up. He circled the paddles furiously while watching...the pitch of the deck."

Then, the paddles dropped. "And I said, 'Here we go!' I released the brakes and we started rolling forward, and as I looked down the flight deck you could see straight down into the angry churning water." But then the deck rose again.

"I pulled up and our plane slowly strained up and away from the ship. There as a big cheer and whoops from the crew, but I just felt relieved and muttered to myself, 'Boy, that was short!'"

Of course, this was only the beginning of a long day of dramatic ups and downs. Burning off their precious fuel every inch of the way after take-off, McElroy and crew had raced westward "just 50 feet above the cold rolling ocean, as low as I dared to fly." Saltwater sometimes splattered the windshield. "It was an exhilarating feeling...I felt as though the will and spirit of our whole country was pushing us along."

They passed an occasional ship on the way to Tokyo, but none that was threatening to them. Then catching the first glimpse of land, the eastern edge of Honshu, they came ashore, still flying low, and were surprised to see people on the ground below innocently waving at them. Realizing they were not in the right place, a course correction took them offshore again and south along the coastline. "I climbed up to 2,000 feet to find out where we were."

That's when they drew antiaircraft fire for the first time. "Then we spotted Tokyo Bay, turned west and put our nose down, diving toward the water."

Ahead, clearly recognizable, was their target, the Yokosuka Naval Base. "Off to the right there was already smoke visible over Tokyo [from the other U. S.

bombers]. Coming in low over the water, I increased speed to 200 mph and told everyone, 'Get ready!'"

Close to the target, McElroy pulled up to 1,300 feet and opened his bomb-bay doors. "There were furious black bursts of antiaircraft fire all around us, but I flew straight on through them, spotting our target: the torpedo works and the dry docks."

McElroy noticed a big ship in the dry dock but kept his focus on flying despite the flak bursts "bouncing us around." At that moment their bombs tumbled free. Then a jubilant crewman yelled: "We got an aircraft carrier! The whole deck is burning!"

Looking back, McElroy caught a quick glimpse of a crane blowing up and falling over and thought, "Take that!"

Though happy with their success, McElroy quickly realized, "We had to get out of there fast!" Even at 30 miles out McElroy could still see "huge billows of black smoke" over the target area they had just attacked.

"Up until then, we had been flying for Uncle Sam; now we were flying for ourselves. We flew south over open ocean, parallel to the Japanese coast, all afternoon. We saw a large submarine apparently at rest, and then in another 15 miles we spotted three large enemy cruisers headed for Japan. There were no more bombs, so we just let them be and kept on going."

By late afternoon, it was time to head for the Chinese coast, across the East China Sea. By now, too, the adrenaline had worn off and a grim realization set in: "We just didn't have enough fuel to make it."

Nor were they able to pick up the promised radio beacon, either. "This was not good. The weather turned bad and it was getting dark, so we climbed up. I was now flying on instruments, through a dark misty rain."

Their chances of reaching land looked hopeless, their situation increasingly dire, when quite suddenly they picked up a strong tailwind and thought just maybe they could make it.

And, just barely, they did. Reaching land, but still over Japanese-held territory, they flew on as far as they could until the B-25 was just about "flying on fumes." Then all five bailed out, with McElroy leaving his plane last and landing safely in a rice paddy. Miraculously, the five were reunited within hours and, with the help of friendly Chinese and Catholic missionaries, were spirited westward over the next couple of weeks—"by foot, by pony, by car, by train and by plane"—until they reached safety in India.

★★★

Additional note: Others among the eighty Army airmen who staged the Doolittle raid on Tokyo did not fare nearly so well. None of the planes actually landed in friendly Chinese territory as planned. One did reach a Soviet base, but the crewmen promptly were interned. The rest of the aircraft, like McElroy's, ran out of fuel and crashed. Overall, four of the heroic fliers drowned, one was killed parachuting from his bomber, and eight were captured by the Japanese, with three of them executed and one dying in captivity. Still, sixty-three others, Doolittle included, successfully parachuted from their fuel-starved planes, found help on the ground, and lived, despite various injuries. Thus, seventy-one of the eighty American airmen who embarked upon the impossible mission of bombing Tokyo just weeks after Pearl Harbor did survive the experience.

Back in Japan, no great damage had been done, but the surprise raid had been a major shock both to the public and the military. As McElroy himself noted, it also "proved to be a tremendous boost to American morale, which had plunged following the Pearl Harbor attack." The American public was further delighted when President Roosevelt taunted the surprised Japanese by saying the bombers had come from a mystical "Shangri-la."

★★★

Based upon the article "Doolittle Raid on Tokyo" by Edgar McElroy in Military, *May 2010 (Volume XXVI, No. 12) Sacramento, California.*

Tokyo's Psychological Shock

ON THE GROUND IN TOKYO during Doolittle's famous raid of April 18, 1942, Father Bruno Bitter, Roman Catholic priest, noticed the alarm sounded at about noon. "Most of the people did not believe it, thinking it was just another drill." In fact, there had been a drill and practice alert that very morning—it was just ending when Jimmy Doolittle's carrier-launched U.S. Army B-25s appeared in the skies over Tokyo and environs.

"But when they learned it was a real raid, nobody could hold them back to go outside, to climb the roofs or the chimneys to get a better view. In other words, it was a thrill rather than a frightening event."

The American planners had not counted on devastating material damage, but they were hoping that the raid from the U.S. carrier *Hornet* would demonstrate

Japan's own vulnerability and thus sap the nation's morale…that the raid would achieve some psychological impact. The effect apparently did seep in.

Toshiko Matsumura, thirteen at the time, was not immediately aware of the raid—it was a few days before she overheard her elders in Tokyo's suburbs "discussing it in hushed tones." What she heard, the gradual effect, indeed was undermining.

"My people had always placed emphasis on spiritual strength and the medieval belief that Japan would never be attacked. As children we had been taught to believe what the emperor and his advisors told us. It was a severe psychological shock to even the most ardent believer when it was officially announced that we had been attacked. We finally began to realize that all we were told was not true—that the government had lied when it said we were invulnerable. We then began to doubt that we were also invincible."

Under "confinement to quarters" in the American Embassy, interned U.S. Ambassador Joseph C. Grew was winding up a meeting with a visitor, the Swiss minister, "…and just as he was leaving before lunch, we heard a lot of planes overhead and saw five or six large fires burning in different directions with great volumes of smoke."

Grew told of their reaction in his diary. "At first we thought it was only maneuvers, but soon became aware that it was the first big raid on Japan by American bombers…." They saw one of the twin-engine U.S. Army Air Corps bombers, "apparently losing altitude and flying very low, just over the tops of the buildings to the west." They thought it would crash, but then realized the pilot was flying low to avoid fighters and flak.

To the east, they saw another plane, closely followed by "a whole line of black puffs of smoke, indicating antiaircraft explosions." Since it didn't look like a bomber, "We are inclined to believe that the Japanese batteries lost their heads and fired on their own pursuit planes."

It was an exciting day for the Allied noncombatants interned in Tokyo. "We were all very happy and proud in the Embassy, and the British told us later that they drank toasts all day to the American flyers."

Elsewhere in Tokyo, meanwhile, Vice Admiral Matome Ugaki, chief of staff for the Combined Fleet, already was at lunch when he received word of the astounding attack. He also kept a diary: "I did not know what was happening, and all I could do was order a pursuit to the east."

He ordered his Third Submarine Fleet "to attack," but none of the Japanese forces attempting to react were able to locate the fast-retiring carrier *Hornet* and her escorts. Jimmy Doolittle's brave B-25s, in the meantime, were headed for the China coast in hopes of finding sanctuary beyond a wide belt of Japanese-occupied territory. In the days ahead, there would be vigorous and cruel response by the Japanese in China, but for now Ugaki felt humiliated. "It is regrettable that I missed my chance three or four times," he wrote in his diary of April 18, 1942. "It had always been my motto not to allow Tokyo or the homeland to be attacked from the air, but today my pride has been deeply hurt and my spirits are low as today I gave the enemy his glory."

★★★

Based upon The Doolittle Raid: America's Daring First Strike Against Japan *by Carroll V. Glines (Orion Books, New York, 1988).*

Tale of Two Ships

ONCE UPON A PREWAR TIME there was a 4,418-ton merchant ship named *Cairo* built at Germany's Kiel shipyards and operated by the Atlas-Levant Line—and no harm in all that whatsoever. Then along came Nazi Germany, the war...and the transmogrification of the placid-looking merchantman into new form, into a potential bully of the sea lanes sprouting guns and torpedo tubes.

Oddly, you might think, her newly appointed commander, *Kapitanleutnant* Horst Gerlach, had his wife in mind when he renamed his armed merchant cruiser *Stier*, which means "Bull" in German. That is to say, he liked the reference to his wife Hildegard's astrological sign of Taurus, also meaning bull.

He took over his warship, designed to be a commerce raider, in April of 1941, but she wasn't commissioned until the end of the year, and she didn't put to sea for her first war patrol until May of 1942. By then she bristled with six 5.9-inch guns, two 37 mm pieces, and four 20 mm guns, plus two torpedo tubes.

Nearly 410 feet in length, with a 56.6-foot beam and 21.4-foot draft, *Stier* the female bull could claim a max speed of 14.5 knots. No greyhound of the seas, she would be a wallowing, pug-nosed bully, her armament hidden until the last second...until needed to surprise and subdue her prey.

Merchantman, cross her path at your own peril!

In America that same May of 1942 a newly commissioned cargo ship named the *Stephen Hopkins* was delivered to the Maritime Administration.

Launched in mid-April at the Kaiser shipyards in Richmond, California, she was one of the first 20 Liberty ships built, with 2,730 more of the same mass-produced merchantmen to follow before war's end. The 7,181-ton *Hopkins* could proceed at eleven knots only. She was lightly armed—one World War I–vintage 4-incher at the stern, two 37 mm guns at bow end, plus six machine guns.

Her maiden voyage under Paul Buck as captain took her first to New Zealand, then Australia, then Africa. It was September by the time she rounded the tip of South Africa and plowed her way northwestward through the South Atlantic, bound for Paramaribo in Dutch Guiana on the South American coast to pick up a cargo of bauxite.

Kapitanleutnant Gerlach's *Stier* had spent the same period of time—May to September—on her own maiden voyage.

Hers, however, began with an unsought baptism of fire. It would continue to produce fireworks, but usually at the bully *Stier's* own instigation.

Her saga opened with a bid—under escort by sixteen minesweeper craft and four torpedo boats—for the open seas from occupied Rotterdam and through the heavily patrolled English Channel. The British noticed, of course, and in the firefight that resulted the Germans lost two of their speedy torpedo boats and the British, one. The *Stier*, though, posing as a slow-moving merchantman, escaped harm and was on her way…poised now to launch her career as a deadly commerce raider.

As reported by Jon Guttman in his 1995 book, *Defiance at Sea: Stories of Dramatic Naval Warfare*, the *Stier* soon, in a matter of days, had nosed into the rough seas of the South Atlantic. "Gerlach—who was promoted to *Korvettenkapitan* on 1 June—and his crew hoped that they might see to it that the sacrifice of their escorts had not been in vain. That could be only done by sinking as much enemy mercantile tonnage as possible, while simultaneously distracting and evading as many Allied warships as possible, for as long as possible."

Gerlach's "*Bull*" drew first blood on June 4, by sinking the 4,986-ton British freighter *Gemstone*, bound for Baltimore with a load of iron ore.

At this point in time, the captain and crew of the *Hopkins* were busy plying pathways of their own in seas on the other side of the world, vigilant against enemy intervention, to be sure, but unaware as yet of the *Stier* and her deadly activities.

In no time at all, the *Stier* found her next victim, the 10,170-ton tanker *Stanvac Calcutta* of Panamanian registry, sunk on June 6 after a brisk shelling and a torpedo round that killed the tanker's master and thirteen of his crewmen. After that came a two-month dry spell…until the armed German raider encountered the British merchantman *Dalhousie* east of Trinidad.

Scratch another Allied cargo ship from the war board. This one of 7,072 tons.

And now came still another lapse in contacts for *Kapitan* Gerlach and crew, except for the fruitless pursuit of two potential victims during the first three weeks of September.

On September 25, *Stier* was joined on the high seas east of South America by the German supply ship *Tannenfels*. Friends from the very first, they steamed together until, in the blotchy weather of Sunday morning, September 27, just before nine o'clock, they were emerging from yet another rain squall.

As for Captain Paul Buck and his crew of the Liberty ship *Hopkins*, they no longer were on the other side of the world. That same Sunday morning, in fact, they found themselves in soupy, rainy, squally weather…east of Brazil. Around nine o'clock too.

Well, make it 8:52 A.M.

Their ship was approaching a rain squall, wrote Guttman, "when suddenly the ghostly silhouette of another merchantman took shape in the rain, followed by yet another." The two strangers were so close, the *Hopkins* had to turn hard left to avoid a collision.

Needless to say, the clean-cut Boy Scout from America had run into a street-smart thug (and his friend) in an alley. It was a blind alley with no escape, since the *Stier* easily could overtake the slower *Hopkins*. Indeed, as the *Hopkins* wisely turned and ran, the Stier not only gave chase, but began pummeling the Liberty ship with her 37 mm cannon, soon followed by a pounding from the armed merchantman's 5.9-inch guns—the same size, by the way, as those on a light cruiser.

"Gunner's mate Paul B. Porter, just in from the 4–8 A.M. watch, had had breakfast and gone to sleep when he was aroused by a sensation like a sledge-hammer hitting the deck," wrote Guttman. "Peering out of the porthole of the starboard midships cabin, he saw two ships, one of which was blazing away at his ship. Grabbing a peacoat, sweater and helmet, he dashed off to his station at the aft .50-calibre mount, passing a crewman whose buttocks had been shot off. Removing the canvas cover of his machine gun, he found that excessive moisture had rendered it inoperative, so he rushed off to assist the 4-inch gun crew."

That lone 4-incher of WWI vintage now became the hapless Liberty ship's chief means of striking back against the *Stier*. The stern-mounted gun became a font of extraordinary heroism, as well.

Also running to help man the piece, Ordinary Seaman Roger H. Piercy saw a horrifying sight. It was the young commander of the U.S. Navy's fourteen-man

Armed Guard unit assigned to the merchant ship, Ensign Kenneth M. Willett, U.S. Naval Reserves. "Ensign Willett was felled by a shell fragment while making his way to the 4-incher, but Piercy saw him arrive, his entrails hanging out from a stomach wound," Guttman wrote in his book.

Ensign Willett carried on anyway.

So did his gun, even though "its crew was being cut down one by one, to be replaced in turn by volunteers." One of the latter was Gunner's Mate Porter, who looked up and saw one of the cargo ship's 37 mm guns up forward simply disappear in a puff of smoke and fire.

Another soon to find his way to the all-important 4-incher would be Cadet Midshipman Edwin J. O'Hara, U.S. Merchant Marine Academy at King's Point, New York, described as the "youngest member of the ship's company." Normally, the youthful cadet would have no business at the gun tub, but Willett, in his spare time, had been showing O'Hara how to operate the gun.

For a while, the 4-incher and the two 37 mm pieces (those two under command of Second Mate Joseph Layman) were making their presence known aboard *Stier*. Fifteen of the bigger gun's shells struck the German ship, while the 37 mm guns landed repeated jabs of their own. The hits by *Hopkins* soon started fires, burst the water lines, and knocked out the raider's electrical power. Its main engine shut down, the *Stier* was adrift, her ammunition hoists no longer operative and her crew forming bucket lines to fight the fires in the absence of water for the fire hoses.

Which is not to say all was going so well for those aboard the brave *Hopkins*. "At length, however, the overwhelming fire of the Germans took its toll, cutting down Layman and his 37 mm gunners and killing or wounding the last of the *Stephen Hopkins'* 4-inch gun crew except for the indomitable Ensign Willett," wrote Guttman.

The end was near. "Even as he [Willett] tried to man the gun alone, the magazine blew up, and he too fell."

Near but not yet quite at hand, for a new hero was about to step forward. First, though, with his weapons all apparently silenced and his engine room afire, Captain Buck had to give the order to abandon ship. "As the crew carried out that melancholy order," added Guttman, "they again heard the harsh bark of their 4-inch gun."

It was young Cadet O'Hara, alone at the gun tub and manhandling the five unused shells he found there. Coming up from the burning engine room, he had seen Willett being carried away, and now the hours of training and practice they had spent together paid off...with a vengeance. In minutes, O'Hara fired off his five shells, "and managed to score hits on both *Stier* and *Tannenfels*."

He then joined his comrades taking to the life rafts. In minutes, the survivors saw their valiant ship slip under the waves, her fires still raging.

It had been an unequal battle from the start, with the name *Stephen Hopkins* certain to join the roster of brave ships lost in battles at sea. But owing to the bravery of the American gunners at the 4-incher, the German commerce-raider *Stier* also went to a watery grave in the South Atlantic east of Brazil that Sunday morning of September 27, 1942.

Gerlach and most of his crew survived the mid-ocean encounter with the *Stephen Hopkins*. Of the Liberty ship's fifty-seven-man complement, though, forty-two were lost—either in the clash at sea or in the thirty-one grueling days the battle survivors spent on life rafts before reaching landfall at a Brazilian fishing village.

Captain Buck, Ensign Willett, Cadet Midshipman O'Hara, and Second Mate Layman did not survive.

However, as some consolation—and honor—their names live on. Willett, posthumously awarded the Navy Cross, was memorialized by having a U.S. Naval destroyer escort named for him, as well as a building at the Merchant Marine Academy. Both Captain Buck and Cadet O'Hara were awarded the Merchant Marine Distinguished Service Medal. A Liberty ship was named for Buck, and a building at the Merchant Marine Academy for O'Hara. Indeed, noted Guttman, "that school remains the only civilian institution in the United States that is allowed to fly a battle flag, in recognition of O'Hara and of its other cadets who served, fought and died in action for their country."

As for the *Stephen Hopkins* herself, she also received a posthumous honor. The Hopkins is one of only eleven American merchant ships granted the U.S. Maritime Administration's title of "Gallant Ship."

Oddly, you will no doubt agree, another of the gallant eleven was another of the *Stier's* victims—the tanker *Stanvac Calcutta*, so honored because, rather than meekly heave to and surrender, she also fought back against the heavily armed German raider.

★★★

Based upon Defiance at Sea: Stories of Dramatic Naval Warfare *by Jon Guttman (Arms and Armour, London, 1995).*

Seagoing Guards

"LOOSE LIPS SINK SHIPS," SAID those wartime posters. And surely they did, although the actual instrument of destruction most often was the enemy submarine, aircraft, warship, or floating mine. And for the enemy, especially with advance knowledge supplied by "loose lips" or other intelligence, what a shooting gallery it was.

All those lumbering merchantmen, those tankers or troopships...what match were they for Germany's wolf packs of U-boats? For Japanese or Italian submarines too? Or the enemy aircraft or occasional warship that found them out as they plied the high seas carrying their vital cargo to the war zones abroad.

These were not exactly gun-bristling American or Royal Navy battleships carrying replenishment across the wide water, but rather your traditionally unarmed freighter. Usually, no creature of war...but often war's helpless victim, yes. *Usually*, but not always, and herein hangs the tale of the U.S. Navy's Armed Guard, a tale told in Justin Gleichauf's 1990 book, *Unsung Sailors*.

Among the millions who served in the U.S. Navy during World War II and among the thousands who went into battle, hardly any saw as much sustained combat (or suffered such heavy casualties) as the 144,000 Americans assigned to protect the merchant ships—the U.S. Naval Armed Guard. These largely unsung heroes were radio operators, signalmen, gun crewmen, and medics shipped out aboard six thousand traditionally noncombatant vessels repeatedly sent into harm's way to deliver their goods.

Gleichauf, a veteran intelligence officer retired from the Central Intelligence Agency, based his history of the Armed Guard (AG) on U.S. Navy files, general and maritime war histories, after-action reports, convoy reports, and personal interviews or correspondence with 150 former Armed Guardsmen.

And the stories they did tell! The punishing conditions they did describe! The dedication they did reveal! And...the sacrifice.

Here's a short diary bit contributed by John Mitchell, who served as a gunner aboard the merchantman *Thomas Hartley*: "Fifth day of storm, getting even worse and also a blizzard to top things off. Everything covered with ice, taking seas over the flying bridge, up to the top of the stack and down inside the engine room. Two portside lifeboats smashed to pieces and washed away...ice freezing on clothes."

Consider, from the same chapter on the epic Battle of the Atlantic, the story of the AG men stationed aboard the Liberty ship *William C. Gorgas* on a run from the United States to Liverpool with TNT, food, steel, and landing craft among the cargo items. The Liberty ship was struck—and sunk—by German torpedoes the night of March 10, 1943.

Fifty-one men from the ship managed to climb aboard rafts and lifeboats, with the skipper, T. C. Ellis, giving up a spot on a raft to a young seaman and then disappearing into the deep. The others were picked up by the British destroyer *Harvester* the next day.

Within six hours, *Harvester* herself was torpedoed and sunk on the high seas. She had been damaged and was limping along after ramming a German U-boat. A French corvette, *Aconit*, ultimately destroyed the U-boat, then picked up *Harvester's* survivors. They, in turn, included the Liberty ship *Gorgas'* survivors, by now reduced to just twelve men, five of them Armed Guardsmen. As one of those five told author Gleichauf, he served "10 long months" as a U.S. Naval Armed Guardsman before "being sent to destroyer duty for a rest."

Overall, as the AG men sailed on their six thousand merchant ships during the war, their voyages nearly countless, their fate from day to day was anybody's guess. Take the crew—and Armed Guard—of the brand-new Liberty ship *James W. Denver*, slowed by engine trouble 250 miles southwest of the Canaries, with a load of P-38 fighter planes aboard…and sunk by two torpedoes.

The survivors were left adrift on the sea. On the second night, a German submarine rose from the depths right under one of the lifeboats and surfaced with the boat stranded on the U-boat's deck. "A German officer asked them where they came from. 'Brooklyn' was the reply. The officer laughed and in English said, 'That's where baseball comes from.'"

He knew they were from a new Liberty ship. His crew gave the Americans a carton of cigarettes, while he provided a course for them to follow in their lifeboat. The U-boat then moved off into the night. "Twenty-three days later, after living on four crackers and two ounces of water per day, fighting heavy seas, and once coming so close to a pod of seven whales that they could have hit them with a stone, they were picked up by a fishing vessel 50 miles off the West African coast," noted Gleichauf's book.

Not so happy an ending could be written for the tanker *Esso Williamsburg*!

Set sail for Iceland in September 1942, navy fuel aboard. Made it from Aruba to the North Atlantic. Forty-two regular crewmen aboard and the Navy Armed Guard of eighteen. Voyage never completed. Reason unknown. Ship simply disappeared.

As the Armed Guard motto said, "Our aim is to deliver." They often did, but it wasn't always easy.

★★★

Based upon Unsung Sailors: The Naval Armed Guard in World War II *by Justin Gleichauf (Naval Institute Press, Annapolis, MD, 1990).*

He Stopped Rommel

TOBRUK SEIZED. TOBRUK UNDER SIEGE. Tobruk fallen.

Back and forth swept the competing armies in North Africa, and with each sweep men would die, men would live. Tragedy and triumph from one moment to the next. Not only in terms of immediate survival, but also for many a man's future fortune.

For instance, British Lt. Col. Charles Morris, commander of the Indian Army's Fourth/Thirteenth Frontier Force Rifles (Tenth Indian Division). His command post overrun by Erwin Rommel's *Afrika Korps* on June 28, 1942, he was captured, made prisoner, and even interviewed by Rommel.

That night, he and his men were placed in a temporary desert compound, but during the same night, a column of more Indian troops accidentally drove "full tilt" into the POW holding area. The result was a confused melee in which both prisoners and their German guards died at the hands of the unwitting interlopers.

In the confusion, however, Colonel Morris and many of his men escaped; they crossed into British lines before the dawn, and later that same day, Morris was to be found briefing his own army commander, Sir Claude Auchinleck. Quite possibly, Morris was "the only officer in the war to be interviewed by opposing Army Commanders in the course of 24 hours," speculates Alexander Greenwood in his biography of "the Auk," as Auchinleck was known. In war, every survivor has a tale to tell and certainly Morris, by combination of cool nerve and bizarre circumstance, had created a small legend all his own.

Another tale cited in Greenwood's *Field-Marshal Auchinleck* tells the story of a Brit taken prisoner earlier in Rommel's drives of 1942 that sent the British reeling back to Egypt. In this case, Sir Walter Cowan had been confronted by two German tanks, his own position overrun. He "emptied his revolver at the tanks before being bodily taken prisoner," and after shouting at his adversaries, "You dogs, I will never surrender!"

His German captors were somewhat surprised, when the dust settled, to find they had on their hands a retired admiral more than seventy years old! With the advent of World War II a decade after his retirement, it seems he had "attached himself" to the Eighteenth Calvary as a "naval liaison officer." (The Germans repatriated their elderly prisoner a year later, by the way.)

With the sweep of events in the same desert, the fortunes of others, great and small, also rose and ebbed.

Indeed, Rommel, in 1942, after capturing Tobruk despite its heroic stand of many months, had swept forward...and forward. Visiting the White House at the time, Prime Minister Winston Churchill was handed a message on pink paper: Tobruk, by now a great symbol, had fallen to the Axis!

And still Rommel was in the ascendancy, sweeping now to Egypt's very borders, beyond which would lie real disaster for the British and their allies. Later (and virtually ever since), Bernard Law Montgomery would take the credit for defeating Rommel at El Alamein. Which he did—in October and early November 1942.

But it was Auchinleck, his former aide-de-camp Greenwood resolutely reminds us, who first stopped Rommel at the threshold to Egypt, at a "First Battle of El Alamein" in 1942.

Later, of course, Tobruk would be recaptured by the British, typical of the rise and tidelike ebb of battle, of campaign...and of men's fortunes. Rommel, of course, returning to an occupied Europe still under the thumb of a maniacal *Führer*, soon was to die, a forced suicide and a conspirator against Hitler. And Auchinleck? Sacked by Churchill, despite the Auk's many credentials.

Sadly, they never had seen quite eye to eye. Auchinleck had stopped Rommel at last, but in the process his subordinate commanders had given away too much North African desert and had lost Tobruk. His fate was a return to his old precincts of India, later to be installed as commander in chief there.

Retired Major Greenway provided much of the rationale on both sides of the sacking decision, together with extensive documentation, but there's no doubting the direction of Greenway's loyalties. The Auk, he concluded, was "a great soldier, destroyed by a politician when about to make his [Auk's] greatest victory."

Possibly, given a bit more time, the Auk himself might or might not have utterly destroyed Rommel and his *Afrika Korps*...we'll never know. All we do know is that at the apparent peak of his military fortune, after "First Alamein," the Auk's fortune also ebbed—and the North African campaign swept on, now without him.

★★★

First published in World War II *magazine, September 1991.*

Spinster Ship

FOUR HUNDRED MILES OUT OF home port in England, the British merchantman was pulling hard for the American east coast, alone on the heaving ocean, when the German bomber found her—and attacked. As Second Engineer Drummond rushed below to the engine room, an explosion outside hurled the engineer against hard metal with stunning force.

But not *totally* stunning…Drummond ordered all the engine crew out of their domain, then turned to the engines, alone. To maneuver at last second from beneath a falling bomb's path, the ship—the *unarmed* ship—would need all the speed that could be mustered.

The second engineer had a reputation aboard ship for coaxing more speed from the engines than any other officer. And how or why might that be? Engineer Officer Drummond's stock answer was: "Oh, I just talk nicely to them. You can coax or lead engines to do what you want; you must never drive them."

If that sounds like a lot of hooey, keep in mind that the same ship's officer lived—when home on leave—in a neat little house in a working-class section of London called Lambeth. It was a house with a yellow door that stood out "like a bright smile on a rainy day." It boasted gay curtains and flowers in the windows. "The short path from the door to the street is paved with flagstones and flowers bloom in the sour soil."

The fact is, three spinster sisters lived in the Lambeth house, all named Drummond—and it was Victoria, *Miss* Victoria, if you please, who "went away" quite often…away to sea, as a thoroughly competent ship's engineer officer.

Now, on this bright Sunday morning early in the war, an entire ship's company depended for its survival on the same Miss Victoria—and the speed she could cajole from her faithful but old engines.

"In ten minutes," related one of the merchantman's male officers later, "she had talked to those engines to such good purpose that our miserable top speed of nine knots had risen to twelve and a half."

The tall, Scottish-born spinster from behind the yellow door in Lambeth had to work with scalding steam hissing right past her head from a sprung pipe joint. The near-miss bomb explosions had fractured pipes, broken tubes, and parted electrical connections, it seems. The steam pipe, though, could have been the real disaster.

"With anyone else less skilled down there, that pipe would have burst under the extra pressure, but she nursed it through the explosion of each salvo, easing down when she judged from the nearness of the plane's engines that the bombs were about to fall, holding on for all she was worth to a stanchion as they burst, and then opening up the steam again. By getting the speed, it gave the helm a chance to move the clumsy hulk."

That, too, was the recollection of Miss Victoria's fellow merchant marine officer. That, and the view he had through a skylight when he one moment looked down, "hoping to be able to shout a few words of cheer to her." She made an unforgettable picture for him. "She was standing under the control platform, surrounded by bullets which had come through the skylight [from the bomber's strafing], one arm stretched straight above her head and her hand pulling down the spoke of the throttle control as if trying by her touch to urge another pound of steam through the straining pipes."

Her face without expression and white as a sheet, she was looking upward that second, toward the sunlight outside her confines, but she didn't see her admiring witness. "From the top of her forehead down her long face, completely closing one eye, trickled a wide black streak of fuel oil from a strained joint."

She—and her ship—would recover their aplomb once the German had flown off after causing strictly cosmetic damage to both the oil-streaked engineer and the ship. Together, they would dock safely at Norfolk, Virginia, where impressed and sympathetic Americans raised $2,500 for a vitally needed service back in Lambeth. Called the "Victoria Drummond Canteen," it was a rolling van-canteen used during air raids. In addition, Lloyd's of London awarded the British Merchant Service's only qualified woman engineer the insurance firm's highest medal for gallantry at sea. Finally, King George of England presented her with the Order of Membership of the British Empire.

In the meantime, a war still on, Victoria Drummond went to sea again...and again. In between, she did her war "bit" at home too—as a helper at the local air raid post.

★★★

Based upon "The Lady Is an Engineer" *by Patricia Strauss in* Vogue's First Reader, *(Julian Messner Inc., New York, 1942).*

Getting from Here to There

THE WAR—IN EARLY 1942—was over there, and the brand-new P-38 Lightnings that were so badly needed over *there* were sitting *here*, waiting for a way to get *there*. Convoys, punched full of holes by German U-boats, were no real answer. The natural way, of course, would be to fly them over. But crossing the Atlantic, flying such a distance in a P-38? *Impossible!*

Or was it? A few in those desperate hours thought not. The latest F model of the P-38 had "phenomenal range," it was reported, and with external fuel tanks added, it might just barely be possible. General "Monk" Hunter, a World War I ace, was given the order to move four hundred fighters from Stateside to England, *Now!*

Mary Lou Colbert Neale told the story in a 1991 issue of *Lightning Strikes*, published by the national P-38 veterans association. And Point A, she noted, was the fact that "no fighters had ever made the trip."

Point B: They would fly via Labrador, Greenland, and Iceland, places where the weather is low, the mountains are high, and the surrounding water is always quite chilly. Greenland would have two hastily built airstrips awaiting the fliers—Bluie West One and Bluie West Eight.

Just before the first band of P-38s took off for Greenland (the Labrador hop being an easy one), ten B-17s set off on the same crossing—big ships, relatively, with four engines, a huge gas supply, and various sophisticated navigational aids, but…"three crashed and six had to turn back to Labrador." In weather that was often harsh and always unpredictable, even the Flying Fort was no guarantee of safe arrival.

On the night of July 1, however, things looked pretty good, "so by afternoon a flight of twenty-four fighters and six B-17s took off for Bluie West One, 779 miles away." All went well until the last set of fighters appeared over Bluie West One, eight of them, supposedly, but…"there were only seven dots in the sky."

Missing on this virgin flight of Operation Bolero was Lieutenant Peyton Mathis. Halfway there, it seems, one of his twin engines failed and he began to lag farther and farther behind his fellows, until they disappeared among the snowcapped mountains that rose from the Greenland coast ahead. "He had no idea which of the several fjords led to the landing base, and none checked with his drawings in his route manuals," reported Neale.

Luckily—and at the last minute—he spotted an odd-looking ridge that reminded him of his preflight briefings. Minutes later, with no room for a go-around, he and his Lightning came down "at 150 mph with a 10-mph tail wind…and screeched to a halt 20 feet short of the end of the runway."

But that (nearly) was nothing! Next on tap was the Ninety-fourth "Hat in the Ring" Squadron of World War I fame—four sections of four P-38s each, plus B-17 pathfinders in front. After hitting foul weather, visibility down to nothing, only five of the sixteen P-38s made it to Greenland. None was lost, but the remainder had to turn back.

At another point, six of the twin-engine P-38s had to crash-land, wheels up, and were lost. Their pilots, fortunately, were all recovered.

Weeks went by with P-38s strung out at various bases across the North Atlantic. After each hop, they waited for an apparent break in the weather in order to continue. On August 15, a P-38 and a P-40 combined to shoot down a German Focke-Wulf Condor off Iceland, apparently the war's first American "kill" in the European theater.

From Iceland, of course, came the final hop to the British Isles, again no picnic in a single-seat fighter. P-38 fighter pilot Jack Illfrey recalls being "numb from looking at dense fog, fighting squalls and storms." And all the while trailing behind a B-17 that in fact was lost. They finally emerged from the soup off the north coast of Ireland, found two British Spitfires, and flew into Ayr, Scotland, with the help of British Beaufighters sent aloft to guide them in. They landed with gasoline tanks "drained to the last drop."

In the end, added chronicler Neale, the P-38 fighters "in large numbers had crossed the treacherous North Atlantic," a "gigantic accomplishment" that went little known or appreciated at the time. The moral here? Not every airman's war tale is of action and combat but instead can be his story of getting from *here to there*.

★★★

First published in World War II *magazine, January 1992.*

Rendezvous for Faithful Companion

Two to four p.m. on the banks of the embattled Tenaru River on Guadalcanal, and the tanks are advancing. It is August 21, 1942, just days since the U.S. Marines landed.

First, much shooting, and then the tanks. Four tanks. "No gun of ours can oppose them."

One of them stopped, however, apparently disabled. After a pause, the other three continued. As they drew closer, their paths diverged somewhat. The number seemingly aimed at Japanese Sergeant Okada's hiding place became two.

On they came as he, lying on the sandy soil, "made like dead."

The first one was not deliberately aiming at him. It was moving very slowly, inexorably. But right at him. "My body was stuck in the sand and I felt two or three pressures on my back. It passed over me! What a surprising! I am still alive!"

It may be that the root of a nearby coconut tree had created a pocket protecting his body. But...no time to think it through, for now here came the second tank.

Near Okada, it mysteriously stopped. The crew is looking for signs of enemy life, he thought. Silent, he slowly pulled at the key from his grenade in case they did see him...but, no, in moments the second tank ground forward again. He felt the pressure of its treads pushing sand onto him, it was so close.

In minutes, the American tanks had moved on. The battle zone in short time was silent, not even any wounded groaning. Around Sergeant Okada, nearly everyone was dead. "Only two men left alive. I and Sergeant Kuragane. He was in deep hole only meters from me. He said that tank passed, though on him, he only got slight bruise because of deep 'octopus trap' in hole he was safe. We talked to each other of course."

They talked about how to escape their predicament. They would have to wait for dark, and then make their way through the lines. *If they could.*

In a short time, their predicament worsened with the arrival of three more tanks and "hundreds of soldiers advancing toward here and shooting at random." Okada thought, "I will be killed, never could be alive this time."

The roar of engines was deafening, and Okada heard the enemy's voices. He continued to play dead while the men of the First Battalion, First U.S. Marines, passed by and stopped, along with the tanks, a hundred meters beyond him. For some reason, they did not examine him to see if he was really dead.

By now, night had fallen. "We, Okada and Kuragane, were left alone in enemy's domain!" They decided to start out about midnight, when their enemy probably would be sleeping.

That decision made, Okada fell into a coma-like stupor that lasted until he felt Kuragane shaking him awake at midnight. To their dismay, the moon was high in the sky and the American marines and their tanks were shooting "at something." Why would they be shooting at midnight? Okada found it very perplexing.

But the two Japanese must make their escape anyway. They split up, and Kuragane went first, "running like a cat." Minutes later, Okada heard machine-gun fire. No doubt, Kuragane had been killed. They wouldn't be meeting, as planned, at another river a mile to the east.

Now, it was Okada's turn, but he wouldn't take Kuragane's route. He would try the sea, since the river emptied into the sea a short distance away. If he could just swim two hundred meters eastward, he would be safe, with his own men.

Parched with thirst, he crawled for thirty meters in the dark and reached the water line, where he drank the salt-laden seawater. Then he walked out in the water until it reached his neck, but the wind and tide kept him from making any headway to the east. "I still carried my helmet and sword. I abandoned them all. I wanted to go back to the beach, but too dangerous, so I crawled in the sea—maybe twenty meters from the shore. This way I could advance. Finally, I crawled out of the water at about three hundred meters east from the Tenaru. It seems safe to me."

There was no sign of the Americans as Okada entered the foliage lining the beach. Recklessly, he plunged into the jungle and ran at full speed for his appointed meeting place with Kuragane. He was not there. Okada thought he was killed for sure. But Okada "returned towards enemy area twice," danger-ous as it was, since "it is disgrace for me to escape before he does."

And still Okada didn't retreat to his own lines somewhere behind him. "I crawled about and once more approached enemy's line, but no avail."

He then finished the night resting by the riverside. At sunrise, he was trapped again because of an airplane in the sky that was shooting at something on the ground. "So I remained there until sunset."

Two days after the ordeal began, on the afternoon of August 23, Okada finally emerged from the Guadalcanal jungle to rejoin his forces at Taivu. There, he found "ten or more" fellow survivors of the fighting on the banks of the Tenaru. There, too, he found Kuragane, safe and well.

Kuragane, it seems, had reached their river rendezvous point after easily passing through the American lines. He waited about an hour for Okada, then heard shooting and thought that meant the worst. "Both thought that the other was not alive," summarized Okada, who was evacuated from Guadalcanal on October 5, 1942, with "heavy illness," never to return to battle but forever the faithful companion.

★★★

Based upon "The Okada Memories of the Tenaru (Ilu)," Guadalcanal Echoes, Guadalcanal Campaign Veterans, July 1986.

Hunt for Tall, Limping Man

FOR THE SIXTY-ONE-YEAR-OLD, five-star general held prisoner in Germany's Konigstein fortress atop a 150-foot cliff, escaping his immediate confines would be difficult enough. Beyond that feat, however, he still would have to elude his pursuers and somehow make his way out of the country itself.

Henri Honoré Giraud's native France, just next door to the west, would be no safe haven, either. Its upper half had been occupied by the German *Wehrmacht* for the past two years, while the collaborationist Vichy administration of Henri Pétain governed the bottom half of France.

Giraud, though, was not a man easily deterred—he had proved that during World War I when he had escaped from a German prison camp in Belgium while still recovering from the wounds of battle.

In the war that followed two decades later, he was captured again, caught in a forward machine-gun post while inspecting the front the very day, May 10, 1940, the Germany of Adolf Hitler launched its offensive against France and the Low Countries.

By April 17, 1942, Henri Giraud was ready to make his attempt at leaving Konigstein. He previously had woven a rope of twine from packages sent by friends and relatives. But it wouldn't hold his two-hundred-pound weight. Communicating by code in personal letters, he had made his needs known at home. As a result, an innocent-looking ham had been the conveyance of a 150-foot coil of copper wire hidden inside.

Giraud was allowed to use a balcony above the cliff face and its sentry circuit at the top. The morning of April 17, he secured his copper-strengthened rope to the balustrade, waited for the sentry to pass by below, then started his trip down the castle wall and then the steep cliff, hand over hand. Even gloved, his hands were rubbed raw, but he reached the bottom safely and hurried into some trees nearby, out of sight.

Temporarily free, he was still in great danger of recapture, if only because he was so easy to spot. He was tall, six feet; he sported a fierce mustache; he walked with a permanent limp from his WWI injuries. Moreover, for the moment, he had only a secreted Tyrolean hat as a civilian garment. His military raincoat might pass casual inspection, but underneath he still had on his informal French general's uniform of blue.

Aware of such drawbacks, Giraud had made his plans carefully. Boning up on his German-speaking capability, he had studied a map of his immediate area—and through his letter code he had made certain arrangements.

First, shaving off the mustache, he made his way to nearby Bad Schandau, and there he met a contact carrying a suitcase full of Giraud's own civilian clothing and a raft of false papers, plus that all-important commodity, money. Without speaking, they boarded the first train to stop at the town, then met in a bathroom.

From then on, his clothes changed, the distinguished-looking Giraud could look and act the part of the industrialist that his false papers said he was. The next step in Giraud's escape would be carried out all on his own, however—having done his part, the contact disappeared from the scene.

But where could the hare find sanctuary? For Giraud, even disguised, to approach a guarded frontier and attempt to cross into France would be sheer madness. Every border guard would be on the lookout for such a ranking escapee with a telltale limp. On the other hand, Giraud was still in the enemy camp; there was no sanctuary for him in Nazi Germany, the most vicious and suspicious of police states.

His solution was risky but simple: For now, until the immediate furor faded a bit, he would ride the trains.

For days, he did just that, on occasion just barely outwitting the Gestapo men aboard the trains or in the railroad stations. He once entered the occupied half of France but was stymied trying to reach the Vichy provinces to the south—the Germans were challenging any man close to Giraud's height.

He resumed his train travel, back into Germany, and now made for the Swiss border. That, too, was tightly closed, but one night Giraud left the rails and climbed a mountain trail that allowed him to slip into neutral Switzerland on foot.

He could have stayed on there, but duty still called, and Giraud was determined to reach unoccupied France. A complicated plan involving a set of cars fooled the Gestapo and enabled him to make the dangerous dash into southern France.

But now Nazi Germany called on the Pétain administration to surrender the escapee—the old marshal of France bravely refused, while Giraud went to ground again to avoid Gestapo assassination squads.

Giraud, a public hero to the French but still a hunted man, would not really be free until just before the Allied invasion of North Africa in early November 1942. Even then, to join the Free French and their Anglo-American Allies he had to escape one more time. On this occasion, working with British agents sent into southern France, he was spirited to a waiting submarine that then carried him safely across the Mediterranean to join his copatriots fighting the long but ultimately victorious war against Hitler's Germany.

Giraud, in the unfolding of that great drama, reestablished the French army and became its commander in chief, although he never got along with Charles de Gaulle and finally retired in April of 1944, a year before the war in Europe ended. He died a free man in 1949, his beloved France by then also free once again.

★★★

Based upon Frederick C. Painton in True Stories of Great Escapes *(The Reader's Digest Association, Pleasantville, N.Y., 1977).*

Escape to Berlin

SEPTEMBER OF 1943, AND IN Paris the dread Gestapo were located on Avenue Foch, close to L'Etoile, the German military headquarters for all of occupied France was tucked into the Majestic Hotel on Avenue Kleber, and just about every day, German troops paraded down the Champs d'Elysées.

From Berlin, one "Joseph Garrat" traveled quite openly by train to Nazi-infested Paris for his wedding—almost as if there were no war or danger at all.

In just weeks, he and Sylvia de German-Ribon, the love of his life, indeed were married, first in a civil ceremony, then, dressed in formal attire, in a church wedding. They honeymooned in the "intimate, 11-suite" Lancaster Hotel, "just off the Champs d'Elysees," among "numerous Germans." Their son, Joe Gatins, further explains in his family history *We Were Dancing on a Volcano*, that on their wedding night "the newlyweds dined…at Maxim's, the legendary gourmet restaurant on the rue Royale, again surrounded by German officers, as one family friend recalled the story."

Next, the young couple travelled into Vichy France, in part by foot and bicycle, to live out the rest of the war in a family chateau "tucked away outside the tiny, remote village of Ahun, in the department of La Creuse, a true, rural backwater lost in the middle of *'la France profonde.'*"

But the happy groom was not really Joseph Garrat, he was Joe Gatins' father, Joseph Francis Gatins, III, who answered to his middle name, Francis. Nor was Francis Gatins as at ease as he appeared. In fact, he would never be at ease until WWII had completely ended. Francis was an escaped prisoner of war, now on his fifth escape from German custody since his original capture in France in the first days of the war.

Born in France to his French mother and an American father who was part-owner of the well-known Atlanta (Ga.) Grand Terrace Hotel, Francis was denied a U. S. passport and dual American and French citizenship before the war broke out. After moving back to France with his mother, Egle de Villelume-Sombreuil Gatins, as a child, Francis Gatins, by now 25 years old, had been serving with a French infantry regiment when he was captured just a month after Nazi Germany invaded France and the so-called Low Countries in early May 1940.

Or, as his son Joe Gatins summed up his father's situation in the *Volcano* family history:

Following his capture on June 14, 1940, Joseph Francis Gatins, III, member of substantial and upstanding families in both France and the United States, bon-vivant, international partygoer and part owner of a well known hotel in Atlanta, landed in the middle of Stalag VIII-C along the Rhine River in [Sagan or Zagan] Germany after a week-long forced march and an uncomfortable ride in a railroad cattle car.

Francis soon was quickly marked by his German captors as an *escaper*, and was sent from one prison camp to another, each one tougher than the last. So escape-bent was the half-American, half-Frenchman that he asked fellow prisoners at one stop-over to help break his arm. That way, he could be hospitalized and avoid an especially undesirable transfer. A prisoner did do him that "favor", but in the end, Gatins still wound up on the outskirts of the Belzec death camp, forced to help unload death-bound Jews from their cattle trains.

His first escape attempt came soon after his capture as he and a fellow prisoner simply walked off a work detail and hid in a barracks latrine. "Squirreled away behind a bathroom partition, Francis could see German soldiers in a mirror, brushing their teeth. But they did not see him."

Once they left the camp confines and took to the surrounding countryside, however, Francis and his companion were recaptured. Still, that was only the first in a series of escapes by Francis, each one followed "by transfer to a different prison camp and two weeks of solitary confinement," noted his son Joe Gatins. The elder Gatins later "recalled coping with solitary by replaying in his mind, hole by hole, every golf course he'd ever played."

His next stop within the German prison camps system was Stalag II-B outside Harnmerstein in West Prussia, "another sprawling barbed wire compound originally built to barrack Polish prisoners of war, and which, like Stalg VIII-C, experienced its own descent into brutality and pain as the war came closer to an end."

In a letter dated January 30, 1942, from this camp, Francis mysteriously mentioned his release from the prison hospital and said his arm was "perfectly set, but severely atrophied." What could that mean? Especially when he added, "I don't know if it's ever going to be as it was before."

His family later did find out, as son Joe wrote:

Faced with probable transfer to another stalag, reportedly on an island from which escape would have been difficult, my father, amazingly, opted to have a fellow prisoner break one of his arms so he could be hospitalized, thus delaying any transfer and, he hoped, stopping it entirely. The first attempt failed. The biggest prisoner in the camp was unable to break his arm. A smaller prisoner, but one with some strength, a butcher in civilian life, then took up a wooden cudgel, as Francis placed his arm between two chairs. The smaller man snapped his right arm with one quick hard strike.

Based upon such traumatic experiences it is not surprising that he wrote his future bride, Sylvia, the daughter of Colombian expatriates, in March of 1942 with the admission, "I've had a rough time."

This plight was soon replaced with hope, thanks to a hint by Sylvia at possible marriage, and furthermore, despite the fact that his right arm now was two inches shorter than the left, he was still at Stalag-II B, as his plans for escape required.

"Don't be surprised if there's a delay, or even a full stop, in my correspondence," he wrote. "But with the spring coming on and my arm getting better, it could be there will be new and numerous disturbances in my life as a prisoner."

What could he mean?

Francis indeed was alluding to his latest plan to escape. "He escaped from Stalag II–B, attempting to get to Hungary, which was then still a neutral country in the war, and was shipped after his recapture to a more forbidding prison camp, Stalag X–B, at Sanbostel, from which he again escaped." The details available are unclear, but he apparently remained at large this time for about two weeks posing as a deaf mute and hitchhiking to Germany's busy port city of Hamburg.

Recaptured yet again, he then wrote Sylvia in August 1942, this time, son Joe Gatins wrote, "from a hellhole of a punishment camp, the notorious Stalag 325 at Rawa-Ruska, in the middle of the Nazi killing and extermination zone on the border between Poland and the Ukraine—birthplace of the Holocaust."

Back in Paris, meanwhile, his French mother Eglé was doing her own bit, and more, to help the Allied war effort—and her prisoner-son. "She sneaked escaped prisoners to the still-free south of France [early in the war], hid papers for Free French forces and aided the budding Resistance as best she could," wrote her grandson Joe Gatins.

She always would remember the horrors perpetrated upon the Jews of occupied Paris. "All the Jews had to wear the Star of David," she once recalled. "First, they could not ride the Metro. Imagine that, poor people. Then, they could not attend the theater, and then they started sending them to concentration camps."

For most, that was a death sentence, as the world now knows.

For nearly 13,000 Parisian Jews, an estimated 75 percent of whom were women and children, the Holocaust began with the five-day "Vel d'Hiv Sweep" starting on July 16, 1942. As related by Joe Gatins: "German forces, clearly with the help of French police, rounded up a total of 12,884 Jews that day…Most of the men immediately were shipped to the French concentration camp at Draney, while almost 7,000 of the remaining hapless Jews were jammed into the Velodrome d'Hiver, or Vel d'Hiv for short, an indoor sports arena in the 15th arrondissement."

Provided little food and water, many of those that were captured were so hopeless they committed suicide. About 100 tried to flee and were shot. For the rest: "There was hardly enough room to lie down and few toilets. Diarrhea and dysentery were rampant." In the end, most were "shipped in cattle cars" to Auschwitz—and death.

Gatins' Grandmother Eglé had tried to help: "'Eglé and the Red Cross went to try to talk the Germans into letting them bring milk for the babies, which the Germans refused,' her granddaughter (also) Eglé said some 60 years after the event. 'She said you could hear the babies and children crying. It was so frustrating not to be able to do anything. She would always get emotional and use the expression *les sales Boches* (the dirty Krauts) when recalling this story.'"

Meanwhile, Francis still languished in the German prison camp system despite his four escape attempts thus far, but back in Paris his mother had become a surprisingly effective helper in his schemes. In his flight to Hamburg, for instance, he used false papers identifying him as one "André Monteil." According to his son's account, it seems clear "that he got crucial aid from his mother to secure the false papers under the name Monteil."

Later, Eglé became even more involved: "Francis, feigning a sweet tooth, often included a special request in his letters to Sylvia: Please have Mother send some of that wonderful honey from Brittany in the next care package. But it was not the honey he loved so much as the currency and gold coins that Eglé secreted in the honey."

With the money hidden in the re-soldered honey tins, Francis had "the key to bribing guards, buying false papers and opening the doors to escape."

Though receiving aid and yet again making plans to escape, Francis was still being held at "the little known but deadly Stalag 325, another punishment camp (like Stalag X-B), this one especially reserved for recalcitrant and recidivist French and Belgian prisoners of war, [and] sited adjacent to the small town of Rawa-Ruska, now just across the Polish boundary line in the Ukraine."

This same Stalag was moved to a nearby town, L'viv, but remained in the vicinity of the infamous Belzec extermination camp. In fact, the new town's rail yards "served as the rail assembly point for cattle cars heading to Belzec."

Here, although the details are neither clear nor fully confirmed, Francis and his fellow French POWs apparently were used against their will—this time not only as slave labor, but also as helpers in the Holocaust pipeline. "He was basically a guard," reported his son Martin, brother of Joe Gatins. "At this point in the war (late 1942) the extermination camps are going full swing...and the French prisoners are considered slave labor. And so his job in the Ukraine is basically...he's a guard or a processor, emptying the rail cars of Jews."

Joe was stunned to hear this fact about his father's participation in the death camps years after their father had died. "Absolutely!" Martin said. "He said he would sit there and open the rail cars. These Jews had been packed like sardines, half of them dead, coming from Poland. I remember him telling me. He'd say, 'My job was opening the rail cars.'"

So horrifying were the conditions at Stalag 325 that it held a prison within the prison for inmates who simply went insane.

Francis himself had been "starved, beaten, tortured, and thoroughly psychologically scarred by the Stalag 325 punishment system." But then, late in 1942, Francis inexplicably received orders that transferred him to Stalag II-A, a "regular" stalag near Neubrandenberg, only 90 miles north of Berlin, "but still some 600-plus miles from home."

Here, he was put to work, but far more innocuous tasks—"pulling sugar beets, work in an underground mine, serving Germans as a waiter in a *gasthaus*."

It wasn't long, though, before Sylvia received one of those letters asking her to tell his mother to send more of that honey from Brittany—another escape attempt was in the works.

From this final escape plan emerged the French "guest worker" Joseph Francis Garrat, aka Francis Gatins, a house painter now living at 38 Tasserdorfer Strasse in Berlin, the capital and very center of Nazi Germany. On May 17, 1943, he was able to write home to his mother, "Berlin is really a very lively city."

Though the events sound simple in retrospect, the escape was bold and surely nerve-wracking in its execution. Francis had used the money he had saved from his mother's latest honey shipment to buy false ID papers, then simply walked off a work detail and hopped a train to Berlin. There, he posed as one of the thousands of Frenchmen turned into so-called "guest workers" and used to fill wartime Germany's insatiable demand for everyday laborers.

Thus, for the next six months or so, "Garrat" was a house painter by day with the freedom to roam the city by night, often staying up until the wee hours of the morning. Francis was never once asked to show his phony ID papers.

Paid an adequate wage, he was "free to eat in restaurants, drop in on nightclubs and go out of town on weekends, since that was when the British usually bombed the city," *Atlanta Journal* columnist Hugh Park wrote after a post-war interview with Francis. And further: "He also had free medical care and was on social security."

He wasn't a totally free man, of course. To arrange his trip to Paris, he, his mother and Sylvia all worked together on a scheme allowing him to come "visit" a fictitious wife named Marie who was desperately ill and needed her husband by her side. His German boss, a painting contractor named Adolph, allowed him to go once his compassionate-leave papers were in order.

Guest worker "Joseph Garrat" never did return to Berlin, and in September 1943, Joseph Francis Gatins, still an at-large POW from Stalag II-A, married Sylvia, and then honeymooned right among the German occupiers of Paris.

Despite an occasional scare when German patrols walked by unexpectedly, the two spent the next year or so at peace. First they lived in her family's castle-like 15th-century chateau, La Chezotte, which was located in a truly isolated rural pocket of France, before returning to live with Sylvia's mother in Paris after the city's liberation in 1944.

After moving to the United States, Francis survived an extended bout with tuberculosis, became a father of six, and finally won his long-sought U. S. citizenship. He and Sylvia divided their postwar years between America and France, sometimes together, sometimes not, but eventually settled together in Atlanta. He died from complications of leukemia in 1983, just after celebrating their 40th wedding anniversary. Sylvia followed him to the grave four years later after suffering a stroke.

★★★

Based upon We Were Dancing on a Volcano: Bloodlines and Fault Lines of a Star-Crossed Atlanta Family, 1849-1989 *by Joseph Gatins (The Glade Press, 2009) with permission of the author and publisher.*

High Drama at Sea

FOR U.S. NAVY ENSIGN GERHART S. Suppiger Jr., convoy duty in May of 1942 did not begin auspiciously. First, one of his nine gun crewmen was hospitalized after he injured his hand carrying a box of supplies. Next, the captain of their merchantman, the SS *Santa Elisa*, went ashore, too ill to carry on.

Then, after largely uneventful days crossing the dangerous North Atlantic from America (one near collision in the fog and two U-boats sunk by escorts), the *Santa Elisa* laid up for forty-six wearisome days at Newport, England, twice onloading, then offloading various war cargo.

Clearly, larger events were in store for the young ensign and the men of his U.S. Navy Armed Guard—those often forgotten, unsung sailors who manned the few guns aboard merchant ships against enemies ranging from commerce raiders to U-boats and aircraft.

Finally, her armament significantly boosted, the *Elisa* joined a convoy of twelve cargo ships and two tankers escorted by a virtual armada—two battle-ships, eight cruisers, five carriers, a flotilla of destroyers. The *Elisa* had become a part of the Royal Navy's Operation Pedestal, with embattled Malta in the Mediterranean as the destination.

The *Elisa* left port in Scotland to join the Pedestal convoy on August 2, 1942. Eight days later, the convoy safely passed through the Straits of Gibraltar (with one aircraft carrier peeling off there), but at nine o'clock the next morning Pedestal's ordeal began.

The action opened with two bombing attacks thirty minutes apart. One of the cargo ships went down. At 10:30, one of the aircraft carriers was struck by three torpedoes. "She sank in seven minutes."

The convoy proceeded as its escorts accounted for two enemy submarines. That evening, though, fresh waves of German aircraft damaged a destroyer and sank two more of the merchant ships. The *Elisa* sailed on.

The next day, August 12, was a continual nightmare—action stations all day long. Wave after wave of Stuka dive-bombers, Junkers, and Heinkel bombers struck, along with Italian torpedo planes. Another Royal Navy carrier was hit and left behind, enveloped in smoke and fire. Of the escorts, all but two cruisers and a "few destroyers" stayed behind too. Intelligence had reported the Italian fleet might sally forth to engage the British battle fleet.

As the diminished convoy pressed on, the air and submarine attacks continued. One of the two remaining cruisers, HMS *Manchester*, went down. At 8 P.M., another freighter was sunk by dive-bombers. The hour of nine o'clock brought "the most concentrated attack of all." Three more merchantmen went down, with "sticks" of bombs narrowly missing the *Elisa*, and not for the first time.

At this point, the convoy remnants scattered, and after two near-collisions in the dark, the *Elisa* had a choice between sailing alone past coastal batteries and an Italian E-boat base, or chancing a known minefield to the west. "We decided to risk the mine field instead of the others," wrote Suppiger in his later report.

At 3:30 the next morning, however, a speedy E-boat found the *Elisa* anyway. In an exchange of machine-gun fire, it was driven off, but then a second E-boat appeared, and this one soon was able to launch torpedoes. At 5:05 A.M., "there was a terrific flash and explosion forward."

With the ship "burning furiously," the crew took to the sea. Survivors were rescued about two hours later by a destroyer. At 7:30 A.M., a new wave of dive-bombers dropped from the sky and sank the *Elisa*.

Upon finally reaching Malta two days later, the Americans learned that five of the original fourteen merchant ships had run the gauntlet. While Ensign Suppiger's contingent and others had lost their ships, a vitally needed few vessels had survived one of the entire war's most difficult convoy operations.

★★★

Based upon The Pointer and the Plane Shooter, *USN Armed Guard WWII Veterans, December 1988.*

Women at War

IN THE MEDITERRANEAN THREE DAYS before Christmas, six thousand troops, four hundred nurses, five American WACS, and *Life* magazine photographer Margaret Bourke-White, together with their former luxury liner's crew, were raised from sleep or torn from nighttime duties by the jolt and slam of a torpedo. And yet…"The torpedo did not make as loud a crash as I had expected," Margaret Bourke-White wrote later, "nor did the ship list as much as it does in the movies." Even so, "Everyone on the sleeping transport knew almost instantly that this was the end of her."

Her electricity snuffed out, the ship was hit hard enough to throw Bourke-White out of her upper berth in the cabin she shared with two Scottish nurses. The women hastily hunted for their clothing items with flashlights. They wouldn't have much time. Despite the urgency, though, Margaret Bourke-White could not help a wry observation or two as she and her cabinmates hurried to get dressed in the dark. "Sister Ismay Cooper scrabbled through the bureau drawers for her money and Sister Violet MacMillan pulled on her trousers and tore the curlers out of her hair."

The trousers were not a commonplace sight for the "sisters" of Queen Alexandra's Military Nursing Reserve Service…not by any means! "We had joked about them during the convoy voyage because the nursing sisters, operating under 'Old Battle-axe,' their strict Scottish matron, had been forbidden to wear slacks except for a torpedoing."

The voyage to North Africa in late 1942 didn't even start well—now, it was to end in death and tragedy for many, with even civilians made casualties of war.

Their convoy just a few days before had gone through the worst storm their own flagship captain had ever seen, "in a lifetime spent at sea." Not only did the dishes in the galley go flying, a flying sofa struck two persons in the head, while many others suffered broken bones or concussions from falls. "One afternoon the piano [in the lounge] broke loose and rushed back and forth like a great beast—until it crashed against the wall with its legs broken."

Storm gone, but seas still rough, their captain insisted upon lifeboat drills two or three times a day. For those unceasing, wearisome drills, "the nurses, almost too ill to stand [from seasickness], marched out with the troops and clung to ropes for 14 minutes of strict silence as the sea boiled about them," wrote Bourke-White biographer Vicki Goldberg.

Fortunate now that they had had the practice! For now, it was no drill but the real thing. "Along the passageways, the troops and nurses silently swelled forward to their lifeboat stations with a perfect discipline instilled by practice drills," added Goldberg.

But not the famous *Life* photographer. By prior arrangement with the ship's hierarchy in the event of action, she dashed to her assigned "action station," an observation point just below the bridge.

"The moon was brilliant, but not bright enough for photographers." Still, she lingered when a crewman told her to go to her boat station. He left her there after she explained her mission, but she didn't stay long. In the distance, the troopship's decks sloping steeply, was the megaphoned voice of a man calling out the order to abandon ship.

Until this moment, her mind had been on her job, her mission—no real fear. "As soon as I knew work was impossible and I must abandon ship," Bourke-White herself wrote later, "I couldn't get to my boat station fast enough." But it would be a slow trek through all kinds of wreckage and metal debris.

And at the lifeboat station, Margaret Bourke-White found her assigned group of American and British nurses "just beginning to climb over the rail into the boat under the calm direction of 'Old Battle-axe.'"

So far, so good, but now came quite a few problems…real dangers, in fact. First, "In the lifeboat I was astonished to find myself in water up to my hips." Reason being: The torpedo hit had lifted a cascade of water into the boats. And if the problem with Bourke-White's Lifeboat No. 12 was water trapped in the boat, the problem with Lifeboat No. 11 was just the opposite—water draining from its bottom. The crew manning that boat had pulled out its "plugs."

Unfortunately for Bourke-White and her companions in No. 12, the other lifeboat was being lowered right above them, with its water "pouring down on us."

Another threat to beware of was "a heavy, dangling chain which swung cruelly back and forth while we ducked and twisted our heads out of the way."

Despite all this, the famous photographer's lifeboat did reach the water intact…but that was no end to the misery, the danger or the loss of life. "The sea, which from above had looked so calm, rose up against us wave after wave and began beating us back against the side of the ship," wrote Bourke-White later. "Our crew strained at the oars."

Her boat's oarsmen, dining room stewards normally, at last "created a small margin" between their lifeboat and the big ship's side, but just then, "down came Lifeboat No. 11 with its load of British sisters." Those now-replaced plugs failed to hold, and as seawater rushed into the lifeboat, up to the gunwales, "a couple of dozen sisters were washed over the side." Some were carried back to the flooded craft by the next wave, others struck out for nearby rafts.

Bourke-White's boat No. 12 tried to move over and assist, but the rudder was broken and the wave action instead pushed No. 12 close, closer…too close to No. 14. "Getting clear of No. 14 was as long a job as I have ever known."

By now, too, the sixty-four occupants of Bourke-White's No. 12 were bailing out water as fast as they could, a task that would last until morning. She, herself, used two cuplike pieces of her camera gear as small bailing vessels.

While she scooped water with all the rest, she watched sympathetically as first one, then at least forty of the nurses in her pitching craft became violently seasick. "I admired the two American nurses opposite me who kept on bailing between spasms of seasickness."

Another sight she would always remember was that of the stricken ship left behind—"In the moonlight I could see that her side was a network of rope ladders and clinging to the one nearest us was a cluster of nursing sisters. The nurse on the lowest rung was being dipped and raised out of the sea time after time, and the end of the ladder was whirling her about dizzily."

Then, "A raft drifted close enough so that we could pull a girl into our boat. She had a broken leg, and the sisters sitting behind me held her tight to keep her from bouncing back and forth with each swell."

Nearby, a soldier on another raft was trying to transfer to Lifeboat No. 14… but with sad result. "Just as…[he] let go of the raft to reach for a rope from the lifeboat, a wave flung the raft against him and cracked his skull." The "skipper" of the lifeboat dived into the water and retrieved the unconscious man, who unfortunately died during the night, added Bourke-White in her account of the torpedoing of her troopship.

"During all this," she added, "we heard a voice from a distant raft shriek out, 'I am alone! I am alone!' over and over. We tried to steer our rudderless craft toward the cry but it drifted farther away until it was lost in distant silence."

Her boat, in fact, drifted a bit too close to one of two destroyers that had stayed behind her convoy in an effort to locate and sink the submarine responsible for the torpedoing. "Keep away from us!" the warship warned. "We are dropping depth charges!" Drifting or not, Bourke-White's lifeboat wasn't really affected, she wrote, "but the deep roar of those depth charges was music to us."

It was a long night, and some of those sharing the misery with Margaret Bourke-White were distaff members of Dwight D. Eisenhower's staff. As the survivors in boat No. 12 began taking over the oars from the exhausted dining room stewards, "a splendid big Scottish girl, Elspeth Duncan, one of General Eisenhower's staff, made the best rower of all."

Another who survived the submarine attack was "blonde, petite, Jeanne Dixon of Washington, D.C., secretary to General Eisenhower." And finally, right in Bourke-White's boat No. 12, there was the "irrepressible Kay Summersby, Eisenhower's pretty Irish driver."

One and all, they spent a night on heaving swells dotted with rafts and other boats, awaiting a rescue unlikely to take place until morning. "From the rafts came snatches of a song: 'You are my sunshine, my only sunshine.'"

In the moonlight, too, silhouettes of their stricken troopship and an escorting destroyer gradually faded from sight. People did their best to keep their spirits up. They joked. Kay Summersby, for one, "announced her breakfast order." Eggs sunnyside, please, yolks unbroken.

Their location well known, Bourke-White and her fellow survivors of course were rescued the next day, in her case taken aboard a destroyer after spending eight hours in Lifeboat No. 12. On a "teeming deck" of the rescue ship, friends greeted friends "with cries of joy." Here, added Bourke-White, "I was delighted to find my two roommates, Sister Violet with a few curlers still stuck in her hair." Here, too, "the beauteous Kay still had two precious possessions, her lipstick and her French-English 'soldier's speak-easy.'"

Poignantly, it was here also that Margaret Bourke-White met a "white-haired" nursing sister from Edinburgh, Scotland, Helen Freckleman, last seen during the dramatic night being whiplashed at the bottom rung of the rope ladder on the side of the wounded troopship, swinging crazily at bottom of her pendulum and repeatedly dipped into wave after wave.

"How long were you on that ladder?" Bourke-White asked.

"Half an hour," was the reply. "I kept telling myself: 'I must concentrate on holding on with both hands.'"

At this, Bourke-White looked down. "I glanced down at those hands which had nursed the wounded of two wars. They were not young enough for such a stern assignment. But they had held."

In this war, WWII, Margaret Bourke-White braved Germany's bombing of Moscow, went along on an American bombing raid of German installations on

Sicily, and survived German shellings in Italy. She was always *frontline*, a cool, often inspired professional, an artist with her camera. Those last moments on the troopship, though, standing in line for the lifeboat was, she later would say, her moment of greatest danger, greatest fear.

She could not stop the fear by resorting to her cameras. But in front of her in line was a young nurse, trembling, "shaking so hard that her sling bag slipped off her shoulder."

The great photographer put it back—and at that very moment lost her own fears—"a trifling thing, but I saw her trembling had stopped, and my own fear had left me."

★★★

Based upon: Margaret Bourke-White: A Biography *by Vicki Goldberg (Harper & Row, New York, 1987, Radcliffe biography series) and "Women in Lifeboats" by Margaret Bourke-White, in* 100 Best True Stories of World War II *(Wise & Co., New York, 1945).*

No Comforts on New Guinea

IF GEOGRAPHY, WORLD GEOGRAPHY, WERE arranged as a zoo, primitive, pestilent New Guinea would be among the most dangerous animals kept behind bars.

From above, of course, high above, the world's second largest island offers a deceptive, even luxuriant, appearance. But that enticing green carpet down there is a jungle—a hard, tough country to beat nearly all others.

For more than two years, invading Japanese fought Australians and Americans on New Guinea, with Allied-held Port Moresby in the huge island's south-eastern quadrant the prize at stake. Advancing through jungle and over the thirteen-thousand-foot Owen Stanley Range, the Japanese fought their way down the snakelike Kokoda Trail to a point just thirty-two miles from Port Moresby before the Seventh Australian Division finally stopped them in late summer of 1942.

After the struggle along Bloody Kokoda, the American Thirty-second and Forty-first Infantry Divisions joined the fight. In late 1942 and early 1943, they finally drove the Japanese out of Gona and Buna, their staging area for the earlier assault on Port Moresby. So tough, so fierce was this fight, that Douglas

MacArthur told his General Robert Eichelberger to get the job done or be killed in the attempt.

And still the struggle for control of New Guinea went on, with the Americans and their Aussie allies gradually driving the Japanese out of Nassau Bay, out of Lae and Salamana on the northeastern coast and Huon Gulf, out of Finschhafen on the Huon Peninsula...then took Saidor, Mindiri and Hollandia, Maffin Bay, Biak Island, among many other points.

In some instances, the Allies leapfrogged Japanese-held sites, then left their isolated, supply-starved garrisons to wither on the vine. It was, in fact, the beginning of MacArthur's island-hopping strategy that eventually won him control of the southwestern Pacific and took him all the way back to the Philippines. It was from New Guinea, in fact, that he began the remarkable, American-led comeback.

As Australian John Brown can attest, New Guinea was a thoroughly miserable place to be fighting a war. No homebound, armchair strategist, Brown knows exactly how miserable—not because he was there then, but because he was there soon after. Let him tell that part of the story—*When I first went to Papua New Guinea with the [postwar] Australian Administration, I worked with several fellows who had fought on the Kokoda Trail. In 1952, I and several others walked the trail to Kokoda, the first since the war. It was overgrown. We found lots of bones, rifles, helmets, etc. It took nine days, and I pitied the poor b———s who had had to fight along it.* Brown traveled widely among the war zones that today once again are largely hidden over by the pervasive and timeless jungle cover—*Later, I walked over the Buna-Sanananda-Gona area, stayed in a model village a friend of mine had laid out and built to replace wiped-out Sanananda, looked at the graves of the missionaries bayonetted by the Japanese at Gona, crossed the Kumusi River, where the Japanese General [Tomitaro] Horii was drowned, and continued on with the patrol I was doing.* Author Brown was interested in the Southwest Pacific theater more generally, in the men and their tales from both sides. He became, though, more than simply a recorder—*I also visited most of the other battlefields in the area, Lae, Salamaua, Wewak, Hollandia, Guadalcanal, Bougainville, and so on, and talked to many individuals, including coastwatchers, who had been involved. Some of the items I picked up, identifications, etc., I sent to the Japanese Embassy in Canberra [Australia]. I then was contacted by an organization of Japanese ex-servicemen who were trying, in a small way, to help the country they had fought over. They called themselves the Japan Papua New Guinea Goodwill Association. I helped them out when parties of them came to Papua*

New Guinea on bone-collecting expeditions, to obtain land for cenotaphs and in other ways—and was made the only non-Japanese member of their organization. I attended their functions, dinners, meetings when in Japan and listened to their stories—some were almost unbelievable.

The final chapter of one story, however, remained unknown to Brown, his Japanese hosts, or anybody else until the 1960s, two decades after the war's end. One day back in the 1940s, it seems, an American bomber lifted off from a New Guinea airfield for a training flight—a "joyride" for some of those aboard. It was headed for a remote interior spot known to the troops as "Shangri-la Valley." The plane did not come back. Nothing was heard of, or from, the crew members and their passengers again.

Two decades later, it was a German missionary who finally stumbled upon the wreckage where the plane had crashed into a densely foliated mountainside. Americans then trekked into the "headhunter" country to carry out the scattered skeletal parts. And, in Tokyo, a Japanese expert was the key man in making the proper identification of the remains for long-postponed burial in the States.

A German...Americans...a Japanese. As with Brown and his newfound Japanese friends, the crashed airplane's rediscovery completed a circle hardly to have been imagined in those not-so-distant days of fighting over possession of a grim and thoroughly primitive land.

★★★

From World War II *magazine, May 1990, and other sources.*

Bully That Never Fought

THE MIGHTY GERMAN BATTLEWAGON *Tirpitz*, for all her brawling reputation, only once fired her big, fifteen-inch guns in anger—and that time at a hapless Norwegian weather station on the island of Spitzbergen, in Arctic waters.

Another time, though, the *Tirpitz* only needed her bully's reputation to scatter and bring about serious damage to a major Allied convoy headed for the northern USSR's port of Archangel.

It was a largely American convoy that set sail from Iceland on June 27, 1942—thirty-four freighters and tankers, together with a ragged escort force of old destroyers, corvettes, minesweepers, and antiaircraft ships. Two squadrons consisting of larger warships under British command stood off in the distance, in case Convoy PQ17 ran into trouble.

It would. The alerted Germans were sending ten U-boats and readying their aircraft—bombers, dive-bombers, and torpedo planes—for all-out attack against the Arctic convoy in the Barents Sea.

The Germans also moved the *Tirpitz* and a couple of cruisers up the Norwegian coast to Alten Fjord, near Norway's North Cape—clearly a springboard for a fast sortie against the approaching convoy.

Alarm ran through the corridors of the Admiralty in London. Signals went out. *Tirpitz* was on the move! The nearest protective cruiser squadron and the convoy itself were ordered to scatter, run for their lives.

Until now, actually, the escort assembly had given good account of itself. The U-boats had been kept at bay, and only three ships had been lost to relentless German air attack. But now, at close to midnight on July 4, the previously well-bonded convoy came apart in pieces.

The next afternoon, the mighty *Tirpitz*, her cruiser escort, and six destroyers sallied forth from Alten Fjord on an intercept course. That night, though, the German warships turned around and went back.

There was no need for them. Able to attack the convoy's remnants piecemeal, the German submarines and aircraft were doing everything that was necessary. In five days, they sank twenty-one ships.

The ship that precipitated such disaster by reputation alone was launched at Wilhelmshaven in 1939, a monster even at birth. Not only did she carry eight fifteen-inch guns capable of piercing thirteen inches of armor from twenty-two miles away, but she could fire torpedoes like a destroyer. Two knots faster than the latest British battleships (she could dash at 31.1 knots), she could defend herself from air attack with 112 antiaircraft guns. Her role would have been as a fearsome raider, but once her sister ship the *Bismarck* was sunk by the Royal Navy early in the war, Hitler sent her to safe haven on the Norwegian coastline.

So inactive was she there that the Norwegians began to call her "the lonely queen."

"The whole strategy of the war turns at this period on this ship," Churchill told his chief of staff in January of 1942. "No other target is comparable to it." Soon after, sixteen RAF bombers sought her out for attack, but not a bomb struck her.

In all, up to twenty attacks were launched against *Tirpitz* as she dodged about Norway's fjords for most of the war. The first telling blow struck against her was that of England's highly secret X-craft submarines in September 1943. They penetrated the submarine nets in her Norwegian harbor to place their explosive charges.

Wounded, but not mortally, the monster ship underwent repairs. The next blow came in April 1944, when nearly four dozen Royal Navy Barracuda dive-bombers managed to score fourteen hits on her, causing *some* damage and killing many of the crew.

She was under repair at Kaa Fjord in September of the same year when twenty-eight Lancaster bombers found her out and scored again, this time with a single six-ton bomb. Her eight-hundred-foot hull suffered a gash forty-eight feet long.

Now simply to be used as a floating battery in the event of an Allied invasion of Norway, the battered *Tirpitz* had been moved to Tromsö when, on November 12, 1944, the RAF came one more time with its Lancaster heavy bombers. Three "blockbuster" hits quickly turned the great ship bottoms up with hundreds of her crew trapped inside. The *Tirpitz* at last had been removed from the war.

★★★

First published in World War II *magazine, July 1986.*

Romance amid Society's Ruins

HE WAS SEVENTEEN AND SHE was sixteen, both from the same corner of Poland near the Russian border. Walter and Olga could have been their names. For forced labor in Germany, each family in the conquered territory must give up one.

That one would go, *must* go.

He was the oldest, and she was the oldest, so each volunteered to go rather than allow a younger brother or sister to be used in that way.

They had not known each other before, and on the train from Dubno they didn't meet. It was a long trip, twelve days, tightly packed into freight cars, standing only, no sleep, guards with machine guns. The train passed though Walter's own town, and there, by the railroad tracks, somehow, were his father, his mother, his younger brother, waving. Last time he ever saw them, waving good-bye.

In Cologne, the camp was quartered in an old theater, girls on one side, boys on the other, boards in between.

They walked to work in a column, four miles. Their factory made engines, motors for subs, trucks, jeeplike vehicles—forty thousand slave laborers working in three shifts. All kinds of displaced, drafted, POW peoples—Russians, Hungarians, French, Yugoslavs, Poles like Walter and Olga.

They arrived June 9, 1942, and stayed until war's end, 1945. Olga, for a short time, was placed out as a nanny in Aachen, then was a blueprints courier in the big factory, running from one section to another, "morning to night."

They met, finally, in one of the interminable camp lines for food and drink. Walter wanted his ersatz coffee ("Some grass in a big bag and dump it in hot water"), and there she was, in the line. He got next to her and said: "That would be a nice pair, you and me."

And so they courted—in food lines, in the column marching to work, in a communal washroom outside the separate toilets for men and women. "You come from work, you are going on lines," she says. "It's dark, so people will sneak with each other."

Actually, she had been "going" with his friend, but that was nothing serious. "He was funny, his friend, he played harmonica and we would all have this fun. Then Walter came and he grab me from behind, he lifted me up and he turned me towards him, like face to face. He said, 'Don't you think we would match together?' So we were joking from that time and having this little going out and sneaking here and there."

After a while, Walter wrote Olga's father for permission, and her father wrote back and said, "I think you are old enough and God bless you."

In the camp, in the war, though, Olga was telling Walter they must not think too much about the future, they must first survive—they couldn't get married just yet.

In January 1944, Olga's father wrote rather cryptically that at home all of the fences have been taken down, "meaning the ghettos." And the trees are down. Just bare ground. And remember the woods where she used to go for mushrooms? "The letter penetrates something. I said, 'Oh, my goodness, the Jewish people were all killed.'"

At the camp, at the factory, in Cologne, one thing and another, alarms, scary moments, always the deprivations, but they both survived. They were, at end, liberated by the advancing Americans.

Finally, it *was* time, but for the wedding she had no dress. She made one for herself, but now she had no shoes. A German gave her a pair of men's shoes, his son's, very large. But Walter went to a Russian camp and swapped a pocket watch from home for a pair of women's shoes.

They were married along with many other couples—thirty people standing about the altar, and when they reached the part about the ring, no ring. They borrowed another couple's ring.

They came to America, "because the Russians took over there [Poland]." They have lived in Southwick, ninety miles from Boston, a married couple, ever since. He began to work in a paper mill upon their arrival and never left. Walter and Olga. Decades gone by. On their kitchen wall a frame around the words, "*Boze Blogoslaw Naz Dom,*" which means "God Bless Our Home." Walter and Olga Nowak, Southwick, Massachusetts.

★★★

Based upon "The Good War," An Oral History of World War Two, *Studs Terkel (Pantheon Books, a division of Random House. Inc., New York, 1984).*

Hitler's Bathwater Purloined

EVEN "GOOD" GERMANS WHO DESPISED the Hitler regime had "black sheep" in their families totally enamored of the man who led Germany into a devastating war. In Gertrud Breier's case, the "black sheep" were her great aunt Lina and her husband, Gustave.

"Gustave was an officer with the military court, who was always wearing his uniform." Great Aunt Lina, though, went a bit further.

She traveled one time to Bad Godesberg, "where Hitler and his big shots would frequently stay for a cure."

Aunt Lina then paid a chambermaid at the hotel that Hitler frequented to obtain some of the *Führer's* bathwater. Aunt Lina provided a small bottle for the chore, and the chambermaid complied. Aunt Lina returned home with her prize, presumably never known to Hitler.

"For years to come, the dirty water was kept in her vitrine for everyone to admire. What a nut she was."

In an obverse way, Lina's son Richard may have outdone his own mother. "He was full of pep and resented his parents. He usually got satisfaction when he could embarrass them."

He achieved that end one day when he managed to raise a chamber pot on a flagpole. "Sure enough, up there, right under the eagle with the swastika, was the chamber pot."

When Cousin Richard was identified as the perpetrator, he was punished by his undoubtedly furious mother, "and he had to apologize openly." At least he wasn't shot—his mother, at the end of the war, was. She died still a fanatical Nazi. "The day the American troops moved into the suburbs of Frankenthal, that stupid Lina took the Nazi flag, saluted and screamed at a group of soldiers. One shot was fired and Lina with her flag in her hand fell to the ground. A neighbor, who had watched it from a small window in his basement, told us it looked as if she wanted to fight those soldiers off."

Son Richard survived both the war and parents who "almost destroyed everything good" in him. "He was a very kind soul. Years later, after the war, he married a very nice girl and let his then-senile father live with them."

★★★

Based upon The Governess *by Gertrud Breier (Vantage Press, New York. 1988).*

Intelligence War

WITH THE BRITISH AT BLETCHLEY Park leading the way, the Allies had achieved solid breakthroughs in their decoding assault upon the German coding machine called Enigma—but then the U-boat fleet came up with its all but indecipherable SHARK radio traffic.

SHARK also utilized the Enigma machines, several of them by now in British hands, but the Enigma put into play by the U-boats in 1942 contained four internal rotors rather than the standard three.

That simple-sounding addition of a single "cog" multiplied the possible variables by a geometrically multiple factor. If, as first seemed the case, the decoders and their machines could not cope with SHARK, what was needed would be a SHARK-modified Enigma from a U-boat, or relevant documents showing how the new system worked. But how to lay Allied hands on such closely guarded material belonging to the enemy?

The breakthrough came in unexpectedly poignant fashion and at high cost.

In the Mediterranean on October 30, 1942, a Sunderland flying boat on patrol off Port Said came across a U-boat skimming the surface seventy miles north of the Nile delta.

Alerted by radio, British destroyers converged and after sixteen hours of hunting and depth-charging finally brought the now-submerged *U-559* to the surface. Under fire from the British *Petard*, the German crew abandoned the submarine. Unknown to the British, but a suspected possibility, the Germans had opened the boat's seacocks in order to scuttle her and keep her out of British hands.

As the U-boat crew swam for a *Petard* whaleboat, Royal Navy Lieutenant Tony Fasson and Able Seaman Colin Grazier leaped into the water, naked, and swam the opposite direction—to the submarine. They were after the U-boat's coding equipment and documents.

By the time they reached the U-boat's conning tower, it barely protruded from the waves, but they climbed down inside anyway and made their way to the radio room.

Although the sub was empty, they soon had company—a ship's canteen assistant named Tommy Brown, who, without orders, also decided to board the stricken U-boat. The fact that Tommy Brown was only sixteen and had lied about his age to join his country's navy was not very well known at the time.

In the radio room, the three found an intelligence bonanza—one of the new four-rotor SHARK machines and documents revealing its encoding keys.

Grabbing those materials by the armful, the older two men handed them to the teenager, who stationed himself by the hatch and then transferred the precious cargo to a whaler pulled alongside.

But the U-boat all this time literally was sinking. At the last moment, Tommy Brown got off, but not the two brave sailors still inside. They went down, two Englishmen, with the German U-boat to a joint grave beneath the sea.

While the intelligence experts subsequently and happily seized upon the prize haul, the two men lost were posthumously awarded Britain's George Cross for their bravery. So was Tommy Brown, at sixteen its youngest recipient ever.

His age, though, was to be his undoing. He was discharged as too young for the Royal Navy and returned home to North Shields. There, two years later, he died the hero's death just barely missed off Port Said in 1942—still a victim of war, he died attempting to rescue a younger sister trapped by fire in their slum tenement, the fire caused by a German air raid.

★★★

Based upon The Sigint Secrets: The Signals Intelligence War, 1900 to Today *by Nigel West (William Morrow and Company. Inc., New York, 1988).*

★ WAR STILL ★ SUPREME

Tapping the Hot Line

BACK ON SEPTEMBER 7, 1941, Leningrad had been under direct German fire for three days. The famous siege of nine hundred days was about to commence. Immediately to the east, at a place called Shlisselburg, troops of the Soviet NKVD desperately resisted advance elements of the German Sixteenth Army. Three hundred aircraft of the German *Luftwaffe* swept in to strafe the holdouts, and by nightfall the city on the shores of Lake Ladoga was engulfed in flames.

Far to the south, but also on the eastern front, *panzer* chieftain Heinz Guderian had turned his tank columns in a drive across the Russian rear in the Ukraine. He soon would meet another German pincer sweep and close the vast encirclement of Kiev. At the center of the eastern front another huge haul of prisoners and territory was in prospect for the German Army Group Center driving toward Vyazma.

A world in such tumult paid little attention to a radio-telephone call late that day from still-peaceable Washington, D.C., to London. In that innocuous pulsing across the Atlantic—also the scene of raging war—a newly arrived British official merely asked his superiors in London to provide him an assistant.

Innocuous as the call may have seemed, the German enemy heard, recorded and understood the conversation—no matter that it was "scrambled." The occasion, in fact, was a red-letter day for a certain set of German eavesdroppers—this was their first intercept of many on the very same transatlantic "line" that Winston Churchill and Franklin Roosevelt would be using throughout the war to discuss Allied strategy, tactics, and policy.

If the Allies had their super-secret ULTRA code-breaking operation as an ear to Nazi Germany's pulse, the Germans, as an intelligence coup of their own, had solved the Allied "scramble" device and could listen in when the two heads of state, or their many functionaries, picked up the scramble phone on either side of the Atlantic.

So secret was ULTRA that only the highest Allied officials and the most select intelligence personnel knew about it. So secret, likewise, was the German radio-telephone intercept that military intelligence was left out of the game almost entirely. Hitler and his closest Nazi Party coterie kept this one pretty much to themselves.

And they could thank the man equivalent to America's postmaster general for the coup, rather than Germany's professional spies.

Ladislas Farago told the story of Reich's Post Minister Wilhelm Ohnesorge's contribution to the German war effort in the 1971 book, *The Game of the Foxes*. The tale actually begins in 1939, when a German agent in New York noticed a story in the *New York Times* that was headlined: "Roosevelt Protected in Talks to Envoys by Radio 'Scrambling' to Foil Spies Abroad."

Roosevelt's scrambler was located in a soundproof room in the basement of the White House. Later in the war, Churchill would do his conversing from a scramble instrument located in his underground War Cabinet Rooms in London. For the moment, though, America was still a neutral party, and FDR's first use of the scramble phone had been to hear about the unprovoked German invasion of Poland on September 1 from his ambassador in Paris, William C. Bullitt.

Developed by Bell Telephone, the A-3 scramble device would break up the frequency band and scatter the voice impulses at one end, all to be sorted out by a descrambler at the other end of the radio-telephone link. From the White House, FDR's conversation was piped into an AT&T security room in New York for the transatlantic transmission in unintelligible form.

The German spy in New York dutifully forwarded his clipping from the *Times*, but in Germany there was no immediate or significant reaction within the intelligence community. Still, the Allied "hot line" did interest one expert outside normal German intelligence circles—Wilhelm Ohnesorge.

As Reichs post minister, Ohnesorge was in charge not only of Germany's postal system, but also its telephone and telegraph network. He was just the man to focus upon the ballyhooed radio-telephone "scramble" link between England and America, which he did without delay. His laboratories and engineers set to work entirely lacking in visible evidence of the highly secret Bell apparatus—no blueprints, models, or the like. But, beginning his work in 1940, Ohnesorge's chief research engineer, Kurt Vetterlein, had developed experimental models of both the scrambling and descrambling devices by September 1941. The first interception was of the British official's call to London from Washington late on September 7, even as Leningrad came under siege.

Keeping their experimental work secret, Ohnesorge and Vetterlein soon perfected their intercept system. They built a monitoring station on the coast of occupied Holland, complete with directional antennas to pick up the radio signals from nearby England. By March 1942, they were ready to begin their intercepts on a regular basis.

At this early stage of the war—for America, especially—FDR and Churchill had a great many military secrets to talk about. The Normandy invasion was still two years away; the Anglo-American invasion of North Africa was still months in the future, and for both Allies, the war in the Pacific against Germany's Axis partner Japan still appeared an unmitigated disaster.

As David Kahn further explained in his 1978 book, *Hitler's Spies*, wartime developments gradually encroached upon the listening unit's original location in a onetime youth hostel on the Dutch coast. Commando raids on coastal radar stations prompted the Germans to move their *Forschungsstelle*, or "research post," to Valkenswaard in southeastern Holland. "Here a compact brick-and-concrete bunker, in the shape of an L, was built for it in the woods...." wrote Kahn. "The men worked in areas guarded by inch-thick steel doors, cooked in their own kitchen, slept in rooms with dormer windows, and relaxed in a living room with a fireplace."

By the fall of 1944, after the Normandy invasion, the exigencies of war forced the Germans to relocate again—this time as distantly from England as Bavaria. "But here the distance from the [England-based] transmitter considerably impaired its results."

The original, early war locale, of course, had been the best for Engineer Vetterlein's operation. That spot, two hundred yards from the sea, "could pick up both the ground wave of the transmitter in England and the back lob of its beam toward America." Vetterlein's equipment included single sideband receivers, filters, modulators, switching equipment, tape recorders, timers and, for the intercepts themselves, two rhombic antennas. The latter took in the Allied signals in their scrambled form, but with the supporting equipment, Vetterlein and his men would find the Allied chitchat "instantaneously disentangled by the apparatus, and tape-recorded in the clear."

As Kahn also noted, Vetterlein did not exactly begin his work from a point zero. His *Deutsche Reichspost* agency had owned an A-3 device allowing radio-telephone communication with the United States. The trick for Vetterlein and his crowd was to descramble, even if they understood the operating principles.

Thus, they first attacked the problem using American transmissions intercepted near occupied Bordeaux, France. They "attacked the problem with oscilloscopes and spectrographs, filters and patience. By the end of 1940, they had reconstructed the A-3's secret parameters—the widths of the subbands, their division points, their inversions, and their intersubstitutions, which changed thirty-six times every twelve minutes."

The painstaking work led eventually to the equipment that would descramble the overheard conversations "as they were being spoken," although it did take months—until fall of 1941—to effectively intercept and descramble the cross-Atlantic messages. Later, when the intelligence operation was in full swing, the

Germans monitored the hot line around the clock, with thirty to sixty calls to choose from every day.

Churchill and his counterpart in Washington would not discuss everything by radio-telephone, to be sure. They did have their wartime conferences; they communicated by other means, and they had many subordinates shuttling back and forth. Many of those subordinates, however, both military and diplomatic, would be using the scramble phone too.

Unknown to any of the Allied principals, the German monitoring station first located in Holland produced an intelligence bonanza from the start. "Its equipment was so efficient," wrote Farago in his book, "that the intercepted conversations could be 'deciphered' instantaneously, losing only a few syllables after each key change (which occurred at intervals of twenty seconds) until the proper key was found automatically. The German transcripts were sent to Berlin on a *G-Schreiber*, a classified teletype that had its own scrambler system. The entire operation, from the interception to the arrival of its transcript in Berlin, usually required only a couple of hours. It was probably the fastest means of intelligence procurement in secret service history."

Reichs Post Minister Ohnesorge waited until the intercept system was working perfectly before informing Hitler of the great success. On March 6, 1942, he wrote the *Führer* to report that his was the only agency in the Third Reich "that succeeded in rendering conversations that had been made unintelligible, intelligible again at the instant of reception."

As a direct result, among other helpful intelligence gleanings, the Germans in July of 1943 were able to confirm that the Italian government, having deposed Mussolini, was seeking an armistice with the Allies.

Various signs had pointed toward the wavering of the Italian ally, but Hitler and his close advisors were unsure what to expect. When Marshal Pietro Badoglio's new government took over on July 25, confusion reigned in Nazi Germany's highest councils.

On July 29, however, Post Minister Ohnesorge's latest intercept, delivered in a sealed envelope marked with a big U, settled the controversy—and resulted in Hitler's next fateful decision. At 1 a.m. that day, Churchill and Roosevelt had talked on their scramble phone about the tumultuous events in Italy. They had discussed the possibility of an impending armistice with the new government.

Since there had been no official peace-feeler by the Badoglio regime, they might have been premature in anticipating such a move just then. And they apparently did speak in a conditional sense, even if their expectations were made quite clear.

Whatever the tone of the conversation, it was enough for the eavesdropping Germans. They saw it as hard evidence that armistice negotiations were under way.

As a result, Hitler's uncertainty was ended. He immediately ordered the occupation of Italy, and soon twenty German divisions stood in the Allied pathway up the Italian boot, instead of the mere eight that were stationed there before the telephone intercept. The Allies would spend the rest of the war subduing the German forces in Italy—at horrendous cost to both sides.

While the *Deutsche Reichpost* had more than proved the value of its listening post in Holland, Germany's military forces were not often to share in the intelligence harvest that resulted. "This was a Nazi triumph, and it was to remain a Nazi operation," wrote Farago. "Distribution of the intercepts was strictly limited. A single copy of the original transcript was sent to Heinrich Himmler to be distributed at his discretion. The [military] *Abwehr* was bypassed, as were the intelligence departments of the Army, Navy, and *Luftwaffe*."

After SS Chief Himmler's scrutiny of the incoming intercepts, the "choicest" were sent on to Hitler. A few went to Foreign Minister Joachim von Ribbentrop, but he apparently was discouraged by the fact that the Allied speakers on the radio-telephone were often guarded even in their scrambled conversations. "Owing to the fact that these conversations are camouflaged," he once complained, "there is very little one can learn from them."

Wiser members of the Third Reich's ruling circles were, of course, more impressed. The Himmler protégé Walter Schellenberg, who had vaulted to head of all German espionage by 1944, recognized an obvious "bull's-eye" when the Holland intercept picked up an FDR-Churchill conversation on May 5, 1944, about an Allied buildup in England. There, straight from "the horse's mouth," was confirmation that the invasion of France was imminent. And when it did take place, just a month later, it wasn't the *Deutsche Reichspost's* fault that Germany was unable to stop it. Germany's postmaster general and his engineers had done their job—what could be done about the information they provided was another matter altogether.

★★★

First published in World War II *magazine, March 1988.*

Brave *Trigger's* Last Patrol

NORMALLY A BRIGHT-COLORED TROPICAL fish, *Trigger* in World War II also was a U.S. submarine—the little (by today's standards) sub that could, to hear it from the underwater boat's official U.S. naval history. For instance, as *Trigger* nosed into the submarine base at Pearl Harbor before her first war patrol, "she was a neophyte, a trifle self-conscious and perhaps apologetic to slip her trim form into the berth of her illustrious sisters."

Pickings were slim on *Trigger's* first war patrol, but never mind, for more was to come. The doughty sub found a very real contact in enemy waters west of Japan soon enough, in October of 1942. She encountered a freighter that tried to ram; she averted the collision and managed to place a torpedo in the enemy ship. Threatened by a patrol vessel, *Trigger* then had to scurry below.

Resurfacing later, she went after the wounded freighter again. As she closed, however, "several large puffs of smoke billowed over the ship, and then nothing was seen." Adds the official (but colorful) history: "The Jap freighter was not designed to submerge, but encouraged by enough torpedoes, she exceeded the designer's expectations on this occasion."

Like other American subs early in the war, *Trigger* experienced the frustration of torpedoes that didn't work. On October 17, she maneuvered into perfect firing position upon another freighter and sent three torpedoes "straight and true for the target." Nothing happened—they were duds. "The skipper could be forgiven if he slammed his cap on the deck."

Just three days later, though, *Trigger* scored two hits on a tanker, then dove to avoid another ramming attempt. "The tanker churned right overhead, dropping a depth charge as she passed. It was her last pass, for *Trigger* had already thrown the lucky pair. A violent eruption; silence from the vessel's screws; the crackling noise of a ship breaking up; a clear horizon. That is how a ship is lost. That is how this one went down."

Returning to Pearl from her second war patrol, "*Trigger* could hold her head higher now." On her third sortie, she scored often, in one case upon an on-rushing Japanese destroyer. "With her bow turned up like an old shoe, the destroyer sank on an even keel."

Trigger's fourth war patrol produced thirteen contacts with enemy ships, but various untoward factors held the sub's score to one ship apparently sunk, another damaged. After replenishment at Pearl in April of 1943, *Trigger* would begin her fifth patrol. Thus, "It was the slender snout of a seasoned veteran that pushed the water aside on her way out."

Off Tokyo in June, *Trigger* spotted a brand-new aircraft carrier and two escorting destroyers coming right at her. She ducked under and held her breath while one destroyer passed overhead; then came the sound of the carrier's heavy screws. "The crisp orders to fire were repeated six times, and each time a swish responded that sent a deadly torpedo on its way. Four solid detonations echoed back…and the carrier's screws stopped."

A fast look showed the giant ship drifting and at a list—"Little white-clad forms scurried madly about the decks." But that same periscope peek showed the destroyers racing furiously toward *Trigger*. And now it was her turn for a beating, a pounding by depth charge that blanked the lights and knocked crewmen off their feet. "The heavy sides of the submarine squeezed in with each reverberating shock.…The temperatures soared, the humidity hit the saturation point and the men worked to the point of exhaustion controlling the flooding…from the tortured sea valves and fittings."

But *Trigger* survived. Survived, surfaced well after midnight, and moved on. "Fresh, cool air never felt so good and the men knew the grateful feeling of returning from the shadow of death."

On her sixth patrol, *Trigger* came across two unescorted freighters in the East China Sea. She unleashed her torpedoes at the biggest of the two, but once again frustration—"two duds thumping the ship's side with nothing more accomplished than putting the Japs on alert."

But now a big show lay ahead—a six-ship convoy that *Trigger* chose to attack from the surface and in the dark of night. Her first six torpedoes struck two tankers, with spectacular results. Flames shot five hundred feet into the air and illuminated the surrounding sea. "Crew members in white uniforms were sprinting forward on her [the first tanker's] decks ahead of the rapidly spreading flames." A freighter beyond the tankers was also hit; it broke in half beneath the stack and disappeared below the surface.

In more than three hours of battle with the convoy, *Trigger* struck a third tanker and a second freighter. In all, four ships were sunk, one was left damaged.

As *Trigger* departed, a glow flared up. It was one of the tankers blowing up. "Huge fires billowed into the air and the bow, bridge and stern of the tanker were incandescent. The hull of the first tanker disappeared and the place where she had been was still burning fiercely with flames lashing up 50 to 100 feet."

And so it went, one successful war patrol after another, as 1943 faded into

1944 for the now-veteran, seagoing fighter *Trigger*. By now, she and her crew had earned three presidential unit citations. Even the proud *Trigger*, though, would find April 8, 1944, a trifle trying.

Sailing her ninth patrol, she encountered a large convoy—ships in four columns—guarded by "a terrific escort force." Indomitable, *Trigger* worked her way among the ships and was about to fire off ten torpedoes for "a mass killing" when a destroyer suddenly loomed not fifty yards away, on a collision course. *Trigger* avoided the ramming, saw a clear lane, and fired four torpedoes down the enemy's path, then was trapped by four of the escorts. "As one tried to ram, the second followed him up with depth charges and the other two were lined up on either quarter. Just then, two hits were heard on a huge, heavily loaded tanker and two more hits were heard on a ship elsewhere in the convoy."

Trigger, of course, couldn't stay for a look at the damage inflicted. She instead "plunged to the depths to take the inevitable working over by the Japanese destroyers." And now came *Trigger's* worst moment yet. Six "very close" depth charges shook her badly. Worse, the submarine hunters would hound her for the next seventeen hours as she lay silent in the deep, her steel hull "buckled in and out." In addition, her pipes and bulkheads "vibrated like guitar strings." Locker doors sprung open. The heat and humidity drenched the shoes and socks of the crew members with sweat. "Lack of oxygen in the air and the nervous strain of the unrelenting depth charges brought some to the verge of collapse."

But *Trigger* at last emerged, made temporary repairs "by mustering spare parts and baling wire," then joined her sister sub *Tang* for further hunting of their own. They found a convoy off Palau. *Trigger* crept to within 2,600 yards and had four ships lined up in her sights as an overlapping mass. With six of her "fish" fired, four made hits. "One of the closer ships blew up from an explosion on her after parts and one of the far ships was seen straight up and down with her course set for the bottom." The others milled about in a state of confusion "that was not unpleasant to see."

Three destroyers gathered close to exchange blinker signals. "*Trigger* decided to add a little more confusion to their conference with torpedoes. A cloud of smoke shot into the air where the middle destroyer had been....The last thing heard...was her load of depth charges erupting in rapid-fire order way down below."

After major overhaul in San Francisco, *Trigger* continued her one-submarine war against the Japanese with a tenth, then an eleventh war patrol. By now it was 1945, the end of that war only months away. *Trigger*, out on her own for a twelfth patrol, was supposed to join her sister *Tirante*.

The day came when *Tirante* arrived on station and called out by radio for *Trigger*. But…no reply. "Silence was the only answer—a silence that has never been broken; a silence that told a wordless story."

Trigger, brave *Trigger*, was gone.

★★★

From U.S. Navy historical files.

Conversation with the Lord

WHEN SHIPS GO DOWN AND their men are cast adrift upon an uncertain sea, nearly any landfall soon begins to look like a good landfall. Nearly, that is.

Take the case of Lieutenant Hugh Barr Miller Jr., U.S. Naval Reserves, shortly after his destroyer, the *Strong*, was torpedoed and sunk during night action in the Solomons, Southwest Pacific, on July 4, 1943. How many men from the *Strong* survived, he could not really estimate. In an "as-told-to" story published later, he said: "I know that there were twenty-three of us in the water that night, clustered on two life nets and some pieces of raft. Eleven days later, there were four of us left alive on Arundel Island, far behind Jap lines."

Far behind enemy lines. Miller's landfall, it seems, was of the *nearly* variety.

Worse, injured internally when his destroyer went down, shaken by a "severe" hemorrhage, Miller thought he was dying. As senior officer in his group of five, he ordered his four men to leave him…to take all remaining equipment and rations and make their way to a coconut plantation down the island coast in effort to find help. Miller gave one barefooted survivor his own shoes and kept only two coconuts, a pocketknife with broken-off blades, and three or four containers of water ("two Jap beer bottles and one or two old cracker tins we found").

It was an emotional parting of shipmates, the young sailor with Miller's shoes "crying like a baby." And, indeed, he never saw them again, never learned their fate. But…not for the reason anticipated.

Miller still thought he would die. "Figuring I wouldn't last long and that

I might as well be as comfortable as possible, I drank all my water that first day—the 15th—after the boys left."

But then, "to my surprise, I was still there the next day, and I began to rally." Two days later, he was still there again! "I got to thinking about myself then and I decided I wasn't showing up as the kind of guy I had thought I was, just to lie down and die without a fight," wrote Miller later.

In fact, Miller now realized he could observe Japanese operations on nearby Kolobangara Island—and provide his own forces helpful intelligence, if he could just manage to live and get the word back.

"So I held a little conversation with the Lord, lying there on the edge of the jungle that evening, and I told Him that if He'd give me a little water, I'd get up out of there and do something about this situation."

Miller then fell off to sleep, and soon, as if in answer to his prayers— "About 9 P.M. it started to rain, and it rained cats and dogs for four hours. The water just poured down. My bed was under a big tree and the water ran in a stream from a large tropical leaf, so I put my tin under the stream and then my beer bottles. I drank four tins of that God-given water as soon as they filled up, replenished the tin and went back to sleep, ready to go in the morning."

That next morning, after a "leisurely breakfast in bed," consisting of more water from the cracker tin, Miller made himself busy. Sometimes supporting himself with a staff his "boys" had fashioned for him earlier, he hobbled back to a spring a mile and a quarter away—he and his "boys" had passed it in their initial wanderings on the island. "The first hundred yards was a major ordeal because I was so weak and the coral and rocks punished my bare feet horribly. In no time they were slashed to ribbons. But I shuffled on and reached the spring just before dark in a state of complete exhaustion. I filled up on water, lay under a log and went to sleep."

By the next day, he had pried open a coconut with his broken penknife, after beating off the stiff husk on sharp coral rock. The bits of coconut meat he obtained were the first solid food he had been able to retain in fifteen days. He was on the way to recovery.

But now, where to camp out...to hide out? His still was a precarious situation, a point that came to the fore in very short order. "As I lay dozing near the spring that night in an old Jap navy blanket I had found, I heard a noise down the beach. I listened carefully. The noise came again. I couldn't be sure just what it was, but my camp was not very well situated for hiding, so I stole back into the jungle. I hid in the underbrush just as a small Jap patrol came into view down the beach."

No great harm done; they never knew he was there…but the lesson was obvious. He had to find a secure hideout, "if I were to live and get some information to our people."

Miller searched the wooded terrain around the spring for the next five days before he found the right place—a pocket among some "great" mangrove trees, "a natural shelter, protected on all sides by thickets and branches."

As an extra bonus, one of the gigantic mangrove trunks rose at a 45-degree angle, then looped over another tree's branch, to create a sort of nest—a perfect lookout post for U.S. Navy Lieutenant Miller.

Of course, as more time passed he grew stronger and stronger.

Soon, too, when an American PT boat shot up Japanese troop barges and supply boats in Hathorn Sound, "in front of my camp," he picked over the battle debris—from an enemy body he obtained shoes and socks, five cans of tinned beef, "a belt, a bayonet, a grenade holder and two very fine grenades."

"That same day I heard a plane coming, so I got out on…[a] salt flat to signal him. The pilot saw me and circled overhead several times. Finally he dropped a small package containing some iodine and some Army D ration, waved and flew away. The iodine, with which I painted my feet, undoubtedly saved my life as it enabled the cuts to heal. They had begun to fester and I was afraid I wouldn't be able to get around much longer."

And "get around" he continued to do, with a vengeance!

It wasn't long, in fact, before the Castaway of Arundel Island was, himself, attacking the Japanese occupiers of the island. For instance, they sent out a five-man patrol after finding the body that Miller had stripped of all useful gear and supplies for himself. It was at night, and fearful of unknown numbers of intruders scattered in the jungle, the five enemy soldiers bunched together, wrote Miller later. One grenade ended that threat.

He stripped and buried the bodies, then managed to elude the added patrols sent out in search of the missing five—and their mysterious nemesis.

After a lull, during which Miller kept arming himself with various weaponry washed ashore in his battle zone, he really went on the warpath. Under the cover of darkness one night, he lobbed grenades into Japanese machine-gun nests he had found along his own shoreline—this just as American planes flew by. He mounted his simulated "bombing runs" the nights of August 10, 12, and 14. Then, the morning of August 16, a Marine Corps Avenger piloted by 1st Lt. James R. Turner found Miller frantically waving a towel on his salt-flat and recognizable as a Westerner "by my red beard and shining forehead."

In short order again, Miller and his intelligence materials, such as stripped Japanese insignia, were gathered up by an American rescue seaplane—a pickup that had its own hair-raising moments, for that matter. "It was a small American seaplane known as a 'duck,'" Miller wrote. His heart in his mouth, he watched as the lightly armed, highly vulnerable "duck" maneuvered within two thousand yards of the Japanese base on adjacent Kolombangara Island in order to land in front of his beach. "But the crew of that plane, composed of absolutely fearless men, didn't hesitate an instant."

Miller started to wade out to his rescuers, but they quickly saw he was too weak to go beyond a reef fronting the beach. "They waved me back, calling that they would inflate their rubber boat and come after me."

All in broad daylight, with the enemy just two thousand yards away.

Miller took advantage of the delay to hurry back to his campsite and retrieve some of the enemy items he had gathered during his stay on Arundel Island. Taking as much as he could carry, Miller then waded out to the reef, where he met both the rubber boat and Marine Corps Major Vernon A. Peterson, commander of the rescue party. After Miller explained the intelligence potential of all the Japanese equipment in his arms, Peterson "loaded it into the boat and took it out to the plane, then came back for me." Miller and Peterson then paddled back to the "duck," which was able to rev up and take off without any harassment by the nearby Japanese.

Miller spent the next two days at recently captured Munda on New Georgia Island being debriefed of his vital intelligence information—many days, many miles, *many pounds*, since the morning he had said good-bye to his last four men and laid down to die on Japanese-occupied Arundel Island.

Castaway Miller's first request of his rescuers, by the way, was for a cigarette. And next...food! "We had returned to Munda in time for lunch that day, August 16, and it was my first real meal since the night of July 4. I had lost forty pounds during the forty-three days I was missing, but I started then and there to get it back."

★★★

Based upon Lt. Hugh Barr Miller and Frank Tremaine in The 100 Best True Stories of World War II *(Wise & Co. Inc., New York, 1945).*

Non-Swimmer's Worst Nightmare

OFF NORTHERN NEW GUINEA IN October 1942, the Australian coastal vessel *Alacrity* was carrying the men of the U.S. Army's Twenty-second Portable Hospital to a forward position near the vicious fighting at Buna when about twenty Japanese aircraft zoomed in to attack. On board a nearly defenseless ship loaded with ammunition, half a mile from the beach, and under a bombing and strafing attack was no place to be if you couldn't swim.

Medic William Vana was such a man, and his first exposure to combat conditions was an unforgettable, searing experience:

The planes were so low that we could see the pilot sitting in the cockpit. Everyone started jumping overboard at this time. The twenty other planes came back and joined in the fun. Then all hell broke loose. The planes started strafing and dropping bombs, and what a racket! I don't think I ever heard as much noise before. The water was full of men swimming and yelling for help or praying.

The *Alacrity* was towing a barge full of added supplies and soldiers, while behind were three more coastal vessels carrying troops and supplies. "I heard a loud explosion and looked behind and saw the last ship blow up. At this time I didn't know what to do. I couldn't swim and there were no life boats."

Vana was not alone in his predicament—"there were about 20 of us still on board and all in the same fix as me."

Vana's first reaction was to fight back. He ran to a nearby machine-gun mount, "and let loose." He had never fired a machine gun before, but he got this one going and "sprayed the sky" until the ammo ran out. A buddy ran to another machine gun and did the same.

The planes kept attacking—strafing the swimmers in the water now. Vana, not knowing what to do, was "running around all over." An attempt to loosen an assault boat lashed to the deck failed; it was too heavy for him and a couple of other men to handle. "There were wounded and killed lying all over."

Vana ran to the stern and yelled at the men there: "What the hell are we going to do? And how the hell are we going to get to shore?"

The two remaining ships of the small convoy were now on fire, and so was

Vana's own vessel. "We expected at any minute for it to blow up, as there were tons of ammunition on board."

One of the men suggested tossing their packs overboard and using them for support in the water.

So I threw mine overboard and started taking my clothes off. I think that was the fastest I ever got undressed. I had my fatigues on, leggings, shoes, and underwear, and in no time I was standing naked on deck. I had on a pair of socks and these were the only clothes I had on. I, for some reason, grabbed a handkerchief and tried to tie it around my watch—and at the same time grabbed a pack of cigarettes. I must have been in a daze, as all at once I wondered what the hell I was trying to do. I threw these down and went to jump overboard. I looked for my pack and couldn't find it anyplace. The damn thing must have sunk!

Frantic, Vana was about to go over the side anyway, "sink or swim," but he happened to see that up near the bow of his burning coastal vessel someone had gotten the assault boat into the water after all. "I ran through a hail of bullets to the bow and jumped overboard. I hit the water and at the same time grabbed onto the assault boat. I was afraid if I was to go down I'd never come up."

In the boat were eight or ten men, including Vana's buddy Herb Grew, while three or four more men were in the water alongside, hanging on. Vana climbed aboard and took an oar; someone else had found a paddle, and together they tried to move the assault boat away from the *Alacrity* and toward the shore, half a mile away.

As he tells the rest of his story:

We managed to get about 20 or 25 feet from the ship and seemed to be getting on pretty good. There were cries of help and prayers filling the air. All at once we heard a plane diving near us and we all looked up—here came a plane straight at us. We could see the tracers coming from it and they seemed to be coming straight at us. We all thought our time was up. We all got excited and the next thing I knew I was in the water.

At first I didn't know what to do—then something told me to keep my head above water and try to get to shore. At this time two chaps who were in the boat with us grabbed onto me—they said they couldn't swim and started to pull me down with them. I yelled to them to let me loose as I couldn't swim either. I then started kicking and finally they let me loose.

I saw Herb Grew at this time. He looked at me but didn't say a word. I guess he knew his time was up—and he died like a real soldier. He was fully clothed and went straight down. I had all I could do to save myself, so I was unable to help him or anyone else. The planes were still strafing and bombing and I started in towards shore. My arms and legs were moving like hell. I knew if my head were to go under I'd never come up, so I held my head up the best I could. Then I started yelling for help and praying.

The air was full of chaps yelling for someone to help them. I hope to never hear anything like it again—and not being able to help them—but it was everybody for himself. Whenever a bomb would explode in the water, I'd get tossed around and get a mouthful of salt water.

After a while my arms and legs began to get tired. My socks felt like they were full of cement. I was tiring out fast and just managed to keep afloat. I knew I couldn't last much longer, and the shoreline seemed to be getting farther away.

I spotted a rowboat on shore and yelled for someone to come out in it. I and everyone else all had the same idea. Everyone was yelling for someone to come out and save us. Two men came out of the jungle and started pushing the boat in the water. I yelled to them to hurry up, as I couldn't last much longer. I was the nearest to shore, so they headed for me. The planes at this time decided they had had enough fun—or else that some of our planes might come, so they left us.

I kept yelling at the two men in the boat to hurry. I was about 200 yards from shore by this time and could hardly move my arms and legs.

Hauled into the rowboat by the two "Aussies" manning it, Vana recovered a bit and helped them in rescuing others from the water. Soon they had twenty-five men in the tiny boat and another five hanging on to its sides as it pulled for the beach.

A few feet away, some of the men jumped out and staggered onto the sand. Some onlooking soldiers ran forward to help. "The first thing I did was drop to my knees and thank God for bringing me through safe and sound. I was naked except for my socks, which I took off and threw away. All I had saved were my ring and watch, which had stopped. The watch stopped at 6:57 P.M. That meant I was on board ship for almost half an hour before going over the side."

While the rowboat went out again to hunt for survivors—and attempt to haul in the barge—the medics left on the beach didn't know if the enemy was in the jungle right behind, or where. "Then our ship started to burn almost all over and the ammunition started to go off. Shell after shell went off and we hit the ground. There was a log lying down the beach, so we made for it. We scooped out a hole to lie in."

A couple of "infantry boys" then told the newly arrived medical corpsmen that the front line was two miles up ahead. In the hours that immediately followed, the Twenty-second Portable Hospital set up shop with what little equipment was left and began treating the wounded from the air attack—including its own personnel. "Someone had found some flashlights and they [the doctors] were using these to see by. The place was full of blood-soaked uniforms and bandages. The doctors were extracting bullets and shrapnel from the boys. All the doctors did a wonderful job with the little medical equipment they had."

With the sky often lighted by the exploding ammunition, the Twenty-second Portable Hospital did its work through the night. Only its CO, Major Parker Hardin, had on any clothes at all—a pair of shorts. In the morning, the medics faced the task of sending the seriously wounded miles to the rear for real hospital care and of treating the wounded coming in from the fighting ahead, and all subject to intermittent bombing and strafing attacks by the Japanese.

In the meantime, they scrounged or made up what clothing they could—one man cut up a blanket to fashion a pair of shorts. Vana, who was awarded the Bronze Star for his action on the machine gun, went barefoot for many days.

★★★

Based upon first-person account by William H. Vana, World War II *magazine, September 1990.*

Constant Companion Cuthbert

NOVEMBER 11, 1942, THE FIRST NIGHT, was clear and cold and American-born Virginia Hall and her constant companion "Cuthbert" still had eighteen miles, plus a back-breaking climb over the Pyrenees in deep snow ahead of them.

Beckoning beyond the mountains, though, were neutral Spain, and a relatively safe journey back to England for consultations with her SOE (Special Operations Executive) colleagues in sabotage, resistance, and spying against the Nazis.

And behind, the Gestapo was on the hunt for her.

By the next morning, November 12, after hours spent trudging straight uphill, "The drifts on the ground were knee deep."

Virginia had to struggle along, often actually dragging Cuthbert.

As the trek led by a hired guide wore on for Virginia and three fellow fugitives, all men, Cuthbert continued to be troublesome. But then, under such strain, that was to be expected.

Finding a short wave radio at a stop in a safe house on the morning of November 13, she messaged her superiors in London that she was on her way out of Vichy France, forced to flee her secret outpost in Lyons.

Okay, they radioed back. Arrangements would be made to welcome her in Barcelona, Spain, but…any special problems?

"Cuthbert is being tiresome, but I can cope," she replied.

Silence.

Then: "If Cuthbert is tiresome, have him eliminated."

She had to smile at that. London knew very well that she called her wooden leg "Cuthbert." Virginia had lost her leg in a shooting accident while hunting before the war, and there was little chance she would do without Cuthbert.

But still, the strain of such a long trek on difficult, uneven ground, the steep upward climbs, the battles with snow, all had combined to produce painful blisters at the bottom of her stump, even with the extra padding she had inserted at the outset.

At the moment, she and her companions were in the rustic home of a friendly young couple on the edge of a mountain village—still in France, not yet in neutral Spain. But their guide Juan promised they were on the final segment of their two-day trek through the mountains. Indeed, as they reached the next summit that same morning of November 13, he "turned to the group explaining that the land that lay below us was España."

Far ahead, thankfully there was no snow to be seen. "Virginia looked behind her, comparing the Spanish vista to what they had spent the last forty hours crossing. The tall, imposing snow-covered peaks of the French side were quite a contrast. They had almost made it."

Almost, true, but not quite. Even at the Spanish border, even though Spain was neutral, there could be border guards who did not exactly welcome clandestine travelers like Virginia and her companions. "When they twice saw ski patrols coming down from the summit, Virginia's party fell to the snow-covered ground at Juan's signal," wrote Judith L. Pearson in her 2005 book *The Wolves at the Door.* "Otherwise, they trod lightly and quietly, picking their way past the village of Meranges and into the Serge River valley. Still on Benzedrine (to give them extra energy), they needed to stop only a few times for a bite to eat before they moved on, arriving at their goal, San Juan de las Abadesas, by early evening on November 13."

Here, their guide collected his money and said goodbye. After all, they were in Spain, they would be quartered for the night in three separate safe houses, and all they had to do next was take the first train out the next morning for Barcelona. They would make their separate ways to the railroad station by different routes and meet there.

Before leaving her safe house the next morning, Virginia, a Maryland native now in her thirties, absolutely had to attend to her worsening blisters. Her hostess lent her some salve, saying she could take it with her. "The donation was truly generous and one from the heart," noted book-author Pearson. "Medical treatments were precious in these hard times. After cleaning and medicating her blisters, Virginia tore up the leg of her long johns to fashion a new stump sock and packed its remains and the salve in her bag."

Arriving at the rail station at 4:30 A.M., she soon was reunited with her three companions, but four Spanish civil guards also showed up and took all four fugitives into custody.

Held for twenty days without counsel or opportunity to notify anyone of her whereabouts, Virginia was finally released to a representative of the American consul in Barcelona, thanks to a note carried out of her Mirana del Ebro prison near Figueras by a young prostitute-inmate Virginia had befriended. As a result, the American-born British spy Virginia Hall and her Cuthbert were back in London well in time for Christmas.

Badly injured from her journey, Virginia Hall didn't have to plunge back into the campaign to free France and probably shouldn't have even considered doing so. But now, disguised as an elderly peasant woman with voluminous skirts hiding Cuthbert, she would anyway.

Leaving the British SOE (Special Operations Executive) for the American OSS (Office of Strategic Services), she soon was back in occupied France, once again doing her remarkable and heroic bit to advance the Allied cause against the common German enemy.

Once again making contacts with the Resistance, again finding isolated fields for parachuted supply (and occasional personnel) drops, again helping to plan, even organize sabotage operations, she added secret radio transmissions to her specialties and became London's conduit for orders transmitted to hundreds of Resistance and Maquis fighters in the days before and after the Normandy invasion.

In just one mid-summer period of four weeks, July 14 to August 14, 1944, her biographer Pearson wrote: "She had transmitted thirty-seven messages to London with vital information. She had organized and received twenty-two parachute drops and directed innumerable acts of sabotage. Her group was responsible for killing over 170 Germans and capturing 800 more." Although some of her French lieutenants balked at taking orders from a woman, she was dealing with a fighting force of more than fifteen hundred by mid-1944.

After the war, reluctantly "retiring" to a desk job at the newly formed CIA (Central Intelligence Agency) in Washington, she married Lieutenant Paul Goillot, one of the Frenchmen who had shared her constant risk in the common fight against the occupying Germans. For her extraordinary war service, she was made a Member of the Order of the British Empire as early as 1943 by King George VI. After the war, she was awarded the American Distinguished Service Cross, presented privately and in person by OSS chief William Donovan, with only her own mother on hand to watch.

★★★

Based upon The Wolves at the Door: The True Story of America's Greatest Female Spy *by Judith L. Pearson (The Lyons Press, Guilford, Connecticut, 2005, 2008).*

Liaison Corps

FOR SPENCER R. QUICK OF Chicago, it wasn't always the Japanese he had to worry about while flying tiny single-engine liaison airplanes in China. The other kind of risk could be a mission as "simple" as flying an American officer to headquarters from some remote outpost—such as the day Sergeant Quick was expected to lift a somewhat impatient lieutenant colonel from a rice paddy near Lungling for a ride to HQ at Paoshan.

After landing—squishing down?—in the unexpectedly boggy rice field, Quick tried to explain that taking off again would be, in a word, "difficult." After some discussion as to who was in charge here, the lieutenant colonel "got very angry and threatened to have me court-martialed for disobeying an order."

Quick, a mere noncom, like all liaison pilots flying Stinson L-5s and Piper L-4s for the U.S. Army in China and elsewhere, finally acquiesced. Rank, after all, is rank.

Up to a point, anyway…and it would be Sergeant Quick doing the flying.

Making a circuit of the rice paddy and its dikes by foot, he had taken notice of a long, somewhat dry rice paddy on the far side of one dike. The takeoff would still be "difficult" to say the least, but a plan had evolved in his head. A plan that he kept to himself.

He told his passenger to leave all his gear behind, even his parachute, to lighten their Stinson L-5. In the process of that briefing, Quick somehow failed to mention the adjoining rice paddy. After all, as anyone could see, it was separated from theirs by an impossibly high dike.

After they climbed aboard, Quick taxied around his wet paddy for a time, steadily revving up his speed, to shake off the mud clinging to his wheels and… well, to make a long story short, he quite suddenly made a fast run at the high dike, "bounced the plane hard" just before reaching the earthen wall, bounced over it, wheels just grazing the top, "mushed down into the adjoining field," the dry one, then really bounced the fast-moving plane and got it airborne.

At Paoshan thirty minutes later, a white-faced, thoroughly chastened lieutenant colonel climbed out and said, "I'll never fly in one of these damned things again," but added his thanks and acknowledged, "I know I almost caused both of us to get killed."

All in standard operating procedure (SOP), it seems, for the incredible, intrepid airmen like Quick who day in and day out flew the L-5 and the L-4 in the tough, unforgiving terrain of the CBI—the China-Burma-India theater of war.

That day's work could also mean carrying artillery spotters, ferrying supplies, transporting the mail, or evacuating the wounded from the ever-changing battlefronts of China and Burma. The risk factor was ever there too.

For one light-plane pilot one day, it was a Chinese horse that stepped in front of his L-4 as it was taking off from a sandbar near Seaton. With repairs, the L-4 did survive. The horse did not. Undeterred, pilot Robert M. Smith of Iron Mountain, Michigan, flew out the L-4—no brakes, loose fabric on the left wing.

Smith, it might also be mentioned, flew air evacuation missions for the famous Merrill's Marauders who fought the Japanese in the near-impassable jungles of Burma. "I had a few adventures during that time," Smith acknowledged in the limited-circulation book *The Unsung Flyers*, a collection of first-person accounts by L-plane pilots from all theaters of World War II.

As one such adventure, Smith cited the time he had to make "an instrument let-down from 5,000 feet with no instruments, a broken air speed indicator, a near-dry fuel tank [and] a stretcher patient." All in a day's work. "I pulled out just before hitting some trees and found our air strip in heavy rain."

Another time, "Again with a patient…I experienced a bad down-draft in very hot air at the end of the strip at the base of a hill." Again, all in a day's work for an L-plane pilot. "I made a flat turn up a creek in among the trees with the throttle fire-walled, the airplane lifted out without touching a thing."

Sometimes, however, the hardworking little planes did "touch" a thing or two—like trees, or mountainsides suddenly rising up in front of them.

This was the land of the "Hump," the vast Himalayan range that had to be crossed to reach China from India's Allied bases. Usually, the flying noncoms disassembled their machines for shipment over the Hump by large transport aircraft, then reassembled them on the other side.

The day came, though, when an extraordinary flight of thirty L-planes took on the Hump crossing on their own, with all but one successfully boring their way through the mountains—and storms that tossed about the light aircraft like confetti.

That one, piloted by Lee East of Highland Park, Illinois, was forced down by a thunderstorm, then hurtled headlong into a tree. East was thrown through the windshield and soaked with aviation fuel, but with the help of area villagers and Chinese bandits, he was able to reach his destination of Kunming, China, anyway. The journey, of course, involved a lot of walking.

Spencer Quick (of bouncing-over-the-dike fame) also had an encounter with Mother Earth in his trusty L-5. Caught in a downdraft and slammed against a mountainside, he yet managed to pancake his plane into a "small, tight draw." Like his compatriot Lee East, Quick was thrown partway through the windshield and soaked with gasoline, but he was able—again with villager help—to reach civilization and safety as well.

But another kind of service, a calling, really, still awaited him. It had to do with his mountainside encounter in the CBI. "As I reflected afterwards on what happened to me," he wrote in fellow L-plane pilot Earl F. Nelson's *Unsung Flyers* book, "I slowly realized that God had in fact provided His saving grace to me—as I called out to Him in my terror and agony."

In 1953, Spencer Quick entered the Virginia Theological Seminary to prepare for his real, his lifetime, calling as an Episcopal priest.

★★★

Based upon Unsung Flyers, *first-person accounts collected by Earl F. Nelson. This account published in* Military History *magazine, June 1998.*

Ship's Piano Purloined

WHILE CHAPLAIN PAUL J. REDMOND of the U.S. Fourth Marine Raider Battalion was ashore at Espirito Santo in the New Hebrides, celebrating Mass at a surprisingly convenient and tarp-covered altar, the skipper of the transport ship *President Polk* was still fuming and fretting over the mysterious disappearance of his piano. Here was a twain which, like East and West, might never meet.

Since the Marine Raiders had just debarked from his ship, though, the skipper wasted no time in going ashore and planting himself before the battalion's Lt. Col. James Roosevelt (yes, FDR's Marine Corps son) to demand satisfaction.

The *Polk*, after all, carried very few pianos as a rule. Just one, in fact. And it was the apple of the skipper's eye.

But Roosevelt explained, quite logically, that no object so large and unwieldy as a piano could have become mixed up with the Raiders' fighting gear. Unimpressed, the skipper "threatened dire repercussions" if the piano were not immediately found and returned to its accustomed place aboard ship.

As the search then began, a few hardy men wisely kept their mouths shut. Only years later, in the veterans' newsletter *The Raider Patch*, did the full story come out…in Weston A. Hartman's account of the piano leaving the ship while the officer of the deck was diverted to an unloading "problem" elsewhere.

When the coast was clear, wrote Marine veteran Hartman, he and a few others in 2nd Lt. Thomas J. O'Connor's company rolled the heavily wrapped piano across the main deck to the port gangway, but then had a bit of difficulty easing it onto the gangway. "We finally had to turn it upside down. The piano played an unwritten symphony all the way down."

Below a lighter was waiting—this was a well-planned operation, meticulous in detail. The lighter headed immediately for the beach, where "a Raider recon truck was waiting."

Also waiting was another helping hand, Harold P. Hart, posted on the beach with thirty-two others to guard the offloaded Raider gear. Sometime before, he had been asked "to leave an open spot right off the beach for a 'Special off-load.'"

And then, "precisely on the hour, here comes an unloading barge from the *President Polk* with one huge object well-covered and escorted by several Raiders."

Hart watched admiringly as the recon truck quickly backed up to the barge and took on the "mysterious object." The entire operation was "short and sweet," and Hart certainly would ask no questions. If it came from the *Polk*, he later said, "I was all for it—they had treated us like hogs aboard." In fact, "When we left the ship, we lifted everything that was loose, and if it wasn't loose, we loosed it."

And where was the piano going after its trip ashore? Enter again the chaplain, Father Paul J. Redmond, whose innocent remark some days before had been that it would be nice to have a piano for Mass.

The Raider "padre" then became *aware*, one might say, that a piano had made its way ashore. But he asked the men not to compromise his conscience by telling him where it was.

Ashore also, he had wasted no time in saying Mass for the island natives in the local chapel. The altar he found there "was very convenient in size and height—covered with a tarp, which should have made me suspicious, but didn't." His altar cloth, covering all, furthered the masquerade as the search went on, with the irate skipper now threatening to contact Washington.

When Roosevelt first asked Father Redmond to return the piano, "I truthfully told him I did not know where it was." Now, on direct order from Roosevelt, the chaplain exerted greater efforts on his own. "I made inquiries and honestly, much to my surprise, I had been saying Holy Mass on stolen property!"

The piano was returned, but "with regret." Aboard ship, meanwhile, Marine Captain Donald Floyd, emerging from sick bay and ready to disembark, was startled when the navy insisted on searching his gear before allowing him to leave the ship. "When I asked the reason for this unwarranted action, they wouldn't tell me, but I remember somebody saying 'Roosevelt and his Thousand Thieves.'"

★★★

Based upon Guadalcanal Echoes, *July 1988,* The Guadacanal Campaign Veterans, *with credits to* The Raider Patch, *USMCR Raider veterans, for piecing together the full story.*

A "Duckling" Transfixed

"SHE WAS BEAUTIFUL, A BRUNETTE, elegantly dressed, and obviously a woman of some considerable means. Our eyes met, and she smiled."

They were in a crowded railroad station. "I was standing with my back to the terminal wall, trying to look nonchalant."

Okay, she was a knockout, and his heart suddenly was racing. So, what was the problem? Their eyes had met from across the terminal, and now...here was trouble. She had pushed forward from her own niche over there. She was crossing the floor. And...uh-oh, she was actually approaching!

Now normally, for a young fighter jock, typically handsome, debonair, et cetera, what a setup!

Since this was no normal situation, though, 1st Lt. Harry Bisher had to wonder...wonder with real foreboding. "Out of all these people in the terminal, why did she pick me?"

But no time to think just now. In seconds, the woman, this gorgeous creature, had made the trip across the floor, and now had stopped, right in front of the young American.

His thoughts joined his heart in racing. What to do? How to discourage her? "Why me?" And...yes, right there, that was the real issue. Why him? "I was sure I didn't 'stand out' in the crowd, and she couldn't have mistaken me for an employee of the railroad because each of them wore special distinctive uniforms."

Normally, of course, Harry Bisher would not have been nearly so concerned. He would have been considerably more receptive, even downright friendly. "Any other time and place, I would have been delighted to see such a smile from such a beautiful lady."

Any other place was the key issue, naturally. Harry Bisher, American fighter pilot, was smack-dab in the middle of France—German-occupied France at that. He was in a bombed-out railroad station in Limoges, famous for its fine porcelain. Further, he was a downed American flyer. A combatant as yet uncaptured and making his escape from occupied France. Trying to, anyway.

Worse yet, he was flanked on either side by companions, fellow Allied air crewmen also trying to escape from France while similarly disguised in civvie clothing. "Ducklings" they called each other, since they were to follow their leader from the French Underground, and each other, like a string of ducklings behind Momma Duck.

To make matters even more difficult for Bisher, the one "Duckling" so suddenly put on the spot at Limoges, he was supposed to be deaf and dumb—an excuse, however transparent, for his lack of French language capability. He might be posing as a Frenchman, but he couldn't speak like one. And now what? Here was this Frenchwoman standing expectantly before him, obviously about to speak. What to do with her when she did?

His thoughts and his heart pumped furiously.

Why him, indeed? And there was no doubt. She had glanced his way. She had locked eyes with him. She had crossed the terminal floor. She had stopped right in front of him, Harry Bisher. He was her target. She was an arrow pointed straight at his heart!

And of course she now did speak to him. Smiling all the while too.

Bisher's thoughts still were racing in circles. "We all heard of the Gestapo techniques used in the entrapment of Allied flyers trying to evade capture, and I was sure she must be one of them," Bisher wrote in a 1988 issue *of King's Cliffe Remembered*, the quarterly newsletter produced by and for the WWII veteran members of the Twentieth Fighter Group Association. "I just knew the bulge in her black leather purse was a fully loaded Luger!"

And now she toyed with him. She spoke—in French of course. She posed a question. But he did know just enough French to figure out the question. She was asking about the trains, about the train schedules. *In a French railroad station crowded with French people, this beautiful woman came up to him, to Harry Bisher, of all people, to ask what time the trains ran!*

And now what? How should he respond? Either he must stick to the deaf-and-dumb ploy or he must answer her in his paltry, mangled French.

Neither option appealed all that much.

By this time, too, the "Ducklings" on either side of Bisher had taken notice of the threat. Moments before, as casually as possible, Bisher had flashed a warning look at the "Duckling" right behind him. "He was aware of my situation and must have read my mind because he immediately focused his attention on the 'Duckling' ahead of me. So I knew that if I was to be taken out, at least the chain would not be broken."

Meanwhile, like a scene in a cheap thriller novel, this gorgeous creature who could be either heroine or villainess stood before Harry Bisher, waiting... waiting for his deathless reply. *When did the trains run?*

Still racing about his head were two options—play dumb or answer the woman. "She seemed sincere—and not the least intimidating. I was sure, though, that those were traits the Gestapo female agents practiced all the time."

What to do? If he played on at being dumb, she might raise her voice and attract attention, even if she were for real—just another pretty face instead of a Gestapo agent.

Bisher finally took a plunge after frantic, split-second thinking. He answered. In his "very best" French, he told her, "I don't know. *Je ne sais pas.*" Nothing else, no embellishments, nothing fancy. Just...about those trains, ma'am, I don't know.

With a terse thank you in French, *"Merci,"* she turned and walked away. Not only did she turn away, she didn't look back, she didn't come back, she didn't signal awaiting Gestapo goons. Nothing.

She simply returned to her niche in the crowd on the far side of the semi-ruined rail terminal, seemingly to await her delayed train.

Bisher, in the meantime, gave a quick glance at the "Duckling" to his front in the escape chain, Lt. Col. Robert P. Montgomery. "I looked toward Bob. He took out his handkerchief, wiped his brow, and I knew he was inwardly grinning."

In short while, with no more heart-stopping thrills just there, Momma Duck and her ducklings moved on, eventually to reach the Pyrenees between France and neutral Spain. After various other adventures, both Bisher and Montgomery made their way to freedom. But, "to this day," wrote Bisher in his 1988 account, "I've always wondered why she picked me."

★★★

Based upon King's Cliffe Remembered, *20th Fighter Group Association, 1988.*

Only Harry

TOM, DICK, AND HARRY WERE THEIR names.

Only a relative few of the men residing at Stalag Luft III at Sagan, Germany, sixty miles southeast of Berlin, ever heard of them or knew they were there.

Of the three, only Harry would go places. Both Tom and Dick came to no good end.

Tom's game was up when the Germans cut down trees on his side of the sprawling POW camp devoted to captured enemy aircrews. Dick capitulated to construction of a new compound right over his head.

That left Harry as the one and only escape possibility for the seven hundred RAF and American airmen held in Stalag Luft III's North Compound—a number that was small potatoes, really, by comparison with the entire camp and its ten thousand POWs of many nationalities.

The men in North Compound who knew Harry best were the leaders of "X Organization" and various moles, forgers, watchers, carpenters, and others conspiring to assure Harry's ultimate success.

The X leader was Roger Bushell, a South African lawyer in civilian life, a fighter pilot in war. Shot down at Dunkirk in May of 1940, he was a known escaper who had been warned he would be shot as a saboteur if he attempted to escape again.

Undeterred by such threats, the POW leadership in North Compound was so determined to mount an escape that it had authorized the simultaneous construction of three separate tunnels—*Tom, Dick,* and *Harry.*

The hard, highly secret work underground called upon talents of Welsh miners, American carpenters, British artists and tailors, and forgers from all over. They were needed, variously, to dig the tunnels and shore them up, to devise fake civilian clothes from available uniform items, to produce false identity papers, railroad tickets, and the like.

This was a massive effort with perhaps six hundred POWs taking part...and only two hundred or so actually expected to make use of a good, completed tunnel in one night of undetected use.

The men had moved into North Compound in April 1943. Work began soon after.

In the summer of 1943, the Americans of North Compound suffered a morale blow—they were moved to a newly constructed South Compound that August. They had to leave the tunnels behind. Then came the demise, strictly through circumstance, of Tunnels Tom and Dick.

Harry, though, grew and grew...until, finally, in early 1944, he was ready for the big breakout...today known as the Great Escape.

The chosen night of March 24, 1944, came at last. Bitter cold, six inches of snow on the ground.

The men, many trembling in anticipation, were ready and eager to go. Everybody had his place in an invisible pipeline running from various barracks to Harry's mouth.

Picked in advance, seventy of them would go first as reward for their effort in building the tunnels, prepping for the escape, and/or their fluency in a Continental language. Carrying their phony paperwork and tickets, they would ride trains and try to distance themselves from Sagan quickly. Another 150 RAF crewmen had won their places in the Harry pipeline by lot. Called *hardarsers* by their fellows, they would try walking to safety...*somewhere.*

Soon after darkness had descended, the escape was under way. In Berlin not so far away, though, an Allied air raid commenced. The lights at Stalag Luft III suddenly were snuffed out; the escape was slowed—only seventy-six men had emerged from Harry and headed for freedom when the Germans discovered the operation and stopped it.

Still, seventy-six RAF airmen were on the loose! Hitler was furious. He ordered the execution of any and all upon recapture. When Field Marshal Hermann Goering, head of the *Luftwaffe*, warned Hitler that such stern retribution would be politically undesirable, Hitler reduced his sentence—not all, but still more than half were to be shot upon recapture.

Sadly, in just two weeks, seventy-three of the seventy-six escapees indeed had been rounded up. Fifty of them were selected by General Arthur Nebe, the Criminal Police Chief of Berlin, to be executed; Roger Bushell was among them. The Gestapo carried out the executions.

That left just three survivors of the Great Escape. Two of them already had reached England by the time their fellow escapees were recaptured. The seventy-sixth escapee, the third man still at large, a Dutchman, reached England six months after the breakout by way of Harry.

★★★

Based upon various sources.

Kilroy Really Was

IN THE MIDST OF ALL the savagery of war, of its long tedium and its outbursts of lethal action, there was that one mysterious name that always seemed to get there first—Kilroy.

Shattered walls, crates of ammo, crude road signs…nearly any object that confronted the American GI worldwide bore that mark: "Kilroy was here."

Painted or chalked, the Kilroy message greeted probably millions in every corner of the globe.

And not only the message, but a drawing of a snoop-nosed fellow with beady eyes hanging on to a fence, peering over it—right at you.

No one will ever know the number of fighting men who thought they were the first to reach some important objective, only to find that "Kilroy" had beaten them to it. "Kilroy was here."

Kilroy, of course, had many helpers, and why not? A little humor in the midst of such carnage and destruction could be a rare positive element, a balm helpful to one's sanity.

There was something about the legendary Kilroy, too, that was uniquely

American. Somehow, it strains the imagination to think of the French, the British, the Russians, or the Chinese indulging in like whimsy on such grand scale. The Aussies? Yes, maybe the irreverent Aussies, but surely no one else.

In any case, Kilroy was a "movement" that spread like wildfire. All over the world, previously pristine surfaces blossomed with the Kilroy message. He truly was everywhere.

Even a murder victim in London was left, strangled, near a message scrawled on her apartment wall that Kilroy had been there, a pathetic aberration that really had nothing to do with the Kilroy phenomenon. The killer, it turned out, was a mental patient living next door—a man named Kilroy. Apparently unaware of the worldwide Kilroy joke, he couldn't understand why it took the police so long to track him down. He had left his name, hadn't he? The police, somewhat naturally, had been thinking in terms of a disturbed American GI.

But who, or what, was Kilroy himself? The original Kilroy?

The theories and the claims were many. After the war, it was time to get serious and ascertain the true facts. The Transit Company of America became a prime vehicle, establishing a contest with a prize for the man who could make the claim and back it up with irrefutable proof.

Jim Kilroy, a former Boston city councilman, Massachusetts state legislator, and shipyard supervisor, heard about the contest and joined more than forty other Kilroys vying for recognition as the "real McCoy."

His story (as one by one other Kilroys were eliminated) was fairly simple but convincing. His shipyard job in Quincy, at the Fore River Shipyard, had required him to check the number of rivets driven into place on a given work shift. He would check them off with a slash in chalk as he went, but the riveters would come along later and erase his mark. It seems they were paid on a piecework basis, and if the rivets could be counted more than once, they would be paid twice over.

When management caught on and complained to rivets-checker Kilroy, he began adding the message "Kilroy was here" as he counted off blocks of rivets done.

For some reason, that stopped the riveters from wiping out his work.

Meanwhile, as the newly built ships left their ways at Fore River Shipyard, the Kilroy scrawl often was still visible on beams and other surfaces requiring rivets. GIs on their way overseas saw the chalked message—and took it with them wherever they went to war.

Jim Kilroy's claim was corroborated by his fellow workers from the shipyard, and he won the Transit Company prize, a trolley car. Strange to say, the man whose name somehow shot ahead of nearly every mud-slogging GI overseas was himself never there in person.

What he and his morale-boosting message had done for the war effort, though, was a good deal more than simply make sure his ships had tight rivets in the right places. (And now if only we could find the inspired wag who added that famous, long-nosed caricature that soon popped up alongside the Kilroy message throughout the world of the 1940s!)

★★★

Based upon Richard W. O'Donnell in Naval History *magazine, Winter 1989.*

Square Balloon

A SQUARE BALLOON? THE GOODYEAR rubber people couldn't quite understand—who would want a square balloon? But the emissary from the squash court in Chicago was quite firm. He provided very exact specs, and they said, okay, one square balloon of rubberized cloth coming up.

About two months later, Goodyear Tire and Rubber Company faithfully delivered the square balloon to that odd address—a squash court under the west stands of the University of Chicago's Alonzo Stagg Stadium.

Once unfolded, the big rubberized square neatly matched the squash court's dimensions—as planned. But erecting the balloon in place was a tricky chore. The scientists attempting to manhandle it couldn't see its top. That was when Enrico Fermi, the Italian emigré and Nobel Prize–winning physicist, mounted a rolling scaffold with a raisable platform. Hoisted on high, he shouted his directions to those below—for some time after, they fondly called him "Admiral."

Indeed, theirs in late 1942 was wartime work, vital work to complete a fantastic project before the enemy might do the same.

With the balloon assembled, they then began to build their pile. "They planned their pile even as they built it. They were to give it the shape of a sphere of about 26 feet in diameter, supported by a square frame, hence the square balloon."

A more crucial reason for the square balloon, though, was the ceiling.

As the world now knows, none of this had ever been done before—no blueprints to follow, no schematic drawings, just theory. And no time to fool around.

The ceiling was high enough, according to theory, but the margin for possible error (or unknown factors such as undetected impurities) was admittedly narrow. If the ceiling were not high enough for their pile to do its expected job, they could improve the pile's efficiency by creating a vacuum around it. An earlier experiment at Columbia University with a "canned pile" had "indicated that such an aim might be attained by removing air from the pores of the graphite." At Chicago, they could, if necessary, enclose their pile in the square balloon and pump out all the air inside.

But that would be decided later. For now, the pile began to grow. Its supports were blocks of wood. Next came bricks of graphite. They left a black powder everywhere, on everyone, the floor black and "slippery as a dance floor."

In six weeks, it was done. It would not be a sphere after all, but instead remained flat at the top. It also did not reach the ceiling. No vacuum appeared necessary, either.

On the morning of December 2, 1942, three young men waited on top of the pile as the "suicide squad." If things got out of control, they were to flood the pile with a neutralizing cadmium solution, since cadmium absorbs, extinguishes, neutrons.

"Suicide squad" was a sort of joke, but who knew, really?

Key personnel and witnesses watched from a balcony at the north end of the squash court. Physicist George Weil was stationed on the floor by one of the cadmium rods inserted into the pile. His would be the last to be withdrawn.

Quite unnecessarily for his small audience of fellow scientists, Fermi explained and instructed step-by-step.

At the beginning: "The pile is not performing because inside it there are rods of cadmium which absorb neutrons. One single rod is sufficient to prevent a chain reaction. So our first step will be to pull out of the pile all control rods, but the one that George Weil will man."

A pen on a graph device would trace a line showing the intensity of the radiation, then, at most steps, level off. "When the pile chain-reacts, the pen will trace a line that will go up and up and that will not tend to level off."

And so it went. Up and up, a process taking hours—interrupted, prosaically enough, for a lunch break. With all the rods pulled out but Weil's, he extracted his by predetermined steps. Even at the first one, the radiation measurably increased. "The counters stepped up their clicking; the pen went up and stopped where Fermi had said it would." And each step after that, the same.

By 3:30 P.M., after many such small steps, they had reached the crucial one. Fermi told Weil to pull out his rod by another foot. Turning to the onlookers in the balcony, Fermi said: "This will do it. Now the pile will chain react."

Again, the pen traced its line, and this time there was no leveling off. "A chain reaction was taking place in the pile."

The suicide squad atop the pile tensed, "ready with their liquid cadmium: this was the moment."

But all went well. In the pile—not only of graphite but also layers of uranium and uranium oxide—the first self-sustaining nuclear reaction created by man had taken place.

Later that day, anxious higher-ups in the Manhattan Project who were over-seeing the development of an atomic bomb received word from the Fermi group in Chicago.

The carefully phrased "word" was: "The Italian Navigator has reached the New World."

The question that came back was: "And how did he find the natives?"

Answer: "Very friendly."

Creation of an atomic bomb now looked very doable.

★★★

Based upon Atoms in the Family *by Laura Fermi (University of Chicago Press, 1954).*

"Mush" Morton Legend

LIEUTENANT COMMANDER DUDLEY ("MUSH") MORTON of the U.S. Navy's submarine service would become a legendary figure of the Pacific War, and he showed why on his very first war patrol as skipper of the boat *Wahoo*.

His initial assignment as the submarine slipped away from Brisbane, Australia, on January 16, 1943, was merely to provide reconnaissance of the Japanese fa-cilities and ships at Wewak, an anchorage on the northern coast of New Guinea.

As events would demonstrate, *reconnaissance* meant one thing to the navy planners and quite another to the aggressive Kentuckian at the helm, once described as "built like a bear and playful as a cub."

As the patrol began, the happy-go-lucky Morton was undismayed by the absence of Wewak from the navy's official charts. A speck in the vast Pacific, it simply wasn't shown.

Pure chance came to the rescue: A motor machinist's mate aboard the *Wahoo* had bought a high school atlas while ashore in Australia. Perusing a map of New Guinea, he happened across Wewak and showed it to one of the boat's officers, who of course brought it to Morton's attention. With the help of a Graflex camera, the submariners blew up the map section to match the undetailed navy charts in scale, then set course for the enemy harbor.

Now coming into play was Morton's conception of harbor reconnaissance— still risky in the absence of elementary navigational information such as water depth, position of reefs, and like details. His conception was *not* to stand outside the harbor and look things over through the periscope. "Hell, no," he said, "the only way you can reconnoiter a harbor is to go right inside it and see what's there."

Which is why, on January 24, the submerged *Wahoo* was to be found picking its way through the channel between two islands at the entrance to Wewak's harbor, a painstaking process accomplished with the aid of the boat's echo sounder. Inside the enemy "chicken coop," however, the underwater hunter found few chickens—at first. Only a tug and two patrol boats could be seen through the *Wahoo's* periscope. None was worth an attack revealing the sub's presence and expending its precious torpedoes.

The skipper and crew were disappointed to find so little after their blind sojourn of the nine-mile passage into the inner harbor at maddeningly slow and careful speed.

Soon, however, the masts of a larger vessel could be seen above and behind a screen of palm trees—moving masts, at that.

"Mush" Morton and his crew discovered that a reef barred a closer approach; the *Wahoo* turned and followed the reef to its end, turned again, and headed toward the mysterious ship. At six thousand yards, they raised periscope for a real look at the quarry and found, for a submarine, the worst of all adversaries— a destroyer!

Worse yet, it was broad daylight and in the clear, shallow waters of the harbor the *Wahoo* had been seen. The Japanese warship already was up to speed and maneuvering, first toward open water, then, after four torpedoes launched by the *Wahoo* missed, straight toward the sub itself. The intent was obvious: ramming!

This was serious. The *Wahoo* quickly fired another "fish" at 1,800 yards, "down the throat," or head-on at the charging destroyer.

Missed. Ran wide of the difficult, bow-on target.

The next one, though, launched at last possible moment, set off on a true track. The *Wahoo* crash-dived, and all aboard steeled themselves for the certain depth-charge attack that would follow if the boat's last fish also missed. In these shallow waters, of course, any submarine would be a dead duck.

Instead, there came a heavy explosion, then…nothing.

After a time, Morton cautiously rose close to the surface and raised his periscope. What he saw was most gratifying for any submarine skipper—a rare sight at that. The enemy destroyer had been broken in two, with the bow end fast sinking.

The Japanese aboard the stern section saw their tormentor and opened fire, but that half of the warship also went down in minutes.

His "reconnaissance" finished, "Mush" Morton set sail for the rest of his war patrol, his first as a submarine commander. Thus began a legend that would inspire and excite American submariners throughout the Pacific during World War II. First war patrol. First enemy vessel encountered, a destroyer. Destroyer sunk.

★★★

Based upon Submarine Warriors *by Edwyn Gray (Presidio Press, Novato, Calif., 1988).*

Plea of the White Rose

HANS AND SOPHIE SCHOLL, BROTHER and sister, were students at a university during the war. Committed Christians, they sent a shower of their anti-Hitler *Leaflets of the White Rose* from the upper floors of the university's main building into the inner courtyard below.

"We must attack evil where it is most powerful, and it is most powerful in the power of Hitler," exhorted their leaflet.

They were caught and executed by guillotine. Sophie went to her death, "as if she were looking into the sun," said associates. Sophie, twenty-two, had to hobble forward to her death on crutches, since the Gestapo interrogators had broken her leg.

Hans, about the same age, had been tortured too. But he faced his frightening death "without hatred, with everything, everything below him."

They issued their appeal to fellow students shortly after the German surrender at Stalingrad, early 1943. Their school was Munich University, in the city where Hitler had his political start. His power had snuffed out their protest... but the leaflets, it is said, "went from hand to hand in thousands of copies through all of Germany."

★★★

Based upon Germans Against Hitler: July 20, 1944 *(English edition; Press and Information Office, Government of West Germany, 1964).*

Soothed into Agreement

BEYOND HIS UNTRAMMELED POWER, THE fear he instilled, the rages, Hitler had yet another weapon at his disposal which he used on his generals (or anyone else). "Hitler had a magnetic, and indeed hypnotic personality," recalled the young *panzer* general who developed the tactics for the Battle of the Bulge, Hasso von Manteuffel. "This had a very marked effect on people who went to see him with the intention of putting forward their views on any matter. They would begin to argue their point, but would gradually find themselves succumbing to his personality, and in the end would often agree to the opposite of what they intended."

Manteuffel was one of those also familiar with Hitler's flair for intimidating his generals with obscure facts and figures, but in Manteuffel's view Hitler himself would fall prey to their mesmerizing effect.

Hitler, he said, "had a tendency to intoxicate himself with figures and quantities." He did use them against others: "When one was discussing a problem with him, he would repeatedly pick up the telephone, ask to be put through to some departmental chief, and inquire—'How many so and so have we got?' Then he would turn to the man who was arguing with him, quote the number and say: 'There you are'—as if that settled the problem. He was too ready to accept paper figures, without asking if the numbers stated were available in reality. It was always the same, whatever the subject might be—tanks, aircraft, rifles, shovels."

★★★

Based upon The Other Side of the Hill *by B. H. Liddell Hart (Cassell and Company, Ltd., London, 1948).*

Brothers to the End

THE WARTIME CAREERS OF THE two Stilinovich brothers of Hibbing, Minnesota, were closely matched until the fearful night of St. Patrick's Day, 1943.

Joseph Anthony Stilinovich, twenty, and his younger brother William Joseph, eighteen, both joined the U.S. Navy on November 17, 1942. Both were sent to the Great Lakes for their training, and both then were assigned to the navy's Armed Guard Center in Brooklyn, New York.

The two brothers were separated, though, in their ship assignments. Joseph went aboard the SS *Harry Luckenbach*, which had a crew of fifty-four and twenty-six Armed Guards. William drew the SS *Irene DuPont*, with a crew of forty-nine and also twenty-six Armed Guards.

They were aboard separate ships, but in the same convoy setting out across the North Atlantic. The convoy was designated HX-229, out of New York.

The waiting German U-boats struck the night of March 17, 1943—St. Patrick's Day. Both the *Luckenbach* and the *DuPont* were hit with two torpedoes. Both ships went down, the *Luckenbach* in four minutes, the *DuPont* the following afternoon, after a second submarine attack.

Both stricken ships got off lifeboats, but only one, the *DuPont*, would have survivors to be accounted for later.

The *Luckenbach* launched three lifeboats, and three or four escort vessels spotted them in the water. In the confusion and turmoil of the U-boat attack, however, the onlookers lost track of the lifeboats. No survivors were picked up—no one from the *Luckenbach* was ever seen again, including Joseph Stilinovich.

Aboard the *DuPont*, brother William had reached a lifeboat being lowered down the side, but it capsized. He wound up in a lifeboat holding eight others—and no oars. They drifted past a ship and someone on deck shouted that they would be rescued. But they drifted away. Nearby, another ship was burning brightly.

The abandoned *DuPont* remained afloat the next day. An escorting British corvette tried to sink her with shelling and a depth charge, but to no avail. Then, in the afternoon, the German *U-91* came across the *DuPont* and sank her.

William Stilinovich and his lifeboat companions were picked up by a British destroyer. Of the *DuPont*'s forty-nine crew, twenty-six Armed Guard, and nine passengers, thirteen had been lost.

William Stilinovich had survived and would continue to sail—aboard two more merchant ships—throughout the war, in all its theaters, before his discharge in early 1946.

The Stilinovich brothers are listed in the *History of the United States Navy Armed Guard Veterans of World War II*, where it says that Joseph's "life ended in the waters of the Atlantic, but he will always be remembered by Armed Guard brother William Stilinovich."

★★★

Based upon The Pointer and the Plane Shooter, *December 1988, USN Armed Guard World War II Veterans*.

Young Man Whittling

A U.S. ARMY PRIVATE CAUGHT up in the Tunisian campaign in the spring of 1943 came across a young German soldier in rough North African terrain near Beja. The German had not noticed the American's approach.

They were twenty feet apart, the young German harmlessly whittling a piece of wood.

The American, lying behind a nearby bush, couldn't bring himself simply to shoot. He wondered, Why should I kill him?

But, failing that, what was he to do? If he spoke, the German would spring to action, and the shooting would start.

The American thought seriously of throwing a rock or moving his bush to end the impasse. It just "didn't seem fair…to up and shoot him."

As the private later told doctors in the U.S. Army's Fifteenth Evacuation Hospital near Beja, the dilemma was resolved by another "Jerry."

The second German, a "patrol," came along, spotted the hesitating young GI and shot him. He had arrived in the hospital tents with gunshot wounds of the thigh and the shoulder.

But *his* wounding was not the end of the story. "Made me so…mad I just used all my strength and shot both of them—the boy whittling had grabbed his gun and I know I killed him."

★★★

Based upon A Surgeon's Diary *by Frank W. Peyton, M.D. (Self-published, 1988, Lafayette, Ind.).*

Death of Leslie Howard

WINSTON CHURCHILL THOUGHT IT WAS because of him. A Roman Catholic priest was called off the airplane by an urgent telephone call that later could not be traced to anyone. Passengers who stayed on board had spoken of unsettling premonitions. British actor Leslie Howard, for one, had gone to neutral Portugal and Spain with "a queer feeling about this whole trip."

The KLM airliner, a DC-3 called *Ibis*, took off from Portella airport outside Lisbon, Portugal, at 9:35 A.M., June 1, 1943, with thirteen passengers on board. Leslie Howard was the only famous person aboard, and he was accompanied by his friend and business associate Arthur Chenhall, a heavyset man who smoked cigars.

Their fellow passengers included Reuters correspondent Kenneth Stonehouse; Jewish-relief activist Wilfred Israel; Ivan Sharp, a mining engineer negotiating vital tungsten imports for embattled Britain; Tyrrel Shervington, Lisbon manager for Shell Oil; two other men, three women, and two children.

Dora Rowe, a nanny, would have been aboard with her young charge, Derek Partridge, son of a Foreign Office official, but they were "bumped" at the last minute to make room for actor Howard and his associate, Chenhall.

Father A. S. Holmes, vice president of the Roman Catholic English College, also would have been aboard except for the mysterious phone call to KLM informing him that "he was to report immediately at either the British Embassy or the Papal Nunciature."

The airliner wouldn't wait, and, as he returned to the terminal, the priest paused momentarily to watch *Ibis* roll down the runway and then take off. "Holmes hurried away to make his inquiries, but at neither the Embassy nor the Nunciature could anyone be found who had made the telephone call that had so urgently taken him off the plane. Nor could the switchboard operators remember one being made. He rang the airport again, but they could only repeat the message they had already given him."

Until that same spring, by tacit agreement of the warring parties, the civil air service between Britain and Lisbon had been allowed to fly its daily flights unhindered. Then, a week before Leslie Howard flew into Portugal for a round of lectures on his films and *Hamlet*, as well as on film distribution business of his own, the same *Ibis* had been attacked off Cape Corunna by six to eight German Ju-88s, but after some hits, it eluded them in a cloud bank and flew on to Portugal. That was on April 19, and until then, KLM, or the Royal Dutch Airline, had been flying the route for the British BOAC, undisturbed, for three years. "It had carried over 5,000 passengers between the UK and Portugal without loss and almost without incident."

Even after the April 19 attack, the daytime flights had continued without further incident. Leslie Howard, who played Ashley Wilkes in *Gone with the Wind*, was nervous about his pending trip to Iberia, in part to "show the flag," but he went anyway. In fact, he told one friend, "Well—what the hell—you know I'm a fatalist anyway."

To his wife, Ruth, however, he acknowledged his "queer feeling" about the trip to Portugal and Franco's Spain, the latter neutral, but a near ally to Nazi Germany.

Before the return trip June 1, fellow passengers Stonehouse and Shervington were apparently nervous. Shervington of Shell Oil dreamed that the plane was shot down with him on board. And journalist Stonehouse told a friend: "I'm not normally frightened but somehow I feel bad about this air-trip. I wish I could go to sleep here and wake up at some English airfield."

As *Ibis* lifted off from Lisbon the morning of June 1, the crews of eight German Junkers prepared to take off from the *Luftwaffe* base of Kerlin-Bastard outside of Bordeaux, France, for a roving mission over the Bay of Biscay. What orders the commander of the Junkers wing may have given to the flight leader are not known. The German Atlantic archives vaguely refer to air-sea rescue and U-boat protection, but there is no evidence to support such activities were specifically ordered that particular day.

Whatever the case, the German fighter-bombers and the civilian KLM *Ibis* were soon flying on intersecting pathways through the air.

In spy-infested Lisbon, there was no secrecy to the airliner's departure. Adjoining German Lufthansa personnel could see the crew and passengers board the KLM plane. Among those on board, who might have incurred German wrath? In Berlin's view, British actor Howard was a propagandist and possible intelligence agent (his most recent films had been distinctly anti-German, anti-Nazi). There is evidence that the Germans considered Shervington a British agent. Israel's Zionist activities and work in rescuing Jews from Nazi genocide certainly made him no friend to the Hitler regime. Altogether, not one of the passengers was a friend.

Churchill, at the time, was in North Africa following his recent consultations in Washington. He was due to fly back to England very shortly. (He did, on June 6.)

In his history of World War II, Volume IV, *The Hinge of Fate*, he wrote that German agents apparently mistook a heavyset man at the Lisbon airport for him, cigar and all. "The German agents therefore signalled that I was on board....Although these passenger planes had plied unmolested for many months between Portugal and England, a German war plane was instantly ordered out, and the defenseless aircraft was ruthlessly shot down."

As Churchill also said, but more accurately, it was "difficult to understand how anyone could imagine that with all the resources of Great Britain at my disposal I should have booked passage in an unarmed and unescorted plane from Lisbon and flown home in broad daylight."

Leslie Howard's son, Ronald Howard, agrees that such a scenario would have seemed improbable "even to the dimmest German mind."

The German *Staffel* of Ju-88s soon met the *Ibis* over the Bay of Biscay, and with six of the eight planes attacking the defenseless civil airliner, shot it down into the sea. All aboard were killed—not a trace of them was ever found. Why has been a mystery ever since.

The *why* part "nagged" at Howard's son for many years, he acknowledged in his book, *In Search of My Father*. In reconstructing the last four years of his father Leslie's life, especially the circumstances of his fateful Iberian trip in 1943, Ronald Howard says he "sought a motive for murder—for murder I believe it was—of all those who died that day in *Ibis*."

But after extensive research, with findings of his own, and with review of what others had found before him, "I am still no nearer a positive solution." The missing piece of the puzzle may be the orders given to the German flight leader by his wing commander, Major Alfred Hemm. But after the war, he could not be found. Nearly all in the Ju-88 aircrews had been killed during the war.

As for Churchill's mistaken-identity theory, that doesn't seem likely even by the most elastic of interpretations, since the first announcement of the shooting came from Berlin itself—with the added specifics that the passengers killed included Stonehouse, Leslie Howard—and his heavyset, cigar-smoking associate Chenhall, the only passenger who could have been mistaken for the heavyset, cigar-chomping Churchill.

★★★

Based upon In Search of My Father *by Ronald Howard (St. Martin's Press, New York; William Kimber & Co., Ltd., London, 1981).*

Shipmates to the End

TED AND PAUL WERE SHIPMATES aboard the U.S. light cruiser *Helena*, pals who shared the same fire-director tub, and before any engagement with the enemy in the South Pacific, Paul would say to Ted, "You protect my back and I'll protect yours."

And for Ted, "It was always comforting to know that Paul was at my back."

When the *Helena* was torpedoed shortly after 2 A.M., July 6, 1943, in the Battle of Kula Gulf, however, the two shipmates were briefly separated in the tumult and confusion of a ship going down. Ted Blahnik, in recent years president of the Guadalcanal Campaign Veterans and editor of their *Guadalcanal Echoes*, remembers the sequence of events very clearly.

At 2:04 A.M., speed 25 knots, their cruiser was struck by a Japanese Long Lance torpedo. The blast tore off the forward end of the ship so completely that a torrent of water, a cascade, poured through the ship and even came over Ted's director shield two decks above the main deck. With him in the director tub at the moment were his buddy Paul—Paul Foster—and two young officers.

As the initial burst of water receded, Ted went to the port side of their tub and looked over the side. "I glanced down toward the water just in time to see the unmistakable tracks of two more torpedoes streaking amidships. Time, 0207. Two more thunderous explosions rocked the ship and broke her back."

That was it...the *Helena* was fatally stricken and soon would be going down. The men from the director tub worked their way down to the main deck and prepared to join those abandoning ship. People were jumping into the water, throwing rafts over the side, sliding down lines. This was the expected. The unexpected, though, was that before leaving one way or another, many of the men turned to salute the flag, just like before hitting the gangway for liberty. *Salute the flag.*

Whether for instinctive discipline or love of country, flag, ship, they did it. "It would be most difficult to describe my feelings as I, too, turned and faced the bravely waving battle flag. As I saluted, I thought, 'Good-bye, old girl.' Melodramatic? Yes!"

Over the side and into the water, Ted Blahnik and the men in his vicinity made haste to move away from the sinking ship and her suction. In twenty minutes, she was apparently gone. "A lady to the end. No fires, no internal explosions."

Paul no longer was with Ted; they had become separated, and now neither was there to protect the other's back. In the black night, on the oil-coated water, however, American destroyers were moving about, dark and silent, as they picked up survivors. After a while, they received orders to "clear the area." As they departed, Ted was among those men left to float "aimlessly during the rest of the night." He was wearing a Mae West life jacket but was afraid it would become waterlogged.

"What daylight would bring, we didn't know. We did know, through a briefing the previous night, that we were in enemy territory."

Dawn brought an unexpected sight—"I saw the bow of our ship sticking straight up out of the water not more than a few hundred yards away. It may sound corny, but I couldn't help but feel that she was still valiantly trying to protect her crew of survivors."

Ted now made his way to the upraised bow, slipped on an inflatable life belt in place of the Mae West—and found many of his shipmates clustered in the water around the bow of their ship. Among them was his buddy Paul. Naturally, the two friends were very happy to see each other.

Among the other sailors, though, were men with injuries. One had broken bones that grated with every ripple of the water. "His cries of pain were heart-rending to all of us." And inside the ship? If any were still alive, "Their world, inside the ship, was slowly filling with water and their time was running out."

There was nothing the men treading water outside could do.

Late in the day, an American B-24 spotted the half-sunken cruiser and her survivors. The aircrew dropped two rafts, and the injured were tenderly hoisted onto one of them. Ted and Paul took turns inflating the second raft by hand-pump, then, with others, began taking turns paddling or sliding back into the water to make room for someone else. There was land visible in the distance, but the ocean current took the raft and its men where it wanted.

During the next night, some men simply disappeared—"drifted off into the night." Ted and Paul still were there, but after a second night aboard or along-side the raft, they and two other sailors decided to strike out for the tantalizing island shores near them by swimming and dog-paddling. "By now the number of men in and around the raft had greatly decreased."

What may not be apparent to those never caught in such circumstances is the fast-building disorientation. "It would seem that physical and mental properties wouldn't leave you so soon, but the two days without food or water were taking their toll. What was before an effort to swim to shore became more a matter of drifting and hoping."

So, Ted wasn't really surprised, or even dismayed—not just then—when sometime on that third day Paul called over to him, "I'm going below." Onboard ship, it was something they said a thousand times. "That would simply mean that he was going to go belowdecks." Here, it meant something else, but here both men by now were delirious. Perhaps Paul really thought he was going below decks. In any case, "He took off his life jacket and went 'below.'"

As for Ted, well, he didn't quite realize. "In retrospect, you might ask, How could you lose a shipmate and close friend of more than two years and not give it another thought? Answer: My own mind was beginning to wander. A female voice called to me and asked, 'Why don't you stop at the gas station and have a Coke?' And I answered by saying, 'I can't seem to get there, can you help me?'"

Ted's ethereal female then said no, she had to go to Paris, but he could meet her there that night. "I replied weakly, 'Okay,' and she was gone."

Meanwhile, Ted could make out the sand on the beach that lay ahead! His thirst was "overpowering." He shouted for help or maybe it was "water"…and passed out.

"When I came to, a native outrigger canoe was alongside and a native was brandishing a long knife over my head, demanding, 'American or Jap?'" Luckily for Ted Blahnik, it was the Americans that the knife-brandishing native seemed to like best. In mere moments, "he hoisted me into the canoe and we headed for the beach."

★★★

Based upon Ted Blahnik in Guadalcanal Echoes, *January 1988, The Guadalcanal Campaign Veterans.*

Stalingrad's "White Rose"

IF STATUES COULD ONLY SPEAK, the memorial sculpture of a comely young woman in the Soviet Union's Donetsk region would tell a Shakespearean tale of triumph and tragedy, romance and bitter revenge.

Lydia Litvak, a Muscovite born in 1921, had been flying for four years when Nazi Germany launched its massive invasion of the Soviet Union in June of 1941. She answered the call for female pilots from the reeling Soviet air force and won appointment to the all-female 586th Fighter Air Regiment. After brief emergency training, she and her companion flyers of the Russian Yak-1 found themselves based at Saratov on the Volga River, just north of Stalingrad…just as Hitler launched his second summer offensive in May 1942. By September, the major battleground would be Stalingrad.

By that time, too, the USSR's standard, all-male fighter ranks had been so depleted by combat with the *Luftwaffe* that women were allowed to fight along-side the men. "Lydia was one of the chosen few, now being assigned to the Soviet Seventy-third Fighter Air Regiment."

She was not guaranteed instant acceptance, however, especially in the Seventy-third, which had earned itself special "free hunter" status allowing its aircrews to range far and wide in search of opportune targets, rather than sit on the ground awaiting alerts to scramble and intercept oncoming German forces. "On her first day of duty, Lydia suffered the humiliation of standing helplessly by her assigned Yak fighter and watching a strange male pilot climb aboard and zoom off into the skies."

Lydia had spent months of air-combat duty defending Stalingrad from German bombers, but that apparently didn't count with the Seventy-third's CO, who had no intention of sending her out with any of his elite "free hunters." Enter, then, the CO's best friend, a future Hero of the Soviet Union with many "kills" to his credit, one Alexei Salomaten. Let Lydia fly at least one patrol as his own wingman, argued Salomaten, and then see if she should stay in the unit or be transferred out. The CO agreed, and off they went the next day.

First, though, Alexei told her to simply follow close behind and duplicate his "every maneuver," rather than worry about protecting him. On their patrol, they went through violent maneuvers; Lydia heard gunfire, and occasionally glimpsed other aircraft in the sky with them. But she concentrated entirely on following her newfound friend.

"Upon landing, the young woman was surprised to learn that her leader had assisted another Russian pilot in shooting down an Me-109. Nevertheless, the beaming Alexei praised her skill in sticking with him, then reported his satisfaction with her wingman performance to their com-mander. Lydia thereafter fought with the 'free hunters' throughout the rest of the battle of Stalingrad."

Not only fought, but soon became known, to German and Russian alike, as the "White Rose of Stalingrad"—for the flowery emblem painted on the nose of her fighter, by now a Yak-9. As her "kills" mounted, they were signified by smaller roses painted on her plane. By the end of 1942, Lydia had shot down three enemy fighters and three transports. She, herself, had gone unscathed, as had Alexei—by now not only her partner in the air, but her constant companion and lover on the ground.

With the collapse of the German Sixth Army's assault upon Stalingrad in early 1943, their Seventy-third Fighter Air Regiment was transferred to the Donbass region. There, while scoring her ninth downed enemy plane, Lydia herself was wounded and forced to make a wheels-up landing in her damaged Yak-9. She recovered, though, and returned to duty in the unusual and prestigious role of a flight commander in the still mostly male outfit.

Known as "Lilya" to her friends, Lydia Litvak would score a total of twelve enemy "kills" as the Soviet Union's leading female ace of the war, but not without personal tragedy. "One day, Alexei took a new replacement pilot aloft to teach him the latest techniques of winning a dogfight against a German. Far below, Lydia watched the graceful aerial duel when, to her horror, tragedy struck. Alexei suddenly lost airspeed in a particularly sharp turn and spun into the earth. The young blonde neither cried out nor shed a tear during the entire episode, but her face was a twisted mask of anguish."

With Alexei gone, Lydia threw herself into one combat after another with "an almost obsessional desire to defeat the Germans." There was no shortage of opportunity in the spring and summer of 1943, and one duel matched her against a *Luftwaffe* ace with more than twenty "kills" of his own. They fought for fifteen minutes before the Me-109 went sailing to the earth below in flames (the pilot managed to bail out first).

As a fateful day in August approached, Lydia herself escaped two close calls: In one case, she again had to make an emergency landing in a damaged plane and in the other she had to bail out of a burning Yak-9.

Then came August 1, 1943, and with "a bullet-injured right hand, the 22-year-old blonde sortied at daybreak." She and her companions encountered bombers and fighters. Lydia briefly disappeared in a cloud while tangling with two Me-109s. Minutes later, through a break in the clouds, one of her fellow Yak pilots caught a glimpse of Lydia's fighter smoking, with eight German fighters in pursuit.

No wreckage, no body, was ever found. If only the memorial statue at the town of Krasny Luch, close to where Lydia Litvak vanished that August morning, could speak, perhaps it would tell the exact details of her final fate.

★★★

Based upon Truman R. Strobridge, Military History *magazine, December 1986.*

★ ALLIES ON ★
ASCENDANCY

"Hey, We're on Your Side"

OFF THE ISLAND OF USTICA, thirty miles north of Palermo, one August night in 1943, the U.S. Navy subchaser *SC 530* was in a bit of a quandary—if ships can be imagined to feel a quandary sort of situation. Earlier in the evening, *SC 530* had finished escorting a slow-moving, freshwater barge to the dry, thirsting island from Sicily's port city of Palermo.

Moving along at all of four knots, the two vessels didn't arrive until the middle of the night. Soon after, radar showed two large blips roaring up on the minuscule subchaser and her ward. At half a mile, visual identification established the two intruders as cruisers.

SC 530's concern at this point was to make it clear that she herself was not the enemy. Allied ships, by mistake, had been known to fire at Allied ships. *SC 530* quite properly "challenged the lead cruiser by flashing light."

The reply was a salvo of cruiser shells—they flew overhead, happily enough.

Disconcerted but stubborn, *SC 530* tried again, after double-checking the correct naval routine. Again a mean salvo from the lead ship.

Still game, *SC 530* next tried turning on her coded recognition lights. Any Allied ship would get the point. This time, both advancing cruisers unleashed their fire.

The moment had come, really, to make sure the cruisers understood whose side *SC 530* was on. *SC 530* turned her twelve-inch signal light on herself, then directed the light at the cruisers.

"That did it," wrote retired U.S. Navy Commander Edward P. Stafford. "The two cruisers ceased firing, reversed course, and sped off into the night."

Naturally, there would be an epilogue. "The next morning, back in Palermo, the *530's* skipper stormed into Operations and complained bitterly about being fired on by his own ships when he had been doing all the right things to establish his identity. But he became very calm and quiet when the duty officer informed him that the ships he had encountered were not friendly but Italian cruisers, probably bound for Palermo to shoot up the harbor. Apparently his illumination had spoiled their intended surprise and they had returned to base."

Indeed, as later established, they had been the *Raimondo Montecuccoli* and the *Eugenio di Savoia*, out of Sardinia and headed for Palermo, but thwarted on their way by the prim and proper *SC 530*.

★★★

Based upon Subchaser *by Edward P. Stafford (Naval Institute Press, Annapolis, Md., 1988).*

"Smoking Too Much"

AT SALERNO THE SECOND WEEK of September 1943, the going for the American and British Allies was rough—so rough that overall commander Mark Clark came within an ace of withdrawing the entire landing force. The British Eighth Army had landed near the tip of the Italian boot earlier, but the Fifth Army show at Salerno, on Italy's west coast, was the big one, the main Allied thrust.

It had to succeed and almost didn't.

The Italians had just surrendered, but the German forces under Albert Kesselring wasted no time in establishing their own control of the country— and moving to block the two Allied armies invading Italy.

Going ashore at dawn on September 9, the American VI Corps (Thirty-sixth and Forty-fifth Infantry Divisions) and the British X Corps (Fifty-sixth and Forty-sixth Divisions) had won their narrow beachhead, it appeared. On September 12, however, Kesselring's forces struck back so furiously that the outcome of the Allied invasion was very much in doubt.

As many as two thousand Allied air strikes and repeated bombardment by offshore navy ships greatly aided the troops ashore in finally turning back the German counterattack. The Eighth Army, moving up from the south under Sir Bernard Montgomery, made its linkup with the newly landed Fifth Army on September 16—the Allies were in Italy to stay, although they still faced a stubborn, vicious campaign that would not truly end until the war in Europe was over in the spring of 1945, a year and a half later.

Richard Plunkett, an American sailor aboard the U.S. light cruiser *Boise*, kept a diary during the Salerno campaign, highlighted by his argument, "The Fifth Army would have been pushed back into the ocean if it hadn't been for the Navy!"

His cruiser was elsewhere the very day of the invasion at Salerno, busy dropping off British Commandos at the Italian naval base of Taranto, since the Italians had just surrendered. The *Boise* then dashed to North Africa, where orders suddenly changed and *Boise* set out for Salerno at high speed.

The warship arrived in Salerno Bay September 12, the day of the major German counterattack, and soon was in the thick of a desperate fight to sustain the beachhead.

Sept. 12: Around 12:30 P.M., six Fw-190s attacked us. Dropped bombs. No damage.

Sept. 13: Germans bombed one of our hospital ships. Another dive-bomb attack. Were Me-109s. Tried like hell to get us.

There were more air attacks that same day, with a near miss on *Boise's* sister ship, the *Philadelphia*.

Sept. 14: Fired 1,500 rounds of ammo. While firing, had air raid. Dive-bombers got one transport and one LST. They came at us again and dropped one radio-controlled bomb which exploded right off our fantail—missed us again (pretty lousy). One plane was shot down.

Sept. 15: We are still in the gun turret firing on the beach, while air raids are going on all day long. Dive-bombers got two more LSTs. Bomb after bomb were dropped all around us. What a hell of a place! Smoking too much.

On September 16, the *Boise* stopped firing at 5:10 A.M. with only 503 six-incher shells left. But thirty minutes later, "we fired all of that." As more *Luftwaffe* dive-bombers appeared, shrapnel flew all around.

Sept. 16: We are very lucky, furious fighting on the beach.

Now, the *Boise* headed back to North Africa for more ammunition, arriving about 11 A.M.

Sept. 16: Loading 3,000 rounds of 6-inch; fuel up. Worked like hell.

Sept. 17: Arrived in Salerno, laid smoke screen to protect ship. USS Savannah hit with radio-controlled bomb on Turret No. 3. Badly damaged. 200 casualties.

But later that same day, for the *Boise* anyway, it was all over.

Sept. 17: Beach under control. Got underway for Palermo, Sicily. Very glad to get out of here, am very tired.

★★★

Based upon letter by Richard R. Plunkett, retired plumber, former U.S. Navy sailor aboard the USS Boise.

Close Call for FDR

THE EXCITEMENT ABOARD THE BRAND-new battleship *Iowa* was brief but palpable one mid-November day in 1943. On her way to Oran, Algeria, with a screen of destroyers, *Iowa* played "target" for a destroyer simulating a torpedo run on a battleship.

The *William D. Porter* wheeled into her "attack." So far, so good…nothing unusual.

But suddenly the destroyer's whistle shrieked in alarm, and the *Porter's* officer of the deck came hard on the radio: "Lion, Lion, Lion: come right, come hard right!"

Inadvertently, the *Porter* had loosed a live one—the *Iowa*, commissioned only the previous February, really was at the wrong end of a torpedo track.

While a visitor on the big ship's bridge continued to watch the flotilla's tactical exercises, the *Iowa* surged into a hard turn. Seconds later, the errant "fish" hit the battleship's wake and exploded, just a half mile astern.

At this point the voice radio did some exploding, as both the *Iowa* and the commander of the destroyer division gave vent to their respective reactions. The language, they say, was purple.

One concern, of course, was the brand-new ship and her crew. Another was that man on the bridge; the one on the first leg of a journey to Teheran for a conference with Joe Stalin and Winston Churchill—the wartime commander in chief, Franklin Delano Roosevelt.

★★★

Based upon John C. Reilly in Pull Together, *newsletter of the Naval Historical Foundation and the Naval Historical Center, Vol. 27, No. 1, Spring/Summer 1988.*

Riding Enemy's Truck

For Lieutenant H. Lathrop, B-17 pilot, January of 1944 provided, if that is the word, one close call after another. First, on a raid over Ludwigshaven, Germany, his faithful Flying Fortress was hit by flak. Number Three engine was knocked out of action.

The big bomber plugged along anyway, crossing back into occupied France. But, Number One engine "was running hot," and the vibration was so bad, Lathrop had to drop out of formation...a sitting duck for any wandering German fighters. He told his crewmen to jump, bail out.

But then he had the plane under improved control and rescinded the order. Perhaps they would all get back to England after all. Coming out from a 1,500-foot cloud cover, however, they ran into fighters. In seconds, Number Two was a goner. Fire broke out behind the cockpit while the elevator controls and right aileron took damage. This time was for real. "Bail Out!" bawled Lathrop as he hit the alarm button.

Elevator control soon gone altogether, his bomber tried to climb a wall and stalled...all her crew gone by now, except for pilot Lathrop. He jumped at only nine hundred feet.

He injured his back when he hit the ground seconds later, but he at least survived the jump. He saw a farmer nearby, a "friendly," ran to the man, and asked—yelled, most likely—"Where are the Germans?" The man pointed his finger, and Lathrop pelted off in the opposite direction.

"As I ran down the hill, I hastily discarded my flying equipment and burst out on a road and almost ran into a car surrounded by German officers."

He and the farmer had misunderstood each other! Instead of running *from* the Germans, Lathrop had run *to* them. Now, "I did a quick about-face and ran as hard as I could in the opposite direction."

He heard shots and plunged into heavy underbrush nearby—and there he remained hidden for the next three hours. The far side of his shrubbery patch was bordered by a path—enemy soldiers passed to and fro constantly. At one point, "seven men stepped close enough to touch me, dropping a pile of the crew members' chutes and equipment while they argued with one another."

There had been a search, with Germans poking staves into pilot Lathrop's small "briarpatch," but never quite in the right place. "I was saved by two of the dumber ones who should have converged on my bush but instead stopped to talk."

This B-17 bomber is obviously doomed. (National Archives)

Darkness fell with the quarry still at large. Lathrop stealthily made his way in the direction the farmer originally had indicated. "It was sleeting now, and my back ached, so I looked for a haystack." He didn't find a haystack, and a local turnip shelter wasn't much help, either. Lathrop walked on.

Spotting a light, he found a stable; inside, he found a young boy "frightened half out of his wits." Calming the youngster, Lathrop spelled out his thirst and hunger by sign language—the boy gave him some beer, then they bedded down for the night.

The next day—daylight—of course would bring new perils for a downed American airman such as Lathrop. For one thing, in his leather flight jacket, he would stick out in the French countryside like the proverbial sore thumb. So, he paid the boy one hundred francs and the leather jacket as a swap for a manure-crusted old black coat that trailed all the way, manure and all, to the American's knees. "Despite this we both were pleased with the exchange."

So equipped, Lathrop decided to head for one of the most dangerous spots he could have picked—occupied Paris. With so many people in one spot, he calculated, his chances of finding help were all the better than in open country. He trudged along a network of roads, hiding in a ditch whenever he heard traffic coming. One time, though, he turned a corner and came upon German trucks and troops halted in the roadway ahead.

To turn and run would have been too conspicuous, so he walked "right through them," odoriferous coat and all. Another obstacle was a roadside work camp with the guards just lining up in formation. Incredibly, Lathrop later said, "[I] elbowed my way through them without difficulty."

Just beyond the work camp, he found a sympathetic elderly man who rushed the downed flier into a run-down house and fed him bread, butter, wine, and a small piece of rationed meat. "I was given pants to wear over my Army trousers and a scarf to hide my shirt. In broken English, they told me the way to the nearest town, and I managed to get halfway through it without attracting attention."

In the town square, though, he stopped to ask a young man for help, in sign language again. No luck—indeed, the Frenchman, who didn't seem to "understand," moved away and headed for the nearest German soldiers.

Moving on quickly, Lathrop hopped a truck-led trailer. Never mind that it was German—the driver and his armed guard up front couldn't see the hitch-hiker on the rear. He, in the meantime, disembarked after a ride of several miles. The jumping off aggravated his back, but no matter...for this indomitable airman from the 364th Squadron of the U.S. 305th Bombardment Group (Heavy), there still was an escape to complete.

First came another ride on a German vehicle, since walking was now painful to the back. This time it was a lumbering brick truck. As it passed people on the road, Lathrop waved amiably, but a man on a bicycle approached, fired some questions, then rode away visibly irritated.

Lathrop didn't understand that the French considered it bad taste, unpatriotic, to ride with the German occupiers in any vehicle.

When the brick truck passed two women on the road, he jumped off to seek their help. A lucky choice, it turned out. The older woman guided him to a nearby farmhouse, where he was given food and arrangements were made for the Underground to smuggle him out of the country.

At last, he had made the appropriate contact! And he did reach safety shortly after, but first there was one more close call. On the way out of France with his Partisan helpers, Lathrop bumped into the same bicycler who had seen him riding the German brick truck. The Frenchman accused him of being a col-laborator and nearly wrecked the escape operation on the spot. "It was touch and go for my safety at first, but fortunately I had proof of my identity, so I proceeded to England."

★★★

Based upon The Incredible 305th: The "Can Do" Bombers of World War II, *by Wilbur H. Morrison.*

"Sure Am Sorry"

THE MULES BROUGHT THEM DOWN from the Italian mountains to a place in the valley where there was a road, a low stone wall, and a cowshed. The dead.

Casualties from the Thirty-sixth Division: Texans mostly.

Ernie Pyle's dateline said January 10, 1944. *From the frontlines in Italy*. In the moonlight, he was down there at the bottom of that long trail negotiated by mules with their awkward, stiff-legged burdens.

"I don't know who that first one was," he wrote for the folks back home to read. "You feel small in the presence of dead men, and ashamed of being alive, and you don't ask silly questions."

He did find out who one of them was, though—Captain Henry T. Waskow of Belton, Texas, a company commander in the Thirty-sixth. Mid-twenties, he was—had been.

Ernie Pyle "never crossed the trail of any man as beloved."

They laid them all down tenderly. By the stone wall, and in a shadow.

He came down and his body was unlashed with four others, and all were laid down there by the wall, end to end.

Something special about Captain Waskow, though.

"After my own father, he came next," a sergeant told Ernie Pyle.

"I've never knowed him to do anything unfair," said another GI.

"He always looked after us," said a third. "He'd go to bat for us every time."

His men didn't want to leave him.

"They stood around, and gradually one by one I could sense them moving close to Capt. Waskow's body. Not so much to look, I think, as to say something in finality to him, and to themselves."

One by one they went close and spoke their good-bye. Or thought it.

Out loud, one of them said, "God damn it," and a second one said, "God damn it to hell anyway."

Another, possibly an officer himself, came close and said, "I'm sorry, Old Man."

A GI followed. "I sure am sorry, Sir."

The first man came back, squatted by his dead captain, and took his hand. He held it for five minutes, looked into his captain's face and said no more, nothing at all.

"And finally he put the hand down, and then reached up and gently straightened the points of the captain's shirt collar, and then he sort of rearranged the tattered edges of his uniform around the wound. And then he got up and walked away down the road in the moonlight, all alone."

★★★

Based upon Brave Men, *by Ernie Pyle (Grosset and Dunlap, New York, 1943).*

Oops, No Parachute

TIME: WORLD WAR II. POINT: Amazing story of survival. Name, rank, branch of service: Reed, R. B., Sergeant, U.S. Army Air Forces. Operational detail? Well, they didn't promise a milk run for the big, square-nosed Liberator, but who would have expected? Who could have predicted?

When the flak hit Sergeant R. B. Reed's Consolidated B-24 Liberator over Bolzano, Italy, the sequence of events for the American tail gunner sped up like a film strip in a movie projector gone wild. The big bomber was on a dangerous mission, to be sure—pounding the Bolzano rail yards at the Italian end of the Brenner Pass. As Reed would say later, "Bolzano flak was famous for its accurate intensity, to say nothing of the daredevils of the German *Luftwaffe*."

The unwelcome American intruder had just reached this hornet's nest—the signal for bombs-away had just been given—when the first flak struck Reed's bomber and "ripped our oxygen lines to shreds."

From his distant position way down at the tail end of the airplane, he watched as the waist gunners scrambled to patch the lines with adhesive tape—tried to patch them, that is, since things were happening too fast…*bad* things.

"It was raining shrapnel," Reed remembered. And there came a hit behind the radio cubicle. It was a hit violent enough to nearly jar Reed's head loose, as he later described it.

And then the waist section was all in flames, the fire spreading rapidly. And…

Reed had left his parachute right up there by the waist window! He would have to go get it. He absolutely needed that chute! This Liberator obviously was not going to stay airborne much longer.

"I started through the flames for it," Reed recalled. "I tore the oxygen lines in my hurry to get to the chute." He later would recall the searing heat. And his trouble breathing. Suddenly, he blacked out. And there he was—unconscious and still back there in the tail section of the stricken bomber. No chute, either.

Next—and who knows how much later it was—came a "rush of cold air." It woke him up. "I found myself alone, speeding earthward in the tail of a B-24," Reed recalled. And where was the crew? "Crew, hell! Where was the rest of my ship?"

As was now evident, the tail had been completely severed from the plane. The facts, like the cold air, were rushing in upon him. "Earth and clouds formed a dizzy pattern as I spun round and round—and no chute for a jump to safety!"

Basically, that was it. He was plunging to earth from twenty-two thousand feet with no parachute, no means of cushioning his fall.

It is not merely prosaic to say twenty-two thousand feet is a long way down… the fact is, it takes a while, and so what would anyone in Reed's circumstance think about (besides a fervent prayer!) on the way down? *Hurry up the trip or slow it down considerably?* Which way would he prefer it? That's what the sergeant thought about all the way down, alone in his severed tail section.

"To say that I braced myself for the shock of landing would not tell the story," said Reed.

"It wasn't easy to brace my mind for it! In a way, I was anxious to get down; at the same time, I dreaded it." Reed suddenly and harshly hit earth. "With a nerve-jarring crash, the tail smashed right through a clump of trees and came to rest on the ground below."

When Reed opened his eyes, he was, incredibly, on terra firma. "I came to lying in the snow, still in one piece," he recalled. "My face was burned and suffered bruises, but no bones were broken."

A German patrol came along shortly afterward, and the enemy had little trouble making a prisoner of war of tail gunner Reed. His fall of twenty-two thousand feet had brought understandable results—a "nervous reaction that made me weak." In fact, at the moment he was captured, he was "too exhausted physically and mentally to care."

★★★

First published in Military History *magazine, October 1994, and based upon* The Shoe Leather Express, Book II, *by Joseph P. O'Donnell, chairman of American Ex-Prisoners of War, Continental Chapter.*

War Story

AH, THE STORIES THEY DO tell! Like maybe the B-17 that made it back with holes in the fuselage big enough for a jeep to drive through! Like the time, on a bombing run against a German airfield near Rheims, France, on March 28, 1944, fighter-pilot Chester A. Hallberg (Fifty-fifth U.S. Fighter Squadron, Twentieth Fighter Group) saw the *Whodat* out of Ridgewell catch a direct flak hit that threw the Flying Fortress into a violent spin.

Flying escort for the bombers, Hallberg and his mates were above, at eight o'clock high. "I watched for parachuters as the big friend spun down—from an altitude of about 24,000 feet, as I recall. There were none. But while I watched, the pilot pulled the plane out of the spin at about 12,000 feet."

Aboard the *Whodat*, both waist gunners and the tail gunner had been killed by the hit. Pilot Daniel C. Henry had rung the bail-out bell. Seconds later, fighting to control the stricken craft, he rescinded the "jump" order.

While Henry and his copilot, Bob Crisler, fought the controls, their rudder cables severed and the elevators jammed at "up," Flight Engineer Sebastian Quarema spliced the cables together with loose wiring. But the result was that pulling back on the controls nosed the ship down, and pushing them forward pulled her up. Just the reverse of normal operation.

Outside, Hallberg took his flight of P-38 Lightnings down to the big bomber's assistance. Obviously, if *Whodat* somehow could stay in the air, she would need close escort all the way home. As Hallberg slowed and pulled in close to see the extent of the damage, however, he was "horrified."

The starboard side of the fuselage "had been blown away from the waist gun to the rear door." On the port side was another hole half as big. "It was a miracle that the crate held together."

But it did, and the *Whodat* staggered back to England, where it was decided that the crew should bail out rather than attempt even a crash landing in their battered ship. Five of the seven flak survivors successfully jumped above their Ridgewell base, then pilots Henry and Crisler headed their Fort over the English Channel before safely bailing out themselves. The big Fort crashed harmlessly in the water.

For years, though, fighter pilot Hallberg had no idea how the difficult flight home really ended. He and his wingman, Philip Pearson, had stayed with *Whodat* as far as the English coast, but then they had to fly for home themselves, their fuel gauges "flirting" on empty. "I never knew if they landed safely or if they lived through the war," he wrote in 1986. Hallberg found out, though, through an article appearing in the *Friends of the Eighth* [Air Force] newsletter; he thus learned that all seven men still alive on *Whodat* after the flak hit did get home safely and that all seven were able to finish their combat hours in Europe unscathed.

Hallberg, like them, had never forgotten the *Whodat* and the crew's feat of getting her home again. "The fighter escort mission on March 28, 1944, was relatively uneventful—except for [that] one unforgettable moment when I witnessed one of the most fantastic displays of skill and courage to be seen in my 74-mission tour of duty in the ETO."

★★★

Based upon King's Cliffe Remembered, *20th Fighter Group Association, Vol. 5, No. 1, January–May, 1987.*

Courage Extended

THE YOUNG MAN NEVER SHOULD have been there. He somehow had managed to avoid the physical examination normally required to enter military service. He later moved on to choose an assignment involving extremely hazardous duty in a hot combat zone.

And yet, look at his medical record.

As a child, he had the usual bouts of both kinds of measles and chicken pox, but he almost died from scarlet fever. He was slower to recover from the normal childhood illnesses than his siblings. The record would indicate even then a bad back, a delicate stomach.

"He went along for many years thinking to himself—or at least trying to make others think—that he was a strong, robust, quite healthy person who just happened to be sick a good deal of the time," his mother once wrote.

At prep school, unfortunately, it was more of the same. He may have suffered from hepatitis or jaundice. Some sources vaguely cite a "blood disease." Whatever the exact cause, the school's headmaster once blamed his "lack of intellectual drive" on "a severe illness" that struck in the teenager's junior year. Said the headmaster also: "Though he has recovered, his vitality has been below par, he has not been allowed to enter into very vigorous athletics, and has not, probably, been able to work under full pressure."

Hardly a recommendation for his imminent role as a commander of men under continually demanding wartime conditions.

Next, in 1935, he would have spent a year in London with the noted scholar Harold Laski of the London School of Economics as his tutor, but the boy abruptly returned home after only a month in England. The young man's ambassador father later wrote, "I took him abroad last year, but he had a recurrence of a blood condition and I brought him home to be near his doctors."

The youth briefly attended Princeton University that fall, enrolling late, in October. He then, in December, entered a Boston hospital for what evolved into an admission lasting for two months, with only fatigue and "general malaise" known today as the cause. He next spent time on a ranch in Arizona, apparently recuperating and regaining his strength.

Applying to Harvard in 1936, he himself wrote that he had attended Princeton the year before to be "closer to my doctors in New York." He pursued his undergraduate college degree for the next four years without encountering really major health problems, but his bad back did make him leave the freshman football team, while a month spent in bed during his second year did mean giving up aspirations to join the swimming team.

In the summer of 1938, an unspecified illness forced an early end to a tour of continental Europe on the eve of Hitler's march into Poland a year later. Returning to London earlier than planned, wrote his traveling companion and college roommate Lem Billings later, "Jack got desperately sick....His face was all puffed up and he got a rash and we didn't know anybody to even get a doctor."

Still, the young man managed to graduate from Harvard on schedule, in the spring of 1940, and *cum laude* at that!

The medical record for the next year and a half is not entirely clear, but Doctors Kenneth R. Crispell and Carlos F. Gomez of the University of Virginia cited various clues to continuing problems in their 1988 book, *Hidden Illness in the White House*. Among them: a note from *New York Times* columnist Arthur Krock expressing hope for "a turning point in the record of your health," plus an unexplained stay in Boston's New England Baptist Hospital.

With war already raging in Europe, young Jack joined older brother Joseph in volunteering for military duty in the late summer of 1941. A routine check of his medical records "would have been enough to disqualify" the eager volunteer at that early stage of the war, noted Crispell and Gomez in their book. "His records would have shown a young man of twenty-four years of age, with a chronically weak back, whose recurring illnesses since childhood had forced him at various times to interrupt his life with prolonged hospitalizations."

Nonetheless, "Jack was sworn in, without a physical examination, on September 25, 1941." His branch of service was the U.S. Navy. By July 1942, he was in officer candidate school at Northwestern University. He heard about the Navy's patrol-boat (PT) units operating in the Pacific, no physical examination required. Enthralled, he applied.

His ambition "to skipper one of these boats was probably ill advised," wrote Crispell and Gomez. "Built out of cheap, light-weight materials, the PT boats were armed with torpedoes and were designed to carry out quick, destructive sorties against larger, more cumbersome Japanese vessels. As they skipped rapidly over the surface of the water, the flimsily constructed boats delivered bone rattling jars to the crew aboard. It was not only dangerous work, but exhausting and enervating as well. It was not the sort of assignment for one with a history of back pains and susceptibility to fatigue, among other things."

The young man had applied...he was accepted. The newly commissioned young ensign graduated from his PT-boat training at the end of 1942. But he did not ship out for the Pacific immediately thereafter. First, he fell ill again and "was out of commission for several weeks." Still in America, he was treated "for what some of his crew remember as back pain, others as 'fatigue.'"

Once he did reach the Pacific war zone, he underwent the exhaustion and stress of haphazard diet, makeshift shelter, and interludes of combat, hot and heavy, with courage and grace. Young Jack Kennedy's heroics as commander of the sunken *PT 109* are well known as an essential part of the JFK story...far less known are the courage and endurance he showed during the year he spent in the Pacific—still troubled, it can hardly be doubted, by his delicate health.

In *The Search for JFK* by Joan Blair and Clay Blair, the widow of JFK's fellow PT-boat commander Lennie Thom is quoted as saying that her husband's letters from the combat zone cited worries "about Jack's health." Further: "He wrote me that Jack was ill—he didn't say what was the matter but that a team of horses couldn't get him to report to sick bay. Lennie said Jack feigned being well, but he knew he was working under duress."

If so, should JFK have continued to be the man most responsible for his crew's well-being? Could other PT-boat crews, other units, rely upon his best performance in combat? Such ethical questions aside, authors Crispell and Gomez point out, "The chronic shortage of fighting men in the Pacific, especially officers, would…have made Kennedy's superiors reluctant to relieve him of command had they noticed that he was less than fit."

Whatever the case, he survived a high-risk combat tour in the Pacific—and the Japanese sinking of his *PT 109* that made castaways of JFK and his crew for nearly a week. Consider, too, "He had served for nearly a year on board a type of ship which the Navy had, from the outset, classified as 'expendable.'"

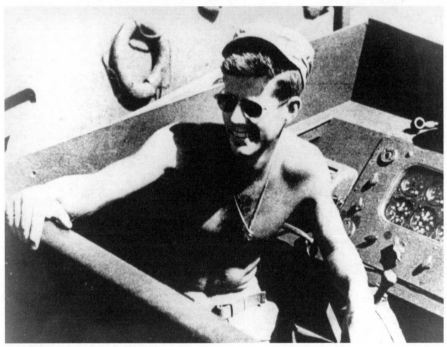

Young John F. Kennedy commands PT 109. (John F. Kennedy Library)

Here was an example, not merely of momentary heroics, but of extended courage. Wise or not, *a profile in courage all his own.*

As for the end of John F. Kennedy's wartime service, Crispell and Gomez reported that while his seriously injured crewmen were shipped to larger base hospitals, JFK "inexplicably languished for several months in the South Pacific." He finally was returned to America, suffering once again from back pain. Then and later, various sources also cited vague reports of fatigue, exhaustion, or—while undocumented in the medical records available—perhaps a bout with malaria.

In the next few years, JFK would undergo two major spinal operations; he also would collapse and/or fall perilously ill on at least three occasions, and he would be diagnosed as a sufferer of the once life-threatening Addison's disease…all before being elected President of the United States in 1960.

★★★

Based upon Hidden Illness in the White House *by Kenneth R. Crispell and Carlos F. Gomez (Duke University Press, Durham, N.C., 1988).*

Strife at High Levels

SPRING 1944, AND IN BURMA the Japanese were driving upon the harried, weakened, and considerably thinned British forces along the India-Burma border. As General William Slim, commander of the British Fourteenth Army, once said of his adversary in that jungled theater, they were "ruthless and bold as ants while their designs went well."

Shortly after the Japanese launched their two-pronged Imphal-Kohima offensive, however, their designs were not going so well as they once hoped. Those hopes, actually, had been pretty much the inspiration of General Renya Mutaguchi, but many of his fellow Japanese generals were skeptical of any victorious outcome for the offensive by his Fifteenth Army. Mutaguchi, nonetheless, committed ninety-one thousand troops to his plan, with Japan's future fortunes in Burma at stake. The pressure was on Mutaguchi, already known for a bad temper.

He drove hard early in March against Slim's Fourteenth Army, and in three weeks the Japanese had succeeded in isolating sixty thousand British and Indian troops. But the undersupplied Allies grimly held somehow and still blocked his attempt to penetrate into India, with the British base at Imphal in Assam Province the first major Japanese objective.

If Mutaguchi was now frustrated, so was his own subordinate, Lt. Gen. Kotuku Sato, commander of the Fifteenth Army's Thirty-first Division. For Sato had been given the unenviable assignment of leading a full division for many difficult miles through jungle, across rivers, over mountain ranges, to tiny Kohima in a four-thousand-foot mountain pass at the India-Burma border as a secondary but vital prong in Mutaguchi's strategy.

Mutaguchi already had encountered problems with the commander of his leadoff Thirty-third Division. When, as early as March 23, that commander's momentum ended, he was replaced. The commander of another attacking division then died of malaria.

After five weeks on the march, meanwhile, Sato and his division had taken heavy casualties from air attacks and had run so low on supplies that his men were eating their own pack mules. He now suggested that his force should retire. The answer was no.

His problems only mounted when his division failed to crack the dwindling defensive "box" at Kohima early in April, then faced an influx of British reinforcements later in the month.

With fierce fighting encountered in the direction of Imphal, also, Mutaguchi saw both his Fifteenth Army and his plan for a grand "March to Delhi" beginning to come apart. But the stubborn general wouldn't back down.

"Continue in the task till all your ammunition is expended," he ordered his men. "If your hands are broken, fight with your feet. If your hands and feet are broken, use your teeth."

By now he had relieved two of his division commanders, and Sato was in a most mutinous mood.

"This is shameful," Sato told his own staff officers. "Mutaguchi should apologize for his own failure to the dead soldiers and the Japanese people. He should not try to put the blame on his subordinates."

After repeated denials of his requests to withdraw, Sato on May 3 radioed to Mutaguchi that he would withdraw his battered division anyway. Retorted Mutagachi, "Retreat and I will court-martial you."

Sato, though, was adamant. "Do what you please," he replied. "I will bring you down with me."

Sato also informed the Japanese Army headquarters overseeing the entire Burmese campaign that the tactical ability of Mutaguchi's staff "lies below that of cadets."

At his own headquarters, Mutaguchi ranted, "He has lost the battle for me."

Since Sato had broken off radio contact, Mutaguchi now had to send his chief of staff into the jungle with personal orders for Sato to rejoin the battle. When they met, Sato shouted that Mutaguchi's Fifteenth Army had failed to send him any supplies or ammunition from the very start of the offensive. "This failure releases me from any obligation to obey the order," he declared. "And in any case, it would be impossible to comply."

That much was certainly true. His own division was shattered. Fifteenth Army was in tatters. The Japanese had suffered the greatest defeat of their ground forces in history.

Fired in the end himself, disgraced, Mutaguchi later was to mourn, "I have killed thousands of my men—I should not go back across the Chindwin [River] alive." Fired also, Sato later was spared court-martial because of a mental condition.

Fair to say that, apart from bodily harm, generals suffer their own kind of wounds.

★★★

Based upon China-Burma-India *by Don Moser and the editors of Time-Life Books (World War II series, Alexandria, Va., 1971).*

Search for "Big Stoop"

SOMEONE, IT WAS THOUGHTFULLY DECIDED in the midst of World War II, should check out the potential invasion beaches northwest of Hong Kong, along China's Japanese-occupied coastline. "My job," recalled retired U.S. Navy Captain Phil Bucklew, "was to carry out the reconnaissance in reverse of what we had done before. This time we went overland."

German defenses on the beaches at Normandy about one month before D-Day. (U.S. Army)

Before, the charter member of the Navy Scouts and Raiders had been a waterborne advance man for the Allied invasions of Sicily, Salerno, and Normandy. Six months prior to Normandy, in fact, he had been ashore at the future Omaha Beach to collect a bucket of sand for engineers involved in the planning of history's greatest invasion.

It was after Normandy that an invasion of the China coast briefly came under consideration. Before anyone thought better of the notion, Scout/ Raider Bucklew was on his way. A combination of wings and wheels took him as far as the Chinese mountain village of Kienyang, but from there it would be a two-hundred-mile trek to the coast—on foot and dressed as a Chinese coolie. "They had come up with a very sacklike coolie suit and a huge straw hat. I was also provided with two hand grenades and a .45 caliber revolver."

Accompanied by ten Chinese guerrillas, Bucklew did his best to fade into the local scenery as his guides took him along mountain trails, through tiny villages, past Japanese encampments with bonfires and sleeping soldiers. "Fading" was a bit difficult, since Bucklew stood six foot two, weighed nearly 240 pounds, and had played professional football in America before the war.

"We'd be walking along and pass another group of coolies, who would just look up at me in wonder," said Bucklew years later. "I was just so out of proportion in size to them and everyone else there. The sandals didn't do too well, either, but later on I got some tennis shoes."

The Japanese soon heard about the mysterious "coolie" tabbed "Big Stoop" and began looking for him. "They knew an American was in the area and they sent out a search patrol. I lost face with my Chinese guerrilla leader because I wouldn't give him one of my two grenades to wipe out this enemy patrol, but my recon mission would have been blown right away."

In one close call, Bucklew hid in the center of a haystack while members of a Japanese patrol ate their lunch nearby. "It was rather foolish, with all my guerrillas sitting completely encircling the haystack. Anyone would have known that something, or someone, was in there."

But they didn't and Bucklew soon moved on.

The reconnaissance trip took about three weeks in all. For the American navyman in Japanese-occupied territory along the China coast, things were surprisingly humdrum. "When we arrived, there were so many fishermen and sampans minding their own business—with Japanese doing the same—that we were hardly noticed. We made our run down the coast and I got the data I needed on the coastline."

The risk, of course, still was great—shunted from one place to another by sampan, Bucklew had to count on the integrity of his Chinese contacts. But... they stood by him.

Not that the mission was completed without further incident. One day, Bucklew's guerrilla leader sold his camera. "He convinced me that he could go into the village and bring back pictures. Later, he told a whopping story that he had been captured by the Japanese, who had both taken the camera and made him work as a coolie for a day."

Another time, joining up with a fellow American sent on the China coast reconnaissance, Bucklew weathered a slight accident. "Rocky Ruggieri and I decided to ride downhill on bicycles that we'd gotten hold of. It was okay until we came upon a sharp, right-angle turn on a three-foot pathway and crashed, flying spread-eagled into a nearby rice-paddy—which wasn't filled with roses! As far as I know, there are still two bicycles at the edge of that path, because we didn't bother to go back. We found a river and cleaned off—I haven't ridden a bike since."

Later, safely returned, Bucklew presented his report in Calcutta, India. The China coast, he advised, offered poor beach conditions for amphibious landings. "From there it was evidently decided to forget about China and go on north to Japan instead."

Fortunately, the war ended before either invasion proposal could be set in motion.

★★★

Based upon interviews by Blaine Taylor, Military History *magazine, October 1987, and this author for the* Washington Star.

Doubling for Monty

FIRST, THERE HAD BEEN THE telephone call from David Niven. You know…the movie actor. Only this was *Colonel* Niven calling. Wartime, you know.

"See if you can come up to London for a film test," he had said.

M. E. Clifton James, a lieutenant in the Royal Army's Pay Corps office at Leicester, then headed for London "in high spirits." Himself an actor for twenty-five years, an army officer since he had volunteered back in 1939, he obviously was in the wrong slot…and now, in 1944, was he at last about to be rescued?

Well, yes and no.

In London, David Niven quickly handed him over to a "Colonel Lester" from MI 5, the Army's intelligence branch. And not for any film test, either.

The colonel came right to the point. "I'm afraid I've got rather a shock for you. You are not going to make any films. You have been chosen to act as a double for General Montgomery."

And, true enough…after a few weeks assimilating all kinds of detail about Britain's General Bernard Montgomery, studying photographs and newsreel footage depicting the famous "Monty," even being assigned to his entourage as an obscure "aide" in order to study him in person, Clifton James faced the greatest acting role of his life.

"I want you to look on this as a play we are producing for the benefit of the enemy," explained Colonel Lester. "Our audience is not simple. We have to hoodwink the German High Command."

The goal, of course, was deception. With the Allied forces massing in England for the imminent invasion of Normandy, the Allies hoped to divert German attention by sending Britain's best-known general on a tour of North Africa to foster rumors of Allied plans to invade southern France, the Riviera…only it wouldn't really be "Monty" showing up at ceremonial stops, it would be the actor Clifton James.

Should the Australian-raised James have been surprised that MI 5 picked him, of all people? Not a bit…not only was he an actor by profession, he really was a near-exact double for "Monty." "I knew, of course, that I looked like 'Monty,'" he later wrote. "My friends had often commented on the striking resemblance. And my picture had once appeared in the *London News Chronicle*, posed in a beret and captioned: YOU'RE WRONG—HIS NAME IS LT. CLIFTON JAMES."

After his first interview with Lester, he plunged into a crash course of preparations for his role, but he really had been stunned to hear of his assignment. As he later wrote, "I had a nightmarish feeling of stage fright." A mere private in World War I, he still had "a schoolboy fear of senior officers." Now, he was being asked to impersonate high on high. But he was given "no time in which to brood."

For all of his study of "Monty" in the abstract, James soon found, nothing could ever replace exposure to General Montgomery in person. The very first time he saw him, in fact, "he was wearing his famous black beret and a leather flying jacket, and I noted that he had his own special salute—a slight double movement of the hand that made it more of a greeting than anything else."

Over the next few days, "I watched him like a hawk," added James in his postwar book *I Was Monty's Double*. "I observed his characteristic walk with hands clasped behind his back, the way he pinched his cheek when thinking, his sudden movements, his manner of eating, his habit of throwing out one hand as he hammered home a point."

British General Bernard "Monty" Montgomery (and Winston Churchill) could draw a crowd of onlookers. (U.S. Army)

James reached the point where he was confident of aping "Monty's" voice, gestures, mannerisms…but the actor still felt unsure of himself in one vital area. He wondered, based upon his own "natural timidity," if he ever would be able "to imitate his unique personality, to radiate the feeling he gave of strength and quiet confidence." James was frank to say after the war, "I doubted it."

As events turned out, a few, nearly casual words of reassurance from Montgomery himself took care of the problem. They came in a private meeting with the great man in person—a meeting in which James found their duplicate looks "uncanny" but, as befitted a professional actor, also took pains to listen carefully to the general's speech pattern. "Trying to record the incisive, rather high-pitched voice and the way he chose his words," is the way James described his actor's method. "He never used high-flown phrases; some people have even described his speech as dry and arid."

Before the actor turned to go, Montgomery said, "You have a great responsibility, you know," and he asked, "Do you feel confident?"

"When I hesitated, he added quickly, 'Everything will be all right; don't worry about it.' And in that moment, such was his ability to inspire confidence, my qualms vanished."

And just as well that they did, because just a few days later, Lieutenant James was stepping off a military airplane at Gibraltar outfitted in "full general's battle-dress and the famous black beret with its Armoured Corps badge."

On that day and at several stops ahead, there were crowds to greet, troops to inspect, generals'-rank officers to stroll with…all the things a publicly visible—and real—General Montgomery would be expected to do.

James was careful—and resolute enough from the very beginning—to step out briskly, to give "the Monty salute," to take old friends of the real general by the arm, head bowed in seemingly earnest conversation. Only a small number of the Brits he consorted with were aware of the deception. Others were fooled… and left fooled, for the time being anyway.

Supposedly, he was seen by a number of German spies who also were unaware of the deception. Landing at Gibraltar, he was told some of the Spanish workers at the airport were spies. Later, at nearby Government House, he looked out a window and spotted a man on a nearby rooftop with a telescope—also a spy, apparently.

He and a companion deliberately encountered a pair of bogus Spanish businessmen in a public garden, with James talking rather loudly about a "Plan 303," then halting rather abruptly and doing his best to look startled and aloof at the same time. Not only were they spies, too, but the Germans soon urgently were trying to find out the nature of "Plan 303." Still more spies—"plants" posing as legitimate contacts—turned up at the impersonator's North African stops later the same week.

In Algiers, for that matter, he was taken on a twelve-mile, "hell-for-leather" dash at top speed for the airport, because of a rumored assassination attempt against General Montgomery. That is, in this case, against his double, Pay Corps Lieutenant Clifton James.

After a week of conspicuous travel in his general's role, James returned to Algiers "without any serious mishap." By that, he meant, "So far as we knew, nobody had doubted that I was General Montgomery."

With D-Day now only a few days off, the actor's job was done. He drove up to headquarters in Algiers "in a final blaze of glory," but then changed back to his lieutenant's uniform and ducked out of sight. "My likeness to the General had now become an embarrassment, for until the invasion was actually launched there was always the danger that my secret might leak out."

James was smuggled out a back door, and next day, "stealthily put on a plane to Cairo—the only city nearby which was big enough to swallow me without a trace—and kept there under wraps until after D-Day."

And how successful was the deception scheme? According to James, very. "Not until after the war was I told how the deception had helped mislead the enemy, drawing away [Erwin] Rommel's armored divisions, and so contributing to the success of the invasion."

But he also eventually learned he had taken greater risks than those normally to be found in the Royal Army's Pay Corps office at Leicester. "When the news of 'Monty's' intended journey to the Middle East first reached Berlin, the German High Command had ordered my plane shot down en route; or, if this plan miscarried, for 'Monty' to be assassinated somewhere….But at the last moment the Germans decided to make sure that I really was 'Monty'; and when they satisfied themselves on this point, the Führer intervened to save my life. Hitler ordered that 'Monty' was on no account to be killed until they discovered just where he was intending to launch his invasion. And this the Germans never did discover until the dawn of June 6 [D-Day at Normandy]."

★★★

Based upon I Was Monty's Double, *by M. E. Clifton James, condensed version in* Secrets & Spies: Behind-the-Scenes Stories of World War II *(Reader's Digest Association, Pleasantville, New York, 1964).*

One Man Army

WHO FINALLY GOT THE TROOPS moving off "Bloody Omaha"—Omaha Beach in the Normandy invasion?

If such a confused, potentially disastrous experience could be said to have been salvaged by the pure grit and leadership of any one man, nominations for that honor must start with a West Pointer, a single-star general in his fifties who was practically elderly in comparison to the men all around him.

That would be Brig. Gen. Norman ("Dutch") Cota, fifty-one, assistant commander of the Twenty-ninth Infantry Division, a veteran of the Allies' North African campaign who spent most of his time with the troops in the field, rather than shuffle papers at headquarters. Both fierce and absolutely fearless in combat, he held to an easily understood credo.

"Now look," he once told a well-meaning officer who suggested that perhaps he should not take so many risks, "I was a poor country boy from the Pennsylvania Dutch country. I heard about West Point, and that it was free, and I went. I made a contract with the government; if they paid for my education, I would serve them. Part of my contract was to die for my country if necessary. I intend to stick to it. If I get killed, then so be it, but I don't expect to be."

After taking over the training of the National Guardsmen who made up the Twenty-ninth, Cota was just about everywhere with his walking stick, while chomping upon an unlit cigar. That was back on the moors of England, beginning in the summer of 1943. There, Cota had done his best to indoctrinate his men in the sights and crashing sounds of battle. And the confusion.

"The air and naval bombardment and the artillery support are reassuring," he told his staff. "But you're going to find confusion. The landing craft aren't going in on schedule and people are going to be landed in the wrong place. Some won't be landed at all. The enemy will try, and will have some success, in preventing our gaining a lodgement. But we must improvise, carry on, not lose our heads. Nor must we add to the confusion."

His prophetic words described exactly the situation on Omaha Beach moments after the first waves of American troops—the Twenty-ninth included—stepped ashore on continental Europe, June 6, 1944. Omaha was a nightmare—noise, confusion, whole units landed at the wrong places, others still far from shore, and just about everybody pinned down by murderous crossfire. And bodies... bodies everywhere, in the water, on the beach itself, draped over the beach obstacles. All of them American.

In the area assigned to the Twenty-ninth, those GIs still living and able to move had scrambled and crawled to the base of a low sea wall 150 yards beyond the water's edge. There, the invasion had stopped. No one dared move. A carpet of men hugged the sand, face down.

General Cota came in with the staff of the Twenty-ninth's 116th Regiment, dropping into waist-deep water from their landing barge fifty yards from shore and wading in from there. Right next to Cota, Major John Sours was hit by machine-gun fire and killed on the spot.

Looking at the masses of men jumbled up, unmoving, behind the sea wall, the German fire only increasing with each passing moment, Cota realized the paralyzed Twenty-niners had to be galvanized into action. Accounts vary on what happened next, but Cota nonetheless was the catalyst.

According to Cornelius Ryan in his famous book *The Longest Day* and to Max Hastings, British author of *Overlord: D-Day and the Battle for Normandy*, Cota scooted to a halt in the sand by the sea wall next to men of the Fifth U.S. Rangers who were mixed in—by erroneous landing—with the Twenty-ninth Division men. "If you're Rangers, get up and lead the way!" exploded Cota (says Hastings). Another version: "Lead the way, Rangers!" (Ryan).

A Fifth U.S. Ranger who was there has got it still another way. According to Stan Askin, the Rangers and their CO, Colonel Max Schneider, had just arrived by the base of the sea wall when suddenly they saw a figure running toward them, "followed by another man shouting, 'Keep down, General, keep down.'" The two were Cota and his aide. "Cota threw himself down beside Max Schneider. 'Morning Schneider,' he said. 'Morning, General,' replied Schneider. 'Well,' said Cota, 'it looks like the Rangers are going to have to get us off the beach.'" (Stan Askins in *World War II* magazine, May 1987.)

By all three accounts, specialists armed with bangalore torpedoes blew vital gaps in the thick barbed wire just beyond the sea wall, and the others then began to follow—a trickle that in time would become a flood, as the German defenders ultimately were pushed back.

Says Askin: "The rest of us followed [the bangalore men] on the double, but found ourselves slowed to a crawl as we began the climb up the steep hillside." The troops pushed and pulled and made their way forward anyway. And the credit for leadership would go to Ranger Colonel Schneider.

In his book *Beyond the Beachhead: The 29th Infantry Division in Normandy*, however, Joseph Balkoski has it another way entirely. The Rangers were there, huddled and pinned like the Twenty-niners, only it was Cota himself who led the breakout at his section of the beach.

Here and there a few brave men up and down the long line were edging forward. Others sometimes followed with discordant but brave sallies forward. Cota "cajoled a motley collection of infantrymen to get up and move." He himself crawled beyond the sea wall to a protective rise five yards ahead. He brought a BAR man to his side to provide fierce covering fire, and another Twenty-niner blew the wire just ahead with a bangalore.

But then, disaster. The first man running through the fresh gap was cut down by machine-gun fire. "Medic," he sobbed, and "Mama!"

With that piteous cry, Cota knew the men behind would be frozen in place. He had to show them it could be done. And so, "He leaped up, dashing across the road and through the gap."

He turned and shouted for others to follow. A few brave souls did, and when they weren't hurt, "their success convinced dozens more to try it."

Soon Cota had a "scraggly column" advancing through a field beyond the beach bluff, the road, and the wire. They passed through minefields, losing several men on the way; they topped the high ground beyond the beaches, encountered German resistance, and forced it back. They reached the French village of Vierville...and took it. All the while, more and more men were streaming up from the beaches behind. One group met Cota on the town's main street, "twirling a pistol on his index finger like an Old West gunfighter." He looked at the newcomers: "Where the hell have you been, boys?"

Not through with his beach heroics yet, Cota then returned to the landing area to speed the flow of men and vehicular equipment such as tanks. The Vierville "draw," a natural depression leading from the beach, still was in German hands. Cota, with six men, took it—from the rear.

Back on the beach, he set about bringing further order to a still-chaotic and dangerous scene. He reported the draw was now clear for troop and supply movement; he cajoled a group of GIs until one finally agreed to drive forward a bulldozer loaded with needed TNT.

Thus, decades later, the accounts of Cota's exact role differ in detail, but they agree in the essential fact that he was a key figure in moving a demoralized mob of men from their pinned-down position at a key point of Omaha Beach.

Not that Cota ceased his aggressive activity with D-Day itself...not at all!

On June 7, adds the Twenty-ninth Infantry story by Balkoski, "Cota was a one-man army again." After prodding and pushing his troops, now toward the village of St. Laurent, he found an infantry captain and some men stymied outside a house occupied by Germans. When asked why they were not trying to eliminate the enemy and take the house, the inexperienced captain said, "The Germans are in there, shooting at us."

Clearly that would never do for a man of Cota's mettle. "Well, I'll tell you what," he said to the young captain. "You and your men start shooting at them. I'll take a squad of men and you and your men watch carefully. I'll show you how to take a house with Germans in it."

The general had been unbuckling two grenades as he spoke, and now he led his men to a hedge, then they dashed toward the house, "screaming like wild men," and threw their grenades through the windows. "Cota and another man kicked in the front door, tossed a few more grenades inside, waited for the explosions, and then disappeared inside the house."

The Germans surviving the assault ran out the back doors and windows, and soon General Cota was able to report back to his stunned captain.

Does the captain now know how to take a house? "Yes Sir!"

"Well, I won't be around to do it for you again. I can't do it for everybody."

But Cota did what he could for almost "everybody," always in the thick of things as the Americans who landed in Normandy gradually fought their way out of the bocage country with its damnable hedgerows, until the Twenty-ninth helped to take St. Lo in mid-July.

Typically, he entered the battered French city "close behind the head of the column." Talking things over with a fellow Twenty-niner shortly afterward, General Cota took a piece of shrapnel in the arm. His colleague noticed blood running from his sleeve, forming drops on his fingers. "He just stood there talking; it didn't bother him in the least."

Cota had a medic tend to the arm and spent the rest of the day with his arm in a sling. That night, he was evacuated for a week's stay in a rear-area hospital. But, typically, he was not down for long.

The end of the month found him in a proud new role—commander of his own infantry division, the Twenty-eighth. And, on August 29, there was Cota, at the head of the Twenty-eighth, marching down the Champs Elysées of Paris and taking the salutes of Charles de Gaulle, Dwight Eisenhower, and Omar Bradley—a long way from that bloody, pinned-down stretch of beach called Omaha.

★★★

From sources cited in the text.

New Hope for "Kitty"

"BAD WEATHER," SHE WROTE MONDAY evening. "Heavy bombardments against the French coast continue."

What could it mean? At eight o'clock the very next morning, she knew. They all knew. The radio in their hiding place spoke.

"This is D-Day. This is the day."

They heard it in English, exactly that way.

Even the German news provided more of the terribly exciting news. English paratroops in France.

English landing craft off the coast, in battle with the German navy, added the BBC.

"We discussed it over breakfast: Is this just a trial landing like Dieppe two years ago?"

She didn't say so quite yet, but their excitement—and hope—in their "Secret Annexe" had to be great.

By 10 A.M., June 6, 1944, the reports were even more thrilling. From the English and given in several languages: "The invasion has begun!" And that meant the "real" invasion.

The hour of 11 A.M. brought more—a speech by "the Supreme Commander, General Dwight Eisenhower."

And at noon: "This is D-Day." In English. Followed by more from Eisenhower, to the French specifically. "Stiff fighting will come now, but after this, victory. The year 1944 is the year of complete victory; good luck."

At one o'clock, more English news, more detail—good, hard, encouraging detail. Eleven thousand Allied planes. Four thousand landing craft depositing their men and cargo between Cherbourg and Le Havre (Normandy, of course). English and American troops "already engaged in hard fighting." And more speeches by the Prime Minister of Belgium, King Haakon of Norway, de Gaulle of France, the King of England, "and last, but not least, Churchill."

By now their reaction has caught fire. "Great commotion in the Secret Annexe! The long-awaited liberation still seems too wonderful, too much like a fairy tale."

Could Eisenhower be right? "Could we be granted victory this year, 1944? We don't know yet, but hope is revived within us. The great thing now is to remain calm and steadfast. Now more than ever we must clench our teeth and not cry out."

Often clenching her teeth and not crying out in all those months since they went into hiding in July 1942, she addressed her diary as a friend called "Kitty." In hiding with her were her mother, father, and sister; another couple with a teenage boy and an elderly dentist. As Jews, they were hiding from what later became known as the Holocaust.

Their hiding place was a group of rooms in the upper rear of a combined warehouse-office structure on the Prinsengracht Canal in occupied Amsterdam, Holland.

"Kitty" had become teenager Anne Frank's only friend in the absence of any social contact beyond the seven persons trapped with her. Obviously, the young Jewish girl longed for friends. "Oh, Kitty," she wrote the day of the

Normandy invasion, "the best part of the invasion is the feeling that friends are approaching. We have been oppressed by the Germans for so long that the thought of friends and delivery fills us with confidence!"

She went on to say the issue at hand no longer was the fate of the Jews in hiding and fear. Rather, it concerned all Holland and all Occupied Europe. Maybe too, her sister Margot had said, maybe Anne could even go back to school that very fall!

Seven days later, she noted the passage of her fifteenth birthday.

And still, "excellent" news of the invasion. Churchill and Eisenhower visited newly liberated villages, she had heard.

On July 21, she noted the "super news" that an attempt had been made on Hitler's life the day before. Hitler escaped real harm, but, "it certainly shows that there are lots of [German] officers who are sick of the war and would like to see Hitler descend into a bottomless pit."

On August 4, however, with the Allies still fighting their way through France, the "Secret Annexe" was raided by the Hitler's Gestapo. All its occupants were shipped off to the concentration camps. Anne's "friend" Kitty was left on the floor, tossed there by the intruders.

Confined to the Bergen-Belsen camp, Anne survived almost to the end of the war, but not quite. In March 1945 she died. The war in Europe (and the occupation of Holland) ended just a few weeks later.

Only her father survived the camps, among those who had hidden in the annex for more than two years. He returned and found the diary exactly where one of the intruders had thrown it in August 1944.

"If he had taken the diary with him," said Anne's father later, "no one would ever have heard of my daughter." As it was, a publishing sensation, her "Kitty" appeared around the world in thirty-two languages and fostered a successful stage play and a widely seen movie.

The annex in the building on Prinsengracht Canal has become a sort of shrine visited by hundreds every day, especially young people like Anne. Others, including many young Germans, for many years visited the Belsen camp site, specifically to pray for the brave and sensitive young girl's soul.

★★★

From Anne Frank: Diary of a Young Girl *(Doubleday & Company, New York, renewed copyright 1980 by Otto H. Frank).*

Only Ike Did It...All

FLOOD TIME IN KANSAS, AND a boy with his brother whirling helplessly about in a flat-bottomed boat in a rampaging stream...until a cowboy hurled them a line.

Then, another time, as a boy, in bed ill, floating in and out of consciousness, with the doctor saying it's going to be the boy's life or the leg, one or the other. But the boy, stubborn, said no to amputating his infected, blood-poisoned leg.

Two weeks later, for whatever reason, he recovered.

Many years later, now grown up, he was almost lost still another time. Flying from North Africa to the British base at Gibraltar, he was told visibility was practically nil, the landing site ahead was difficult, and there wasn't enough gas to turn back. Even so, the military aircraft landed safely, and Dwight David Eisenhower continued on with life—with an extraordinary and historic career.

If, at any of these crisis points in his life, he had not survived, someone else would have been in charge of the Allied landings in North Africa. Someone else would have planned and directed the Allied invasions of Sicily and Italy. Some other general would have been the Supreme Allied Commander for Operation Overlord—the Normandy invasion—and the subsequent conquest of Nazi-held Europe. Surely, too, someone else would have been the thirty-fourth U.S. president.

But could someone else really have done it all?

Maybe, as the critics sometimes have argued, George C. Marshall should have been the SHAEF commander instead of remaining in Washington as army chief of staff. Maybe some British general would have been better. Maybe "Monty," as Sir Bernard Montgomery was called, was another Duke of Wellington whose advice should always have predominated in the Allied councils of war. And maybe Douglas MacArthur was the most brilliant of American generals, and maybe George S. Patton was unfairly chastised and so on. Many were the criticisms of good old affable "Ike," sometimes dull-looking and by the time he died at age seventy-eight, retired president, a kindly, worn-shoe sort of face.

The critics, with all their maybes and implications, sometimes forget that the war was won, the invasion of Europe ultimately was successful (as were those other invasions earlier), and the man at the helm was, indeed, Eisenhower.

He was born October 14, 1890, in Denison, Texas, but the family moved almost immediately to Abilene, Kansas, where he spent his boyhood. That was where the cowboy rescued him and brother Edgar with a lasso, where a very young Ike refused to allow amputation of his leg (and brother Edgar slept at the bedroom door to keep the doctors away!).

Like Napoleon, Ike considered a naval career. But, too old for the Naval Academy at Annapolis, he went to West Point instead. He was a football star, a running back, until a ruined knee sidelined him. He then became a part-time football coach, a sideline that nearly ruined his post–World War I army career, since he often was assigned new duties based on a post-commander's need for a good football coach.

Along the way, though, he befriended Patton and served happily under both Marshall and MacArthur.

Only a fair student in earlier years, but always an avid reader of military history, he began to shine as a career officer—first in his class at the Army Command and General Staff School at Fort Leavenworth, Kansas, and a widely publicized star at the Louisiana Maneuvers of 1941.

After Pearl Harbor, he served in Washington as chief of war plans for the War Department. Named Commander of Allied Forces in North Africa in the fall of 1942, he could boast in one year that all German forces had been driven out of Africa…and Sicily. Further, Italy had declared itself out of the war, although at the cost of German occupation.

In the end, it was former aide Eisenhower who was chosen as Supreme Allied Commander, rather than Marshall or MacArthur. It was "Ike" who had to grin and bear it during the bombing of civilian rail yards in France as preparation for D-Day. It was "Ike" who sweated through those two eleventh-hour decisions that "made" D-Day—one holding back the Allied invasion force due to bad weather, and the other unleashing that massive force one day later, despite gossamer-thin predictions of improved weather.

Someone else might have done some of it, perhaps even all of it, but they didn't. Only Ike did.

★★★

First published in World War II *magazine, November 1990.*

Two in Single-Seat Fighter

NOT SO REMARKABLE FOR WHERE they were going but rather how to get there were two intrepid American airmen winging their way north in June 1944 from one of those difficult air raids on the Ploesti oil works in Romania.

Headed for a Russian air base at Poltava as their nearest sanctuary, Lieutenants Richard T. Andrews and Richard E. Willsie sallied hastily along in their single-seat, twin-engine P-38 Lightning.

Normally, of course, the World War II fighter carried a "crew" of exactly one. But this wasn't "normally." To begin with, American P-38s from the Fifteenth Air Force had been sent to the hot Polesti complex in an all-fighters saturation strafing raid, rather than risk still another bomber strike.

While strafing trains, trucks, and German air facilities in the oil field area, Willsie related years later, "I could feel the bullets hitting the aircraft and they actually made my feet bounce on the rudder pedals." As he saw oil leaking from his left engine, it lost all pressure. "I feathered that prop at once."

Willsie pressed on with his one good engine at full power, but then he saw coolant streaming from the right engine. "Knowing that I had only a few minutes left, I reported that I was going down."

Enter, at this point, nineteen-year-old Dick Andrews of the same Eighty-second Fighter Group, a youngster with only one hundred hours in the P-38 and guns already emptied. "Pick a good field," Andrews radioed tersely, "and I will come in after you."

Willsie was too busy to dwell on the startling message. With his remaining engine popping ominously and a fresh hit cracking his windshield and causing a bloody head injury, he made for a freshly plowed field just ahead. "As I slid over the last obstacle and touched down, with wheels up, I placed my head against the rubber shield on the gunsight for protection. But my nose still took a pounding as the plane skidded to a stop."

Willsie got out in a hurry, destroyed his plane with a small phosphorous bomb (as instructed for such circumstances), then ran for the cover of nearby trees.

Beyond the trees, truckloads of German troops were racing toward the field. Six Me-109s appeared in the sky above. But here came Andrews anyway, his landing gear down, in line with the field's furrows. "You just can't leave a man like that to walk back through enemy territory," Andrews later explained in a letter to his mother. "I was determined to get him out of there."

While fellow P-38 pilots tangled with the Me's in dogfights above, Andrews made his landing, and Willsie sprinted for the Lockheed Lightning that could be his salvation.

But would they both fit in the single-seat cockpit? As Andrews tossed out his parachute and other gear to make room, there wasn't time to think it through. "We both jumped into the cockpit with miraculous precision," said Willsie later.

Seconds later, with senior pilot Willsie taking the controls at Andrews's suggestion, they were rolling down the soft, furrowed ground, their canopy securely locked. Willsie was on the front edge of the bucket seat, and Andrews was scrunched behind, one cramped leg draped over Willsie's shoulder.

They barely cleared the trees at the end of the field, then they ran into "weather" and lost their fighter escort and had to fly instrument. They had no map of their route to Poltava, and they just might expect "friendly" Russian fire at their unfamiliar plane, but to make a long story short, they made it.

The next day Lockheed technician Richard "Stumpy" Hollinger asked the intrepid pair to pose in simulation of their contortions for what may have been the first rescue of a downed combat pilot by a modern single-seat fighter landing on enemy soil. But…they couldn't do it. "They could not both get in and close that canopy," said an admiring Hollinger later. "No matter how hard they tried, it was impossible to fit in tightly."

In fact, when word spread of their feat and others tried to emulate it, there were so many casualties that American pilots were forbidden to attempt such a rescue procedure. In the meantime, Andrews was awarded a Silver Star for his heroic rescue feat.

★★★

Based upon interview notes and supporting material supplied by Mary Lou Colbert Neale, Coeditor, Lightning Strikes, *P-38 National Association.*

A General and His Dog

AS THE MEN OF GEORGE S. Patton's Third Army could attest, rare is the bond to equal the unique relationship that seems to develop between a general on campaign and his pet dog.

And, in World War II, if Patton had his famous bullterrier Willie, General Charles Gerhardt, commander of the Twenty-ninth Infantry Division, had his own handsome pup of black-and-white coloring, longish hair, hound-dog ears—and distinctly mixed (but French) parentage.

The pup had appeared in the division's headquarters area on June 12, 1944, just six days after the Twenty-ninth landed on "Bloody Omaha" as a leading element of the Normandy invasion. For Gerhardt and the months-old dog, it was bonding at first sight.

Gerhardt, known to his men as "Uncle Charlie," named his new constant companion "D-Day." In no time at all, the division would see the general's jeep racing about the advancing front with only a driver, general's aide, general, and D-Day aboard.

The French-born dog usually occupied the rear jump seat with the aide, Lieutenant Robert Wallis. D-Day soon realized his exalted status and took full advantage of it. "The pup rides around in the general's jeep and his behavior is such that he seems to sense that this vehicle sports a red sign with two stars and that he is something special," reported the alert division newspaper, *29 Let's Go.*

Gerhardt was an aggressive, no-nonsense general. One of his pet peeves, for instance, was the loose chin strap attached to one's helmet. If the general was in the area, the men of the division knew they had better buckle their chin straps, pdq.

Thankfully, though, his pet D-Day became a sort of early warning system. Given nearly total freedom to roam where he chose, he often appeared in the van of the visiting general. Thus, a frontline spy would have seen large numbers of grown-up men buckling straps, smoothing down rumpled uniforms, and otherwise primping as best they could when a mere dog hove into view. The general, of course, would not be far behind.

D-Day, clearly, was no mere dog. Soon quite used to artillery, he stuck to the general like glue. He slept on the general's cot. He had K rations with the general and his staff at mealtimes. He dashed in and out of headquarters with no apparent restraint.

Their bond was such that the general one moment would fulfill his reputation by delivering a fierce tongue-lashing of momentarily wayward officers, and in the next, turn to D-Day with cooing "baby talk" that was most unsuited to the general's usual image.

D-Day had his faults, naturally. His greatest sin—with ample opportunity to indulge—was the impulse to chase jeeps and trucks. This particular flaw could ruin a perfectly good day for Gerhardt's driver, Sergeant Robert Cuff. At the sight of an enticing convoy, D-Day thought nothing of leaping from the cruising jeep and giving chase. At the alarmed general's quick order, Cuff was forced to pursue and collar the wayward dog, hoping all the time that they would not be blown up together by unmarked mines.

The same character flaw was very nearly D-Day's undoing. One of the trucks he chased accidentally struck the dog and left the animal near death.

A distraught General Gerhardt allegedly told the truck driver: "If that dog dies, you're history!"

Happily for all concerned, a division surgeon managed to tend D-Day's wounds, and the dog recovered. He recovered in such exemplary fashion, in fact, that he was able to accompany General Gerhardt back to Stateside after the hostilities were all over. He then assumed a more normal dog's life for another ten years.

One day, though, former Sergeant Cuff heard again from his wartime commander. "D-Day is dead," said the sad note. If the general's onetime driver shed a tear, was it one of soulful sorrow—or delayed relief syndrome?

★★★

Based upon Beyond the Beachhead: The 29th Infantry Division in Normandy *by Joseph Balkoski (Stackpole Books, Harrisburg, Pa., 1989).*

Faint Sound in the Distance

AMBUSH. SOMEHOW, THE WORD SMACKS of ancient tribesmen lying in wait around the next bend for the interloper. In the more modern world, it rings of jungle fighters or insurgent guerrillas. Whatever the case, at Normandy three days after D-Day, it clearly was not a thought uppermost in the minds of the weary men making up the 2nd Battalion of the U.S. 29th Infantry Division's 115th Regiment.

In the past twenty hours, they had marched fifteen miles, effected a difficult river crossing, and then warily threaded their way along the road leading to St. Lo. As they plunged more and more deeply into the bocage past the Aure River and its swamps, they saw less and less of the enemy.

The troops, six hundred of them, were tired, merely trudging along, and they were hungry. They were ahead of most other American units and behind them, unknown to either side at first, was a retreating task force of the German 352nd Infantry Division.

Long after dark—at 2 A.M., actually—the exhausted infantrymen were guided off the road into the bivouac area their officers had found for them, two pastures enclosed by the hedgerows and embankments that crisscross the Normandy landscape as a giant maze. Just to the north stood several houses—the French hamlet of Le Carrefour, meaning "crossroads."

The Americans didn't know the German task force was right behind them. The Germans, however, had discovered the presence of the American column ahead—and its bivouac area.

In the pastureland, the Second Battalion threw up its sentries, while the main body of men simply spread out and found places to sleep. No foxholes, for once, were dug. Men fell asleep in minutes without even shedding their packs.

"From somewhere in the distance sentries could hear the faint sounds of vehicle engines—probably the jeeps of the 3rd Battalion, they figured. The 3rd was supposed to be somewhere east of the 2nd."

In a stone farmhouse by the road, Lt. Col. William Warfield, commander of the Second Battalion, was still up, conferring with his staff. None of the Americans had any idea the Germans were so near...so near they had virtually surrounded the bivouac area, filtering behind the hedgerows, emplacing their machine guns and mortars, even bringing forward three motorized assault guns, *Sturmgeschutze*, that looked like tanks.

With flares suddenly lighting the two pastures, the Germans behind the hedgerows let go with all their ordnance at once—machine guns, mortars, and the three *Sturmgeschutze* with their long-barreled cannon.

"The 29ers never stood a chance. With no time to set up a coherent defense, the frantic 29ers ran to and fro looking for a way to escape the death trap, but the Germans on top of the surrounding embankments could easily pick off the Yanks. Along one hedgerow, a platoon of dozing 29ers had only just risen when most of the men were cut down by a burst of machine-gun fire. As the GIs were hit, they tumbled back against the hedgerows in heaps."

Those who tried to fight back couldn't see anything beyond the flare-lit fields. Still, they managed to silence two of the assault guns with bazookas. "It was terrible," said a survivor later. "We had crawled about 100 yards away from the field when we heard a lot of the guys screaming. I think the Germans may have been making a bayonet charge."

The entire firefight consumed all of twenty minutes. Fifty battalion members were dead; another one hundred were either wounded or captured, while the rest fled singly or in small groups, to slowly wend their way back to the American lines to the rear.

At the farmhouse quartering Warfield and his staff, the situation was no better. The Germans had shouted, in English, their demand that the officers surrender. The stunned Warfield shouted back, "Surrender, hell!" He and his staff then attempted a dash to the bivouac area, but they, too, were cut down by machine-gun fire.

To the rear, Division Commander Charles Gerhardt had been concerned at the lack of reports from the 115th all during the day of June 9. A staff officer, Major Glover Johns, finally located the regiment's command post about dusk, but learned the personnel there "had no idea where any of the 115th's three infantry battalions were."

Apprised of this news, an angry General Gerhardt turned up at the command post at about 2 A.M., about the time of the ambush. There still was no news until, about 4 A.M., the first survivors of the ambush began to straggle in with their grim report. Gerhardt couldn't believe what he heard. "No security!" he shouted. "They just went into the field and went to bed!"

He and Johns set off by jeep at dawn to find the ambush site, with Gerhardt ignoring the possibility that the area ahead might now be under German control. On their way, they encountered two dozen more survivors, traveling together. As Gerhardt heard their accounts, he praised their decision to stay together and determined to award them all a Bronze Star.

A mile up the road, he and Major Johns came upon the ambush site itself. Two elderly French women were placing flowers on the bodies. They didn't know any details of the fight. Nearby was Colonel Warfield's body, his Colt .45 still in his hand. "If you have to die," said Gerhardt bitterly, "that's the way to do it."

The German task force that had struck during the night was long since gone. It had continued its retreat as ordered earlier—the 352nd was by now taking up defensive positions south of the Elle River.

All during the day of June 10, more and more Second Battalion survivors filtered back to their lines. With one hundred replacements, a new CO, and a battalion reorganization, it set out again later in the day on the same road to St. Lo. By the time the reconstituted Second Battalion again approached Le Carrefour, the bodies had been removed. All three battalions of the 115th moved forward that day without encountering any significant numbers of the enemy. One battle, an ambush, was over. Many battles still lay ahead for the Blue and Gray Division before it would end its wartime duty in Germany's industrial Ruhr and Klotze Forest in May 1945. But still, on the early morning of June 10, 1944, that was one terrible ambush.

★★★

Based upon Beyond the Beachhead: The 29th Infantry Division in Normandy *by Joseph Balkoski (Stackpole Books, Harrisburg, Pa., 1989).*

Hitchhiker to the Rescue

LIMPING FROM A SEVERE LEG wound suffered a few weeks before, the hitchhiker on the battle-scarred road to St. Lo, France, was a U.S. army captain determined to catch up with his company of the Second Battalion, Sixtieth Infantry Regiment, Ninth Infantry Division. With his men in tough battle again, Captain Matt Urban, a native of Buffalo, New York, had checked out of the convalescent wards in England and made his way back to France on his own. They might need him.

Arriving at the Second Battalion Command Post at 1130 hours, July 25, 1944, he found that his unit had jumped off at 1100 hours in the first attack of "Operation Cobra."

Cobra, quickly following on the heels of St. Lo's capture, was the operation that finally carried U.S. forces beyond the hedgerows of Normandy's bocage country, where they had been stymied and held to small advances ever since D-Day, June 6.

Captain Urban had suffered his leg wound just about a week after the Normandy landings. At Renouf on June 14, he and his company ran into two German tanks and heavy small-arms fire. The tanks soon were "unmercifully raking his unit's positions and inflicting heavy casualties."

With his company's very survival at stake, Urban grabbed a bazooka, worked his way forward among the hedgerows despite the "barrage of fire," and drew near the tanks.

He brazenly exposed himself to the enemy fire and, firing the bazooka, destroyed both tanks.

With that, his men routed the German infantry ahead and moved forward. Later the same day, though, near Orglandes, Urban suffered his severe leg wound—"by direct fire from a 37mm tank gun."

Refusing medical evacuation, he saw that his men were settled into defensive positions for the night. At dawn the next day, he led them in still another attack—an hour later he suffered another wound. He was then evacuated to England.

During his convalescence, however, he heard about his unit's heavy casualties in the bitter fighting that continued in Normandy for several weeks. With the "big push" on for Operation Cobra in late July, he couldn't stand to sit still any longer and "hitchhiked his way back to his unit near St. Lo, France."

Now, still limping, he caught up with his men just as they were again held up by strong opposition. Two American tanks supporting them had been knocked out, while a third stood by, "intact but with no tank commander or gunner." It simply wasn't moving.

Urban found the young officer, a lieutenant, in charge of the tanks and with him worked out a plan of attack against the German strongpoint ahead. But when the lieutenant and a sergeant climbed aboard the immobile tank to get it rolling again, they came under fire and were killed on the spot.

That left the job to the infantry captain himself.

Captain Urban, though physically hampered by his leg wound, knew quick action had to be taken. He dashed through the scathing fire and mounted the tank. With enemy bullets ricocheting from the tank, Captain Urban ordered the tank driver forward and, completely exposed to the enemy, manned the machine gun and directed devastating fire on the enemy.

Inspired, indeed "galvanized" by the sight, the entire Second Battalion now sprang into action. They attacked and eliminated the German position that had been holding up the Americans.

Urban, though, was not yet through with the war or his heroics. About ten days later, he suffered a chest wound from shell fragments and again refused recommended evacuation. He took command of the entire battalion on August 6, and on August 15 was wounded a fourth time, but still insisted upon staying with his men.

As the Allies now mounted their relentless march across France toward the German homeland, they came upon the same Meuse River that the German *panzers* had crossed in May 1940 to bring about the collapse of France early in the war. Urban and his Second Battalion were ordered to effect a crossing of the river near Heer, Belgium, in early September.

The enemy planned to stop the advance of the Allied army by concentrating heavy forces at the Meuse.

As the battalion attacked toward its assigned crossing point, German artillery, mortars, and small-arms fire stopped Urban's men in their tracks. Leaving his battalion command post to take the lead personally, Urban reorganized his forward elements, then led a charge against the German strongpoint ahead. The advance took him and his men across open, exposed ground, and he suffered still another wound, a serious neck injury.

Although unable to talk above a whisper from the paralyzing neck wound, and in danger of losing his life, he refused to be evacuated until the enemy was routed and his battalion had secured the crossing point of the Meuse River.

It should be no surprise that Captain Matt Urban, twenty-six, for his "personal leadership, limitless bravery and repeated extraordinary exposure to enemy fire (June 14 to September 3, 1944)," was awarded the nation's highest military decoration, the Medal of Honor.

★★★

Based upon Lt. Col. Matt Urban's Medal of Honor citation.

Marooned in America

OH-OH! ON LIBERATOR 107 AT twenty thousand feet at 2 A.M. on June 21, 1944, an engine caught fire. And then all four of the big-nosed bomber's engines quit. *Bail out, bail out,* bawled the pilot, and navigator, bombardier, and flight engineer did exactly that.

Their ship at a more friendly twelve thousand feet by now, they dropped into the Stygian darkness below by way of the bomb bay.

But this, as events turned out, was not to be the last flight of Liberator 107. Still aboard were pilot, copilot, and radioman, none anxious to jump quite yet, their plane still nosing downward…when, at about eight thousand feet, three engines coughed and caught on after all. Number 107 was back in business again! She landed safely a short while later at an army airfield.

And now, about those three crewmen who followed orders and jumped—Where were they? How to locate and bring them home again? What kind of rescue operation would be needed?

Good questions. The same, surely, that struck 2nd Lt. Charles "Goldie" Goldblum, the plane's bombardier, when he realized he had come down in a "hole of some sort." One moment he was floating earthward in his parachute, the lights of some town clearly visible although distant from him. And in the next moment? "Suddenly they blinked out completely, as if someone had drawn a blind over them," he later said. The edge of the "hole" had cut off his vision of the distant lights, he had to conclude.

And rightly so. When he came down on terra firma, it was with a wrench, as his chute snagged on something above. With quite a few bumps, he hit a hard and rough wall of some kind. The real shocker, though, came with daybreak.

Good thing, he then discovered, that when he crawled up on a nearby ledge in the night darkness, he didn't unbuckle his parachute harness and try to wander around!

"At first light, he could see that his chute had snagged the edge of a 'great cliff, 1,200 feet above a river,'" wrote Norm Tessman in the July 1997 issue of *Arizona Highways* magazine. "Had he unbuckled his harness, the released tension might have pitched him off balance and over the edge."

Since that still could happen, Goldblum, a "city boy" from Pittsburgh, turned and used his parachute shrouds to climb up the rock face to the top of the cliff. And…what a sight! "He stood on the edge of a cactus-covered plateau. Beyond this platform soared great red-layered cliffs, the most distant gray-white toward the top and capped with trees. Behind yawned the precipice he so nearly had drifted over. To his right, a side canyon deepened across the plateau. In all directions he saw cliffs and peaks of every shape, their faces blazing with early morning sun."

The fact is, he and his two fellow crewmen from Liberator 107, barely two weeks after the D-Day landings at Normandy, had come down in America's own Grand Canyon…and it would be ten long days before they could all be "rescued" from the deep gash in the Arizona landscape. It is, after all, a very deep gash.

On his first day within canyon walls, Goldblum came across fellow crewman (and 107 navigator) Maurice "Mo" Cruickshank, who was hobbled by a broken foot. Needing water, they worked their way down Tuna Creek to the Colorado River…and drank thankfully.

Next day, proceeding downstream alongside the river, they encountered Corporal Roy R. Embanks, flight engineer of their B-24 Liberator. They first spotted him on a ridge above their riverside route. He was fine, and he thoughtfully had spread his chute out on flat ground, weighted down by rocks, to attract the attention of potential rescuers looking for them.

Now the trio experimented with the idea of floating out of the canyon on a log raft, but when they tested the idea by shoving a large tree trunk into the flooding river, "It thrashed-end-over-end, convincing them there would be no escape via the river."

The third day they were stranded in the canyon was June 23, and after hearing the sound of passing aircraft far above, they decided to risk leaving their water source. They would return to Tonto Plateau in hopes of being more easily seen from the skies above.

They began the climb the morning of June 24 and, after "a long tortuous ascent up a side canyon," at last reached the plateau. They heard "bomber engines" and to the east, where Embanks had spread his chute as a marker, they saw the rising plume of a smoke bomb. After yet another difficult struggle in their weakening condition, they reached the spot and found only a "blackened circle."

It seemed to indicate that someone knew they were there, in the canyon, but they prayed that night anyway.

The next day, June 25, help did appear—in the air. First one aircraft, a B-24, passed overhead, then came a second plane. It dropped K rations and canteens cushioned against breakage in blankets. Still other drops gave the wanderers a fifty-pound radio, additional food, clothing, shoes…their own shoes, although Cruickshanks' fell into the river.

Also arriving had been a message saying, "Greetings! You are in the Grand Canyon. Do not leave your position until notified by message dropped from an Army airplane."

The stranded air crewmen were amply supplied, but, as the saying goes, they weren't out of the woods yet. Mounting the first attempt to rescue them was a team sent to negotiate a trail from the canyon's South Rim down to the riverbanks opposite the trio's campsite. The mule-borne team carried a "two-piece rescue boat" and a line-firing cannon, but upon seeing the river's angry flood-waters and the granite banks opposite, the rescuers decided their line would never penetrate and hold. Giving up the idea of crossing the river at that point, they faced a long climb back up to the South Rim.

Now, another attempt was under way—a two-man team plunging downward from the North Rim. One was Alan MacRae, a frequent canyon hiker who taught at a seminary in the East. He interrupted his honeymoon to join Ranger Ed Lawes in the attempt to reach the air crewmen and lead them out.

They left their jumping-off point, Grama Point, the morning of June 28. At noon the next day, "they strode into the airmens' well supplied camp." Lawes took one look and wryly commented, "You boys sure are suffering in comfort."

It was 12:45 P.M. the next day when all five men finished the climb back to Grama Point—"to a waiting crowd of newspaper and radio reporters, photographers, military brass, and park service officials." The plight of the stranded airmen and the rescue attempts had been big news despite all the dramatic war events in Europe and the Pacific. And soon, after days stranded in America, they themselves were back on duty.

Two of the trio, Cruickshank and Embanks, survived the war, but Goldblum did not. Assigned to a B-24 Liberator unit in the Philippines toward the end of the Pacific War, he was reported missing in action.

★★★

Based upon "The Rescue of the Liberator 107 Crew" by Norm Tessman, Arizona Highways *magazine, July 1997.*

Fear and Trembling

IF HITLER STRUCK FEAR AND trembling in his generals, this was especially true after the open attempt on his life on July 20, 1944, an event that was not isolated unto itself but came as the Allies were breaking out from their continental foothold at Normandy. Hitler's vengeful wrath was expectantly terrible, and among those who went to their deaths as a result was Erwin Rommel (as a forced suicide).

Lesser-known was the military governor of occupied Paris, General von Stuelpnagel, who, upon hearing the erroneous news that Hitler was dead, revealed his role in the conspiracy and then failed in a suicide attempt. He later was hanged.

Also affected by the bomb plot, and in his case not a directly involved conspirator, was Field Marshal Günther Hans von Kluge, who had replaced Gerd von Rundstedt as commander of German forces in the western part of France shortly before July 20. According to his chief of staff, General Günther Blumentritt, Kluge knew there was a plot against Hitler, but had declined to take part in it. Nonetheless, his name turned up in the investigation that followed the abortive July 20 attempt.

Worse, cut off at the front by artillery fire during the Battle of Avranches, he was out of touch with his own headquarters for more than twelve hours one day. Hitler's suspicions were immediately excited; his orders to Kluge became "brusque and even insulting," recalled Blumentritt later.

268 ★ Best Little Stories from World War II

Kluge, the commander charged with stopping the Allies, now carried a double burden. "All this had a very bad effect on any chance that remained of preventing the Allies from breaking out," added Blumentritt. "In the days of crisis Field Marshal von Kluge gave only part of his attention to what was happening at the front. He was looking back over his shoulder anxiously—towards Hitler's headquarters."

So were many others. "He was not the only general who was in that state of worry for conspiracy in the plot against Hitler. Fear permeated and paralyzed the higher commands in the weeks and months that followed."

Shortly after July 20, the German front in the West collapsed, and, unannounced, Field Marshal Walther Model arrived to replace Kluge. "His arrival was the first news of the change that Field Marshal von Kluge received—this sudden arrival of a successor had become the customary manner of dismissal at this time."

A crestfallen, fearful Kluge left for home the next day. In the evening of the day after, Blumentritt received a telephone call informing him that Kluge had suffered a fatal "heart attack." Two days later, the report was changed to "cerebral hemorrhage." Then, he was to receive a state funeral, with Rundstedt slated to deliver a resounding funeral oration.

But then, there would be no state funeral. "I then heard that Field-Marshal von Kluge had taken poison—my opinion is that he committed suicide, not because of his dismissal, but because he believed he would be arrested by the Gestapo as soon as he arrived home."

Narrator Blumentritt had fears of his own, for that matter. He, too, had been privy to discussions about the plot against Hitler, about who was in it, and who was not. And now came his own summons to Hitler's headquarters.

He visited with his family in Marburg on the way east ("in case of what might happen"). While at home, he quivered every time the telephone rang or he heard a car approaching the house. He pressed on to Hitler's headquarters in East Prussia, where he first was told that Hitler was too tired to receive him but to attend the daily conference at noon.

Arriving at the appointed place, he found a group of fellow generals informally gathered in front. Among them were Heinz Guderian, recently appointed chief of the General Staff, and William Keitel, headquarters lackey who later was hanged as a war criminal. The apprehensive Blumentritt noticed that Guderian made no attempt to shake hands, "while Keitel and others stood aloof." Even worse, Guderian in a loud voice said, "I wonder you dare to come here after what has happened in the West (the Normandy debacle)."

As it turned out, Hitler was very cordial to Blumentritt. When his fellow generals learned that the *Führer* had been so pleasant to him, they suddenly became very pleasant too. Keitel even invited Blumentritt to tea. And the reason for his summons to headquarters, by one account, was Hitler's wish to award him the Knight's Cross of the Iron Cross in person. Replaced by a more experienced man as chief of staff in the West, Blumentritt was to return to that fighting front in command of his own army corps. As he left Germany's military command center, he felt, "I had a lucky escape."

★★★

Based upon The Other Side of the Hill *by B. H. Liddell Hart (Cassell and Company Ltd., London, 1981).*

Destruction, Destruction Everywhere

FOR A TIME DURING THE German campaign against the great Black Sea naval base of Sevastopol in the winter of 1941–42, the defenders and residents of the city thought their ordeal had ended.

During December 1941, the advancing Germans had pushed to within six miles of the city. The German offensive was halted, however, by amphibious landings the Soviets mounted on the Kerch Peninsula to the German rear, an operation pressed forward despite the wintry weather.

In the respite, lasting for a few months, Sevastopol's citizens returned to their homes from caves and other shelters and began repairs to the damage wrought before the Kerch landings. The expectation was that the Soviet troops to the east soon would liberate the entire Crimea—the diluted German forces at the city's gates would be driven off.

Instead, the offensive to the northeast was a disaster, and soon the German Eleventh Army once again was drawn up before the city at nearly full force. The German shelling then resumed in earnest.

Both before and after, however, the defenders and citizens of Sevastopol responded in ways that inspired song, poetry, and the stuff of legend. "The Five Sailors of Sevastopol" were five Black Sea navy men who threw themselves bodily under German tanks with hand grenades. In the city, underground factories turned out mines and hand grenades, clothing and footwear, while children learned their lessons in subterranean schools.

Pounded into submission, the Sevastopol of Crimean War fame at last fell. But then it would be the turn of the German occupiers to withstand a siege and vicious, constant shelling by their resurgent enemy at the gate. Once again, the population went underground…their city above given no such refuge.

Two years later, after the Soviets finally recaptured their Black Sea port, Russian-born British journalist Alexander Werth visited Sevastopol. The once lively and beauteous Crimean city, he found, was dead. "Even in the suburbs… there was hardly a house standing. The railway station was a mountain of rubble and twisted metal; on the last day the Germans were at [Sevastopol]…they ran an enormous goods train off the line into a ravine, where it lay smashed, its wheels in the air. Destruction, destruction everywhere."

Werth came across an inscription scratched into an old navy monument by the sea. It was probably written during "the last days of agony of July 1942," he decided.

"You [Sevastopol] are not the same as before, when people smiled at your beauty," it said. "Now everyone curses this spot, because it has caused so much sorrow. Among your ruins, in your lanes and streets, thousands and thousands of people lie, and no one is there to cover their rotting bones."

The sidewalks of the newly liberated city were deserted, Werth found in 1944. The mayor explained that survivors living in the outskirts still looked upon the city proper as verboten. Werth walked the empty, shattered streets recalling historical accounts of the Crimean War of the 1850s, of the fort, still visible across the bay, where a young Leo Tolstoy had been stationed.

Now, in 1944, proceeding to the Khersones Promontory, where some 750 German SS men had fought to the last, Werth found the ground had been "ploughed up by shells and scorched by the fire of the katyusha rockets." The ground was littered with German equipage and "thousands of pieces of paper— photographs, snapshots, passports, maps, private letters." Floating in the surrounding bay waters were rafts and the bodies of men who had tried to escape but could not.

★★★

Based upon Russia at War: 1941–1945 *by Alexander Werth (Dutton, New York, 1964).*

Million and One Heroes

AT CAP CAVALAIRE ON THE French Riviera the morning of August 15, 1944, Sergeant James P. Connor's infantry platoon stumbled into a German minefield just beyond the invasion beaches. He tried to shout a warning, but too late. His platoon leader, Lieutenant John J. Criegh, tripped the wire of a hanging mine. In the explosion that followed, the young officer was torn to bits and Connor was blown ten feet away.

Stunned, bleeding from fragmentation wounds in the neck, Connor got to his feet and helped regroup remaining members of the platoon for the dash to the "safety" of the nearby coastal road. The road, though, was nothing but a bowling alley for depressed 20 mm German flak guns.

Vastly superior in numbers, the Germans were entrenched on a peninsula affording them a commanding view of the road and the beaches where men and equipment of Connor's U.S. Third Infantry Division were still landing as part of the Allied invasion of southern France. It was his platoon's job to penetrate several thousand yards of terrain that were alive with the shot and shell of the flak guns, of mortars, machine guns, and sniper-held weapons. They were to destroy the fortified enemy position—and all with utmost speed.

As Connor's patrol pushed forward to a road bridge just outside the village of Cavalaire-sur-Mer, he shot and killed one enemy rifleman who jumped into view not ten feet away. Seventy-five yards beyond the bridge, he killed a second sniper, but still another had killed the acting platoon leader. Connor, a native of Wilmington, Delaware, was left in charge of the thirty-six-man platoon.

The number of men still available to him had been reduced to twenty, however, and now they were anxious to take cover from the heavy mortar fire dropping all about them. But no, get the hell out of here, he ordered them. The *only* way to escape the mortar fire was to advance and attack its origin, the enemy strongpoint on Cap Cavalaire.

They started forward again. A nearby machine gun opened up and caught Sergeant Connor in the left shoulder. As one of his men knocked out the machine gun with a BAR, he refused medical attention and directed his platoon members in a flanking movement against nearby snipers. The platoon continued its assigned course, through groups of buildings and light woods; it began the ascent on the Cavalaire side of the enemy-held point above the invasion beaches.

Rising from a hole in the ground ahead, a German now shot Connor in the leg, his third wound of the day. He fell. He tried to stand, but couldn't. "Nevertheless," says his official citation, "from his prone position, he gave the orders and directed his men in assaulting the enemy. Infused with…[his] dogged determination, the platoon, though reduced to less than one-third of its original 36 men, outflanked and rushed the enemy with such furiousness that they killed seven, captured 40, seized three machine guns…and took all their assigned objectives."

With more than ten million Americans in uniform for World War II, Connor was one of 434 who received the Congressional Medal of Honor. In the eyes of his own nation, the 434 are a special number, members of an exalted order, but there were millions of other heroes too. They were the American GIs sent to continental Europe like Connor; they were the GI's sent into the Pacific War; they were sailors, marines, Coast Guardsmen, spies, airmen, generals, and admirals who served world wide too.

Not all the war's heroes were Americans, nor even combatants. They were, too, the soldiery of the Allies; they were the Resistance, and they were the civilians pushed, pummeled, and pilloried by war.

Compared to both allies and enemies in World War II, America entered the fray a most unwarlike nation, its experience in war, or taste for it, limited. But its ten million quickly adapted. "What was really amazing," said German Field Marshal Erwin Rommel at one point, "was the speed with which the Americans adapted themselves to modern warfare." They succeeded in an unprecedented way Rommel also noted. "Starting from scratch, an army has been created in the very minimum of time, which, in equipment, armament and organization of all arms, surpasses anything the world has yet seen."

★★★

First published in World War II *magazine, May 1986.*

Marooned in Modern France

TOM MALONEY MIGHT AS WELL have been shipwrecked, marooned on a remote island in the Pacific. Within easy view was a "tower-type" structure. Normally, it would take him only minutes to walk over to it.

In August of 1944, it took Tom Maloney five lonely days to reach the tower.

In the middle of the European War, in the days immediately after a massive invasion of southern France pitting hundreds of thousands of fighting men against each other, Tom Maloney had found himself marooned in a world of pain and desolation on the coast of the same modern but war-racked country, with all those thousands of soldiers, and their civilian onlookers, quite close by.

On August 15, 1944, Maloney was healthy, young…a hotshot P-38 pilot with the Fifteenth Air Force's Twenty-seventh Fighter Squadron, First Fighter Group. On that day, on his sixtieth mission, the twenty-year-old ace shot down two German Me-109s over St. Tropez, France, to give him a total of eight victories for the war thus far. This date would stand out in his memory also as the day the Allies mounted their second invasion of France, a near-perfect amphibious exercise that landed thousands of Americans, French, and British troops along the French Riviera.

For the fighter pilots based at Foggia, Italy, the invasion meant a flurry of combat missions over the next few days. Thus, Maloney flew his sixty-third and sixty-fourth missions in one day, August 19—with number sixty-four destined to be his last.

Dive-bombing a German truck convoy near Avignon, France, Maloney hit one truck so squarely that he saw "the back half of the truck, with the wheels still attached, going end over end by his airplane, plus a heavy concentration of debris." In no time at all, his twin-engine Lightning lost oil in the left engine, which he quickly shut down. He turned for the coast, thirty miles distant, while his right-hand power plant was still going.

He reached the Allied-controlled Mediterranean, but with his right engine also failing due to low oil pressure. He made the fateful decision to ditch his *Maloney's Pony* five to six miles offshore between the Gulf of Lions and the Côte d'Azur, and so far, so good, considering. The plane nosed quickly into the water, like "a submarine," but he managed to wriggle out, inflate a dinghy, and head for shore.

In the hours ahead, two sea rescue boats cruised by without spotting him in the tiny dinghy. They turned and passed him again.

He put to shore, finally, near the mouth of the Rhone River. By now, it was after dark.

He walked inland a short ways, just forty to fifty feet, when "he heard a click, as though someone was cocking a hand gun." He froze on the spot, rooted.

It hadn't been a handgun, of course. It was a mine, and he was practically standing on it. The explosion drove steel shards through his feet, severely lacerated his left hip area, and caused numerous other shrapnel injuries.

With such injuries, Maloney was left immobilized. Semiconscious for a while, he rallied and somehow managed to pull some of the steel shafts out of his feet, the larger ones. He lay back…and three days later awoke, still in the same spot, still alone, still grievously injured. He awoke with a terrible thirst. Forty to fifty feet away there were some green bushes—perhaps there would be water nearby.

Half a day later, he reached the bushes. He could move, barely, by sitting, pushing himself backward with knees bent, then arms taking up the slack, a bit like rowing.

At the end of the fifty feet, there, indeed, was a puddle of water! "Tom says he will never forget the moment!"

Now he could see the tower structure, and in five days, he reached that goal too.

Nothing there. But a short distance away was "a lodge-type building." He backpedaled to it, pushed the door open, and on the floor found some rotten carrots. He couldn't stomach them and couldn't break down a hard chunk of old black bread. Obviously, he would have to move on.

"The area was quite marshy, so Tom was able to fashion a raft of sorts. With this new mode of transportation, he slowly made his way toward what appeared to be a small settlement of the French. He finally reached the settlement and got the attention of six men who were standing around an old truck."

From there, Maloney was carried to a French hospital three miles away, and from it he was taken to an American field hospital and then to a U.S. Army hospital at Naples, Italy. There, the doctors wanted to amputate both legs, but held off at his insistence and that of his group commander, Colonel Robert Richards.

He recovered eventually, at last leaving his many hospital beds in September 1945, more than a year after he suffered his injuries. He married his childhood sweetheart back in the States, Patricia Jean Driggs. In future years, he would undergo further operations and medical treatment, graduate from Oklahoma State University, run his own oil drilling business, and serve his community as a school board clerk, city planning commission chairman, and chairman of his church finance committee. Nor would he be any slouch on the golf course, either.

★★★

Based upon Irv Styer in the 1st Fighter Group Association News, *Fall–Winter, 1986.*

Resistance at Auschwitz

THE MAN REPAIRING THE ROOF, armed with a smuggled camera, was a spy. Earlier, saboteurs within the tightly guarded complex had damaged the roof with planned deliberation. That was the excuse for insertion of the "roofer" now watching, waiting, with his hidden camera.

The camera had to "go in" ahead of him, since he naturally would be searched upon his arrival.

That problem was solved by building a false bottom in a large soup kettle. Protected by a watertight cover, the camera was hidden beneath soup carried into the compound every day from kitchens located outside.

The workers inside had places to hide the camera until the day the "roofer" arrived.

He did, and he reported to the *Obershafführer* in charge, a one-eyed man named Moll.

As usual, this widely dreaded sadist minced no words. "I want you to stay at your job like a dog chained to his post. If you move away from there for one minute you will not come out of here alive. You hear me, you *Schweinhund*?"

David Szmulewski meekly agreed, but when Moll left the compound to meet one of the frequently arriving "transports," the roofer took the camera from a waiting coconspirator and secreted it under his flimsy jacket. He squeezed the lens through an enlarged buttonhole and while working upon the roof was able to snap three key photographs of the secret activity below.

He wrapped the film in a rag and hid it in his roofing tar, while others hastily buried the incriminating camera on the grounds of the compound. Szmulewski finished his repairs and left the compound uneventfully, the film safely hidden in the roofing tar.

He himself wouldn't go far, since he had merely stepped from one prison compound into the far larger boundaries of another one at Auschwitz. The film, though, would be smuggled out; it would show a group of naked women on their way into the gas chamber. Two other shots would reveal bodies being burned in open pits. The place where the "spy" had done his work was the crematorium compound at Auschwitz II, or the Birkenau camp built next to the original death camp, and both on marshy, pestilent ground 160 miles southwest of Warsaw.

Himself an Auschwitz inmate, Szmulewski had arrived in March 1942, while the camp was still being built. Volunteering as a "roofer," though he really wasn't, he had avoided the usual fate of the Auschwitz inmates by being classified "as a prisoner with special skills needed by the administration."

He eventually earned a *Passierschein*, or permit, allowing him "to move about the camp unguarded, including Auschwitz II [Birkenau], where the gas chambers and crematoriums were located." Thus, he was a vital liaison man for the Resistance cells scattered throughout the huge death camp—and the perfect prospect to obtain photographic evidence of what was going on in the new crematorium compound, "whose smoke-belching chimneys were visible to thousands of prisoners in the Birkenau barracks."

The camera itself had been no problem—the Nazis had whole warehouses full of personal belongings left behind by the condemned, some of whom innocently brought cameras with them to Auschwitz.

The camp Resistance was so well organized that the film now was smuggled out and sent to the Polish Underground at Crakow, together with a report from Jozef Cyrankiewicz, a leader in the camp underground who years later would be premier of Poland. The report from Cyrankiewicz was a warning that the Nazis had begun a hideous massacre of Hungarian Jews "transported" to Auschwitz. (Indeed, the 400,000 Hungarian victims killed at Auschwitz would outnumber those from any other nation under Nazi Germany's rule, including Germans.)

The photos that Szmulewski took "provided the outside world with the first photographs of Nazi atrocities inside Auschwitz, giving visual support to the word-picture painted by Cyrankiewicz in his secret report to the P.P.S. [Polish Socialist Party]."

The camp Resistance, however, was not yet through with the crematorium compound. In this dread place, the workers were always several hundred Jews sequestered from the rest of Auschwitz and forced to operate the incineration system. Called the *Sonderkommando*, they themselves were gassed and burned to ashes every two or three months, only to be replaced by a new group performing the same terrible task.

"But the brotherly hand of the underground extended even into the ranks of the *Sonderkommando*. Though cut off from the rest of the prisoners and condemned by the Nazis to spend the last months of their agonized lives burning the bodies of fellow Jews, the underground kept alive within them the spirit of revenge and revolt."

Thus, they had been happy to help David Szmulewski in his photography assignment. Thus, too, in the weeks before October 7, 1944, a young Polish woman by the name of Rosa Robota was a chief organizer in an underground chain that had been smuggling tiny bits of dynamite and other explosives into the crematorium compound.

The source of these forbidden materials was a munitions factory at Auschwitz employing prisoners as slave laborers. Rosa had seen her own family and other Jews from her hometown of Ciechanow marched off to the gas chambers on her arrival in late 1942, and she was more than willing to help the Resistance when a contact told her what was needed.

She organized twenty factory "girls" in a smuggling operation that carried out the explosives in the form of tiny "wheels" that looked like buttons. The women stashed them in matchboxes tucked into their clothing. The "buttons" then went, through many hands, to a Russian named Borodin who was a demolitions expert. He created "bombs" with empty sardine cans as the casings. Rosa herself was again involved in smuggling the explosives into the crematorium enclosure. "The explosives she received were hidden in the handcarts on which corpses of those who had died overnight in the barracks were taken to the crematorium."

Other bombs or their ingredients filtered throughout Auschwitz, since the inmates planned a general uprising, but inside the crematorium enclosure, the *Sonderkommando* learned their turn for liquidation had come. With no time to waste, they blew up Crematorium III (one of the four in use) on October 7, 1944, threw one of their four German overseers into the oven, killed four SS guards, injured many others, then cut through the barbed-wire fence and fled en masse.

They were about six hundred, and they still were within the larger Auschwitz bounds. A "large contingent of SS" men hunted them down and shot them. The subsequent investigation led the SS eventually to Rosa Robota. After interrogation and torture, she was hanged with three other young women conspirators, but not before she was able to scribble a farewell message to her fellow Jews, the Hebrew greeting of *Hashomer Hatzair, Khazak V' Hamatz*—"Be strong and brave."

She and many others had been.

★★★

Based upon Yuri Suhl in They Fought Back: The Story of Jewish Resistance in Nazi Europe, *edited by Yuri Suhl (Schocken Books, New York, paperback edition, 1975).*

Record Set Escaping

HOW MANY LIVES TO A cat…how many escapes allowed to a single man, even in wartime? Especially in wartime. Such a query might well be directed to Grover P. Parker, lieutenant, U.S. Air Force, photo reconnaissance pilot, Twenty-seventh Squadron, Seventh Photo Group, out of England. In only six months' time, he was shot down three times, evaded capture, escaped all three times, and kept returning to base to fly again…and again.

In his first such meeting with unfriendly people, it was southern France, where enemy ground fire brought him down from the sky in early September of 1944—the Allied armies then roaring across France toward the German borders. "Within a week he was back flying missions," reported the veteran-produced *7th Photo Reconnaissance Group Journal*.

The last of his three episodes came in February of 1945, after the Battle of the Bulge, with Germany now in her death throes. This time a German jet fighter—yes, jet, an Me-262—brought him down in the Peenemunde area where all the German rocket scientists had been assembled earlier in the war to work on secret weapons such as the V-2 missile. On this occasion, Grover P. Parker bailed out and "walked back" to liberated territory "via Poland and Russia."

With those two traumas accounted for, the really dramatic interlude was his second shoot-down and escape, the shoot-down part taking place on September 19, 1944, over Holland on the eve of the Anglo-American Operation Market Garden (*A Bridge Too Far* was the book and movie version).

His P-38 Lightning all shot up, Parker was forced to end his photo mission by landing on a beach near Knocke, Holland. Landing *wheels up*, that is—no wheels!

Surviving his jolting return to earth, Parker was captured by onlooking German soldiers before he could set his plane afire—he was marched off to begin a series of stays, a day to several days at a time, in various POW facilities. Neither he nor his German hosts had any idea that he soon would embark on a short career as a guerrilla fighter and raider based on a fleet of barges in the middle of German-occupied territory! But there you have it—that's exactly, in his impatience to get clear, to get home, to get going again, what Parker did.

First, though, there was the small matter of eluding his captors, true. Held in an old warehouse surrounded by a stockade, and quite anxious to move on, he waited for the frequent ritual that attended the arrival of new POWs, always a moment of confusion and commotion. One day, one afternoon, that moment did come again, and slipping unnoticed into a ramshackle building to the rear of the compound, Parker managed to ease out the back unseen, climb the barbed-wire fence at the rear of the stockade, then pass through a few other buildings. In the end, he reached an apartment house and found an elderly couple willing to take him into their apartment on a temporary basis.

He stayed with his brave seniors for about ten days, through various alarms stirred by German search parties, while awaiting contact with the Dutch Underground. Its representatives finally transferred him to an area north of Geertruidenberg. There, with an Englishman, he fell in with an aggressive Resistance band hiding out by day on old river barges and raiding German positions along Holland's many canals and rivers by night. The Resistance group was well armed, well fed—and so successful in its harassment of the hated Germans that it held fifty German prisoners of its own.

The band had to break up and flee one time—it was under direct attack by German SS troops. When the Resistance fighters regrouped later, they found their German prisoners had elected to stay on as prisoners rather than accept liberation by the SS, for fear of either Dutch or German reprisals.

Finally, the Allies reached the Geertruidenberg area, albeit after shelling the Resistance hideout by mistake. Parker, avoiding harm once again, managed to reach the British lines, explain his presence, and resume a rudely interrupted trip home from Holland.

Oddly enough (but perhaps not, considering his proven resourcefulness), he soon was flying his photo reconnaissance missions again. Somehow, he had eluded all the homegrown bureaucracy and red tape that "prohibited combat flight after evading."

In any case, with his third and final shoot-down behind him just a few months later, he did set an apparent record—as the only Allied pilot in the ETO to endure, to evade, and escape after three shoot-downs.

★★★

Based upon Claude Murray, editor, 7th Photo Reconaissance Group Journal.

Apology Between Enemies

UNLIKE THE ALWAYS UGLY PACIFIC War, the American GI sent to Europe some-times was able to maintain an odd relationship of sorts with the German enemy. They shot and killed each other, true…but when the firing died down (and excluding the SS fanatics) there was this personal, sometimes almost intimate bond present. They could speak, interact, soldier to soldier. Or…young-boy-sent-to-war with young-boy-sent-to-war.

U.S. tanks pass through Huertgen Forest in late 1944. (U.S. Army)

While not universally true, many an American veteran can recall the stories of unexpected battlefield camaraderie.

Elliott Johnson, for instance. An artillery lieutenant with the Fourth Infantry

Division, he landed at Normandy, made the crossing of France, and wound up at the end of 1944 in the terrifying tangles of the Huertgen Forest.

His experience was not only with visible German troops taken prisoner, but with the enemy's invisible artillery, directed in many cases by a forward observer like himself. Sometimes it became a personal thing, a duel of sorts.

One day in Normandy, he was approaching a "huge old chateau" protected by a slimy moat. He heard the sound of a deadly German 88. "You could tell from the sound when it was pointed at you. I heard this *chok!* and knew it was mine."

Johnson leaped from his position in the middle of a road over the nearest hedgerow and landed in the moat, "all covered with green slime." The round missed.

Now he had to go back. He dashed across the road and behind a hedgerow on the far side. But—"Not before he took another shot at me. He was up in that church steeple, and he had a telephone going straight down to that guy. When he'd say fire, the guy'd pull that lanyard. I was the target."

The German artillerists were fast and accurate, Johnson realized. He had one more road to cross. They were waiting.

He took a running start and made the dash. The 88 fired again. It was a shade too low, and all that Johnson got was a piece of shrapnel in the thigh. Nothing serious.

A few days later, his friend Fitzpatrick ("a wonderful young man") was hit directly by an 88 shell. Nothing left.

So it went for Johnson, in combat across Europe from June of 1944 until May of 1945, end of the war in Europe. Killing or be killed, advancing, taking prisoners, friends lost, wounded, permanently maimed.

And yet—"I avoid using words like 'kill a man' because I like to divorce myself from that. We recognized that we were in a war, but we recognized that they came from families like we came from families and that they had loved ones and they were good guys and they were bad guys. We were called on by our government, that our country was in jeopardy. Therefore, we had to fight for it. Personally, I had no malice at any time toward the Germans."

The SS was a bit different—brainwashed and difficult to deal with. "Those people made me angry." The regular German, though, the ordinary boys they took prisoner, were just "glad to be out of it." The Americans would take off their shoes and send them down the road to the rear to be processed as POWs. "The last thing they'd do is come back and either shake hands with us or embrace us."

One day in December, near or at the Huertgen, Johnson as artillery observer looked down a steep bank into a small, tight valley and saw "enormous numbers" of German tanks and other vehicles move into a block of forest. He called in his artillery, a massive barrage of burning white phosphorous and one-half posit fuses that would explode just above the ground. "The devastation on that little piece of land, the accuracy of those boys in firing, was incredible. It's one of my bad memories, the suffering."

Then in the Huertgen Forest itself one time he was locked in an almost friendly artillery duel with a German counterpart, a fellow artillery observer. With his crew of three, Lieutenant Johnson had gone forward with their radio equipment to a forester's tower. At the base, they propped up some logs as their shelter from all the artillery tearing up gouges in the deep forest. They did their work, spotting, from the tower above.

On the second day at the outpost, Johnson saw another forester's tower. "There was a German lieutenant looking right at me. We waved at each other. I marked him on the map. I got my guns zeroed in on him, and I know in my heart he did the same thing to me."

Johnson had a view of a road that was a pathway for German tanks. They were Johnson's target. "He would watch my shooting. He was interested in my effectiveness."

And so Johnson brought in the artillery whenever a target presented itself. One day, however, three German ambulances held down the middle of a vehicular convoy—"hands off." Johnson was letting them go by, unmolested...but suddenly the American artillery came in anyway, ambulances or no ambulances.

Frantically, Johnson looked at his lieutenant counterpart and shook his head, "hard as I could." But the German thought Johnson had called down the fire. Johnson saw him pick up his telephone, and that was enough to "hit the ladder" and get down from the tower and into the little log shelter at the bottom.

Seconds later, the German artillery rolled in. The tower almost came tumbling down, but not quite. It nonetheless was "his [the German spotter's] precision shooting."

As soon as the firing stopped, Johnson scrambled up his ladder to the tower cubicle. "I had my hands up and I was waving and shaking my head: not me."

The German looked at Johnson...studying. After a moment the German carefully and symbolically took off his helmet. "That was his apology to me."

★★★

Based upon "The Good War," An Oral History of World War II, Studs Terkel (Pantheon Books, a division of Random House, Inc., New York, 1984).

Wildly Varied Lot

ONLY THE MOST WILD-EYED dramatist could dream up such an array of often pitiable, yet professionally able, characters as the real-life historical figures populating Nazi Germany's most exalted army ranks. If only they had been a bad joke, these men left now to posterity's judgment!

We speak here of "the Rubber Lion" and "the Lackey," of "Clever Hans," "the Leader's Fireman," and "the Noble Lord." And quite a few others, all recalled in historian Samuel W. Mitcham's 1990 book, *Hitler's Field Marshals and Their Battles.*

Cute little names they acquired while nations trembled and wept before the might of their armies.

They all worked for "the Bohemian Corporal," as one of their number insisted on calling Hitler. Another of their company of course, was "the Desert Fox."

They began World War II all together, but not necessarily in philosophical or political agreement. Far from it!

They achieved brilliant victories in the field, one after the other, as their enemies reeled before them.

Short-term would be their hour, however. Long-term would be their undoing.

Nineteen in number, their group finished out World War II with only two still actively serving their country's ground forces. Five had died and one more was on his deathbed. And all those still alive soon would be prisoners of the victorious Allies.

Although several at one time or another did conspire against their leader, most had made their Faustian pact with the devil, and those who chose to live by such a sword indeed were destined to die by it, either physically or spiritually…or in many cases, both. Such was the fate even of the fence-sitters like "Clever Hans," otherwise known to the world as German Field Marshal Günther von Kluge (before war's end, a suicide). He did *not* take part in the plot to assassinate Hitler the summer of 1944, but he knew about it.

Looking back with the aid of a historical "telescope" like Mitcham's book, it is difficult to believe such bizarre personalities once lived, once ruled great military forces, once allowed such mad and evil genius to rule over *them*! And if it all begins to seem so wild and almost…well, fanciful to us who lived at the same time, what must it seem, what will it seem, to later generations?

As noted, the bizarre characters could be both bumbling or cruel and evil.

For instance, the "Rubber Lion." That was the brave-looking War Minister Werner von Blumberg, who visibly lost his nerve in moments of crisis and then made the mistake of marrying a far younger woman who had a past as a prostitute. (At war's end, he was an Allied prisoner dying of cancer.)

The "Lackey" was Hitler's longtime right-hand man, Wilhelm Keitel, a real yes man and toady whose name rhymed with the German word for lackey, a coincidence not exactly lost upon his *Wehrmacht* brethren. Another of their descriptions was "the Nodding Ass." (Keitel at war's end was executed as a war criminal.)

The "Desert Fox," just about everybody knows, was Erwin Rommel of *Afrika Korps* fame (by war's end also a suicide). Hitler's "Fireman" was Walter Model, tough and reliable (from Hitler's point of view) to the very end (also a suicide).

The "Noble Lord" was Friedrich Paulus, the man who surrendered his Sixth Army at Stalingrad because he had to (and because Hitler would not allow a breakout attempt). His nickname came about because, in happier times, he bathed and changed clothes twice a day. (He survived Soviet captivity and returned to a life in East Germany.) More to historian Mitcham's serious point, the trouble with Paulus was "he lacked decisiveness and had convinced himself that Hitler was an infallible military genius—a fatal combination."

Mitcham, pointing out the strength and weaknesses of Hitler's army marshals, chose as most brutal, Ferdinand Schoerner; as "perhaps the most neglected and underrated," Siegmund Wilhelm List; as the man with talents "most misused," Ritter Wilhelm von Leeb; and he clearly thinks Gerd von Rundstedt was, while capable, "not of the first class." It was Rundstedt, incidentally, who habitually referred to Hitler as the "Bohemian Corporal."

Many of the field marshals actually were anti-Nazi or simply apolitical; a few, such as Walter von Reichenau (felled early in the war by a heart attack) were rabidly pro-Nazi. One active anti-Nazi, Erwin von Witzleben, was hanged before war's end for his admitted part in the anti-Hitler assassination plot of July 20, 1944.

Author Mitcham seems to go along with the reputation for genius attending both Rommel (on a tactical level) and Erich von Manstein, but says: "One conclusion I drew from this study was that Hitler's field marshals, on the average, were surprisingly mediocre military commanders." Even so, their stories may remind us all, present and future, of the kind of Germans who very nearly conquered the Old World for a mad "Bohemian Corporal."

★★★

First published in World War II *magazine, March 1991.*

Prepare to Attack Fleet

WHEN THE JAPANESE SENT A powerful column of cruisers and battleships as battering rams against the back door of Leyte Gulf of 1944, few would have drawn the slightest equation to the flatlands of Oklahoma in distant America. Even more remote would have been any thoughts of the Native Americans who roamed the virgin continent before the technologically advanced Europeans learned to bridge entire oceans in their great ships.

Indeed, what could have been less relevant in 1944, as the world's modern fleets gathered for the greatest naval battle in history? Relevant...except that it was a Native American, a Cherokee from landlocked Oklahoma, who led the counterattack against the seemingly overpowering Japanese column at the critical moment of battle.

Among the 216 American ships engaged in the Battle of Leyte Gulf in the Philippines against 64 Japanese vessels...among the 143,000 American personnel (and 42,800 Japanese), few ships or sailors will be remembered so well as the U.S. destroyer *Johnston* and her fighting skipper, Commander Ernest E. Evans, an Annapolis graduate from Pawnee, Oklahoma.

As the situation unfolded October 24, 1944, on a gigantic chessboard of 500,000 square miles, Admiral Takeo Kurita's Center Force, approaching the island of Leyte from the rear, had been badly battered and turned away from the San Bernardino Strait. Or so it seemed.

During the night of October 24–25, the Japanese Southern Force had been caught negotiating the narrow Surigao Strait and mauled so badly that the lower arm of a giant Japanese pincer appeared cut off. Meanwhile, the American invasion of Leyte—MacArthur's return to the Philippines—continued apace, apparently not to be overly disturbed by the last great sortie of the Japanese Imperial Navy.

But Kurita, last seen hightailing in the opposite direction after losing the *Musashi*, one of Japan's two "super" battleships, on October 24, was not to be so easily denied. Unknown to any on the American side, he had turned his Center Force about during the night and now, early the next morning, was barreling down the San Bernardino alleyway after all.

Lt. Comdr. Ernest E. Evans at the commissioning of his destroyer the Johnston, *October 1943. (U.S. Navy Historical Center)*

And no one was watching its handy exit above Samar Island.

"One might have been in the age of Drake," wrote naval historian Samuel Eliot Morison later. "Lord Nelson would have left a frigate to watch…and give him advance notice of the approach of an enemy fleet. How could such a thing happen in broad daylight, in the age of air power and electricity? And to top it all, as if the god of battles wished to test the Americans, he shielded Kurita's fleet from the probing invisible fingers of radar almost until the lookouts sighted it with their own eyes."

Including Japan's second "supership," the *Yamato*, Kurita's juggernaut burst upon "Taffy 3," a weak flotilla of six slow-moving escort carriers and their seven "small boy" escorts. It was sharks against ducks in a millpond.

Blowing smoke and spitting torpedoes, though, the incredibly brave *Johnston* turned to the attack despite the hopeless odds. As other destroyers joined in, even destroyer escorts, the hits they made, the confusion they sowed, the time they gave most of the unprotected carriers to escape, all combined to throw Kurita off stride. Also beset by a swarm of attacking aircraft, with his powerful

Yamato soon sent scurrying to avoid torpedo tracks, Kurita in the end did not plunge on into the vulnerable Leyte landing zone.

Why he didn't brush aside his waspish attackers has been a matter of debate ever since, but one major reason was the unexpected ferocity of the "small boy" attacks, with "General Quarters Johnny," the *Johnston*, showing the way.

Fondly called "Chief" by his men, Evans never faltered in pressing his attack or his interdiction tactics, even when the torpedoes were gone, when his upper clothing had been sucked right off him by the blast of arriving Japanese shells… when he had lost two fingers of his left hand. Or when, at the end, with all guns but one five-incher out of action, his *Johnston* was surrounded by a ring of enemy ships.

As she went down, a Japanese destroyer skipper was seen to salute the gallant *Johnston* from his own bridge.

Later, a grateful nation bestowed upon its Native American son the Medal of Honor. Sadly, it would be posthumous, since Commander Evans was one of the 186 *Johnston* crewmen lost in the memorable battle. But he undoubtedly knew those odds before taking his *Johnston* on what naval historian Morison later called "her mad, brave course" into the teeth of the oncoming Japanese column.

Prepare, Evans had told his crew at the very outset of the battle. *Prepare to attack major portion of Japanese Fleet.* And no exaggeration, they did.

★★★

From various sources.

Agent's Unexpected Role

LACONIC AND TACITURN, JACK TAYLOR was not entirely your stereotypical orthodontist solely interested in retainers and braces. That was the California resident's civilian occupation before the war, true. But he also was a ham radio operator, a licensed pilot, a yachtsman (races in the Hawaiian islands and to Bermuda under his belt), and he once spent two days trapped inside a collapsed gold mine in the Yukon. Quite a résumé…but hold on, there soon would be more.

When he signed up for the U.S. Navy as a lieutenant, he spurned the relative safety of the medical corps to become a line officer aboard a subchaser.

The American OSS was taken with his extracurricular profile and soon had him instructing trainees in boat-handling, underwater demolition, navigation, and related specialties. In short order, he himself was in the field as a behind-the-lines agent. Based in the Balkans, he survived fifteen such missions in Corfu, Yugoslavia, and Albania. Taylor was tall at thirty-three, a handsome man with short-cropped brown hair.

He did not, for all his various attributes that appealed to the OSS, always enjoy the luck of the draw. On one mission, he had endured forty-five days of isolation upon an enemy-occupied island off Albania. His survival was a testament to his inner resources, but the parallel fact was that he had been stranded there helplessly, and his sub-rosa colleagues had been forced to rescue him.

Then, on his very next mission, a parachute drop into Austria at the head of a four-man team, he was captured. As of late 1944, it appeared that his luck finally had run out; that even if he were fortunate enough to survive the horrors ahead, the war was over for him.

But fate had not counted upon the resilience and remarkable courage of the orthodontist from California.

Taylor was beaten into unconsciousness at the moment of his arrest, and from the first his interrogation at the Gestapo headquarters in Vienna's Metropol Hotel was accompanied by slaps and kicks. To his amazement, Taylor learned he "knew" one of the interrogators—a fellow ham radio fan who had "talked" with him before the war.

The peacetime contact did Taylor little good, though. Held for months in solitary confinement at the Metropol facility, he survived bouts of dysentery and pneumonia. He was under threat of death for espionage, but he argued he was a visible combatant, a soldier in the war, since he had operated in Austria dressed in a brown Navy officer's ground-combat uniform.

In early March 1945, American bombs heavily damaged the Metropol—along with other Gestapo prisons. Taylor was moved to a commandeered villa, also in Vienna. He regained some of his strength working outdoors pruning trees, splitting wood. But then came a final ruling from Berlin. Uniform or no, he was considered a spy. The sentence would be execution, to be carried out at the widely dreaded Mauthausen concentration camp near Linz, Austria.

Taylor had no way of knowing then, but the move to Mauthausen would take him to the most deadly of all German concentration camps (not to be confused with "officially designated" extermination camps like Auschwitz).

By war's end, Mauthausen would lead all concentration camps by sending thirty-six thousand inmates to their deaths. But Taylor needed no briefing to appreciate Mauthausen for what it truly was—a torture chamber and center of extermination, whatever its official designation. He was put to work with labor gangs building a crematorium that would double the camp's number of executions.

Typically for Mauthausen, Taylor's greeting upon his arrival on Easter morning, April 1, 1945, was a three-hour beating by SS men and the shooting of a prisoner who allegedly had attempted to escape some time before. In all other respects, Mauthausen was a worst-case scenario of concentration camp horror—sadistic guards, starvation diet, unremitting labor, overcrowded, unsanitary living quarters. A chilling specialty at Mauthausen, though, was its gigantic rock quarry by the banks of the romantically storied Danube.

Not only was the primitive quarry work hard and dangerous for the emaciated inmates, but the guards had a game called "parachutist." That involved dropping a prisoner from the quarry's lip to the rocky floor 150 feet below. If the victim somehow survived, he was carried up the 186 "Steps of Death" to be dropped a second time.

"Official" executions were carried out by gas, hanging, or shooting (in the back of the head), usually in a building known as the "Death House."

Although still under a death sentence himself, Lieutenant John ("Jack") Hedrick Taylor, USN, now found the real wartime role that fate had designed for him.

Clearly, he was a rarity among German concentration camp prisoners. As an American officer, his fellows realized, he could be a compelling postwar witness to the brutalities they were suffering at Mauthausen—if any of them survived, Taylor included. The European nationals with him, many of them professionals with strong anti-Nazi credentials, conceivably could be considered too "political," too anti-Nazi and vengeful to be taken literally in their horror claims.

The American among them would be a far more believable witness. "Thus, they unburdened their most painful memories on him, a litany of men torn to pieces by trained dogs, injected with magnesium chlorate in the heart, tossed into cement mixers, and given hot showers followed by naked exposure in sub-zero temperatures while having hoses turned on them. For each story, Taylor insisted upon two eyewitnesses. Then, he committed the accounts to memory."

On May 5, 1945, forward elements of George S. Patton's Third Army liberated the camp. Weighing a mere 112 pounds and still suffering from dysentery and fever, Taylor was sent to a U.S. Army hospital at Regensburg.

Three weeks later, though, he was back at Mauthausen, to help gather evidence against its surviving wardens and their collaborators. He found eighteen "death books," a meticulous record of the executions carried out at the camp—and prime evidence against its captured war-criminal personnel. He also discovered that his own execution had been scheduled for April 28, but that a fellow inmate, a trusty, had burned the order.

A year later, temporarily recalled to active duty, Lieutenant Commander Jack Taylor was at Dachau for the war crimes trial of the Mauthausen personnel. He was the lead-off witness for the prosecution. His testimony was a major factor in the guilty verdicts that resulted—"the major surviving officials of Mauthausen were convicted and executed."

A year after V–E Day, Jack Taylor went back to his orthodontist's practice in California, his unexpected part of the war finally done.

★★★

Based upon Piercing the Reich: The Penetration of Nazi Germany by American Secret Agents During World War II *by Joseph E. Persico (The Viking Press; Ballantine Books, New York, 1979).*

Presidential Unit Citation

FOR AMERICAN BLACKS, TOO, THE war began with Pearl Harbor. One was Dorie Miller, Mess Attendant Second Class—a common job for a black soldier or sailor at the time—on the battleship *West Virginia*, a big man who also was the ship's heavyweight boxer.

As the Japanese planes bore in on the Sunday morning tableau at Pearl, Miller was serving the nearly empty junior officers' wardroom. Suddenly, for all, frenzied activity aboard ship. Up on the bridge, flying shrapnel from the *Tennessee* alongside struck down the *West Virginia's* skipper, Captain Mervyn Bennion, a fatal wound that nonetheless left him conscious for some time.

Another officer, racing for the command center that was the bridge, encountered Dorie Miller and brought him along. As a result, notes Dorie Miller's Silver Star citation, the sharecropper's son from Waco, Texas, "assisted in moving his Captain, who had been mortally wounded, to a place of greater safety." Assisted while under "serious fire."

Minutes later, Miller was busy with a nearby machine gun—by some accounts he shot down two of the attacking aircraft before he was finished for the
day, before his ship sank. In the interim, he had earned the first Navy Cross to
be awarded to a black soldier…yet he died later in the war aboard the torpedoed aircraft carrier *Liscombe Bay* (November 24, 1943) still a mess attendant.

And so it was for most blacks, for most of the war—menial jobs in manual
labor and housekeeping chores for the most part. Typical of America's all-black
outfits—for there were some—was the Ninety-sixth Engineers (Colored),
which was commanded by a white civil engineer and which spent a good part
of the war building airstrips, docks, and roads in New Guinea and other Pacific
islands. Vital work to be sure, but short on heroics or glory. Exceptions to
the pattern were the few all-black combat outfits, such as the intrepid airmen
known as the Black Eagles (99th Fighter Squadron, later grown to the 332nd
Fighter Group).

The flyers tended to get the publicity, but on the ground there were a handful
of other all-black outfits (often led by white officers)—infantry, artillery, antiaircraft, tank destroyer, and tank units. One was the belatedly recognized 761st
Tank Battalion, which, while nominally assigned to the 26th Infantry Division,
was in actuality on "roving" assignment that broke ground for several divisions
in the long march across France and through Germany.

Broke ground? "The average life of a separate tank battalion was from ten to
twelve days. Then they'd just redline it out and the few men who were left were
attached to somebody else. So when there was a bad spot, they'd send the separate
tank battalion in the area and the division would just bypass it. You were just gun
fodder really. We went 183 days without relief and damn few replacements."

In the 183 days, also recalled former Battalion Commander Charles A. Gates,
himself black, the battalion began with 750 men and ended with 35 killed in
action. "We had 293 who received Purple Hearts. We had 60 who received
Bronze Stars. We had 11 who received Silver Stars. Remember, these awards
were granted through the divisions with whom we'd been attached. A division
naturally is gonna take care of its own first. So for us to have received that
many awards meant to me that any man who received a Bronze Star should
have received a Silver Star and any man who received a Silver Star should have
received a Congressional Medal of Honor. Because we got only the crumbs. So
we must have done a very creditable job."

Later, back home, hostilities over, the tankers of the 761st Battalion discovered at least twelve of the units they had served on temporary status had been
awarded Presidential Unit Citations. Why not the 761st Battalion, apparently

the first black tanker unit to be used in combat—and for 183 days immersed in combat?

"We had tried at the close of World War Two to get someone interested in reading our record and hadn't been successful. In '66 it was introduced in the House and it died as usual; '67, it was introduced and died. After President [Jimmy] Carter'd got into office, he said, 'Write the White House if you have a problem.' I wrote him a letter. On January 24, 1978, he signed our award for a Presidential Unit Citation."

★★★

Based upon: "The Good War" by Studs Terkel (Pantheon Books, New York, 1984); Strength for the Fight: A History of Black Americans in the Military, *by Bernard C. Nalty (The Free Press, New York, 1986); "0755": The Heroes of Pearl Harbor by Donald and Helen Ross (Rokalu Press, Port Orchard, Wash., 1988);* Day of Infamy *by Walter Lord (Henry Holt and Company, New York, 1957).*

Escape from Auschwitz

AT AUSCHWITZ, RUDOLF VRBA'S JOB was to greet the incoming transports and get the dead, dying, and sick out of the boxcars and into a truck that would go straightaway to the crematorium. "The whole murder machinery could work on one principle: that the people came to Auschwitz and didn't know where they were going and for what purpose. The new arrivals were supposed to be kept orderly and without panic marching into the gas chambers. Especially the panic was dangerous from women with small children. So it was important for the Nazis that none of us give some sort of message which could cause a panic, even in the last moment. And anybody who tried to get in touch with the newcomers was either clubbed to death or taken behind the wagon and shot, because if a panic would have broken out, a massacre would have taken place on the spot, on the ramp. It would already be a hitch in the machinery. You can't bring in the next transport with dead bodies and blood around, because this would only increase the panic. The Nazis were concentrating on one thing: it should go in an orderly fashion so that it goes unimpeded. One doesn't lose time."

The man "speaking" here, born Walter Rosenberg rather than Rudolf Vrba, had arrived at Auschwitz on June 30, 1942; two years later, he was a clerk in the huge extermination facility's "quarantine camp," a post allowing him relative freedom of movement and access to information on the "deportations, selections, and extermination of prisoners in Auschwitz." His friend Alfred Wetzler, also a clerk, was in a similar position.

Both were active in the Auschwitz Resistance, but by April 1944, Vrba had concluded there was no chance of fomenting a general uprising. He saw that the Resistance "is not geared for an uprising but for survival of the members of the Resistance." He and Wetzler decided to escape and "inform the world" of what was going on at Auschwitz. "And I thought that if this would be made known by any means within Europe, and especially within Hungary, from where a million Jews were to be transported to Auschwitz immediately, in May—and I knew about that—that this might stir up the Resistance outside and bring help from outside directly to Auschwitz. And thus the escape plans are finally formulated and the escape took place on April 7."

What "took place" when the two Slovakian Jews vanished from sight that day was not what the searching guards assumed. Vrba and his companion had not yet really escaped; they had not yet really gone anywhere; they were still in Auschwitz itself. They merely had gone underground—into an excavated pit hidden by boards and pieces of wood filched from the camp barracks. "They protected themselves against police dogs by scattering gasoline-soaked tobacco around the bunker."

They stayed in their "bunker" for three days and nights, not five hundred yards from a block commander's office. Only when the initial hue and cry over their escape had eased up did they move. With the perimeter guard deployment back to normal by the evening of April 10, they crawled their way out in the darkness and took to the countryside. "After a ten-day-long flight that was full of dramatic experiences, Wetzler and Rosenberg [Vrba] crossed the German-Slovakian border. They rested for three days and nursed their injured feet in the house of a farmer named Cansky in the Slovak community of Skalite." They then reached Zilina, where they made contact with Jewish leaders and imparted their account of the genocide being conducted at Auschwitz.

As their eye-witness details were being filtered through various organizations to a not-always-listening world, still another escape plan was developing back in Auschwitz, where in May the camp "conveyor belt" reached a record extermination figure of nearly twenty-thousand men, women, and children reduced to ashes in one twenty-four-hour period.

In Camp BB-II-d, where escapee Wetzler had served as a clerk, Jewish leader Arnost Rosin was suspected of complicity in Wetzler's escape with Vrba.

"Rosin was called in for questioning and torture." As punishment, he was assigned to hard labor in a gravel pit. But there he met another determined Jewish prisoner, Czezlaw Mordowicz, a Pole. And they discovered in the wall of the pit "a short, narrow passageway—a bunker—that had been filled in with broken stones after the escape of other prisoners."

After surreptitiously preparing the hideaway while at their gravel-pit labors, they "vanished" the night of May 27. Like Vrba and Wetzler, they stayed hidden for three days, and when the initial alarm was lifted, with a lightening of the perimeter guard force, they, too, crawled free, swimming the Sola River and making their way toward Crakow. To avoid a roundup of forced laborers, however, they had to change their plan. Riding on the roof of an overcrowded passenger train, they headed instead for Rosin's native Slovakia, which they reached after a trek through forestland. They also made the right contacts and reported on the events in Auschwitz, and still the outside world did little in response.

All told, there were 230 escape attempts by the thousands of prisoners sent to Auschwitz during the war years. Only about eighty inmates were successful. Eighty was a handful, relatively, but what a remarkable handful!

★★★

Based upon Erich Kulka's "Five Escapes from Auschwitz" in They Fought Back, *edited by Yuri Suhl (Erich Kulka, with his twelve-year-old son, escaped from Auschwitz during its evacuation by the Germans in January 1945 prior to its dismantling); and upon* Shoah: An Oral History of the Holocaust, *text of the film by Claude Lanzmann (Pantheon Books, New York, 1985).*

★ FINAL THROES ★

Remarkable Delaying Action

A SMALL-TOWN BOY LIKE ALVIN York, he came from Right, Tennessee. He joined the New Deal's CCC—Civilian Conservation Corps—at age seventeen, and he joined the U.S. Army on December 1, 1942, his twenty-first birthday.

Two years later, on another December day, Tech Sergeant Vernon McGarity was a squad leader in Company L, 393rd Infantry Regiment, 99th Infantry Division, on the line near a place in Belgium called Krinkelt. That morning, December 16, 1944, the great German counteroffensive to be known as the Battle of the Bulge opened with an intensive artillery barrage. McGarity suffered a painful wound right then, but he was not yet ready to bow out.

He made his way to an aid station, received treatment, and then refused to be evacuated, choosing to return to his hard-pressed men instead.

With German tanks and infantry swarming from out of the snow-clad Ardennes, they needed him.

The fury of the enemy's great western front offensive swirled about the position held by Technical Sergeant McGarity's small force, but so tenaciously did these men fight on orders to stand firm at all costs—that they could not be dislodged despite murderous enemy fire and the breakdown of their communications.

Squad leader McGarity braved the same fire at one point to go forward and rescue a wounded comrade. During the night that followed, he continued to exhort his men to fend off the swarming Germans.

When morning came and the Germans attacked with tanks and infantry, he braved heavy fire to run to an advantageous position where he immobilized the enemy's lead tank with a round from a rocket launcher.

That done, his squad laid down murderous fire of its own that again drove off the German infantry, plus three supporting tanks. McGarity, in the meantime, rescued another wounded American, then directed "devastating fire" on a light cannon the Germans had brought forward.

But now the squad's ammunition was running short—McGarity knew there was more ammunition stashed in a hole about one hundred yards ahead of his squad's defensive line, in the direction of the enemy. He went and retrieved the ammo, despite "a concentration of heavy fire."

The Germans, meanwhile, circled the squad's position and managed to set up a machine-gun emplacement to its rear—along the squad's only prospective route of withdrawal.

Unhesitatingly, the gallant soldier took it upon himself to destroy this menace single-handedly. He left cover and while under steady fire from the enemy, killed or wounded all the hostile gunners with deadly accurate rifle fire and prevented all attempts to re-man the gun.

But a squad is only a squad, and eventually McGarity and his men fired their last round. They would be POWs for the rest of the war, but they had done their bit—especially squad leader Vernon McGarity.

The extraordinary bravery and extreme devotion to duty of Technical Sergeant McGarity supported a remarkable delaying action that provided the time necessary for assembling reserves and forming a line against which the German striking power was shattered.

Like his fellow Tennessean and army sergeant, Alvin York, Vernon McGarity returned home after war's end to a Medal of Honor and various other military decorations—in McGarity's case including the Purple Heart and the POW Medal.

★★★

Based upon The Checkerboard, *99th Infantry Division Association, June 1989, and* Medal of Honor Citation: McGarity, Vernon.

What to Call the Battle?

SUDDEN. IT WAS SO VERY sudden, that morning of December 16, 1944. The fog was closing in when the artillery suddenly erupted, when the big ugly *panzers* clanked forward, and the infantry fanned out from behind. Column upon column of armor and infantry.

The ground was hard and cold…and the fog, the overcast—all perfect for Adolf Hitler's great plan. Allied air cover was *kaput*, grounded.

An incredible twenty-five divisions had been scraped together for the last-gasp effort. Seventeen of them would attempt the opening punch through the paper-thin American front stretched along a hundred-mile, hilly, forested line in the Ardennes at the German-Belgian border. There in the fog and snow a line belonging to the U.S. VIII Corps consisted only of four divisions—two of them unseasoned as yet, the other two fully seasoned but worn and tired out by the race across Western Europe since the breakout from Normandy back in July.

All, in fact, were at the far, far end of a spaghetti-fragile supply network straining to keep up with the combat troops. And, now, in the wintry pre-Christmas weather, the exhausted Allies had paused for the moment at Germany's front door before knocking it down.

Hitler for months had anticipated this moment and had secretly assembled his forces, primed his factories, and exhorted his skeptical generals.

With the Belgian port of Antwerp and a split of Allied ranks as the ultimate goal, Hitler's strategy was to drive his armor through the center while using infantry above and below (north and south) the *panzer*-led thrust to protect its flanks. What Hitler got, at the expense of the surprised and thinly posted Americans on their line, was *not* exactly a clean, penetrating arrowhead on his battle maps.

The line did bend—the cost to both sides was terrible—but the line did not break.

In Paris, the night of December 17, 1944, U.S. Army historian S. L. A. Marshall took a telephone call from an operations officer with General Dwight Eisenhower's Supreme Command. "There's a battle going on up front," said the officer.

Marshall already knew that, although the scope of the German offensive was not yet fully appreciated on the Allied side. For one thing, so many frontline units and their communications links had been wiped out that the rear echelon didn't yet know what was happening up front.

At any rate, historian Marshall was asked what to call the unfolding battle. It needed a name, even as it needed to be fought. He said, "Call it the Battle of the Ardennes."

His caller objected, "But there have been other battles of the Ardennes."

To which Marshall replied: "Wrong. In the past, much fighting in the Ardennes, but never a Battle of the Ardennes."

The caller then suggested the Ardennes Defensive, but Marshall said that wouldn't do, either. Suppose, he pointed out, that the Allies—the Americans, primarily—take the offensive before all is said and done, "and score big?"

A scene typical of the Battle of the Bulge. (U.S. Army)

After all, despite Hitler's most fanatical encouragement to his men, they simply did not have the resources, the manpower, the energy (or, in many cases, the will) to carry out his grand scheme. The Americans were just about certain to regroup, take the offensive, *and score big*, as Marshall said. "Then you will have the battle misnamed."

The caller at this point "tossed in the towel," and, officially speaking, "the Battle of Ardennes" it became.

Of course, as we know today by the sacrifice and heroics of thousands upon thousands of American troops (an incredible 77,000 killed, wounded, or missing), their allies, their supporting air forces—and many a Belgian citizen too—Nazi Germany's great offensive was turned back, with significant materiel and human cost to the enemy side as well. It would be mid-January 1945, though, before the situation was back to normal, more or less, and the Anglo-American forces could begin to roll forward again.

In the meantime, the issue of a name for the battle—one of history's greatest in physical scope and strategic outcome—had been decided. Even on that night of December 17, "Slam" Marshall could look at the maps and see "a great enemy bulge was developing and coming our way."

What he did not yet realize was that the battle's name would soon emerge, "simply because several million GIs so willed it." Back in 1944, *the Battle of the Bulge*.

★★★

First published in Military History *magazine, December 1994.*

Ripple Effect

WITH 600,000 AMERICANS EVENTUALLY INVOLVED in the fighting, the Battle of the Bulge quite arguably was the most dangerous moment for the Allies in Europe. Flaring up along a hundred-mile front in Belgium and Luxembourg just on the western edge of the Ardennes, it would result in 100,000 German and 77,000 American casualties before Hitler recognized defeat and allowed his units to begin withdrawing in the second week of January 1945.

The German counteroffensive took the Americans and their allies completely by surprise. Such a massive offensive exploding from the difficult, winter-mantled Ardennes Forest at that late stage of the war seemed so unlikely that the Americans had been calling their thinly manned line the "ghost front."

Unlikely it had seemed to many of Germany's generals too. When Hitler first told Field Marshals Gerd von Rundstedt and Walther Model, along with other senior strategists, of his plan, they warned him of its risks and proposed less ambitious objectives for the war-weakened German *Wehrmacht*.

Hitler, insisting upon his proposed drive to Antwerp, said: "If we succeed, we will have knocked out half the enemy front. Then let's see what happens."

By battle's end, one of his Bulge commanders, General Hasso von Manteuffel, was struck by a lasting image of his doomed commander in chief. What Manteuffel saw was a "stooped figure with a pale and puffy face, hunched in his chair, his hands trembling, his left arm subject to violent twitching which he did his best to conceal, a sick man, apparently borne down by the burden of his responsibility."

The Bulge had a far greater ripple effect than the immediate issue of halting the Western Allies in their advance into Germany—or, as it turned out, *failing* to halt that advance. The Americans, after the initial confusion and setbacks allowing a sixty-mile German penetration, reacted strongly and soon threw the Germans back, even if their victory was a costly one in personnel and war materiel.

More, the surprise initiative of the Germans was an embarrassment that did not strengthen President Franklin Delano Roosevelt's hand at the Big Three Yalta Conference just weeks later, in early February 1945. Along similar lines, the German focus on the Ardennes counteroffensive made the Red Army's advances from the east all the easier during the same period. Indeed, argued military historian J. F. C. Fuller in his three-volume *A Military History of the Western World*, "Since Hitler had committed his entire strategic reserve in the Ardennes offensive, Stalin decided to open the Russian winter campaign in mid-January; he hoped that by the time the 'Big Three' met, his armies would have overrun the whole of Poland and he would be in a position to present his allies with a *fait accompli*."

Opening on January 12, adds Fuller, the Russian offensive "burst like an avalanche" against the German eastern front. By the time of the Yalta Conference (beginning February 4), the Red Army had reached the Oder River at Kustrin and Breslau—Stalin indeed had won for the Kremlin "the fleeces of Poland and several other countries."

★★★

Based upon various sources.

"Miracles Do Happen"

FROM HIS OWN B-24 LIBERATOR ABOVE, navigator Jackson W. Granholm was sickened to see pilot Charles Giesen's B-24 nosing down, out of their formation over the snowcapped terrain upon which other men were fighting the Battle of the Bulge.

It was Christmas Eve, 1944, and the flak that day was incredibly heavy. Those people could really shoot, had been Granholm's unhappy thought. And now...now, he saw the flak burst right underneath Giesen's big ship, and it nosed down. "There was no external sign of damage to his airplane...no fire, no feathering engines."

Yet, "Suddenly, the whole tail section of Charlie's airplane fell off, taking the tail gunner down."

Mesmerized and horrified, Granholm had to keep on watching.

"I looked anxiously for hatches to open, for crewmen to leap out, for the bomb bay to spill forth escaping people. There was nothing, no sign of anyone bailing out."

As Granholm's own Liberator churned onward, Giesen's stricken ship hit the ground with an impact creating a "vast ball of fire." It appeared the entire crew rode the ship into the ground.

From another angle, another U.S. Eighth Air Force crewman saw a slightly different, albeit still grim, scenario. He saw the ship break into three distinct parts—front complete with wings, tail end alone, and midsection of the fuselage.

Still, with such a midair "hit," how could anyone have survived?

Al Wolak of Foley, Minnesota, did. He was the left waist gunner that day, and he agrees with Granholm that the flak they ran into "was to be the most accurate and intense of any mission we'd ever been on." (For Giesen and crew, this was, in fact, Mission 23.)

Wolak recalls two hits, and then he blacked out. He came to in his waist section of the Liberator, apparently alone. He was unsure how long he had been "out." The waist section was "floating down like a falling leaf."

Wolak tried to gather his wits, figure out what was next. "[I] got to my knees and wiped the blood from my eyes and face, saw my chest pack lying beside me and snapped it on. My steel helmet was lying there, too, with the front part smashed in, and that is how I got knocked out, I believe."

Oddly, Wolak felt in no great rush to depart from his gently falling waist section. His unreasoning impulse was to stay with this light, balanced "leaf" floating in space. Fortunately, he knew better, and he leaped free, to truly float down to earth beneath a parachute.

On the ground, the Germans were waiting—Wolak would be retired from the war as a POW. No surprise in that, considering the circumstances, but just ahead would be a joyous and unexpected discovery after all. "I met the tail gunner and our co-pilot in a German prison camp!"

Their stories? The tail gunner, after his lone and severed section careened downward on its own, had bailed out at two thousand feet. The co-pilot very nearly went all the way down with the Liberator's front section. Shaken by one flak hit, he was looking about the damaged cockpit "and then there was another explosion, and when he came to he was hanging in his parachute just above the ground."

U.S. B-24 Liberators release bombs over Tours, France, July 1944. The white plumes are smoke markers. (National Archives)

Chancing many years later upon Granholm's eyewitness account of that day, Al Wolak in Foley, Minnesota, not only leaped from his chair, but also hastened to write: "As terrible as it looked to you, Mr. Granholm, and to the other boys up there that day, believe now, as I do, that miracles do happen."

★★★

Based upon Jackson W. Granholm and Al Wolak in World War II Magazine, *May and September 1988.*

Platoon's Heroics at the Bulge

BASTOGNE, ST. VITH…SUCH ARE the place-names that usually symbolize American heroics and stubbornness in the Battle of the Bulge. But there also was a small town named Lanzerath, just south of the Losheimergraben cross-roads on the northern shoulder of the long battle line that became known as the Bulge.

Lanzerath, you might say, was at the western end of a funnel through the Ardennes—at the opposite end was the German village of Losheim. The corridor in between was the Losheim Gap. Germany had used the corridor to pour her troops into Belgium in World War I, and again at the start of the campaign against France and the Low Countries in May 1940. Rommel himself came right through the same Losheim Gap.

As the Battle of the Bulge began, eighteen young Americans would be posted on the northern lip of that same funnel into Belgium, on a hillside overlooking the town of Lanzerath. And as the great German counteroffensive of the war opened December 16, the main thrust was assigned to the Sixth SS *Panzer* Army in the same sector of the Ardennes front. A swarm of infantry, closely followed by tanks, would lead the desperate attack.

Aligned opposite the Germans here was the U.S. First Army, stretched out along a lengthy front reaching from Aachen to lower Luxembourg. In the center of the thin Allied line was the American V Corps, and of its three infantry divisions, the newly arrived Ninety-ninth held the center front's southern sector, from Monschau down to Lanzerath and the Losheim Gap, a twenty-one-mile stretch of the "ghost front's" tough terrain and forests that were expected to impede any German attack. As fate would have it, the division's 394th Infantry Regiment held the V Corps' southern flank and was positioned directly athwart the Sixth SS *Panzer's* proposed thrust.

Tanks of the Seventh Armored Division move down a snowy road during the Battle of the Bulge. (U.S. Army)

For the Germans attacking all across the Ardennes front, north, center, and south, speed in reaching key objectives was the name of the game. They had to shock their enemy, overwhelm his thin lines, disrupt his communications, and penetrate as quickly as possible. The offensive could not otherwise be sustained.

And they did shock and stun, they did disrupt communications, they did penetrate in many sectors…but they soon began to fall behind the all-important timetable. On the northern shoulder, one major reason was the 394th Infantry stationed all around Losheimergraben.

In the confusion of battle and deliberate disruption of communications, it was a series of small-unit, sometimes even individual actions that held up Sixth *Panzer* Commander Sepp Dietrich's powerful thrust westward.

The artillery barrage announcing the Battle of the Bulge began at 5:30 A.M. It lasted for two hours.

The 394th's Intelligence and Reconnaissance Platoon was posted that morning at the town of Lanzerath to help fill a gap of more than seven miles between the V Corps' southern flank and the next American corps to the south, the VIII. The platoon thus was the southernmost unit of the V Corps.

Holding the south flank of his regiment, division, and entire corps was platoon leader Lyle Bouck, a first lieutenant about to turn twenty-one the next day. He had established his men in log-covered foxholes on a small hill northwest of, and looking down upon, Lanzerath. Situated in the town itself were elements of a tank destroyer outfit that represented the VIII Corps' northernmost unit.

Bouck was counting upon the Americans in the town to provide warning of any German attack, since they had a better view of the approach from the German end of the Losheim Gap, the only natural funnel of appreciable size on the Ardennes front.

The opening artillery barrage December 16 only briefly struck in Bouck's vicinity and soon lifted for more distant targets to the west, behind. But Bouck then was dismayed to see the men of the tank destroyer outfit hurriedly pull out—the village of Lanzerath suddenly was left empty.

Hustling down to the village with a few of his men, Bouck found a vantage point in the top floor of a building, looked down the road beyond the small town, and saw a German column headed his way. He left two men in the town as an outpost and radioed the information to his headquarters staff. He was not entirely believed (the scope of the Ardennes offensive took hours to become fully appreciated at many points up and down the American front).

Soon, lead elements of the crack German Ninth *Fallschirmjäger* (Parachute) Regiment, Third Parachute Division, reached the village streets while Bouck watched from his hillside position. He would have waited for more of the Germans to come into range, but a blond-haired girl ran into the street and apparently alerted them. Bouck's platoon, seventeen men, immediately opened fire, catching many of the enemy before they could take cover.

At least a full battalion now was alerted to the American platoon's presence. And it responded to the seemingly minor impediment with predictable fury.

For reasons unknown, however, the Germans foolishly, time and again, attacked across more than one hundred yards of open ground before the hill, with no artillery support. They were cut down time and again. Bouck himself called for artillery fire from his distant rear but received little. Below him, as the minutes, then hours, passed, the dead Germans piled up. His men didn't like shooting such easy targets.

Radioing headquarters for instructions for his vastly outnumbered platoon, Bouck was told, "Hold at all costs."

The day, the untenable situation, stretched on, a mere platoon holding off the lead battalion of an entire German regiment. By afternoon, though, the platoon's ammunition was practically gone. Bouck told his radio operator that they had done all they could do, and anybody who wanted to leave, withdraw, could do so.

His radioman, Private William J. Tsakanikas, said he would go only if Bouck left too. But Bouck said: "No, I have orders to hold at all costs. I'm staying."

In the end, no platoon member left the isolated position, except for two messengers Bouck used as runners to regimental headquarters. The Germans, in their overwhelming numbers, finally eliminated the stubborn obstacle in their path with an assault from one flank. They systematically "cleared" the line of foxholes with MP40 submachine guns until every American was killed or taken prisoner. Bouck was among the latter. So was his radioman Tsakanikas, horribly wounded.

By then it was late afternoon; it had taken the German paratroopers eight precious hours to eliminate the few stubborn Americans holding them up at Lanzerath.

Likewise, all up and down the V Corps' southern flank, various elements of the 394th had held up the German advance at various points during the same day. One of those actions was at the Losheimergraben crossroads itself. By late afternoon, December 16, the advancing Germans had cleared most of the crossroads area, but a small group of Americans in houses at the intersection still blocked the way for the German 48th Grenadier Regiment. Finally, the Grenadiers' commander, Wilhelm Osterhold, shouted from behind a nearby building in English that there was no way the handful of GIs could hold out any longer. He threatened them with mayhem from an American antitank mine thrown through the window of their building if they didn't surrender. They did, and Osterhold personally led them out of the building, and soon they shuffled down a road into Germany as POWs.

They could hold their heads high, though—they and their fallen compatriots at the crossroads had held up Osterhold's entire regiment for a full day.

Individual initiative at small-unit level is what the military calls it…and that's what the scattered pockets of the 394th practiced that grim day in the face of overwhelming assault by a long pent-up torrent of enemy forces.

The delays thus inflicted would be fatal to the German timetable on the key northern shoulder of the Bulge.

It often was the same story all up and down the American line. Neither the 394th nor the entire American force along the Ardennes was able, on that first day, to turn back Hitler's great counteroffensive, but small, brave actions here and there contributed to eventual victory with the delays they cost the enemy. Every delay like Lanzerath placed the Sixth SS *Panzer* Army further behind its crucial schedule.

Massive and overwhelming attack up and down the line at dawn the next day, December 17, forced the 394th's withdrawal to Hunningen and, later, to the Elsenborn Ridge. Thanks to the small-unit actions at places such as Lanzerath or the Losheimergraben crossroads, however, Sepp Dietrich's Sixth *Panzer* Army was off to a fatally slowed start.

★★★

Based upon "394th Infantry, Battle of the Bulge," by Captain Stephen Rusiecki in The Checkerboard, *99th Infantry Division Association, February 1989; and* A Time For Trumpets: The Untold Story of the Battle of the Bulge *by Charles B. MacDonald (William Morrow and Company, Inc., New York, 1985).*

Playing Possum

JUST ABOUT EVERYBODY KNOWS HOW possums often escape harm by playing dead. And, well…it's been known to happen on the battlefield too—*people* playing possum to escape further harm. But…repeatedly, three, even four times in a row at the same battle scene?

Meet Matt Miletich, a brand-new replacement thrown into the Battle of the Bulge in December 1944, just seven months after he left high school in Albia, Iowa. He was sent up front to join the 333rd Infantry Regiment, 84th Infantry Division, in the Ardennes on Christmas Day…he and two buddies, Eddie Miller of Ames, Iowa, and Harold Moneypenny of Akron, Ohio. He had met them on the long training-and-assignment pipeline from high school to raging war.

Now, facing a flat and snow-covered field, their First Platoon, Company I, was looking for a German machine-gun emplacement near two Belgian villages, Lamorneil and Freneux. It was early afternoon, January 5, 1945, as the American GIs stepped out of the dark firs along an icy road and viewed the flat field. Where was the machine-gun nest? Beyond the field, two hundred yards away, a farmhouse stood alone. But to the right, just one hundred yards from the Americans, was a "pile of black dirt," and, "That, I thought, is the enemy machine-gun, dug into frozen ground," wrote Miletich later.

It indeed was, and since the machine gun commanded both the flat field and the road, the GIs making up the platoon were amazed to hear their lieutenant order: "Fix bayonets and follow me into the field."

That was crazy, but the men followed their leader anyway. Miletich was certain it would be better to work their way up the roadside ditches or to go by way of the forest and its cover. "But I was new to combat and a raw, green rookie at that. The only rank lower than a buck private rifleman in the infantry is a prisoner in the stockade. And that's where I might have been sent if I tried to suggest a better plan. I probably would have been court-martialed."

The men fixed bayonets and, crossing a barbed-wire fence, stepped out into the field, Miletich and his buddies Miller and Moneypenny included.

Snagged on the barbed wire for a moment, Miletich had to hurry to catch up as, insanely, the company started walking toward the German machine-gun. Just then, "*Zing!* A bullet shot by my ear!"

By reflex, the young GI dropped flat in the snow and began firing at the machine gunners with his rifle—POOM, POOM, POOM! "My rifle roared as loud as a cannon in the snowfield."

After eight shots and while inserting a new clip, it dawned on the Iowa youth that all he could hear was the machine gun and his own weapon—nothing else. "God, all the others must be dead, I thought. What chance have I got, fighting a machine-gun with a rifle!"

And true, the Germans in their dug-in emplacement really had mowed down the platoon and were now zeroed in on the lone GI in a dark uniform sprawled on a white tablet. Their machine-gun rounds "were digging huge, gaping holes in the snow all around my head and shoulders." How he avoided being hit was "more than I'll ever know."

The only way Miletich could think to escape his hopeless-appearing situation was to play dead. He allowed his rifle to drop in the snow. He let his head and body suddenly go limp in a parody of death.

Miracle of miracles! The shooting stopped. And then, silence. A long silence while the boy from Iowa wondered about his buddies, wondered what to do. "I laid as motionless as I could for about an hour in the cold of the January afternoon."

The longer he waited, the more he worried about the possibility that some of his fellow platoon members would be lying wounded or "dying from exposure and lack of medical attention." That thought bothered him more than the cold seeping through his uniform from the snow. He had to get help.

Finally, he made his move—of sorts. "Dragging my rifle with me, I inched along, crawling about three feet toward the fence." He caught a glimpse of another platoon member, Calvin Bock, in a crouch and also moving. But the machine gun stopped all that as it suddenly burst into life again. Bock dropped from Miletich's sight; Miletich himself went limp and again played dead. The machine gun fell silent.

Another agonizing hour passed. That fence and its inviting ditch were so near too! Only three or four feet. "I thought I could sneak to it and roll under the bottom strand of barbed-wire and into the ditch."

Inching along again, Miletich reached the fence, poised to roll—and then, "Suddenly, a furious burst of bullets from the machine-gun sawed off a fence post inches from my face, spraying a fountain of wood chips right in front of my eyes. The top of the post dangled on the strands of barbed-wire and danced crazily back and forth and up and down."

Once more, the Iowa youth played possum. "My head lay right next to the sawed off post and my body was at an angle with the post."

Another uncomfortable hour passed. He still might roll under the wire and into the ditch, he was thinking. Then, he'd be out of the machine gunner's line of fire.

He thought, he agonized, he finally moved. He rolled into the ditch. He started to rise for a dash across the road and into the woods. But no good! Now, a German "burp gun" opened up, just twenty or twenty-five yards away...*from* the woods! He hadn't known they were there too!

Once again, there could be only one escape from the lethal enemy fire—"I wheeled around and did a backward swan dive, pretending to be hit. I let my rifle fly into the air."

This time, the fourth time, thought Matt Miletich, he had better really play dead! Play dead, wait for dark, then see...think what to do. "I lay as motionless as I could, my head hanging back on the road and my legs sprawled crazily in the ditch."

Only after darkness fell did he stir again. Safer now, he could have found some way to crawl away from the day's nightmarish scene, but he paused... hesitated. In the field still, the wounded. He called softly: "Hey, is anybody alive in there?" There was one reply, a private shot in the right leg and stranded just several feet from the fenceline. In low voice, he told Miletich all the others apparently had been killed. Miletich started to drag him from the field, but it was too painful for the wounded man. They decided Miletich would go in search of their unit and its medics. Wending his way through the woods, Miletich indeed did find help in a short while.

But he soon learned that only he and Calvin Bock had escaped totally unharmed—Bock had found his own way out of the deadly field. Miletich's two buddies had been killed, both of them, along with the platoon-leader lieutenant.

The next day, survivors Miletich and Bock were among the Americans who "smashed" their way into the village the machine gun had been defending. Miletich saw the blood-marked field where it all happened the day before. He looked away, toward the fir trees. There, next to the trees, was "a big pile of dead American soldiers."

He never, the rest of his life, forgot that sight. The Iowa boy's eyes by chance lit upon one face in particular. He knew the face. His buddy from Akron, Harold Moneypenny.

★★★

Based upon Matt Miletich in The Bulge Bugle *(Official publication of the Veterans of the Battle of the Bulge, Vol. VIII, No. 4) November 1989.*

Practice Makes Perfect

IN LATE DECEMBER 1944, 1ST Lieutenant Harley L. Brown of the Fifty-fifth Fighter Squadron, Twentieth Fighter Group, was at twenty-five thousand feet over friendly territory test-firing the guns on his P-51 Mustang. He began a "big slow roll" to see how his speedy mount would react while he fired the guns on his back—upside down.

The Mustang didn't react well at all. "When I pulled the trigger, my Mustang stalled and I fell into an inverted spin."

After dropping several thousand feet, the startled young pilot recovered, but his ship then fell into a normal spin. And still dropping.

This went on for quite a while. First one spin, then recover, only to revert into the other spin. Ground coming up pretty fast by now. "I lost 15,000 feet fighting those damn spins."

Finally recovering at ten thousand feet, Brown realized what his mistake was, took his ship back up to twenty-five, and threw her into another spin, intentionally this time. He recovered in three thousand feet and in short time flew on home to base in England.

Three weeks later, those spins—and his mastery of them—probably saved his life.

This time he and his faithful Mustang were above German territory, near Magdeburg. Two to three thousand feet below, he spotted a German Me-109. He nosed down into a dive to take on a dogfight that either would establish him as an ace with five kills…or possibly end the other way. One never knew.

He closed, and the German headed straight up, into a vertical climb. The American P-51D followed right behind. "I kept giving him short bursts and pieces of debris kept falling all around me." The moment finally came when Brown and his Mustang were within twenty yards of the 109, just under him… but neither plane was destined to reach the crest of their hill. Both now faltered and at nearly the same moment stalled out.

That meant, naturally, that each would collapse into a spin. And they did. "We fell several thousand feet spinning almost in formation. That black cross on his fuselage looked big as a barn!"

But this is where Brown's earlier practice session came into vital play for him. "I recovered from the spin and got on him just as he recovered."

Brown now had the advantage, but even then, it wasn't easy. This was his "toughest" dogfight, and the German pilot the smartest he ever had encountered in the air.

"The next three or four minutes he used the most evasive tactics I ever experienced, turning left and right, climbing and diving and slowing down." At one point, Brown had to drop his flaps, lower his landing gear and fire his six 50 calibers to keep from plowing right into the suddenly slowing 109—or streaking on past, to become the hunted instead of hunter.

In the end, though, his guns found the mark. The 109 in front abruptly blew up, with just the wing tips and tail left "fluttering to the ground."

Brown "in a way…was sorry to see him go." But he also knew the practice spins three weeks before had saved him, since otherwise "Jerry would have recovered first and probably got me!" Instead, 1st Lt. Harley L. Brown reached ace status with his fifth air victory.

★★★

Based upon King's Cliffe Remembered, *20th Fighter Group Association*, Vol. 6, No. 2, Summer 1988.

Fateful Tea Party

THE TEA PARTY WAS HELD at the home of Elizabeth von Thadden, former head-mistress and founder of a boarding school in Germany. Present were several associates in the German Resistance movement—among them, the Widow Solf and her daughter and Helmuth James Graf von Moltke, legal adviser to the German High Command and great-grandnephew of the famous Field Marshal Helmuth von Moltke.

Forced by the Nazi regime to leave her beloved school, hostess Thadden had joined the Red Cross and the sputtering German Resistance. She and Frau Solf, widow of a former colonial minister for prewar Germany, were the leaders of the *Solf Kreis* (Circle) near Heidelberg. Frau Solf and daughter Grafin Ballestrem had been active in quiet opposition to Hitler and in helping Jews to escape Nazi persecution.

Moltke, a distinguished young lawyer, had used his position as an adviser in the foreign office of the High Command to help hostages, prisoners of war, and forced laborers, but would be best known for his *Kreisau* Circle, composed of bright young Germans who hoped to replace the Hitler regime with a morally based government.

The "Solf Tea Party" was fateful because of the presence of a newcomer to the group, a young doctor named Reckzeh who claimed to be a Swiss national. He persuaded Frau Solf to entrust him with a letter she wanted smuggled to contacts in neutral Switzerland.

Four months later, in January 1944, all who had attended the tea party, the hostess included, were arrested—Dr. Reckzeh had been a spy for the Gestapo. As a result, both the *Solf* and *Kreisau* circles were broken up.

As time passed, all were executed, one by one—Elizabeth von Thadden on September 8, 1944; Moltke on January 23, 1945. All, that is, except for Frau Solf and her daughter. Their turn was coming, though. They would go on trial early in February 1945 before the widely dreaded People's Court Judge Roland Freisler, who had sent Moltke and many others to their deaths for plots or imagined plots against Hitler and the Nazi regime.

Totally without mercy, Freisler was noted for the abuse he directed at the helpless prisoners brought before his bench. He had sent Moltke, a conscientious Christian, to his death with the comment: "The mask is off. Only in one respect are we and Christianity alike: we demand the whole man."

Certain death also awaited Frau Solf and her daughter as their turn came for an appearance before Freisler's court in the plenary chamber of the Berlin Law Courts. But that very morning, February 3, 1945, a bomb from an American daylight air raid on Berlin ripped into the building and Freisler was killed right in his courtroom. Destroyed with him was the dossier on the Solf case.

A few weeks later, on April 23, the miraculously spared widow and her daughter were released from the Moabit Prison—by mistake. The war in Europe ended two weeks later. They were the only surviving conspirators from the tea party held on September 10, 1943, at the home of Elizabeth von Thadden.

★★★

Based upon the Encyclopedia of the Third Reich *by Louis L. Snyder (Paragon House, New York, 1976).*

Southpaw's Cruel Fate

EVEN IN THE MIDST OF HOT combat there can be the most accidental, totally chance tragedy, startling and dismaying to even the most battle-hardened onlookers. During the liberation of Manila, for instance, sheer accident called upon U.S. Army 2nd Lt. Robert M. Viale, a native of Bayside, California, to make the supreme sacrifice.

It was February 5, 1945, and Viale was leading his 1st Platoon, 148th Infantry Regiment, 37th Infantry Division, toward a small bridge. Held up by fire from three Japanese pillboxes nearby, he and two companions dashed across the bridge behind a grenade-laid smoke screen. He knocked out one of the pillboxes; the other two were taken out by various of his platoon members.

Fatefully, Viale had suffered "a painful" wound in his right arm. He and his platoon couldn't stay where they were, either—their planned pathway into the city had been blocked minutes before by enemy demolitions. Now, after crossing the small bridge, they pushed ahead "through mortar fire and encircling flames." Ahead, though, their only path was blocked by a machine gun placed at a street corner.

Searching for ways to overcome the latest impediment, Viale led his men into a nearby building. In one room were civilians "huddled together." In another, close enough to the machine gun for his intended purposes, was a high, small window with a ladder leading up to it.

One of his men, a right-hander, tried to toss a grenade from the window, but the angle was wrong. As a left-hander, Viale decided he could get the angle with a southpaw throw.

Taking an armed grenade, he started up the ladder. But his wounded right arm failed him—as he tried to steady himself, the armed grenade fell to the floor of the room.

In the five seconds before the grenade would explode, he dropped down, recovered the grenade and looked for a place to dispose of it safely. Finding no way to get rid of the grenade without exposing his own men or the civilians to injury or death, he turned to the wall, held it close to his body and bent over it as it exploded. Second Lieutenant Viale died in minutes, but his heroic act saved the lives of others.

★★★

Based upon Medal of Honor Citation: Viale, Robert M.

"They're Still There"

NAVY DOCTOR RICHARD HAMILTON HAD never seen anything quite like it in his young life. He was aboard the transport attack ship U.S.S. *Mellette* offshore from a small volcanic island in the far Pacific, as for three days the big U.S. Navy ships around him simply pounded the island. From the battleships behind, the shells whistled overhead, and on the hapless island looming in front, there were leaping bursts of black, volcanic dust.

And then came the aircraft, what appeared to be hundreds of carrier-based dive-bombers. Surely their added ordnance would "sink the island." And surely, nobody on that island could survive so awesome a pasting!

But an officer with the grimly awaiting men of the Fourth Marine Division thought otherwise. "Don't let this fool you," he told Hamilton, a recent graduate of the medical school at Kentucky's University of Louisville. "They are still there."

In 1,500 fortified caves, in a network of interlocking tunnels, pillboxes, blockhouses, and plain old trenches, *they*, twenty-one thousand Japanese defenders, *were* still there. For the pasting of their island a mere seven hundred miles south of Japan, they merely ducked under. They didn't fire back. Figuratively, they didn't move. They merely waited.

Even before the marines climbed down to their landing craft the morning of February 19, 1945, the young medical officer felt the somber mood that had taken over the transport ship. "There were no more jokes, no laughing, only silence. It was obvious that some were praying. He saw fear in their eyes. Some were trembling with fear. It was very serious now."

Hamilton, left behind on his ship, idle for the moment, could only watch as the first landing wave went in, the beaches black with their volcanic sand. And...nothing! With his binoculars, "he could even follow his navy medical team as they landed and set up their aid station without a shot being fired." And still, "It was like watching something going on across the street." He watched the marines move in from the beach. So far he on his ship and his medical team on shore had nothing to do—no business.

One second they didn't, the next they did. As in concert, the waiting defenders and their instruments of death filled the air with noise, with shot and shell for all those distant tiny men on the beach shelf, and for the landing barges still nosing in. So intense was it, as well as so sudden, that Hamilton now was sure the marines couldn't possibly cling on. Either they'd "be killed or be pushed back into the ocean."

In minutes, too, the thirteen doctors and forty medics aboard his ship were overwhelmed with the wounded hurriedly carried back from shore. And nothing in his training was preparation for the sights that now greeted him—a leg gone, a face shattered, or even worse. "But the most difficult thing for him were the combat fatigue cases..., the stress of battle with noises, sights, orders and constant threat to life and limbs was too much for some men."

They were, he recalls, "scared to death!" Many of them, trembling uncontrollably, could not calm down. "He learned that no medicine would relax them like two 2-ounce bottles of brandy."

Some he could send back to battle, others not.

For the navy doctor, the Battle of Iwo Jima lasted for ten nightmarish days before his ship moved on to Saipan; for the marines on Iwo, those surviving it all, the battle would last until March 26, more than a month.

Off Okinawa not long after (April 1–July 2, 1945), Hamilton more personally came to know the fear of imminent death, just as his patients ashore did, since at Okinawa the supporting fleet endured weeks of *kamikaze* air attacks by suicidal Japanese pilots (who sank twenty-six ships in the process). Later still, the war by now stopped, the young American doctor was near

Nagasaki. He saw a group of Japanese children who responded to the presence of Americans in sheer panic. "They ran into each other, and into things
as they tried to get away. It was like a wild animal trying to outrun a bigger
and faster predator."

Still, he wouldn't change the way the war ended—with *the Bomb*. "Without
it, we never would have whipped them."

★★★

Based upon Col. Arthur L. Kelly, USA (Ret.), in the Springfield (Ky.) Sun, *May
25, June 1, June 8, 1988.*

Flag Raised at Iwo

THE FIRST AMERICAN FLAG RAISED upon the crest of Mount Suribachi on Iwo
Jima was a small one—54 by 28 inches. It was carried up there by members
of 1st Lt. Harold Schrier's platoon, Second Battalion, Twenty-eighth Marines,
on D-day plus Four at the instigation of the battalion commander, Lt. Col.
Chandler Johnson.

Bill D. Ross, a U.S. Marine combat correspondent who himself was on
bloody Iwo, has told the story.

Heavily defended Suribachi was strangely quiet as Schrier, his forty-man
platoon, and Sergeant Louis R. Lowery, a staff photographer for *Leatherneck*, the
official Marine Corps magazine, made their climb. At the rim of the dormant
volcano, though, they engaged in a short skirmish with Japanese defenders
hidden in caves.

"While the melee was at its height, two men—Corporal Robert Leader
and Private First Class Leo J. Rozek—had found a seven-foot length of iron
pipe from a rainwater cistern and they had attached the flag to it." And they
raised it.

But that's not the end of the story. For one thing, Colonel Johnson, watching from the foot of Suribachi, had a new thought. "Some s.o.b.," he said, "is
going to want that flag as a souvenir, but he's not going to get it. That's our
flag." In minutes, relates Ross, a lisping corporal called "Wabbit" was sent
scampering to the beach to find a new flag.

Meanwhile, Associated Press photographer Joe Rosenthal also had been watching. While "Wabbit" was on his errand, Rosenthal set out for the summit of Suribachi to see about a panoramic shot of the besieged island. He was accompanied by two marine photographers, Private Robert Campbell, a still-photographer, and Sergeant William Genaust, a motion-picture cameraman.

A sergeant dispatched to the summit with the new flag and the three photographers all arrived close together. As Ross, author of the book *Iwo Jima: Legacy of Valor*, tells the tale:

The new flag—twice the size of the original, measuring eight feet by four feet, eight inches—was quickly lashed to a longer length of pipe. Six men were having trouble shoving it into the rubble. The photographers watched for several seconds and then scurried for positions to shoot the action.

Rosenthal frantically piled rocks to get better elevation to make his picture. He focused, and the Speed Graphic's shutter clicked just as the struggling marines hoisted the new flag.

Rosenthal's negatives were flown to Guam that night along with the day's output of copy and photos from correspondents covering the action. When they were processed, darkroom technicians knew in a flash that Rosenthal's Suribachi photo was very, very special. It didn't fit the formula of a conventional news picture—the face of only one man was clearly visible, the rest were either hidden by hands and arms raising the flag, or their heads were turned.

But it was a masterpiece of composition and lighting that captured the mood of the unfolding drama on Iwo Jima. Its stagelike setting and powerful position of the men gave it the graven look of a posed statue—so much so, in fact, that cynics suggested the photo was staged.

The next day, the photo was on the front page of virtually every newspaper in the United States, and it became an instant symbol for millions on the home front—an indelible portrait of patriotism and determination.

The picture won the 1945 Pulitzer Prize. It later was reproduced on a U.S. postage stamp and was re-created in minute detail as the world's largest bronze statue, the memorial that now stands adjacent to Arlington National Cemetery...

Bill Genaust never saw what he shot, he was killed a few days later making more footage of marines in battle. But millions saw his film in movie theaters across the nation. Lou Lowery, the Leatherneck photographer who made pictures of the first flag-raising, received scant attention for his work, as did Bob Campbell.

The call came from Lt. Col. Johnson at the command post to raise the flag at the peak.
(National Archives)

And so, the true story behind the war's most famous photograph, taken by
Joe Rosenthal.

★★★

First published in World War II *magazine, July 1987.*

Aboard "Apartment Ship"

SMALL-TOWNER WILLIAM ROWE DECIDED on the navy for its "better life" than the other branches of wartime service. "You had a decent place to sleep, no C-ration, no foxholes. As long as the ship was not shot out from under you, I figured it would be okay."

As long as…

After his initial training at Great Lakes Training Center near Chicago, he received his orders. Troop train to the West Coast. Then another train up the coast to Bremerton Navy Yard on Puget Sound, near Seattle, Washington. He then saw his "decent place to sleep" for the first time—the newly built U.S. aircraft carrier *Bunker Hill.*

She struck him as quite a sight. "When I first saw it, I thought to myself, 'I'm going on there?' I thought I was looking at an apartment building. It was a little city, with its own library, canteen and chapels."

Perhaps more impressive yet, her "crew of 3,200 men totaled almost as many people as I had left back in Painesdale [his hometown in Michigan]."

The *Bunker Hill* set sail for the Pacific, and she soon was on station to support the American landings at Iwo Jima. "I had experienced a large volume of noise from the drilling in Michigan copper mines, but Iwo Jima was something else. I'll tell you, the noise was really deafening, with both ships and planes hitting the island."

Seaman Second Class Rowe, a loader for a 20 mm gun mount, began to see—and experience—things that would not have been commonplace for the infantry or the air corps. Like when, in that famous 1945 typhoon off Okinawa, the ship swayed so much her flight deck dipped into the water on one side. Or: "Sometimes the screws lifted out of the water, and when they did, the whole ship vibrated. That was scary."

One time, too, Seaman Rowe was on overhead lookout, a four-hour watch that he undertook by lying on the deck and staring straight up—I was to focus my attention on the airspace immediately above the carrier."

He did, but still he was pretty startled when suddenly, "a Jap bomber broke through, coming right at us." Rowe was supposed to holler a warning to the other guys in his gun crew, "but I was so scared that nothing came out."

U.S. Aircraft Carrier Intrepid (CV-11), October 1944. (National Archives)

The enemy craft then released a bomb—"and it looked like the bomb was coming right at me, but it fell 50 feet short of our carrier."

When his crewmates upbraided him for failing to yell a warning, Rowe explained he simply had frozen. "So they said, 'Next time, Rowe, say anything at all—like son of a bitch, or something.'"

Next time, though, would be a lot more serious. During the campaign against Okinawa that April, the Japanese responded with their most intense *kamikaze* effort yet—suicide planes willfully crashing into American ships. The sailors aboard all ships felt the danger, but especially those on the carriers, prime targets in anybody's navy.

"We were living 24 hours a day on a floating target. This thought was always present, but especially so at Okinawa where Japan used the *kamikaze*. We constantly thought of being an open target....It was like living on a large bull's eye."

And then came May 11, 1945. The men of the *Bunker Hill* were at "Condition Easy" at 10:45 that morning—manning battle stations, but with the leisure to read or write letters while others kept watch. Quite suddenly, not one, but two, *kamikazes* broke through the nearby clouds. How they eluded the fire of surrounding lesser ships was a question no one had time to ponder. They were there, upon the *Bunker Hill*, before anyone could react.

The first one, a Zero, dropped a bomb that penetrated the wooden flight deck, went through a section of hull, and exploded over the water. The Zero itself, however, turned for the thirty American planes bunched up on the after flight deck, all fully armed and loaded with aviation fuel—twelve thousand gallons of it. The Zero hit the aircraft parking lot directly, then bounced on into the ocean, an inferno springing up behind.

Just thirty seconds later, the second *kamikaze* came in—a dive-bomber coming down in "an almost vertical dive" until it struck. "The plane hit midships, about 40 feet away from me, flipped over, hit the superstructure [the carrier's 'island'] and shook the whole ship." The dive-bomber's heavy engine careened onward by itself and killed fourteen men in the "flag office" of task force commander [Admiral] Marc Mitscher.

As the two suicide planes impacted and set off explosions and massive fires, Rowe was on a catwalk beneath the after flight deck. Stunned by the first impact, he explained before his death in 1988, "I ran out to my battery and yelled, 'What the hell is this?'" Moments later, the after section of the ship a lake of fire, he had a momentous personal decision to make. With his area hemmed in by advancing flames, the only escape was "over the side." But over the side meant a risky drop to the ocean far below. Rowe climbed over a gun mount's splinter shield and was hanging on to the outside of it. "It must have been an 80-foot drop to the ocean, so I tried to get back into the gun mount because I didn't want to jump. I couldn't do it, though, and that probably saved me from burning to death."

What *did* he do? "Finally, I let go—it's amazing what you'll do when you have to."

Rowe hit the water safely enough, despite the long drop, but he was not yet out of danger. He had no life jacket, and he landed in the huge ship's wake. The tumbling water action pushed him down like a giant hand. He tried to claw back to the surface, "but it was more difficult than I imagined." Finally, though, he did.

He found a floating life jacket, grabbed it, then shared it with an injured shipmate who had none. Soon four survivors in all had formed a small supportive ring in the ocean waters, three helping the injured man.

After two hours, a destroyer picked them all up.

Aboard the *Bunker Hill*, meanwhile, surviving sailors and their officers were doing their best to save the grievously wounded vessel—three of her decks on fire from amidships to stern; flight deck buckled; armor plating peeled away; aircraft elevators hamstrung; the thirty targeted planes in ashes.

Crewmen tossed hot bombs and rockets overboard. The ship's skipper, Captain George Seitz, did his valuable bit by making a difficult, seventy-degree turn that shifted the carrier's list in the opposite direction and thus sent quantities of fuel and ammunition spilling harmlessly off the flight deck into the ocean. He also had turned broadside to the wind, a maneuver blowing the smoke and flames away from the ship.

With such effort, the *Bunker Hill* was saved; she limped all the way back to Bremerton Navy Yard outside Seattle under her own power for extensive repair, with William Rowe once again aboard his "apartment" ship—but on this cruise helping to clean up and prepare dead shipmates for burial at sea.

When the *Bunker Hill* arrived Stateside, *Time* magazine said she "ranked next to the *Franklin* as the most cruelly ravaged U.S. ship ever to reach port under her own power." For both the *Bunker Hill* and William Rowe, the Pacific War ended before they could replenish themselves and return to battle. Rowe, like many others, was just as glad.

He heard about the end of the war on board his battle-scarred ship. "I was in the shower getting ready to go on liberty when I heard hooting and hollering. A guy came in and said the war was over. I didn't go on my liberty. Instead, I thought how wonderful it was to be over and that I was alive, and I realized I wouldn't have to go into battle action again. Funny, I could go on liberty like all the rest of the crew, but I wanted to be alone at a time when everyone else wanted to be together."

★★★

Based upon interview by John F. Wukovits, Military History *magazine, December 1988.*

Obituary

ARTHUR GOLDBERG, HEAD OF THE American OSS Labor Bureau in London and later destined to serve on the U.S. Supreme Court, looked at the woman before him. She was dressed plainly, even severely. A radical Socialist, she always eschewed makeup and wore her hair pulled back in a tight bun.

She would be one of the first American-recruited agents to infiltrate Germany and Austria in the latter half of 1944, and Goldberg felt "a strange foreboding" as she prepared for her mission.

Code-named "Crocus," she was to establish a network of fellow Socialists in the Vienna area. She would "go in" by way of Switzerland, along with Anne Kappius, another Socialist-labor movement believer. They would then split up, with Kappius joining her already-planted agent-husband in the Ruhr and running courier duty for him back to neutral Switzerland.

Escorting them through reoccupied France to the shores of Lake Geneva, American Lieutenant Anthony Turano of the London OSS Air Dispatch Section was struck by the severe and studiously drab appearance of both women.

They stayed the night with a French family, and when the host somehow produced a fine dinner consisting of a large roast and white bread, the two ascetic-looking women ate only the bread. Turano felt constrained the next day to shake their hands in farewell, rather than try the comradely kiss that he normally would have bestowed.

While Anne Kappius was soon with husband Jupp and running her courier missions, "Crocus" didn't enter Austria until early 1945. When she arrived, though, she quickly put together her planned network.

Soon the time came for her to return to Switzerland with her information. At the Austrian-Swiss border, however, she was spotted by a patrol of the German SS. A sharpshooter hit her in both legs. Still conscious and reasoning despite the pain, she placed her cyanide-filled "L Pill" between her jaws and bit down.

Hilde Meisel, a quiet woman in her early thirties, died before the Germans could reach her.

★★★

Based upon Piercing the Reich: The Penetration of Nazi Germany by American Secret Agents During World War II *by Joseph E. Persico (The Viking Press; Ballantine Books, New York, 1979).*

Freedom March

NOW THIS…THIS WAS NEWS INDEED! No mere rumor again sweeping the camp, this was solid news, real development…but a change affecting one and all, a change offering both hope and risk. At *Stalag 357*, north of Hanover, Germany, RAF Warrant Officer James "Dixie" Deans, 29, asked just how the "transfer" would be made.

He could guess the answer—with their country falling apart in the final weeks of the war, the Germans invariably moved their POWs on foot. The guard contingent would be light in number and the mobile POW "camp" would be told to live off the countryside, to forage for food and other essentials.

Sure enough, Camp Commandant Hermann Ostmann, a World War I veteran with a bad arm, told Dean the prisoners would "march in columns," all twelve thousand of them.

And where to? Deans also asked as they confronted one another over Ostmann's desk. "Northeast of here," Ostmann said. "Exactly where I do not know, but I'll get instructions on the way." Whatever the case, the staff and the POWs would set out "immediately."

As Deans and his camp colleagues hurriedly gathered their few belongings, they knew from their hidden radios that the Allies to the west had advanced beyond the Rhine and even now were rounding up German forces in the industrial Ruhr. Colonel Ostmann, however, knew the situation more precisely—the British were fifty to sixty miles from his *Stalag*, and the Americans, fifty.

To keep discipline under the difficult conditions ahead, he knew Deans would be the key. Elected as the POW spokesman, the onetime RAF navigator could claim absolute loyalty from his men. A prisoner of war since 1940, he knew all the prison-camp ropes by now. He knew how to deal with prison-camp commandants too. ("You simply give the blighters hell all the time.")

If in Ostmann's mind Deans would be the man to hold things together, the POW leader was thinking along similar lines as the entourage from *Stalag 357* took to the road. "Using every ruse he could think of, from slow-ups to sit-downs, to minor mutinies, Dixie Deans somehow intended to reach the Allied lines with all twelve thousand men of *Stalag 357*," reported Cornelius Ryan in his 1966 book *The Last Battle*.

Ten days later, neither leader—the Briton or the German—could be sure what the future held, not even what the next day might offer. Food was in short supply; the POWs, already weak and emaciated, had only tatters as their uniforms, and Ostmann obviously didn't have very specific orders from on high…wherever *that* was at the moment. "I don't think he has a clue from one day to the next where the devil we're going," Deans told a comrade.

And Ostmann told Deans, "There is just nothing I can do."

The POWs marched two thousand to a section, and Deans kept an eye on them all by weaving back and forth on a bicycle with a patched-up front tire. Germany, as yet-unconquered Germany, shrank day by day. And as the columns now turned for Gresse to pick up precious Red Cross food parcels, Deans tried to persuade Ostmann to stay at Gresse and allow the advancing British to find them all there.

In the meantime, whenever the POW army reached a German village, two Scottish bagpipers shouldered their instruments and broke into the haunting wail unique to the pipes—a sound not often heard in Germany, especially the wartime Germany of the 1940s. It had been Deans's more general instruction for all his POWs to "spruce up even if it hurts" when they passed through a village, "and show these bloody supermen exactly who won this war."

At Gresse, as promised, they found the Red Cross parcels—thanks, in fact, to Deans. He had talked Ostmann into allowing a few of the POWs themselves to drive supply trucks to a Red Cross center to load up the parcels. And now they were here—manna from heaven for the semistarved POWs.

But here also, up in the sky, were nine fighter planes. They were British, and the twelve thousand POWs at ground level below of course were British. The men up in the sky didn't know. The men on the ground were in a delirium of delight—the parcels contained both food and cigarettes. "The arrival of the parcels was a plain miracle," said Flight Sergeant Calton Younger many years later, "and we promptly invested Deans with the qualities of a saint."

Deans, in the meantime, wheeled around on his frail bike urging his men to save what they could, "because we don't know what Jerry still has up his sleeve."

Up in the sky, the RAF Typhoons circled the happy scene. Then they peeled off and screamed into a dive, one after the other. "Someone said, 'My God! They're coming for us!' Men scattered wildly in all directions."

It was over in minutes—rockets and antipersonnel bombs.

Sixty were dead, others grievously wounded, and all the rest deeply shaken.

Their own planes! "We're your mates!" many had shouted as at least eight of the Typhoons pressed the mistaken attack. (The ninth at last second held its fire, "perhaps realizing the mistake.")

That was it for Deans—no more games of protocol with Ostmann. Telling the German in no uncertain terms that "this sort of thing must never happen again," Deans demanded a pass and permission to plunge ahead of the POW mob and find the British lines as quickly as possible. When Ostmann, taken aback, wavered, Deans reminded him in cold tones that surrendering to the British instead of the advancing Red Army could make a vital difference for the German officer and his men.

After a brief pause, Ostmann agreed to write a pass for Deans, to provide him a decent bike, and to allow a favorite German guard to accompany the British POW leader. The Briton set out that very evening for the front, with German Corporal "Charlie" Gumbach as his only companion.

Days later, in the cellar of a German house east of Lauenburg, with Berlin now in its final throes, Deans and "Charlie" heard the news of Hitler's suicide. The *Hausfrau* "was in tears," but Deans, of course, was delighted. Liberation couldn't be far off now…even if he and his companion still must find a way through the heavy fighting at the frontlines just ahead.

Deans fell asleep that night thinking about how to persuade the Germans to allow passage. He awoke with a tommy gun in his side and a rough voice saying: "Okay, chum, on your feet."

The man was a Brit! Sixth Airborne! The British, it seems had captured the area during the night hours. Liberation was at hand!

Deans quickly established his bona fides, then worked his way up the chain of command with his pleas for fast action to rescue the POWs left behind. Finally brought before Lt. Gen. Evelyn H. Barker, commander of the British Eighth Corps, Deans told the tragic tale of the attack by British Typhoons. When Deans pointed out the whereabouts of his men on a map, Barker hastily issued a stop order—stopping still another attack scheduled for the same sector.

That done, he told Deans not to worry, the British would "overrun" the POW columns in forty-eight hours or less. Deans had done his job, and now he could take it easy, stay there, and enjoy his own liberation.

"No," said Deans, "I promised Colonel Ostmann that I would return." And so, still accompanied by Charlie Gumbach, Deans did—in a captured Mercedes draped with a Red Cross flag.

Two days later, it was a finally and truly liberated Deans who watched as both Colonel Ostmann and Charlie marched into a British compound with their German comrades—now POWs themselves. Just a short while before, Deans and his precious twelve thousand had marched smartly into the British lines—with the skirling bagpipers at the lead, and all free at last.

★★★

Based upon The Last Battle *by Cornelius Ryan (Simon & Schuster, New York, 1966).*

Sink Sank Ship

ARTILLERY SPOTTER LEONARD SINK, A young lieutenant with the U.S. Army's Sixty-sixth ("Black Panther") Infantry Division, was cruising along in his little Piper Cub aircraft above German-held Lorient harbor in France when he noticed an enemy steamer below had edged a bit too close to the Sixty-sixth's latest field artillery positions.

In the past, German boats had been able to ply the harbor waters with impunity from the Sixty-sixth's guns, thanks to prevailing fogs, the extreme ranges involved, and possible counterfire from the really giant guns the Germans had massed around their submarine pens at Lorient.

Once the spring weather arrived, however, the screening mists had lifted. The Panthermen had wormed closer with their field artillery, and on this particular day, someone aboard the passing German steamer became a little too careless.

"What the heck," mused Sink in his spotter plane above. A 155 howitzer shell might not reach, but why not give it a try? Siinto S. Wessman's smoothly written Sixty-sixth Division history tells the rest of the story.

Sink radioed the coordinates to the Sixty-sixth's Lieutenant J. T. Mack, and in seconds there came the splash of a howitzer shell. It was a miss, but only a near miss. The artillerymen on the ground, excited by the possibility of finally discouraging the enemy harbor traffic, bent to their work with such zeal that German gunners began counterfire on the American battery.

This led to a fast and furious artillery duel in which the German guns actually were silenced. Now, it was the careless steamer's turn again. The fire shifted back to that initial target, wrote Wessman in his division's history. "Fifty-nine rounds were fired in record time at the ship that was now trying its best to zigzag out of its precarious position. About half of the 59 struck the vessel. The 300-foot boat, full of holes, sank in 15 minutes."

Also sunk was a salvage barge that attempted to resurrect the stricken vessel. One result was that Sergeant Robert Premoshi's gun crew claimed theirs was the first American field artillery piece in the European theater to sink an oceangoing vessel. Another result was the proud, epigrammatic line that, of all U.S. Army units fielded in Europe during World War II, only the Sixty-sixth Infantry Division ever could boast: "Sink sighted ship; Sink sank same."

The more surprising aspect for many of us today, though, is the vision of any U.S. Army field artillerymen, infantrymen, or artillery spotters engaging the German enemy on the coast of France as late as spring of 1945—almost a year after Normandy and only weeks before the hostilities in Europe ended altogether on May 8!

The fact is that when the Allies swept across France during the summer and fall of 1944, they left behind a very few pockets of German forces to be dealt with later. These were fully active fighting forces left in the war's wake. And not so minor in size or threat, either.

It was the Sixty-sixth Infantry Division's task to contain the Germans left in two principal "pockets" on the French coast—Lorient and St. Nazaire, both long-standing bastions known for their U-boat pens.

All told, an estimated fifty thousand Germans became trapped at the two ports, along with thousands of French civilians. The enemy couldn't break out, but his submarines were able to continue using their base facilities, and the Allied forces available weren't enough to "break in," either. The result was a sort of standoff marked by artillery duels as the surrounding American forces squeezed the two port perimeters more and more tightly.

V-E Day ended the standoff, but not before the Black Panther artillerymen had sunk fourteen vessels at Lorient, knocked out huge 340 mm German guns on nearby Quiberon Island (despite their nineteen-mile range), imposed such a rain of accurate artillery fire that only the underground sub pens offered safety…and, of major importance, too, had begun a German-American negotiated evacuation of civilians caught in the lethal siege.

★★★

First published in World War II *magazine, May 1991.*

Who Are You?

BANGING AGAIN AND AGAIN ON the door in the stricken city was a terribly injured man, Herbert Kosney. The woman opening the door, then shrinking back in horror, was his wife, Hedwig. And what did she have to say? "Who are you?" she said.

And he? "I'm Herbert." Then he collapsed.

Grievously injured, or not, he would live…as the only postwar survivor of a massacre that took place in the last hours before Berlin fell to the Red Army. The perpetrators were not the Russians, but his fellow Germans, and the victims not really the enemy, but again…Germans.

Herbert Kosney had been swept up and imprisoned in the furor that followed the July 20, 1944, attempt on Hitler's life. His "involvement," if it could be called that, was after-the-fact and strictly peripheral. A doctor friend asked Army *Corporal* Kosney to help in transporting a stranger by military ambulance. Unfortunately, the stranger was General Arthur Nebe, Gestapo official, Chief of the Berlin Criminal Police—and, in the official frenzy that followed the assassination attempt, wanted man. Never mind that Nebe, as commander of the Minsk-based *Einsatzgruppe* B, was "credited" with responsibility for forty-six thousand executions in Russia. That was early in the war, and in late 1944 he would be, himself, executed for alleged complicity in the plot against Hitler. (It has been suggested that he worked with the German Resistance all along and was not directly involved in the pogroms to the east; it also has been alleged that he escaped execution in Germany despite what the official records may say.)

The doctor who asked the favor of Herbert Kosney was a member of a Communist resistance group along with Herbert's older brother, Kurt. Two years before, Kurt had been so determined to stop his younger brother's return to the eastern front that he took a rifle and broke Herbert's arm with it. Thereafter, their mutual doctor friend repeatedly certified Herbert should remain on light duty with a reserve battalion in Berlin.

As a result of the ambulance ride and Nebe's arrest, however, the doctor committed suicide and Herbert was given a death sentence. He awaited his fate in the final months of 1944 and those of early 1945 in Wing B of the notorious Lehrterstrasse Prison with many of the alleged anti-Hitler conspirators, many of them totally innocent—even proved innocent in trials, but held anyway.

Possibly two hundred souls waited in Wing B for final Gestapo disposition. Prisoners came and went, many never to be seen again.

Not far from Herbert's cell, unknown to him, was his brother Kurt, rounded up for his communist involvement. Herbert, it also seems, "had been on the fringes of various Red underground groups since 1940," but he was not, himself, a communist. The two brothers learned of each other's presence during an Allied air raid in early April 1945. When the incendiaries penetrated the roof of Wing B and set myriad fires below, the prisoners were set loose to fight the small fires. It was then that Cell 244 discovered Cell 247—brothers Herbert and Kurt!

More time passed in anxiety and tension; of the two, Herbert was in the greatest danger, thanks to his death sentence that only needed rubber stamping by a military tribunal. Kurt, on the other hand, was charged with no crime; he was being held merely as a suspected Communist.

With the Red Army at Berlin's very gates late in April, Kurt was able to walk out with a fellow prisoner's conscientious objector's release slip. Kurt took it after the prisoner said he would rather wait for the war's end in the relative safety of the prison. Kurt first had offered it to his brother Herbert, but Herbert, thinking of the death sentence that set him apart, realistically argued: "You'll have a better chance [of slipping out of prison with the release]. You go."

Kurt, joining a group of Jehovah's Witnesses in a processing line, soon found himself outside the prison, on a street where the air was "thick" with shrapnel. He was free, but Herbert? Still a condemned prisoner.

By evening of April 22, the atmosphere for those left behind in the prison was electric. The rumor was of freedom! In the afternoon, twenty-one men had been released. That evening, a guard arrived in the cellar where the prisoners now were housed as protection from bombing (and kept from possible escape through breached walls above). He read out sixteen names, Herbert's among them.

The sixteen were taken to an office and given their personal belongings. The six SS men in the office were drunk; one said to Herbert, "Well, you'll see your wife pretty soon."

Within hours, though, the sixteen were led under gunpoint from the prison, marched down the street, stripped of the same personal effects, then prodded onward, "each prisoner flanked by an SS man with a machine pistol on his back and a gun in his hand." The group was led by a lieutenant colonel wearing a helmet. It was dark outside and it was raining. Rumbling, Berlin was under siege, in its final throes.

At nearby *Invalidenstrasse*, the group was turned into a skeletal exhibition hall, a ruin held in place by big concrete pillars.

Few now had to be told…each SS guard suddenly took his prisoner by the collar and pushed him against a wall, all about six or seven feet apart. Some of the prisoners begged for mercy. Herbert felt cold steel touching his neck. A sergeant barked the dread order: "Fire," and Herbert jerked his head, turned away.

He heard the volley all around, and he felt the blow. Somehow, motionless, he then was on the ground, but aware…still in the hell of Berlin. A man walked down the line. He fired shots one by one. The lieutenant colonel was shooting the prisoners in the head. One by one, just to make sure.

He reached Herbert. He didn't shoot. He said, "This pig has had enough."

In moments, the SS men were gone. "We must hurry," the officer had told them, "we have more work to do tonight."

Now alone, Herbert was bleeding heavily, but he was alive. Turning his head had saved his life. Still, he was bleeding, he couldn't use his right arm or leg—he had been weak to begin with, thanks to his long prison stay. And he was far from home and safety.

But he couldn't stay where he was.

He crawled to the street outside, still *Invalidenstrasse*. After that, he was able to get to his feet and stagger along. He stopped at one point to discard his shoes—he was so weak, "they felt too heavy."

He escaped harm in an encounter with some Hitler Youths who allowed him to pass after noting his injury. In a daze, he was exposed at some point to artillery fire…in a daze, not recalling too many details nor how long it had taken him, he finally reached his own home off *Franseckystrasse*.

The woman responding really was Hedwig and the man knocking—banging—on the door, his face masked by blood, really was Herbert, "the only living witness to the *Lehrterstrasse* Prison massacre."

★★★

Based upon The Last Battle *by Cornelius Ryan (Simon and Schuster, New York, 1966).*

GI's New Boots

LET'S SEE NOW. WORLD WAR II, you say? Wasn't it those really colossal events? You know—Pearl Harbor, North Africa, Guadalcanal, and Normandy. The Bulge and V-E Day. Then, over in the Pacific, the final throes leading up to V-J Day and war's end—Leyte Gulf, Iwo, Okinawa, China-Burma-India, and...The Bomb!

And that's it, right? That *was* it. The war, except for a few assorted firefights here and there?

Wrong. How wrong? Well, for one rather large omission, just ask the guys from General Mark Clark's Fifth Army, who fought one of the longest and toughest infantry campaigns of the entire war...of any war in history, for that matter. Just ask the GI Joes who slogged and fought their way up the Italian boot, all of it; who had the "misfortune" to walk triumphantly into an abandoned Rome on June 5, 1944—the day before that most famous "D-Day" of all D-days, Normandy. *Misfortune*, you could say, because their accomplishments would be eclipsed by the great Normandy-cum-dash-across-Europe campaign of the Allies; because the Fifth Army would remain widely overlooked even though the fighting and slogging against an implacable, well-led German foe continued north of Rome until the very last days of the war in Europe.

Eclipsed? Absolutely. In the fiftieth anniversary commemorations of 1994, the media coverage, the pomp and ceremony, was all about D-Day and *not* the fall of Rome, *not* the campaign in Italy.

Still eclipsed fifty years after the fact? As a post-anniversary issue of *The Blue Devil*, the newsletter published by the Eighty-eighth Infantry Division Association commented: "Media coverage of the anniversary proceedings in Nettuno and Rome ranged from ludicrous to excellent" but with "very few excellent ratings."

No irony or argument intended, the same issue—like many veterans association newsletters—carried first-person GI Joe stories from the war, and one in particular recounted the author's combat experiences in strikingly matter-of-fact style. Absolutely deadpan.

But then, that was Italy, where death and destruction were nearly routine.

Luther F. Werner of Attica, New York, and his I Company, 349th Infantry, were checking out an apparently empty house near a place on the Gothic Line called Battle Mountain one day in October 1944. As they approached the building, German mortar shells began "walking" toward the Americans. Werner dashed for the open door as a fresh round hit close by. Sliding under a table and crashing into a wall in his haste, he still caught enough flying rock and shrapnel in his back to make it bleed, but nothing too serious.

As the company moved on, over terrain ragged with ridges, Werner recalled: "Our company commander was taken to the rear. One platoon leader was lost." But…the war went on. Werner spent the night in a slit trench that slowly filled with water from an underground spring.

On a nearby mountaintop next evening, his friend "Jiminez" investigated a noise in the brush nearby and was…well, "shot and killed by some Germans." Werner saw more enemy behind a machine gun below his position; he cleared them out with two hand grenades.

A German prisoner brought in for interrogation suddenly bolted into the dark. A sergeant's rifle shot sent the man's helmet flying. "We yelled *halt*; why did he have to run?" the sergeant asked.

Next day, while moving forward, mortars started falling around them again. "When they landed close, we dove into the mud," Werner recalled. Werner lent his rifle to a new man, who then lost it. No great matter. A dead GI a couple hundred yards back was lying next to a perfectly good M-1. He wouldn't be needing it.

And so it went. Probably the same in a hundred, a thousand, infantry offensives, probes, or patrols before the grueling campaign was finally over.

But this one, for Werner, did have its climactic moment. That very night, Werner and his comrades found themselves trapped in a farmhouse behind German lines. Platoon leader Jack S. Parker had been stunned by a German grenade, and when he went to look around the corner of the house, he was killed by machine-gun fire. Surrounded, his surviving men took refuge in the farmhouse, with at least three machine guns firing at them in the light of parachute flares.

Werner, caught outside the house, was told to go get help…and he did do his best. He crawled past Germans in the dark; he ran past the Germans. He fell into a berry patch. He ran smack into a face-high German communications wire. He tried to leap a stream, but his feet slipped into the water—the water made his boots squish loudly as he ran, but when he stopped to empty them, shots whizzed by. Close by.

He abandoned his boots, and soon his socks were gone too. He ran and he ran, on field stubble, on dirt roads…and finally, he reached the Eighty-fifth Infantry Division command post. The Americans there notified Werner's own Eighty-eighth Division of his trapped platoon's plight. Unfortunately, his story wasn't immediately believed. After all, the GI would have had to cross German lines twice to reach the Eighty-fifth Division's lines.

But he had, as was confirmed the next day. His company meanwhile, its few survivors, anyway, had held out through the night in their farmhouse, he then learned. Seventeen men, with ten of them killed or wounded.

But still the war would go on. Werner, given a battlefield promotion from private first class to staff sergeant, simply moved on to new ridges, new fire-fights, new deaths all around him.

He had new boots too. Well...not exactly new, but a gift from an officer who explained, "Try these on—I lost one of my boys last night." They were size 9½D, exactly Werner's size.

★★★

From Military History *magazine, March 1996.*

Fifth Army Fortunes

LIEUTENANT GENERAL MARK CLARK'S FIFTH Army was "born," you might say, in North Africa in early 1943, about the time that the Anglo-American Allies began planning their assaults upon Sicily and Italy, known as the "soft under-belly of Europe." While Clark organized and trained, Dwight D. Eisenhower commanded the joint invasion of Sicily in July, with George S. Patton's U.S. Seventh Army as the chief American contribution to Operation Husky. As Eisenhower later noted in his diary, Clark was anxious to see action too.

"Within a month after taking command of the Fifth Army," wrote Eisenhower in May 1944, "he and some of his staff began to plague me as to their future. They became very fearful that the war in the Mediterranean would be won, and they would never get into it, although I assured them that their troops sooner or later had to get into action. I showed them that such an outcome was inescapable."

Even so, added "Ike," Clark and his staff remained "most unhappy through-out the whole spring."

The sometimes bitter irony is that once the Fifth Army indeed was commit-ted to action—at Salerno, September 9, 1943—it would spend the rest of the war virtually on the same, never-ending campaign—Italy. Even in May 1944, Ike noted "this army has been in action continuously since last September 9."

With the "soft underbelly" proving to be a hard shell instead, none of it was ever easy for the Fifth Army—its men were thrown into heartless battles in Italy's heartless mountains and river valleys; its commander Clark was dogged by one controversy after another; its High Command eventually was British rather than American; and its German foe was extremely tough, able, and tenacious in fighting a defensive campaign.

After its shaky start at Salerno, Clark's Fifth Army moved on to capture Naples on October 1, 1943, but twenty miles to the north was slowed in its march to Rome by German resistance at the Volturno River. After that ten-day delay, the Fifth then ran aground as it encountered *Generalfeldmarschall* Albert Kesselring's Winter Line and Gustav Line in the Monte Cassino and Rapido Valley area. With winter weather also conspiring against further advance in the mountainous terrain, the Fifth remained bogged down until May 1944.

Since the Allied invasion of France (Normandy) appeared imminent by then, the dogged fighting in Italy was often forgotten or overlooked; supplies and equipment often were diverted for the "Big Show" to the northwest, with Italy and the Mediterranean becoming a secondary theater of war.

In the meantime, a second Allied landing on the west coast of Italy, at Anzio on January 22, 1944, had provoked a strong German response and an even longer struggle to establish the lodgement and breakout than at Salerno. It was March 1 before that invasion point was considered secure. As at Salerno, Clark took much of the blame despite mitigating factors not always under his own control.

Worse yet, the Thirty-sixth Infantry Division's disastrous attempt to cross the Rapido River by his order in late January had provoked criticism, as did the bombing of the famous Benedictine monastery atop Mount Cassino in February (ironically, against Clark's own objections and better judgment).

Clark then riled his British colleagues with his controversial decision to strike for Rome after the breakout from Anzio in May 1944. The city offered no defense as his troops entered on June 4–5, but the shift in direction had left the Valmontone corridor north open to Kesselring's forces in the south. They would take full advantage of that omission to man new defensive lines in northern Italy, where the German forces would not surrender until May 1945—to Clark in Florence.

He had many admirers and many detractors it seems, but either way, there is no doubt that his Fifth Army saw little else but action from its very first moments on the pebbly beaches at Salerno.

★★★

First published in World War II *magazine, January 1989.*

Horror Story

RELATIVELY FEW WOULD SURVIVE THE grim process of elimination at work in the movement of American POWs from the Philippines to Japan aboard the Japanese "Hellships." For one such group, in fact, the trip meant the horrors of three different *Marus*, since two of the crowded transports were shot out from under the POWs.

The tortuous cruise began late on December 13, 1944, aboard the *Oryoku Maru*, jam-packed not only with 2,000 Japanese women and children returning to Japan, but also with 1,600 American POWs (and 37 British). The Japanese dependents had the topside living quarters for their own; the prisoners, already weak and sickly, were jammed into the cargo holds. For the dependents, the hell would begin the next morning. For the prisoners, it began right away.

Packed tightly together in the dark airless holds, they had to share food buckets and latrine buckets that passed hand to hand, often indistinguishable in the dark until too late. Many had dysentery and uncontrollable diarrhea. The air was foul, fetid. The heat was overpowering. Men could only sit or stand—no room to lie down.

The transport left Manila about 5 P.M., in the company of four additional merchantmen, a cruiser escort, and several destroyers. Night came. Men starved for water. Men died. Men went insane. Many killed one another. "All through the terrible night, the men in hold #5 fought, clawed and tore at each other for a breath of air. Madness, induced by the lack of oxygen, caused many men to pair off and attack their comrades. They slashed the wrists of the weak and drank the blood. Others urinated into their own canteens and drank the fluid."

The next day was hardly any better. It began with fifty of the POWs already dead. Then came the American planes—the convoy had been caught out. "The prisoners stirred apprehensively, knowing that a successful attack might be their death knell. The entire ship vibrated as each bomb straddled the vessel. After their bombing runs, the planes made wide circles and returned, strafing the ship from one end to the other. In hold #2, ricocheting bullets splattered into the [POW] doctors and corpsmen."

The airborne firepower broke open hatch covers or pierced deck planks, at last giving the POWs a breath of fresh air. At the same time, blood from wounded or dead Japanese on the ship's upper levels dripped down on the nearly naked prisoners through the same holes. Topside, the decks were covered with Japanese casualties. The ship's steering gear was knocked out. That evening, it ran aground three hundred yards from the beach at Olongapo Naval Air Station. The POWs still were kept in the airless cargo holds, some of them crazed enough to scramble up the ladders and be shot.

The next morning, American aircraft struck again as a lifeboat was leaving the damaged ship with a few of the sickest POWs. They strafed the lifeboat, then went after the big transport itself—most of the POWs still trapped in the holds. The guards fled, and when they realized, the POWs streamed up the ladders, onto the deck above and into the water alongside. But many were killed first in the cargo holds.

Outside, the American pilots now noticed the bodies in the water by the ship were white and "waved in recognition."

By now, 250 POWs apparently had died aboard the *Oryoku Maru*; the rest were herded from the water and marched—barefoot over coral ripping their feet—to a concrete tennis court at the naval station. They stayed there in the heat of the day, the cold of the night, for 5½ days. "Every morning a roll call was made and a burial party was formed for those who had died during the night."

The American pilots still attacking every day knew the prisoners were there and avoided the tennis court with their ordnance. On the sixth and seventh days, the POWs were moved by truck to San Fernando, Pampanga, where they were housed in both a provincial jail and a movie house with its seats removed.

They received their first hot food since leaving their Bilibid prison camp December 13. It was now December 22. On December 23, 15 of the sickest men were taken out of town by truck and executed by a large open grave— beheaded or bayoneted. On the 24th, Christmas Eve, the rest were packed into railroad boxcars for a ride to Lingayen Gulf, where they were "housed" at an empty school. Christmas dinner was "a half cup of rice and one cup of water for every two persons." The men denuded a hibiscus hedge around the school building, consuming berries, leaves, and all.

On December 26, they were marched to the shoreline. They spent another night with no cover—on a "beach" that was sand covering "hundreds of drums of high-test gasoline buried beneath them." The next day, men dropped from sunstroke on the same hot sand. On December 27, too, the men were taken by barge to two more *Marus*—the *Brazil Maru* and the *Enoura Maru*. The two transport ships soon set off in convoy with four others and destroyer escorts.

The men aboard the *Enoura Maru* were in a stifling hold most recently occupied by horses. They had to clean up the manure underfoot with their hands. Horse flies swarmed over them and into their small rice ration. Every hour or so, a man died "from dehydration, diarrhea, or untended wounds." Most of the same conditions prevailed aboard the *Brazil Maru*. Headed for Formosa, the convoy of six was attacked at sea by American submarines. Two transports ran that gauntlet; the rest were lost. The two were the prison ships carrying the POWs in their cargo holds.

They spent New Year's Day aboard their two *Marus* in Takao harbor, Formosa (Taiwan today). They stayed for several days, except that on January 6, the *Brazil* complement was transferred to the *Enoura Maru*—a total at this point of about 1,200 men still living.

Early on January 9, American aircraft attacked—the *Enoura Maru* was hit by a bomb that exploded against the hull and by at least two more striking elsewhere. Three hundred POWs were killed instantly or mortally injured, with many others wounded as well. "Despite the fact that the *Enoura Maru* was in a heavily populated harbor with doctors and hospitals in the vicinity, the Japanese refused to give any aid to the wounded Americans."

Both the wounded and the dead remained on board. "For three days and nights, the living shadows of men wandered shocked and dazed among the decaying corpses. In the crowded holds it was not uncommon to see men sitting on stacks of dead bodies."

After three days, the exhausted prisoners themselves were ordered to remove the bodies and provide a "burial" party—ashore, the men of the burial party formally saluted farewells as their three hundred comrades were turned over to the Japanese for cremation. The remaining nine hundred prisoners now were transferred to the *Brazil Maru* for continuation of the nightmarish voyage to Japan.

On the *Enoura Maru*, they had died at the rate of about one an hour; on the *Brazil Maru*, as it cruised into colder climes, with an icy blast of air whistling into the cargo hold, they died at the rate of about forty per day. They called the frigid swirl of air the "Wind of Death." And all knew about the "Zero Ward"—a hatch cover about eight feet below the main deck. "Whenever a man felt he could no longer go on, he would say, 'Well, boys, I have had enough. I'm going to sleep in the Zero Ward tonight.'" Death was the only escape from the Zero Ward.

Madness still afflicted the suffering men. Back on the *Oryoku Maru*, U.S. Navy Commander Frank Bridget had been a voice of reason among the men trapped aboard the grounded prison ship. "For God's sake, men, don't leave your place," he had warned. "Every move you make generates heat. Keep fanning the air. There are people in the back who are going to die unless you sit still and keep fanning."

Now, on the *Brazil Maru*, sadly, he had suffered too much, too long. "Commander Frank Bridget was wandering about the deck, dazed and incoherent. He was discovered by the Japanese and beaten. He was thrown back down the hold, where he died the same night."

The *Brazil Maru* plodded northward toward Japan over a span of eighteen days, from January 13 to January 31, 1945. During that period, and before, Chaplain William Cummings had been "a tower of religious strength" for his fellow POWs. Once a day, in the evening, he spoke simple homilies to them and offered prayer. Three days out from Japan, however, "dysentery finally caught up with the priest." He nonetheless went through with his evening ritual—lifted by others so that he could do so. That night, too, he retired to the Zero Ward, where, in hours, he joined the dead.

By the time the *Brazil Maru* docked at Moji, the nightmare voyage finally completed, only 425 survivors were left of the 900 men who had climbed aboard two weeks before. Before going ashore, the shivering men were hauled onto deck, told to strip naked, and sprayed on the spot with a delousing disinfectant. Pulling on his clothes a few moments later, one POW officer paused and dropped dead.

Of the surviving 425, in the days ahead, 135 were hospitalized, and 80 died. The others, the "healthiest," were sent to prison camps near Omuta and Fukouka. In six weeks, 235 of those men also died.

In the end, that is, at war's end, of the 1,600 who set out from Bilibid in early December, 300 survived. Said one of them: "When you speak of the good and the heroic, don't talk about us. The generous men—the brave men—the unselfish men—are the men we left behind."

In his view, the Japanese had been "bad," yes, "but we—the 300 living—we were devils too. If we had not been devils, we could not have survived."

True or untrue? Who but God would presume to judge?

★★★

Based upon A. B. Feuer in Bilibid Diary: The Secret Notebooks of Commander Thomas Hayes, POW, the Philippines, 1942–45, *A. B. Feuer, editor (Archon Books, Hamden, Conn., 1987).*

Rescue by Drunk Driver

WAS CORPORAL ROGER FOEHRINGER ABOUT to look a slightly flawed gift horse in the mouth? No way, not when it was a fully qualified, bona fide American jeep smack-dab in the middle of the town square of Versbach, Germany, just outside of Wurzburg. A U.S. Army jeep complete with driver, that excited-looking fellow sitting on the hood and brandishing a .45 at a ring of Versbach's citizenry.

Foehringer, after all, an artilleryman with the U.S. Ninety-ninth Infantry Division, had been captured in the Battle of the Bulge. He had been marched through snow and ice as a POW. He had been shipped into the heart of Germany in tightly-packed boxcars. He had lost weight, but survived, on a near-starvation diet. He hadn't seen a sign of a Red Cross parcel.

He and his buddies had worked in a Wurzburg military bakery as forced labor.

They had survived American strafing of a rail yard they frequented. They had survived the British night-bombing of the Bavarian city with incendiaries that turned the place into an inferno—"it was the most tremendous wind you've ever felt in your life, and the whole sky and city of Wurzburg seemed to be in flames."

He and his buddies then spent two or three days helping to clean up the debris and remove the bodies beneath, carrying them first to the street curb, then piling them into horse-drawn carts for mass burial.

For the next night or two, Foehringer and his four buddies of the bakery detail "saw the sky lit up and we started to hear rumbles and we knew the front was coming." On Easter Sunday, April 1, 1945, their captors decided to move them back, away from the advancing Americans.

It was on foot, by a side road. At a rest break, the five took a planned nature call in the nearby woods and simply didn't go back. Their POW column moved on without them—no one seemed to care.

Friendly Germans a day later showed them a cave in a hillside near the village of Versbach. They hid there for a few days, with two young boys bringing them food once a day. Then, late one afternoon, the two boys showed up with the news that the Americans had come!

Rushing down to the village square, the five American escapees found the waiting jeep and its sergeant-driver.

The only trouble was, he was what today we call a DUI—drunk! He didn't have the vaguest idea where he was, or how he got there. Moreover, he was far ahead of the frontlines—he was totally alone.

A mechanic with a tank destroyer unit, he had been drinking somewhere to the far rear and decided to "go up to the front and find out where his buddies were, the guys that drove the tank destroyers."

Soon lost, he "had just come through the lines with the jeep—nobody had bothered him, he had just drove [sic] right down the road toward Wurzburg."

Now, of course he wanted to find his way back. Foehringer and his fellow POWs were more than glad to oblige—and ride along.

First, they opened up the jeep's foot locker and spread its "goodies" among the onlooking townspeople—cans of food, candy, K-bars, and the like. The POWs thanked their benefactors, climbed aboard the jeep, and began their return after pointing the driver to the highway back to Wurzburg.

They soon came across the signs of battle—"burning German half-tracks, dead soldiers lying outside the road."

At first there was no sign of their fellow Americans, but then, quite suddenly, "along came a line of infantry on either side of the road and of course it was an American infantry and on their helmets were their insignias." It was the Forty-second ("Rainbow") Division—a welcome sight for the escaping POWs. And they a welcome sight themselves for the wary GIs of the Forty-second, who were "expecting Germans before they saw a jeep with a bunch of Americans hanging on the sides."

★★★

Based upon Roger Foehringer in The Checkerboard, *99th Infantry Division Association, Vol. 42, No. 2, March 1989.*

FDR's Last Visit

HE HAD RETURNED TO HIS beloved Warm Springs only three times since the war started…once in April 1943, then late in 1944, during the Battle of the Bulge, and now, spring of 1945, here he was again, back for an extended visit, it did appear.

One Monday afternoon, an April day it was, the polio-crippled FDR put aside his official papers and called for the specially rigged Ford Phaeton he liked to drive around the Warm Springs complex, throttle, clutch, and brakes subject to hand controls rather than foot pressure. It was about three o'clock, and he was off in a very few minutes, his Secret Service entourage scrambling to keep up as he headed down Pine Mountain.

He proceeded serenely on old Route 41 until it met up with Route 208. There, pulled off the road, was a Cadillac convertible. In it, waiting for him, was an old friend—an old sweetheart, in fact—Lucy Mercer Rutherfurd.

Now, quite true, he recently had begun to violate an old pledge to his wife, Eleanor, never to see Lucy again, but this was no private tête-à-tête of the romantic kind. For waiting in the car with Lucy were the artist Elizabeth Shoumatoff and her photographer Nicholas Robbins. Lucy did ride back to Warm Springs sitting up front in the Phaeton, next to FDR as he drove.

He told her about a barbeque party scheduled for later in the week, for Thursday evening, April 12.

The next day, Tuesday, April 10, FDR was in his car again, this time accompanied by four Secret Service agents. As they sailed past wire service reporter Merriman Smith, who was aboard a frisky horse at the moment, FDR called out, "Heigh-O Silver!"

By now, just about everybody with FDR had noticed how his mood had improved—his pale skin color too—since the presidential party's arrival eleven days earlier. The positive changes reminded many of the "good old days" when he visibly revived in both body and spirit after only a short time back in Warm Springs.

The drive on April 10 took FDR to the top of Pine Mountain, to an overlook he loved, Dowdell's Knob. Pulling to a stop, he asked his four Secret Service guardians to leave him alone for a while. He would honk the horn when ready to go back down the mountain.

They walked back down the road a short ways and smoked a few cigarettes while FDR remained at the overlook, alone with his thoughts. Soon, he did honk the horn, they rejoined him in the car...and the party returned to the Little White House halfway down the mountain slope.

We may never know what his thoughts were up at the overlook that day. He said nothing to the Secret Service agents.

The next day, April 11, the president was busy in the morning working on his annual Jefferson Day speech, to be delivered later in the week by radio from his small study at the Little White House. He worked with Dorothy Brady, an assistant to FDR's secretary, Grace Tully. He said he would work with Grace herself the next day, Thursday, on the address he was preparing for the all-important opening of the United Nations Conference in San Francisco. With the war in Europe visibly winding down, it was time to lay the foundations of the postwar peace.

Miss Tully's postwar book, *FDR: My Boss*, avoided any gossipy comment about Lucy Rutherfurd's arrival. Miss Tully simply said that while she was talking with FDR's cousin Polly Delano at the Little White House Tuesday morning, April 10, "Madame Elizabeth Shoumatoff, the artist, came into the room." Miss Tully's explanation: "Mrs. Winthrop Rutherfurd, who had commissioned her to do the portrait [FDR's], had accompanied her to Warm Springs. Madame Shoumatoff had done an earlier portrait of FDR and was very excited at her concept of a new one."

They talked about the artist's idea of depicting FDR holding a scroll, his navy cape draped around his shoulders—the scroll intended "to represent the treaty of peace that will come soon, we hope."

About that time, an aide wheeled FDR into the living room and study from his adjoining bedroom. "He looked quite rested, was cheerful in his greeting to us all and readily approved Madame Shoumatoff's plans," wrote Miss Tully.

Incidentally, in addition to a navy doctor, the Secret Service gang, a few reporters, a press secretary, and other staff personnel, FDR was accompanied on this trip to Warm Springs by still another cousin, Daisy Suckley, the family benefactor who had presented FDR with his famous Scottie, Fala. In fact, Fala was on hand too.

As was often the case during FDR's sojourns in Georgia, Eleanor was busy with her own agenda elsewhere.

On Wednesday, the eleventh, as FDR worked on that Jefferson Day speech, a number of local citizens were busy preparing for the Thursday afternoon barbeque featuring a Brunswick stew and grilled hog and lamb. That afternoon, FDR took his two cousins, Polly and Daisy, for a drive in the countryside. That night, he entertained his friend and cabinet member Henry Morgenthau, Secretary of the Treasury, with a dinner of waffles…waffles because Morgenthau had given FDR a waffle iron at Christmas.

FDR retired to bed that night with a mystery novel titled *The Punch and Judy Murders*. He stopped at page seventy-eight, at a chapter entitled "Six Feet of Earth."

It was the next day that FDR died in his bed. He had been sitting in the living room for Madame Shoumatoff's latest portrait, doing some light work at the same time, with Lucy Rutherfurd also sitting quietly in the room and FDR's two cousins coming and going, when he complained of a "terrific" headache and put a hand to his head.

He immediately fell unconscious. A valet and mess boy from the traveling presidential party carried him into the adjoining bedroom. Doctor Howard Bruenn, one of FDR's two physicians, did what he could, but the massive stroke could not be denied. FDR died in his narrow, simple bed at 3:35 P.M.

Eleanor flew down to Georgia from Washington that night to be with her husband's body and to take charge of the funeral arrangements. Lucy Rutherfurd of course had left by then. The barbeque had been canceled.

Hours before Eleanor arrived, Daisy Bonner, a local woman who always served as FDR's cook when he was in town, penciled a note on the pinewood wall above the cottage's kitchen stove. "Daisy Bonner cook [sic] the first meal and the last one in this cottage for the President Roosevelt," she wrote.

Her note still can be seen at the Little White House, now maintained as a historic site by the Georgia state government. Madame Shoumatoff's "Unfinished Portrait" of FDR still stands on an easel in the living room. FDR's specially rigged Ford convertible sits in the nearby garage, still bearing its 1945 Georgia license plate: "FDR-1."

A finished version of the Shoumatoff portrait can be seen in a museum—within the same complex—that is packed with all kinds of FDR memorabilia. Down near the base of Pine Mountain is the Roosevelt Warm Springs Institute for Rehabilitation, founded by FDR in 1927 as an aftercare facility for polio patients like himself, but more recently operated by Georgia's Division of Rehabilitative Services and annually serving three thousand patients with a variety of disabilities. Covering much of Pine Mountain itself is Georgia's ten-thousand-acre Franklin D. Roosevelt State Park, including Dowdell's Knob… including log cabins, a swimming pool, and other recreational facilities built by the Civilian Conservation Corps (CCC) that FDR's administration created during the Great Depression.

Among the memorabilia on view at the museum in the Little White complex is a roster of the Marine Corps members who once were assigned to FDR's security detachment here and later were killed in World War II, all fourteen of them in the Pacific. Nearby, too, is a "guest book" in which visitors can record where they were when they heard of FDR's death.

Among the comments to be seen in the book is that of a man who lived on a farm with no telephone in 1945. A passing trucker told him about FDR's death. Another visitor heard about it while operating a streetcar in Philadelphia.

A third was an American POW in Germany at the time. A French prisoner with a hidden radio had passed the word.

★★★

Excerpted from author's presentation at the Miller Center of Public Affairs, University of Virginia, April 1997.

Aliases for FDR

IT HAD STRUCK HARRY TRUMAN as an odd, indeed a foreboding remark. In a luncheon meeting at the White House on August 18, 1944, he and Franklin Delano Roosevelt were discussing their plans for the 1944 presidential campaign. For the fourth time, FDR was at the head of the Democratic ticket, and for the first time, Missouri Senator Truman would be FDR's running mate.

Roosevelt had not attended the Democratic National Convention that nominated them, and so Truman had not seen the president and commander in chief for a while.

He was appalled at what he saw on this day—a man who "talked with difficulty," who shook so badly that he missed his coffee cup when pouring cream from a small pitcher, who physically was "just going to pieces."

But he was mentally alert. Innocently, Truman said something about his using an airplane in the upcoming campaign. Oh, no, said FDR—"one of us has to stay alive."

The fact is, Roosevelt was suffering from cardiovascular disease and never should have run for a fourth term…not in normal times. But this was war, and perhaps that's what he had in mind when he publicly announced he was seeking reelection in 1944 as a "good soldier."

But was he fit to continue as commander in chief? How would the voters have reacted if they had known just how ill their polio-crippled president was? Only his doctors and the inner circle of the White House were aware that in the three to four months before the Normandy invasion of June 6, 1944, illness kept Roosevelt away from his Oval Office half of the same time period. Only a privileged handful were aware that the same sick man visited the Bethesda Naval Hospital at least twenty-nine times from 1941 to his death in 1945—using twenty-nine aliases, such as "Mr. Delano," "James D. Elliott," "Ralph Frank," "Rolphe Frank," "George Adams," or "John Cash."

President Roosevelt (center) and Winston Churchill (smoking cigar) in a conference aboard ship. (National Archives)

That FDR himself felt the shadow looming over him can hardly be doubted, and not only because of his remark to running mate Truman. They won, of course, and on inaugural day itself in early 1945, FDR huddled with son James to ask help in ordering his papers and other affairs, to explain his will and, on the spot, to pass on a family ring that FDR removed from his own hand.

James was upset, naturally, and later he said that 1944 campaign was his father's "death warrant." From the time of the campaign to inaugural day, January 21, 1945, he saw his father only twice, and, "Each time I realized with awful irrevocable certainty that we were going to lose him."

Eleanor Roosevelt asked the White House staff "not to push the President too hard."

Still ahead for FDR in those closing weeks of the war in Europe was the all-important Yalta Conference with Winston Churchill and Joseph Stalin. Simply to make the trip, much less debate the postwar shape of Europe with such titans of the world stage, FDR had to travel eight days by ship, fly another 1,200 miles (at low altitudes due to his precarious condition), and finally drive 80 miles on a Crimean road so bad that the drive alone took six hours.

The argument over FDR's alleged concessions at Yalta have persisted ever since. Did he, mesmerized or bullied by Stalin, "give away" Eastern Europe? Did he, recognizing the reality of Red Army presence in Eastern Europe already, win Stalin's agreement to FDR's own goals, such as continued support for the establishment of the United Nations? Or was FDR too ill to hold his own in any case?

Participants at the conference were stunned and saddened at FDR's appearance. His ambassador to Moscow, Averell Harriman, saw "signs of deterioration" that were "unmistakable." And Churchill, old ally and friend Churchill, was unhappily struck too. "His captivating smile, his gay and charming manner, had not deserted him, but his face had a transparency, an air of purification, and often there was a faraway look in his eyes."

The difficult conference ran from February 4 to February 11. Roosevelt then met with Middle East leaders in Egypt (with Churchill again), then returned to Washington, where he faced an address to a joint session of Congress. For the first time in a congressional appearance, he spoke while seated, explaining in attempted jest that he was tired out by "so much metal" on his legs (his braces).

With the San Francisco conference launching the UN soon to come, FDR then traveled to his favorite resting place of Warm Springs, Georgia, where he would prepare his keynote address for the UN gathering that meant so much to him.

That was on March 29, and shortly before, somewhat mysteriously, a Secret Service detail appeared on Vice President Harry Truman's circuit for the first time. Margaret Truman, his daughter, later wrote that the assignment was arranged by Truman aide Harry Vaughn, but Vaughn in a postwar interview asserted the Secret Service just appeared one day with no explanation for their presence.

It was April 12, still in Warm Springs, of course, that FDR awoke with a slight headache. It passed after a light massage, and later, about midday while going over paperwork and sitting for his latest portrait, he suddenly started, rubbed his forehead, and slumped forward with those last words, "I've got a terrific headache."

He remained unconscious but alive until 3:31 P.M., when his breathing stopped. (Although he was pronounced dead at 3:35 P.M.) Harry Truman, late that afternoon, was called to the White House. He arrived at 5:25 P.M., and Eleanor Roosevelt, who had not yet left for Warm Springs, told him what had happened. Truman was sworn in as FDR's successor shortly after 7 P.M. in the White House itself.

Churchill, on hearing the news, felt "a physical blow." Stalin's Soviet Union lowered its flags to half-mast and bordered them in black. Hitler's propagandist Josef Goebbels called his *Führer*, and said: "I congratulate you—Roosevelt is dead." And in Japan, the other great enemy, oddly, Prime Minister Kantaro Suzuki, offered the American people "profound sympathy" for the loss of a leader who could take credit for "the Americans' advantageous position today."

★★★

Based upon Hidden Illness in the White House *by Kenneth R. Crispell and Carlos F. Gomez (Duke University Press, Durham, N.C., 1988).*

Parachuting into Enemy Territory

PAINTED BLACK AS THE SKY above them, the eight Liberator bombers set a course for the distant North Sea after lifting from runways in England with a thunderous roar. Aboard, men anticipating action settled in for the long flight and fought down their nerves as best they could.

The lumbering B-24s droned on, their "target" a frozen lake in the mountainous north of German-occupied Norway. It was late in the war—March 24, 1945—but Norway still was a battleground tying down seventeen German divisions. One major reason was *resistance*, and the highly trained specialists aboard the eight Liberators comprised an OSS-sponsored team planning to parachute into Norway and add to the widespread sabotage, harassment, and sporadic mayhem already afflicting the German occupiers.

The men of the American OSS Norwegian Special Operations Group (NORSO) were headed by a slightly built, bespectacled American major who five years earlier had been a college boy about to graduate from Princeton—William Colby. A veteran of similar behind-the-lines operations in France, the youthful Colby already knew how easily even the best-laid plans could go wrong.

This night would be no exception.

Colby and his team of Norwegian-Americans had been awaiting their night drop for two months—their aircrews needed moonlight to reveal rivers and lakes on the ground as navigation points. Bad weather had aborted planned drops in January and February. But now it was March, and Operation RYPE was under way at last. The drop, inland from the Norwegian coastline, would be on frozen Lake Jaevsjo, north of the port of Trondheim. The NORSO team's mission, as later explained by Colby himself, was "to sabotage the Northland Railway over which the Germans were moving 150,000 troops toward the final battle of Germany after having been pushed out of Finland."

At the last minute, the NORSO group had to change both the intended sabotage target and the planned drop zone—from a Norwegian exile newspaper in London, the OSS (Office of Strategic Services) learned that the Germans had beefed up their defenses in the originally intended target area. Now the target would be the Grana rail bridge in the heavily wooded mountains north of Trondheim.

At least, that's what Colby thought when the time came for his jump over the frozen lake close to midnight.

He landed without incident or injury, then made his way through a ground mist until he spotted a bonfire. That should be his contact with the Norwegian Resistance. Colby saw "a tall figure" awaiting him as he walked carefully forward. He drew his pistol, "just in case."

As they met, Colby stated the prearranged password in his basic, hastily learned Norwegian: "Is the fishing good in this lake?"

The contact man was supposed to say, "Yes, particularly in the winter." Instead, the stranger looked at Colby "rather quizzically" and said, "To tell you the truth, it's no good at all."

Although Colby was startled for the moment, it was only a minor crisis— the contact man was very much for real. Soon Colby's other NORSO team members were gathering; the OSS men collected their supplies and parachutes from scattered points on the frozen lake.

"We established a camp in the woods with our parachutes for tents, so that we would not be seen by Easter skiers. Our local Norwegian reception committee, six resistance team members, a reindeer herder and guide, and an isolated farmer, told us the Germans were in Snaasa Valley, twenty miles west."

For the moment, though, Colby was forced to wait. Only four of the Liberators leaving England the evening before had reached the drop zone in Norway—three of the big Liberators had been forced to turn back before completing the long flight, and a fourth had dropped its OSS men fifty miles inside the borders of neutral Sweden, where they apparently would be interned.

If Colby and his team were to be momentarily stymied, that does not mean that resistance in Norway ground to a halt. Nor had the Resistance been awaiting this latest Allied "insertion" as a signal to rise up at last. Far from either proposition, Norway had been difficult and restless ever since its seizure by Nazi Germany in a rapid campaign five years earlier.

Colby, destined later in life to be director of the U.S. Central Intelligence Agency (CIA), would be in Norway to war's end, but in late March of 1945, he had no such inkling. All he knew was that he was in enemy-occupied territory, and in theory he didn't have enough men to carry out his assigned sabotage mission.

Even so, accompanied by six Norwegian Resistance members, he and his sixteen NORSO team members set out for the Grana bridge, one hundred miles and six days away by cross-country ski trek.

They reached the Northland Railway without incident, but they found the German force guarding the Grana railway bridge too large to take on with such a small number in their own party. Consulting his maps, Colby found a smaller bridge at a place called Tangen. "We arrived about dawn, set our charges, and waited for a possible train, in hopes of repeating the sabotage operation that our Norwegian colleagues had pulled off nearby some months before. There, a German troop train had run straight into the stream at Jorstad, some hours after the bridge had been blown."

Colby posted lookouts armed with walkie-talkies up and down the tracks—if a train came along, he wanted to be sure it wasn't a passenger train full of Norwegian civilians. "Finally, the wait becoming too long, we blew the bridge and left our small American-flag shoulder patches to show who had done it and, hopefully, protect the local population from German reprisal."

The team's days-long trek by skis back to its base camp at Lake Jaevsjo was a roundabout one, with the skiers hard pressed to outdistance expected pursuit by truck-borne patrols. Exhausted, Colby used Benzedrine as a stimulant for the hurried ascent of "one long, steep climb" on the way.

At the lake, where the team's hideout now was a farm, Colby was delighted to find his five men who had been dropped in Sweden by mistake, then interned. They, "with a conspiratorial wink from the Swedish intelligence authorities," had been allowed to leave and rejoin the OSS team across the Norwegian border.

After a few days' rest, Colby's group next attacked the railroad in small teams assigned to blow intermittent rails with minor explosive charges. Colby's own group was just finishing its work on the rail line about midnight when another team's charge went off down the line. Fifty yards from Colby, a German flare suddenly lit the sky—"a bullet kicked a pebble against my forehead."

Colby wouldn't allow his men to respond to the German fire with automatic weapons, since that would alert the enemy to the presence of a "regular" unit. Instead, the OSS men retrieved their skis and slipped away in the dark. "Applying the lesson of my drop in France, I made the group keep going all the way back to the base, taking a roundabout route to point the German patrols in the wrong direction until a friendly snowstorm covered our tracks."

Later, as elsewhere in Europe the war was coming to an end, a five-man German patrol did stumble across the NORSO group. In the skirmish that followed, all five Germans died.

Later, too, a Lapp reindeer herder reported the wreckage of an airplane on high ground not far away. The investigating NORSOs found the bodies of an aircrew and four of their own original team members—the plane had crashed while trying to drop the additional four men.

Soon, on May 8, the war in Europe officially ended. Colby and his men were left awaiting further orders. On May 11, they received word to proceed to the Snaasa Valley, twenty miles away, and receive the surrender of the German garrison there.

With two six-foot sergeants as escort, and the rest of the NORSO team covering from behind, a somewhat apprehensive Colby approached the gates of the German camp. As it turned out, however, "The German commander was more nervous than I, and he quickly assured me that all German units would remain in their camps in perfect discipline."

After a triumphant march down the highway to Trondheim, every village turning out a throng of excited, cheering Norwegians, the NORSO group still had one more chore to perform. Sixty miles up the coast was the town of Namsos, temporary home of ten thousand German troops awaiting final orders and repatriation. The Norwegians there wanted "some visible reassurance that the war indeed was over." The Allied Command sent Colby and about thirty of his men.

It was, at first, a tense situation. German sailors in the harbor were chanting *"Sieg Heil,"* while on the streets German soldiers were "accidentally" bumping shoulders with the NORSO men. The solution of the twenty-five-year-old Major Colby was to announce an inspection of the German naval craft in the harbor.

"Taking three NORSO members, all former Norwegian merchant mariners, I climbed aboard each ship despite the sullen looks of the crewmen. And that put an end to all demonstrations; the message was clear to all that the war was indeed over. Inspection made the point to German as well as Norwegian."

Back in the United States some months later, with the war in the Pacific also ended, William Colby was awarded the Silver Star for valor in combat. In Colby's view, however, it often isn't a combatant's response to action that is the measure of heroism, but rather the earlier, voluntary commitment to unknown dangers.

"Later on, when the mission itself is underway," he wrote years later in his autobiography *Honorable Men*, "all sorts of irresistible factors come into play that require a man to behave bravely, independently of his will, very often without a second thought." Among those factors, he listed peer pressure, the instinct for survival, or plain, simple comradeship with others facing the same danger.

To OSS volunteer Colby, now deceased, it was "in the tranquility of an office, before any of these factors begin to have any force [that] a man does measure his courage and decide whether he is willing to risk his life, and why."

The outcome of the war naturally did not turn alone upon the contributions of Colby and his NORSO team in its final weeks, but he and each of his team members had made their own, individual commitments long before their eight blackened Liberators lifted off from friendly territory for the night drop over a frozen lake in German-occupied Norway. The outcome of the war did turn, however, upon like individual commitments made by thousands—no, millions—of brave souls just like Colby and his team members, whether the eager volunteer showing up in an army recruiting office, or the volunteer spy-saboteur willing to insert him- or herself in the enemy camp.

★★★

First published in World War II *magazine, September 1987.*

Flowers on Their Graves

IN WARTIME GERMANY, "THE MOOD of the people became rather bad." People didn't smile anymore. "Many families had lost a son, two sons, a father, or a husband fighting on the Russian front or in the Balkans. Many came home seriously wounded or maimed for life."

Gertrud Breier's two older brothers were drafted. "Helmuth, a flyer, didn't return from a flight over the Atlantic. My older brother, Fritz, deserted the air force and found a safe refuge in Denmark with a farmer."

Gertrud's mother had moved her younger children and their governess, Kate, to a small cabin in a mountain village, away from the small industrial city of Ludwigshafen, since it was a prime target for air raids.

Gertrud's schooling was interrupted by a year at a labor camp for girls her age—a year spent in Spartan barracks, cold showers, dull, ugly uniforms, and farm work in the surrounding countryside. A friend who was half Jewish fled and with her father successfully escaped to Denmark, where they also found refuge on a farm for the rest of the war.

After the year's labor camp assignment was completed, Gertrud, nearing age twenty, was not allowed to go home and resume her schooling. "When the year was over, most of the girls were sent to ammunition factories or other important war plants. I was sent to the south of Germany to get some training as a meteorological technician."

After that, she was assigned to a *Luftwaffe* base in France, just south of Paris. She found "a nice group of pilots," but, "those pilots didn't have much to do, as there was no more gasoline for their planes."

Came the invasion, the Normandy invasion of June 1944, and all fled for German territory by road. "Only once did American planes attack us on the highway. Fortunately, we had found a safe shelter and didn't get hit. Over the border we were attacked again, and there were many wounded and several killed. When the caravan reached Vienna, I felt so desperate to feel safe again, but where?"

Gertrud deserted, leaving her mobile headquarters on foot and walking for days back toward the west. She begged food and milk at remote farms and slept in barns, on straw (very similar to the labor camp pallets, actually).

Her "march" through Bavaria and across the Rhine took nearly two weeks, even with an occasional ride on a freight train. Her mother, two sisters, and younger brothers were at the mountain cabin—she finally reached them shortly before Christmas of 1944, during the Battle of the Bulge. As a deserter, she "tried not to be seen by the people in the village."

But she wasn't safe after all. "On December 21, 1944, the little mountain village was bombed. It was the most devastating, horrible, indescribable, sad happening in my life."

The American bomber crews had mistaken the small mountain village for another one by the same name five miles away in a nearby valley. The intended target had a railway station, and the small mountain village did not. "No one expected a thing when suddenly small aircraft unloaded their deadly bombs. For days to come the survivors had to search for bodies....Months after the war, there were corpses still being dug out of the destroyed houses."

Gertrud was among those who ran to pick through the smoking rubble for possible survivors. She found a small boy without legs—dead.

During the raid, she and her mother saw one of the attacking airplanes crash into the side of a nearby hill. They went the next morning to look for any survivors.

"When we got there, two dead American air force men were still in the plane. The bodies were already stiff. We had a hard time putting them in the little wagon we had brought along. We both cried."

They took the bodies home, where, as in biblical times, Gertrud's mother wrapped them in hand-woven and embroidered sheets that had been a part of her trousseau years before. They secretly buried the American flyers in "the very back of the cemetery." First, Gertrud's mother carefully saved their dog tags, rings, and watches. "She hid them under her mattress. We knew then that soon the war would be over."

Then, on a beautiful spring day at their village of Esthal, American tanks appeared—they could be seen "moving on the other side of the mountains in the woods."

Gertrud's mother opened an upstairs window and hung out a white flag— ten minutes later, two American GIs arrived at their doorstep. The war was over for Gertrud and her family. Nearly over, that is, since there was one more matter to take care of.

Asking the Americans for an officer, Gertrud's mother solemnly handed over the dog tags and other personal items from the two airmen who had crashed into the hillside. "We told them where we buried them. We took him to the cemetery about eight hundred yards from our house, and what did we see? Someone had put flowers on the grave."

★★★

Based upon The Governess *by Gertrud Breier (Vantage Press, New York, 1988).*

Brothers/Sisters of the Sea

THEY WERE THE SUPERSHIPS of the war and their skippers an exalted threesome who, toward war's end, would share the same grim fate.

Mounting giant eighteen-inch guns, *Yamato* and *Musashi* came out of the yards and feverish pre-war secrecy as 72,000-ton behemoths of the sea, the mightiest battleships ever built. Their sister hull, the *Shinano*, emerged by a change in plan as a giant aircraft carrier.

Their combined fate, though, was to contribute surprisingly little to Japan's war effort. *Yamato*, first of the trio to visit the waters of the Pacific, merely stood by in the Battle of Midway, a disaster for the Imperial Japanese Navy (four carriers lost, to America's one, the *Yorktown*). Their first real action was in the three-day, multipronged Battle of Leyte Gulf. *Musashi* should have stayed home, and *Yamato* might as well have.

They were with Vice Admiral Takao Kurita's Center Force approaching Leyte in the Philippines by the "back door" route of the Sibuyan Sea on October 24, 1944. At *Musashi's* helm was Toshihira Inoguchi, sailing his last day as skipper of the powerful warship.

Spotted and attacked in the South China Sea by two U.S. submarines the day before (October 23), Kurita's Center Force came under swarming air attack, with the two giant battleships the main target for the American dive-bombers and torpedo planes.

The first wave came in about 10:40 A.M., but the two superships steamed on, their heavy armor-plating allowing them to "shrug off" torpedo and bomb hits. The ordnance tended simply to bounce off.

At noon, in came a second wave of U.S. fliers braving the ring of flak around the two capital ships. Again, no serious injury inflicted. At 1:35 P.M., a third wave of U.S. Navy aircraft appeared. All attackers this time concentrated on *Musashi* alone. And she merely plowed onward…it seemed at first.

But three torpedoes had struck home in her starboard bow and bent vital plates. Her skipper, Inoguchi, ordered counter-flooding to stabilize his monster ship. Her speed now slowed to just 22 knots. Her doom was near.

At 2:30, another fifty air attackers swept in, and at 3:10, still another hundred swarmed angrily about the Japanese fleet. They focused upon any apparently damaged Japanese ship. In that lot, the giant *Musashi* stuck out like the proverbial sore thumb. She took more and more torpedoes. Inoguchi had been forced to flood three of her four engine rooms to keep his even keel. Her bow was underwater and she staggered along at 6 knots.

He made for the closest land in order to ground the great ship and at least prevent her sinking. But now her last engine failed. Dead in the water, Inoguchi gave the word to abandon ship.

The first of the three skippers to meet shared fate, he stayed on his bridge—still there when the behemoth suddenly rolled to port and went down, with 1,100 crewmen and their skipper still aboard.

Kurita took his Center Force through the San Bernadino Strait the same night, *Yamato* still tagging along, but after encountering a startled U.S. task force of jeep carriers and small escorts the next morning, he unaccountably reversed course before exacting any damage on the U.S. landing force in Leyte Gulf. *Yamato*, turning away to avoid torpedo attacks, contributed little to the morning action of October 25 and retired with the rest of Kurita's Center Force.

Shinano's turn came next, about a month later—and quite unexpectedly. Just off her shipyard ways and in her first sea trials, the giant carrier was taken by surprise in Japan's own home waters—the Kumano Sea. The American submarine *Archer-Fish* had found her, an incredible target for Commander Joseph F. Enright's submersible prowler.

Four torpedoes tore into *Shinano's* hull without warning. Her skipper, Toshio Abe, still had faith in his "unsinkable" ship, however, and he steamed for a nearby safe haven at 20 knots. Soon, though, the internal fires boiled up and she listed badly. He, too, ordered abandon ship. He, too, remained on the bridge. And he, too, was still there when his ship went down.

That left only *Yamato*, the original of the three mighty sisters of the sea, and her skipper, Kosaku Aruga, to face the final days of the Pacific War. And they stayed out of harm's way for weeks, then months.

With the American invasion of Okinawa in April of 1945, however, the admirals of the shattered Imperial Navy decided upon a last desperate sortie to the aid of Okinawa's defenders. *Yamato* would be the flagship for Vice Admiral Seiichi Ito's Second Fleet in the grim run—some say it was a one-way suicide sortie from the very outset, with no fuel available for the return voyage to Japan.

As the last of the Imperial Navy's big ships started for Okinawa, it was shadowed by U.S. reconnaissance planes and submarines. The sortie would be no surprise, and ahead waited the American carriers and their swarms of aircraft.

The action began the morning of April 7, 1945. Wave after wave of airplanes went after *Yamato* in a battle lasting three hours in all. Holed by torpedoes and hammered by countless bombs, the mighty *Yamato* soon was staggering, her end obviously near.

On the bridge, his ship dying beneath him, Aruga gave orders to be tied to the compass stand. "I am one with *Yamato*," he told his executive officer, Jiro Nomura.

Oddly, he also said he might work free and swim away later. So near was the end, though, that Nomura was swept off the bridge even while strapping his skipper to the ship's binnacle. Like his two brothers of the sea, Aruga then went down with the third and last of Japan's three most powerful sisters of the sea.

★★★

Based upon various sources.

Waiting to Be Shot

FOR A JEW IN NAZI Germany during World War II, every added day of survival was an escape from the Holocaust daily consuming Europe's Jewish people. Young Klaus Scheurenberg, only fifteen in 1940, was among the millions rounded up. He was packed into the cattle cars; he was sent to the concentration camps; he was put into forced labor; and he was stood before the firing squad, all like so many others who didn't live. And yet…he did.

His first escape, you might say, came when he was thirteen, in 1938. Beaten up years before (at age eight) by the physical education teacher at his "normal" school in Berlin, young Klaus now attended a Jewish school where such things did not happen…yet.

Then came the infamous *Kristallnacht* (Night of Broken Glass) of November 9, 1938, when bands of Nazis, their followers, and plain vandals attacked Jewish stores and synagogues with impunity. That day (or the next, possibly), the children in Klaus's Jewish school were assembled and told to go straight home because of anti-Jewish demonstrations. But the children in the "normal," Aryan schools had been released too. They had been told "to go over to the Jewish school and beat up the Jewish kids," said Scheurenberg many years later.

The children of Germany fought their own internal war in those prewar days. "We got our bicycles, made the girls walk in the middle, and with our bicycle pumps in our hands, fought our way through."

For Jews like the Scheurenberg family, however, the situation would only become worse. As Nazi Germany plunged into war in September 1939, then entered a struggle for its own survival, the Scheurenbergs did remain free for a surprisingly long time. One day, though, their respite abruptly ended. "On May 1, 1943, I saw two men from the secret police enter our house. They were wearing long coats and large floppy hats. They looked so 'secret' you could tell who they were a mile away. The building we lived in was almost empty, since most of the tenants had already been deported. The men had come to get us."

For Klaus, then seventeen, the choice was to run away before he could be taken, or to stay with his father and mother in hopes of somehow being a help to them. He stayed, and together they were placed in a so-called transit camp in Berlin. Then came their assignment to Auschwitz. At dreaded Auschwitz, they surely would die.

But, miracles of miracles, Klaus's father ran into an old acquaintance, a *Herr* Sasse, "who used to work at the police station in our neighborhood." They had cooperated and become "sort of friends," since Mr. Scheurenberg was administrator of the local Jewish House. Sasse, drafted into the Gestapo earlier, now worked at the transit camp.

"He took one look at my father and said, 'Scheurenberg, what on earth are you doing here?' My father told him: 'We're supposed to be sent to Auschwitz. We already have our numbers.' Sasse said: 'That's absolutely out of the question! Come with me!'"

As a result, another respite—the Scheurenbergs were sent to Theresienstadt, the notorious camp in Czechoslovakia with a pretty, but, as eventually shown, phony façade. "We knew very well that no one was gassed there yet. It was the so-called waiting room for Auschwitz, but at least we knew we had a little more time."

So passed a few more months in relative safety. But then, in 1944, young Klaus was sent as forced labor to SS Officer Adolf Eichmann's headquarters near the Sachsenhausen death camp—the same Eichmann who after the war would be tried and executed in the newly created state of Israel for the liquidation of millions of Jews. Klaus was now at a place called Wulkow, where he would see Eichmann frequently over a period of six months.

Because of frequent air raids, it seems, the Gestapo in Berlin had a secret headquarters "built in a thick forest," reported a grown-up Klaus many years later. "Jewish prisoners, whom they planned to liquidate later on, had to build the new headquarters. Many of my friends were killed, but the Nazis forgot about me once again." The commandant at this work camp himself shot some of the prisoners, but his greatest pleasure was beating them to death with a chain.

Still a survivor after a period at that labor, too, Klaus was ordered back to the "pretty" camp in Czechoslovakia in February 1945, too late in the war for transport to Auschwitz (located in Poland), since it already had fallen to the onrushing Red Army. But the young Jew and his comrades from Wulkow knew too much—and now came his most incredible escape of all.

On the way back to Theresienstadt, his captors made a stop, determined then and there to shoot their prisoners, Klaus included. "I was already standing in front of a firing squad waiting to be shot when at that exact moment, the German front [nearby] broke and a flood of German soldiers retreated right across our field."

Despite the disarray, the foiled guards rounded up their prisoners and packed them into a railroad cattle car—ninety-four men in Klaus' own carrier. "Many of them died. We traveled for eight days and eight nights until we finally arrived in Theresienstadt."

Surely, time was running out by now for the eighteen-year-old Jewish kid, even if he was "an experienced, expert prisoner who knew all the tricks of the trade." But no, lying to obtain assignment to a fairly safe SS bakery, Klaus found fresh sanctuary—hastily learning the bakery skills he had claimed—until he was freed on the last day of World War II in Europe.

He returned to Berlin, a rare survivor of the Holocaust.

★★★

Based upon Voices from the Third Reich: An Oral History, *by Johannes Steinoff, Peter Pechel, Dennis Showalter (Regnery Gateway, Washington, D.C., 1989).*

Farther than Any Army

AT WAR'S END IN EUROPE, George Patton thought it appropriate to honor his Third Army troops:

    Headquarters
    Third United States Army
    APO 403

General Order Number 98, 9 May 1945

Soldiers of the Third Army Past and Present

During the 281 days of incessant and victorious combat, your penetrations have advanced farther in less time than any other army in history. You have fought your way across 24 major rivers and innumerable lesser streams. You have liberated or conquered more than 82,000 square miles of territory, including 1,500 cities and towns, and some 12,000 inhabited places. Prior to termination of active hostilities, you captured in battle 956,000 enemy soldiers and killed or wounded 500,000 others. France, Belgium, Luxembourg, Germany, Austria and Czechoslovakia bear witness to your exploits.

All men and women of the six corps and thirty-nine divisions that have at different times been members of this Army have done their duty. Each deserves credit. The enduring valor of the combat troops has been paralleled and made possible by the often unpublicized activities of supply, administration, medical services of this Army and of the Communications Zone troops supporting it. Nor should we forget our comrades of the other armies and the Air Force, particularly of the XIX Tactical Air Command, by whose side or under whose wings we have had the honor to fight.

In proudly contemplating our achievements, let us never forget our heroic dead whose graves mark the course of our victorious advances, nor our wounded whose sacrifices aided so much to our success.

I should be both ungrateful and wanting in candor if I failed to acknowledge the debt we owe to our Chiefs of Staff, General [Hugh C.] Gaffney and [Hobart] Gay, and to the officers and men of the General and Special Staff Sections of Army Headquarters. Without their loyalty, intelligence, and unremitting labors, success would have been impossible.

The termination of fighting in Europe does not remove the opportunities for other outstanding and equally difficult achievements in the days which are to come. In some ways the immediate future will demand of you more fortitude than had the past because, without the inspiration of combat, you must maintain—by your dress, deportment and efficiency—not only the prestige of the Third Army but also the honor of the United States. I have complete confidence that you will not fail.

During the course of the war, I have received promotions and decorations far and beyond my individual merit. You won them. I, as your representative, wear them. The one honor which is mine alone is that of having commanded such an incomparable group of Americans, the record of whose fortitude, audacity and valor will endure as long as history lasts.

G. S. Patton, Jr.
General

★★★

Thanks to Charles H. Miller, 549th AAA Battalion, C & D Battery, and the Eighty-seventh Infantry Division Association's Golden Acorn News *of December 1997, in which the foregoing appeared, verbatim.*

Greatest Invasion Averted

AS VICE PRESIDENT OF THE United States, Harry S. Truman didn't know his country was close to perfecting the atomic bomb. He didn't even know that it was being developed under the aegis of the supersecret Manhattan Project.

President Truman's first glimmer came at the end of an emergency cabinet meeting he convened in the White House just minutes after he took his oath of office on the evening of April 12, 1945, to replace the deceased Franklin D. Roosevelt. Secretary of War Henry L. Stimson lingered briefly to alert the new president to "an immense project" developing an explosive "of almost unbelievable destructive power." That's all he told Truman for the moment.

In far-off Japan, the enemy knew even less. The Japanese, clearly on the defensive at this late stage of World War II, were fully occupied with more immediate events. America's island-hopping Pacific campaign was drawing closer to the home islands; from the air, the war already was crashing down upon the homeland.

On March 26, after incredibly fierce fighting, U.S. Marines who first landed February 19 finally secured the island of Iwo Jima, just 750 miles from Tokyo.

Worse, though, U.S. bombers on March 9 had opened a new phase in the air war against Japan proper. While bombing by long-range U.S. B-29s had achieved only desultory effect before, 325 of the new "Superfortresses" on this night leveled sixteen square miles of Tokyo and killed 85,000 to 100,000 persons in a single incendiary raid. Curtis LeMay's bomber force would carry the same firestorms to many other Japanese cities by war's end in August, the port city of Hiroshima one of the few to be "spared."

On April 1, U.S. forces invaded the island of Okinawa, just 340 miles south of Japan, to initiate another fierce battle that would last until late June before final American victory. By now, the invasion of Japan itself looked imminent.

"Fat Man" stands ready for its journey to Nagasaki. (U.S. Department of Energy)

In the West, Roosevelt had died on April 12, to be succeeded by Truman. On April 30, Hitler committed suicide—Germany was just about out of the war. Berlin fell to the Russians May 2; Germany surrendered unconditionally May 7. Japan was now alone.

On July 4, Douglas MacArthur could announce the full liberation of the Philippines from occupying Japanese forces. All U.S. war effort now could be devoted to the invasion and final defeat of Japan.

Okinawa, however, had been a sobering lesson for the American and British strategists laying their invasion plans. For one thing, Okinawa—and the surrounding seas—had been the scene of hundreds of *kamikaze* attacks by suicide-bent Japanese defenders. As Winston Churchill noted later, though, there had been another kind of suicide too.

"I had in my mind," he wrote in *Triumph and Tragedy*, "the spectacle of Okinawa Island, where many thousands of Japanese, rather than surrender, had drawn up in line and destroyed themselves by hand-grenades after their leaders had solemnly performed the rite of hari-kari." Allied strategists concluded the Japanese would not submit easily to invasion of their homeland—rather than any surrender to overwhelming force, casualties would be in the millions.

On July 16, at Alamogordo, New Mexico, however, the secret Manhattan Project, costing some $2 billion, involving thousands of workers, creating two entire cities (Oak Ridge, Tennessee, and Hanford, Washington), inaugurated a new age. In a test detonation, "Fat Boy," the first plutonium bomb, had worked beyond all expectations. News of "Fat Boy's" success was flashed to Truman and Churchill at their Potsdam Conference with Joseph Stalin in Germany.

Just a month earlier, Truman, War Secretary Stimson, and the U.S. Joint Chiefs of Staff had given conditional approval to Operation Olympic, MacArthur's plan to invade Japan's southernmost home island of Kyushu on November 1—at expectedly horrendous cost. Wrote Churchill later: "Now all this nightmare picture had vanished. In its place was a vision—fair and bright, indeed it seemed—of the end of the whole war in one or two violent shocks."

On July 26, the United States and Great Britain, with China as a cosigner, issued their Potsdam Declaration demanding that Japan surrender unconditionally or face "complete destruction" of its armed forces and "utter devastation" of the homeland.

For ten days, its Supreme War Council split between die-hards and moderates, Japan did not respond clearly or officially. By President Truman's decision to end the war quickly as possible, America's plan to use one or both of its only operational atomic bombs went forward. The first, a uranium bomb called "Little Boy," was dropped on Hiroshima August 6, and the second, another plutonium bomb, on Nagasaki August 9.

By some accounts, Russia's last-minute declaration of war against Japan August 8 shook Japan policymakers more than the blow at Hiroshima two days before. Still, even after Nagasaki, the Supreme Council remained split, until Emperor Hirohito settled the issue August 14 by urging surrender without further quibble.

★★★

Based upon various sources.

"I Saw the Mushroom Cloud"

"ON THE CLEAR, HOT SUMMER morning of August 6, 1945, I was aboard the B-29 airplane called *Enola Gay* as it flew from Tinian Island in the Marianas island group to any one of three possible target cities in Japan."

Not many months before, young Jacob Beser had been attending classes at Johns Hopkins University in his native Baltimore as a student of mechanical engineering. Now, at the climactic moment of World War II, he was on his way to a place called Hiroshima.

Three days later, Lieutenant Beser was aboard a second B-29 winging its way toward Japan…in this fateful instance, toward hapless Nagasaki. For his would be a unique distinction among all American veterans of World War II. No one else flew aboard both B-29s that dropped the atom bomb on Japan—on both Hiroshima and Nagasaki.

That first morning in Tinian was hot and clear…on the mission to Nagasaki three days later, however, delays and bad weather threatened the outcome. As Beser later wrote, "If everything had gone according to plan and if the weather forecast had held up, the flight could have been completed in an uneventful manner. But such was not to be the case."

First, though, Hiroshima on August 6.

"We had left Tinian in the wee hours of the morning and would appear over our chosen target between 8 and 9 in the morning," Beser wrote years later in a first-person account appearing in *World War II* magazine. The *Enola Gay*, piloted by Colonel Paul W. Tibbets, carried the bomb known as "Little Boy," nearly 10 feet in length, 28 inches around the middle…and 9,000 pounds in weight!

Hiroshima had been the primary target all along. "It housed the headquarters of the Japanese Second Army and was the designated command and control center from which resistance to our projected invasion of the Japan homeland would be directed." Kokura, a steel town, was listed as the secondary target and Nagasaki, also an industrial center, was the possible third choice that grim and momentous day.

As fate would have it, reports from advance weather observation planes left Hiroshima as the mission's primary choice. *Enola Gay* forged on.

For the first three hours after liftoff from Tinian Island, it seems, the exhausted Beser had slept—he had been so busy preparing for the *Enola Gay's*

The crew of the Enola Gay. Jacob Beser is the last man on the right in the back row. (U.S. Air Force)

moment of destiny on August 6 that he hadn't slept for the previous forty hours, according to the book *Enola Gay* by Gordon Thomas and Max Morgan White. But he was awake and ready for action as the plane approached Japan.

Beser's responsibilities as radar countermeasures observer included keeping a lookout for evidence of early warning or gun-laying radar activity in the B-29's path. He also monitored Japanese radio fighter-control frequencies for signs of sudden interest in the *Enola Gay*. "Although I did not understand the Japanese language, radio telephone procedure had distinct characteristics and I could measure the signals," he wrote in *World War II* magazine. "The signal from a pursuing aircraft would become stronger with each ensuing transmission."

Then, too, "As our aircraft neared the target area...it was necessary that I monitor that area of the radio spectrum in which the electronic proximity fuses installed aboard our weapon would operate." The point was to guard against outside signals that could "interfere with our proximity fuses, making sure nothing would jam them or set them off prematurely."

In the event of electronic jamming, however, the crew still could resort to backup systems built into "Little Boy"—barometric-pressure switches or, if "all else failed, conventional bomb-nose and tail impact fuses." Aside from that aspect, Beser was confident that "whatever happened, short of a prematurely induced detonation, we as the delivering agents would be relatively safe."

That continued to be his impression as *Enola Gay* arrived in the target area under clear skies...no flak and no sign of approaching fighters. Now, Beser readied himself for one additional duty on that historic day—it would be his job to record the entire crew's reactions to the bomb drop.

Command Pilot Tibbets reminded his crew members that whatever Beser recorded would become a historic document—"So, keep it clean, fellows."

Minutes later, the *Enola Gay*, "lurched as if on an updraft." The 9,000-pound bomb was gone.

Nor was that the only mid-air gyration for the Superfortress. "The air-operated bomb bay doors were slammed shut and a violent escape maneuver was initiated—the idea was to turn hard to the right for 158 degrees, lose about 3,000 feet in the turn and put as much distance between us and the explosion as possible before detonation."

In seconds, after a brilliant flash of light, the men aboard the *Enola Gay* would be stunned by the force of two shock waves that reached out and shook their plane. According to the book by Thomas and White, tail gunner Robert Caron saw the first one coming up from the ground, a mass of compressed air moving at the speed of sound. It looked, he later said, like a discernible planetary ring coming after them.

He tried to shout a warning but no one understood, and then the shock wave hit, "bouncing the plane higher," wrote Thomas and White. Then came Caron's shout again. "There's another one coming!" And it hit with "a spine-jarring crash" that "tossed" the big plane, "tipping [radio operator Richard] Nelson half out of his seat and sending Beser tumbling."

By Beser's own account, meanwhile, the internal interphone system aboard *Enola Gay* was momentarily silent in the first seconds after the two shock waves tossed the big bomber. The first spoken reaction to the bomb's effect below came from co-pilot Robert Lewis, recorded for posterity—"My God! Look at that sonofabitch go!"

Wrote Beser also: "The airplane was now circling the target area, giving one and all aboard a chance to observe what had happened. Colonel Tibbets then informed the crew that they had seen history's first atomic bomb in action. As I recorded the conversation with a specially designed disk lathe, he queried each and every man aboard for his reaction."

Those reactions, unsurprisingly, "ranged from astonishment to disbelief."

As for Beser's own:

When I was able to get to the window, I never saw the city of Hiroshima. I saw the mushroom cloud that had climbed above our flight level, and beneath it was a churning, boiling mass of flame and debris where only minutes before had been a thriving city.

The scene was so bizarre that it defied belief. It was difficult to comprehend that one airplane and one bomb had created all that havoc.

Volumes of course, can be—and indeed have been—written about the horrific results on the ground, where more than seventy-one thousand people would be killed outright by the first atomic bomb used as a weapon of war (not as many, true, as the eighty-five thousand victims of a single nighttime firebombing of Tokyo just months before).

Two miles from the blast epicenter, for instance, a stunned 2nd Lt. Matsuo Yasuzawa emerged from an air base building and thought of chasing the distantly visible *Enola Gay* in his small trainer out on the airstrip. He saw…looking up from the ground at Hiroshima, he actually saw Beser's departing Superfortress and two accompanying B-29s assigned to monitor the bomb effects.

Rushing to his plane out on the field, he noticed that every other aircraft was wrecked. For that matter, most nearby buildings were structurally damaged and most windows in sight had been blown out. His trainer, it also turned out, "was bent like a banana" (Thomas and White).

But he climbed in and managed to start it up anyway.

Only then did he see the most horrifying sight yet. As described by coauthors Thomas and White: "Coming onto the airfield was the vanguard of a procession of 'living corpses.' Bleeding and blackened, their skins hanging in shreds, their hair scorched to the roots,…many were naked, their clothes burned from their bodies."

Yasuzawa's real mission now would be to "get out and report what had happened to Hiroshima." Somehow, his plane flew, and he did.

Meanwhile, another task assigned to American Lieutenant Beser that historic day was to brief *New York Times* reporter William Laurance on this culmination—and first revelation—of the long-standing Manhattan Project that had developed the nuclear weapon in great secrecy.

According to coauthors Thomas and White, Beser did his briefing of Laurence with significant success. "Beser's vivid descriptions helped Laurence later to collect a Pulitzer Prize for his work," they wrote. Among other histories, Beser appears as both participant and source in Richard Rhode's Pulitzer Prize–winning book, *The Making of the Atomic Bomb*. In addition, Beser told his version in his own book, *Hiroshima and Nagasaki Revisited*.

In all that's been written about the explosive dawn of the Atomic Age, the focus has been Hiroshima and the *Enola Gay*. But there was more…the second strike, the tragedy of Nagasaki. How many today, for instance, can name the second B-29 that delivered an atomic bomb in those fateful August days of 1945? How many are aware that the second B-29 to drop a nuclear weapon on Japan—for the record, it was *Bock's Car*—first traveled through stormy skies to Kokura, the steel center, found it hidden by smoke, then, with fuel running low, turned for Nagasaki, that day's secondary target?

The nose of Bock's Car, the B-29 that dropped "Fat Man" on Nagasaki. (U.S. Air Force)

Beser, who was aboard *Bock's Car* for history's second atomic bomb drop, explained the switch from Kokura this way: "Kokura was situated east of

Yawata, the 'Pittsburgh of Japan,' and it had been firebombed by other groups of the 20th Air Force just two nights previously. The city was still burning. With Kokura situated downwind…our target was obscured by the smoke and debris of the still burning city."

Not that Nagasaki looked much better when *Bock's Car* arrived overhead that industrial center…arrived lugging "Fat Man," a plutonium bomb more than 10 feet in length, 60 inches in diameter, and 10,000 pounds in weight. The fuel level by this time was so low that *Bock's Car* wouldn't be able to fly all the way home to Tinian, or even to Iwo Jima. Okinawa now appeared the destination of choice—"One pass at Nagasaki, pray, and head for Okinawa," recalled Beser.

The problem at Nagasaki was the "essentially solid" undercast below the bomber, "with only an occasional hole here and there."

As *Bock's Car* initiated a bomb run by radar, bombardier Kermit Beahan spotted one of those momentary breaks in the cloud cover ten to fifteen seconds before the radar-controlled automated drop and exclaimed: "I have a hole. I see it. Bombs away!"

Later, the crew was relieved to know their hastily aimed bomb "had hit the center of the industrial area…and not the densely populated residential area." (Even so, "Fat Man" is considered responsible for 70,000 deaths at Nagasaki by the end of 1945 and 140,000 within the next five years.)

And now it was time to head for Okinawa—as rapidly as possible. Ironically, the men in *Bock's Car* could look down as they left Japanese skies and see other aircraft, fellow Americans, busy below the big B-29 bombing Japanese targets of their own.

At Okinawa soon after, Beser's fuel-starved B-29 broke into a crowded landing pattern firing warning flares and streaked for the runway. Touchdown was "hot and fast," Beser later wrote. And just as well at that! "As we flared to land, nose up to touch down, the two inboard engines coughed and died." Out of fuel.

After the war, "Jake" Beser returned to his home and his studies at Johns Hopkins. He earned his degree in engineering and spent his working career at Westinghouse, three decades in all.

Any second thoughts after all those years about the two atom bomb strikes on Japan? Not really, it seems. As Beser said in his 1991 article for *World War II* magazine, "The fact is, the Japanese were digging in to resist the invasion they knew had to come, but they then were persuaded to alter their plan of resistance and to accept the terms of surrender that were evolving.

"In essence, the horrible effects of the atomic bombs that were dropped on Hiroshima and Nagasaki were sufficiently persuasive to change their minds."

Wouldn't the "conventional" air attacks, the firebombings, with their tremendous loss of life, have brought Japan to her knees anyway? Not in B-29 crewman Beser's view, even decades later. "It can be argued, of course, that Japan was already beaten, and that with several more weeks of conventional bombings, the results would have been the same," he acknowledged. But he went on to say that while Japan certainly "had suffered terribly under the conventional onslaught of the B-29s," the Japanese had shown such a "will to fight to the death in each of the Pacific island battles" that there was "no reason to expect that they would do otherwise in resisting our invasion of their homeland."

★★★

Based upon Jacob Beser article, "Deploying Gimmick," in World War II *magazine, March 1991.*

Momentous Word Flashed

EVENTS PILING UPON EVENTS, THE leader of a warring people had a difficult announcement to make one day in August of 1945. "The war situation," Emperor Hirohito told his people that historic August 15, "has developed not necessarily to Japan's advantage."

And there, with that understatement of understatements...there it was. The end of World War II!

What joy, what relief, flashed around the world!

In Naples, Italy, the Andrews Sisters were doing a show for the troops. And, sure, the European phase of the war had been over, shut down since V-E Day, May 8. But this was a glum crowd, nonetheless, an audience loaded with about eight thousand of the most unhappy-looking soldiers they had ever seen, recalled Maxine Andrews years later.

"They were hanging from the rafters," she once explained. "All these fellas were being shipped out to the South Pacific. They hadn't been home in four years, and it was just their bad luck. We were trying to get them into good spirits."

That was when a note was delivered to the troupe's backstage managers, along with instructions to read its message on stage. The message announced the war was over. Japan had surrendered.

The "fellas" wouldn't have to go invade Japan after all! They could relax.

At first, nobody there in Naples believed it. Thought it was a gag, somebody's really bad gag.

Maxine went out on the stage with the note and tried to give it to Patty, who was just finishing a skit.

Patty said, "Stop your kidding. We can't read that here. We've got to finish the show."

When Maxine insisted the message be read aloud, Patty relented.

"All right, I'll go along with the gag," she said.

Without looking the note over first, she read it aloud to all the onlooking, wondering, unhappy troops.

Not a sound. Dead silence.

Patty looked at Maxine and looked at the note again. It was from the depot's commanding officer. The CO.

No gag.

"So she said, 'No, fellas, this is from the CO. This is an announcement that the war is over, so you don't have to go.'

"With that," Maxine recalled, "she started to cry. Laverne and I were crying."

Even then, there was no reaction from the stunned onlookers. Not a peep.

"So she read it again, 'This is the end, this is the end.'"

"All hell broke loose," Maxine remembered. "They yelled and screamed. We saw a pair of pants and a shirt come down from above. Following it was a body. He came down [from his rafter perch] and fell on the guys sitting downstairs."

So much for the pending invasion of Japan proper, scheduled for November 1 of that same year.

Scheduled, you could also say, to produce millions of casualties on both sides.

The atomic bomb drops on Hiroshima and Nagasaki had taken place on August 6 and August 9. And it still took until August 14 for Emperor Hirohito to end the argument between hawks and doves within the Japanese Supreme Council and insist upon the surrender.

Say what you will of President Harry S. Truman's decision to use The Bomb, it was done. He made the tough decision to go ahead.

The Allies, on July 26, did warn Japan. Surrender, they demanded, or face "prompt and utter destruction."

Japan did not budge.

And so, with two "violent shocks," as Winston Churchill later called them, the fighting did come to an end, but with much suffering and pain still to be alleviated among so many nations around the globe.

President Harry S. Truman and U.S. Army Chief of Staff George C. Marshall with Emperor Hirohito's signature on the Japanese surrender proclamation. (Harry S. Truman Library)

And now came the memories, both difficult and joyful.

Patty Andrews years later entered a hotel elevator in Cleveland.

"Hey, 'member me?" said the elevator operator.

Should she? she asked.

"Yeah," he said, by Maxine's subsequent account in Studs Terkel's "*The Good War*." "Remember Naples? Remember the guy who fell off the rafter? That was me."

★★★

First published in Military History *magazine, August 1992.*

Escape from New Menace

IT WAS ON THE SKI slopes in the Bavarian Alps that a young Jane Archer, American actress, met Horst Schillbach, physics student from Munich University. They fell in love and married in Berlin in 1938.

Opposed to National Socialism from the outset, the couple had to endure the Nazi Party and the war until 1945.

When the Third Reich crumbled into defeat and a Soviet capture of Berlin was imminent, Schillbach was determined that he and his wife would never live under a totalitarian regime again. He arranged his wife's escape from Berlin in April 1945, but his own escape attempt had to wait until August. By that time, Germany was partitioned into three zones. Berlin was an island in the Soviet Zone, an island divided among the Soviets and the Western Powers.

Late one day Schillbach proceeded as far west as he could legally go. He arrived at a small village and questioned the natives. The natives told him: "Yes, the Reds had erected three fences of barbed wire on the border. Yes, there were constant patrols." A stretch of the Iron Curtain already in place… and World War II not yet officially over! "But around 2 A.M., those Russian sentries were less attentive, not like the German patrols!"

Schillbach waited until midnight and then started out, crawling from bush to bush, edging toward the border. He lay in a gully until he heard a nearby church bell sound two o'clock. He started crawling across a field that had been stripped bare of vegetation—a no man's land. Anyone seen on it provided target practice for Russian sentries.

He was helped by a night storm brewing. He crawled on, finally reaching the woods beyond.

Then, in order to avoid making the slightest sound, such as a footfall on a breaking twig, he put his arms around a tree and lifted his body until he saw, in a flash of lightning—the border! In pelting rain, he ran forward, heaved his knapsack high over the first two fences, then fell on his knees and started digging in the rain-softened earth beneath the barbed wire. He squirmed under the first barrier, ran to the second, fell on his knees and started digging again. He slipped under the second. Just as he heard the shot of a rifle, he squirmed under a third fence. Then, slipping and sliding in the rain, he staggered forward, fell and finally crawled for shelter under a farm wagon. A farm wagon in the British Zone.

Three weeks later, Schillbach joined his wife in Bavaria. They later moved to the United States.

★★★

First published in World War II *magazine, Vol 5, No. 4, 1990.*

Humanitarian in Budapest

ONE OF HUMANITY'S HEROES WAS in Budapest when the house of horrors erected by German Nazis and Hungarian fascists came crashing down under the pounding of the Red Army in early 1945.

He was a Hungarian priest and, like Swedish diplomat Raoul Wallenberg, he had risked his life helping others escape the Nazi terror. Like Wallenberg, too, he was "swallowed up" by advance elements of the onrushing Soviet juggernaut. He also disappeared, utterly.

But by chance, by God's help, however to name it, Bela Varga slipped free—to become, in Hungary's immediate postwar years, president of its Parliament. Nor would his short incarceration by the Soviet MVD early in 1945 be the only Communist trap he had to elude. Another would be laid in 1947, as Hungary fell into captive nation status.

Tall and husky, Bela Varga was the peasant son of a Hungarian farmer who twice worked in America to earn the money that enabled him to buy his farmland in Hungary. "I was educated in the spirit of American," Varga once said. "My father loved America very much."

As a strapping young man, Bela Varga became both a priest and a follower of Gaston Gaal, the popular leader of the Smallholders political party. Future Hungarian Premier Ferenc Nagy met Father Varga at Gaal's funeral in 1932, and was struck when the parish priest from Balatonboglar told him: "I was with Gaston Gaal every day. Through him, I know your party, and with my heart and soul I identify myself with its aims. If you take me in, I shall march with you and help you as much as I can. I have no other goal than to serve the people of Hungary."

Nagy and his associates did take in the youthful Catholic priest, and by the time World War II broke upon Europe, Father Varga had been elected to the Hungarian Parliament as a Smallholder. The Smallholder Party advocated social and land reform, among other democratic ideals, but as Hungary's leadership consorted more and more closely with Hitler's Germany, those goals gradually were lost to sight.

Varga's humanitarian concerns were not so easily derailed, however. He turned his rectory in a village on Lake Balaton into a camp, then a school, then a major stop on an underground railroad for thousands of refugees from war-torn Poland to the north.

Both Jews and future freedom fighters for Poland were among those who escaped the Germans with the aid of Varga's ever-growing network. For a time, his makeshift school was "the only institution of higher education the Polish people had anywhere in the world," Nagy later wrote. As for Father Varga himself, "There was no end to his labors on behalf of the suffering Poles."

With the relative immunity he enjoyed as both a cleric and a member of Parliament, Father Varga had links to the Resistance beyond his refugee in-terests. He was able to hide radio equipment in his rectory. He eschewed the Underground's sabotage or assassination activities, but he did inform the Allies that barges full of Turkish chromium ore were traveling up the Danube River for shipment to Germany. In short order, the originating mine in Turkey not-so-mysteriously was blown up.

Another time, a Polish contact approached him with hard evidence of both the Nazi pogrom of the Jews in the Warsaw Ghetto and the "extermination" program begun in Nazi death camps. Father Varga accompanied his contact to neutral Switzerland, his companion disguised as a fellow priest, but no one among the Allied intelligence sources they contacted would believe the story. They couldn't conceive of such a thing, Varga later explained.

His parish rectory on Lake Balaton, meanwhile, had become a major Resistance headquarters—at one time, the village pastor had thirty-five Jewish orphans hiding in his own house. But then, in 1944, the Germans suddenly occupied their ally Hungary with major fighting forces. They began the systematic assault on Hungary's own Jews that Swedish diplomat Raoul Wallenberg tried to stem. With a Gestapo price on his head, Varga was forced to go into hiding—ordered to do so by his own prelate, Cardinal Mindszenty. He hid in the crypt of a monastery near Budapest.

Oddly, it was there that Soviet agents found him in early 1945, the battle for Budapest still raging nearby. "The Russians came into the monastery, and we thought they were liberators," Varga later explained. "I came up from the crypt, I spoke with them. After a few days, they came again; two officers in tuxedos, one Hungarian interpreter. They said, 'We are so happy to see you.'"

They told Varga a Soviet army marshal wished to see him—to express the gratitude of the Russian people for his anti-German activities during the war. Suspicious, Varga tried to stall by pleading it was time for him to say Mass. But they were insistent.

"We will bring you back after a few minutes," they told him through the Hungarian interpreter. "I saw in his eyes, the way he said it, he knew they were lying."

Knowing he couldn't turn and run, Varga went with them. The first two men took him to a barracks and left him there—no Soviet marshal, of course. Two more appeared and took him to a house in what might be called the suburbs of Budapest. *They* left him.

Finally, a third pair took Father Varga to a bunker outside the besieged Hungarian capital and locked him in the barren concrete structure. Like Raoul Wallenberg, the humanitarian effectively had "disappeared."

But why? In Varga's view, rather than his being a political leader dedicated to his people and democratic ideals, he "suffered" in Communist eyes because during the war he had passed to the Allies information on the Soviets' mass execution of Polish officers at Katyn Forest. He had been an intermediary for Poles carrying photos and other documentary evidence of the notorious massacre.

Interrogated relentlessly, fed only garbage for food, and locked in a windowless, subterranean room in the bunker outside Budapest for nearly two weeks, Varga then was moved to still another suburban house—for his "trial."

A new interpreter assigned to him for the proceedings told Varga the outcome already was decided. "You are condemned to death because you are a link to Katyn," the priest's fellow Hungarian said. "We know that you are. Stalin gave direct orders to kill everybody who knows anything about Katyn."

Still, in a semblance of judicial process, Father Varga would be granted the right to appeal.

And it was as predicted, to the letter. His interrogator from the bunker presiding, the lower "court" quickly convicted Father Varga as an enemy agent, sentenced him to death, and granted the automatic plea for an appeal. The appeal would have followed the same, preordained course, but for the interpreter—a self-proclaimed atheist and communist whose early life as an illegitimate child in a small Hungarian village had been especially embittering. Only the village priest had been kind to him, according to the fablelike story he poured out to Father Varga in their pretrial meetings. And Father Varga reminded him of that priest, who in fact had taken the child into his rectory and raised him for four years.

At first, Varga didn't quite believe the story. "I thought he might be an *agent provocateur.*" Before the appeal proceeding, however, the interpreter carefully coached Father Varga. "You say, 'I am a priest, a peasant, and I had no connection with the Americans or the sabotage Underground,'" he urged.

Then during the appeal appearance before a dignified-looking Russian colonel, the interpreter did not seem always to translate Varga's answers exactly as given. While he didn't speak Russian himself, Father Varga sensed that the interpreter was more or less "giving his opinion."

Then, it was over. The judge told a startled Father Varga: "You are free, you are a friend." The interpreter, it seems, had convinced the appellate official that Varga was not the man the Russians thought he was. A day later, after his lie was found out, the Hungarian translator was shot in the garden of the same suburban house, Varga later learned.

Varga, though, was free, unlike the ill-fated Wallenberg. As a political figure of some note, Father Varga soon was in the public eye—he could not so secretly be spirited off again by the Soviets occupying Hungary at the war's end.

In postwar elections, which the Communists at first tolerated, both Varga and his Smallholders Party briefly held sway—Ferenc Nagy became premier and Varga, as president of the Parliament, was in a post equivalent to Speaker of the U.S. House of Representatives. But the Communists, Russian and Hungarian, squeezed the fragile coalition government ever more tightly, wrung from its key figures various "confessions" to treasonable "conspiracies," staged various "incidents," and by the spring of 1947 were ready to take over the country.

So it was that Varga one May morning called to order an extraordinary meeting of thirty parliamentary deputies. Flanked on either side by his vice presidents, he studied the faces before him in vain hope of finding, even then, new allies in his fight to stop the Communist takeover.

The Communists in the group stared back with barely concealed triumph; Father Varga's fellow democrats, many of them, looked on with real fear in their eyes. Their coalition government had collapsed. In the past few days, the occupying Russian forces had produced a "confession" from a key Smallholder official to an anti-Soviet conspiracy among the party's leaders, Nagy and Varga himself allegedly among them.

Nagy, vacationing in Switzerland, had been forced to resign as premier; the nation's aging president, a largely titular figure anyway, was isolated and rendered ineffectual. Only the priest Bela Varga was left, and it would be only a matter of days before his arrest.

Everyone knew. Old friends and political associates were afraid even to talk to Varga—he had become a leper.

The meeting of the Parliament's special political committee had been called to select a new government; the Soviets had their handpicked candidate all lined up to take office. What Varga's longtime colleagues in the room feared now was that the stubborn priest would nominate his own choice for premier, even at this eleventh hour. Few wanted to choose between a true leader and a Communist favorite.

But, Varga, to their relief, kept his own counsel. For the important task of forming a new government, it was a remarkably short meeting. No objections voiced at all.

Parliamentary President Varga started to adjourn the meeting, then, almost as afterthought, added that he would convene Parliament as a whole the following Monday, June 2, to ratify the committee's "choice." More relief. That proposal also was approved with no dissent.

Varga in fact had made his choice too. He could stay on in Hungary, he later explained, and die for his beliefs, his reputation muddied by Communist accusations. Or he could try somehow to inform the outside world of the police-state tactics by which the Soviets and their puppets were taking over not only Hungary but all of Eastern Europe.

On Monday, June 2, as the Parliament convened in war-shattered Budapest on the banks of the Danube, its presiding officer, oddly enough, was nowhere to be found. As the Communists soon would discover, he was on his way to the West, the meeting of the Parliament his "cover." A day or two later, making his way through a remote forest alone and on foot, he crossed the Hungarian border into Austria—ready, he later said, to knock down anyone who might stand in his way, to use whatever violent means necessary to carry his message to the outside world.

★★★

First published in the Washington Times, *April 1985. Based upon personal interviews.*

Last Missing WASP

THEIR FLIGHT SUITS WERE ALWAYS miles too big, it seemed, but there's nothing exaggerated about the 60 million miles they flew from 120 Army Air Force bases around the world in every U.S. military aircraft put into operation during World War II. Amazingly, too, out of 1,102 serving in uniform, fewer than four percent were lost.

"They" were the WASPs—the little-known U.S. Women Airforce Service Pilots.

Not content to be stay-at-home moms or sweethearts, nor even a Rosie the Riveter in a key assembly plant, these were women, mostly young women to be sure, eager to fill a key gap left by the men sent overseas. Young women eager to fly, too.

And that's where they came in so handy—ferrying U.S. military aircraft from one place to another in lieu of the male pilots who normally would (and sometimes did) do the same obviously needed task.

As further explained by Mark "Sharky" Alexander, a U.S. Air Force Reserve senior NCO for more than 20 years and head of Sharky's Underwater Expeditions, "During WWII, thousands of new airplanes were coming off assembly lines and needed to be delivered to ports on the East and West coasts, for shipment overseas."

With all the men gone, he added in the February, 2010 issue of *Military* magazine, "the government launched an experimental program, the WASPs, to train women pilots to fly military aircraft." He also noted that many people did not believe that these women could take to the air in these "powerful warplanes."

And yet they did. "WASPs ferried 78 types of planes over 60 million miles, a huge contribution to the war effort." This big contribution is even more impressive since these young women defied the female conventions of 1940s America and stood in line to voluntarily sign up for the often-dangerous ferrying and aircraft-testing duties. "Over 25,000 women volunteered for the WASPs, but only about 1,000 were chosen for this unique opportunity to serve," Alexander also wrote in *Military* magazine.

According the website, "WASP on the Web" (www.wingsacrossamerica. us/wasp/), the actual number chosen was 1,102 women, 38 of whom "were killed flying for their country." In its November 2007 issue, Waco, Texas' city magazine, the *Wacoan*, reported on one such case in which California-born Bettie Mae Scott was killed flight-testing a recently repaired aircraft at Waco Army Air Field on July 8, 1944—just 18 days before her 23rd birthday.

The *Wacoan* article, "On a Wing and a Prayer" by Lynn Bulmahn, also noted that although Scott's assignment to test-fly recently damaged and repaired aircrafts was inherently dangerous, many WASP pilots were also risking their lives towing aerial gunnery targets or flying around in the night skies as practice for searchlight personnel.

Though they were highly trained, the jobs these women did voluntarily was very dangerous and, as with Bettie Mae Scott and 37 others, sometimes fatal. Just ask underwater diver "Sharky" Alexander, who spent time in 2009 deep in the waters of Santa Monica Bay off Los Angeles looking for a long-missing WWII vintage P51-D Mustang fighter—and its female pilot.

As he related the story behind his hunt in waters 215 feet below the bay's surface, "It all started on 26 October 1944, long before I was born, when an attractive ferrying pilot named Gertrude Tompkins [Silver] took off from what is now Los Angeles International Airport. She was a member of the elite Women Airforce Service Pilots (WASPs). She flew into an off shore fogbank and was never seen again."

It was Silver's P-51 Mustang that Alexander and members of the Missing Aircraft Search Team (MAST) were seeking in the depths of Santa Monica Bay, but unfortunately to no avail.

As he had learned before undertaking the dive, Silver disappeared after taking off last in a group of 30 ferrying Mustangs flying from Los Angeles to Newark, New Jersey, with plans to make an initial stop-over at Palm Springs, California.

Spurred by the death of a sweetheart, an American flying with the British RAF early in the war, she had taken private flying lessons, then applied for acceptance into the WASP program. Trained at Avenger Field in Sweetwater, Texas, Alexander also learned, "She was so good that she was selected for fighter pursuit school, and became one of a handful of top women pilots trained to fly the P-51 Mustang, the most powerful American fighter."

With all of the remaining WASPs accounted for and either living out their old age or already passed away, other sources have provided further details about the final days of the last missing WASP flier.

"She was 32 and a bride of just one month," the *Los Angeles Times* reported in 1997. Even more dismaying, her flight plan apparently was misplaced and she herself wasn't missed for three days. "A search, including the scanning of Santa Monica Bay by military boat with new husband Henry Silver on board, failed to turn up any trace of the young pilot or the newly built single-seat pursuit plane she was to fly across the country for shipment overseas."

The *LA Times* story focused on California high school history teacher G. Pat Macha, "a widely recognized expert in 'aviation archaeology'," as one of those both moved and intrigued by the mystery of the WASP pilot's disappearance. Macha, it seems, became involved in the effort to solve the mystery after publishing a guidebook on historic aircraft crash sites in the mountains and deserts of California.

"It caught the eye of a former WASP who had known Silver, and, eventually, some members of Silver's surviving family. Macha was hooked on the search project after those relatives approached him for help," the newspaper noted.

"As a history teacher, I feel it is my duty to do my bit," he himself explained. "I think the nation owes her, and we need to do what we can."

The information available about Silver's activities on that fateful day in October 1944 places her in the cockpit of a brand-new and perhaps unfamiliar P51-D at old Mines Field (later became part of Los Angeles International Airport). Cleared for takeoff at 4 p.m., she "ascended into an overcast sky shortly after that," the *LA Times* reported, but "no one in the tower saw her departure, and the tower never had contact with her once she was cleared for takeoff."

Reviewing the same scenario, Macha "believes that Silver met her fate within moments, that something caused her plane to plunge, nose-first, into the ocean." He further theorizes that "She may not have been familiar with the then-new model of the plane, which had a fuel tank just behind the cockpit. When full it could have shifted the plane's center of gravity, sending it into a low-altitude stall from which it could not have recovered."

The Los Angeles paper also cited former WASP pilot Iris Critchell's recollection from those hectic wartime days that "many of the planes that we picked up had never been flown before." Or if they had been flown it was only "at least for 10 minutes or so by factory pilots," the Times account said. "Fortunately," Critchell also recalled, "their reliability was very high."

★★★

Based upon sources cited, but it's worth special note that the WASP website cited, WASP on the Web (www.wingsacrossamerica.us/wasp/) was created by former WASP pilot Deanie Bishop Parrish and daughter Nancy Parrish.

End Is Seen

LEROY NICHOLSON WAS JUST SIXTEEN years old and all of ninety-eight pounds when he joined up in August 1942—"just a little squirt working in a cotton mill." The U.S. Marines already were going ashore at Guadalcanal. How much war could be left?

Enough so that he saw his action aboard the light cruiser *Montpelier*, a ship of twenty-six invasions, of fifty-three shore bombardments, of thirteen battle stars before it all was over.

And so, in the Pacific, as a young man in a quadruple 40 mm antiaircraft gun mount, he saw gun battles at sea, such as the Battle of Empress Augusta Bay the night of November 2, 1943, in which Rear Admiral A. Stanton ("Tip") Merrill's Task Force 39 of four light cruisers, plus destroyers, took on two heavy and two light Japanese cruisers, plus their destroyers, in order to protect the American transports landing the marines on Bougainville.

Merrill's tactics in that American victory are still considered classic. As the engagement unfolded, however, few on board the *Montpelier* were thinking of textbook naval battles, even if she were the admiral's flagship.

When their [the Japanese] 8-inch shells landed, they threw up enormous mountains of water, and the light from the outer shells colored the water green and red and orange. Our gun tub was close to a passage that led from one side of the ship to the other. When the 8-inch shells started landing on the starboard side, we would run to port. When they started ranging on the port side, we'd run to starboard. There was always a danger of shrapnel from those big, beautiful waterspouts, you see.

Right on the scene like that, he could really see what was happening, all right.

You could see the flashes from their guns. And we got a good view of one of their cruisers, the Sendai, *going down. She was on fire from one end to the other, part of her hull looked like it was glowing. You had to feel sorry for the men on board…*

but not too sorry, because if it hadn't been for Admiral Merrill's getting the drop on them, it might have been our ship instead.

He had had to obtain parental permission to join up, and now, out in the Pacific, he also saw what it was like to be under intensive air attack. He saw that the morning after the nighttime engagement at Empress Augusta Bay—

As I remember it, we were too busy to be frightened. They threw about 100 planes at us in the space of seven or eight minutes....Our ship burned up about 6,000 rounds of 40 and 20 mm ammo in those eight minutes—it was incredible how much firepower we could throw out. [Merrill had circled his ships in wagon-train style to fight off the air attackers.] The prettiest hit I saw that day, however, was not by one of the antiaircraft guns, but by one of the big, 6-inch turrets. It was tracking a plane as it flew off to the north, and when it fired you could see the big tracer just arch out over the water. The 6-inch round landed right beneath the Japanese plane, and this enormous column of water came up and knocked it out of the sky, end over end—just like swatting a fly.

He was there when *Montpelier* and *Cleveland* traded blows with Japanese shore guns—

I kept thinking how it would be our turn next, and how big a target a 600-foot-long cruiser makes. Sure enough, when we came into line and opened fire, 8-inch rounds started landing nearby. I heard one of them come overhead, right between the mainmast and the smokestack—50 yards shorter and it would have landed on us. Next thing I knew, they bracketed the bow of the Montpelier. *These were just near-misses, mind you, but the force from them was enough to rip one of the 20 mm guns off its mount, and the whole front end of the ship was sprayed with big hunks of red-hot shrapnel.*

He later saw man's most violent weaponry at work too—

We actually saw the Nagasaki bomb go off, a big flash off in the distance. We thought one of our carriers had taken a bad kamikaze hit and blown up. It wasn't that at all, of course.

Strangely, though, it was also at Nagasaki that Leroy Nicholson saw an end to the war, and its battles, its hatreds—

A month later, when we were allowed on shore, it was a weird experience. What can I say, except that the city looked just like the pictures you see—utter devastation. We didn't know what to expect, but it was logical to assume the Japanese would feel very hostile, so we all went ashore armed with 45s. We were walking down the street when suddenly these little children came out, maybe half a dozen of them, six or seven years old. They were adorable and well-mannered—they bowed politely and held our hands and we walked around with them, gave them some candy, and suddenly it was as if the blackness of the war had lifted from our minds. The hatred most of us had felt for the Japanese during the past few years just went away. We had all been bragging about how, boy, when we get to Japan, we're gonna show 'em who's boss… and suddenly, standing there in a devastated city, holding hands with some smiling children, it was impossible to feel that way any longer. I think that was the day the war really ended for most of us.

★★★

Based upon interview by William R. Trotter, Military History *magazine, August 1989.*

Among the Former Enemy

IT SEEMED THE NATURAL THING. MacArthur would be in Tokyo in a few days to accept the Japanese surrender. For a trio of long-held POWs, Americans all, the question was hardly a question. Why not take the train north from Kobe and be there when the advance U.S. occupiers arrived?

You know, the train from recently firebombed and completely leveled Kobe, home of a million or so Japanese.

After all, the hostilities were over…had been since August 14. For two U.S. Navy physicians and a dentist companion, there seemed no reason to remain confined at the makeshift new quarters for the International POW Hospital at Kawasaki, near the largely destroyed old POW facility at Kobe. Hadn't they already had been told, "For you…the war is now past?"

They indeed had. "Yesterday we were prisoners of war under the Japanese in a foreign land," wrote one of the three, navy dentist Stanley W. Smith, years later. "Today," he added, "we were free, almost, and carried away with the knowledge of our liberation although still in a hostile environment, a factor we seemed to have overlooked in our exhilaration."

A British friend, also a POW, cautioned that he thought their proposed trip was a "rum" idea.

Never mind that, added Smith. "Three of us were imbued with a perfectly ridiculous notion to go on a 250-mile journey to Tokyo to be there when General MacArthur and his advance forces arrived to sign the peace terms."

And so, down to the small Kawasaki station they went, to catch the electric tram over to a railroad station in Kobe, which only weeks before had been leveled—burned out—in a firestorm created by U.S. B-29s dropping conventional bombs.

They, themselves, had seen the armada of three hundred B-29s approach, arrive nearly overhead, and turn everything within a five-mile radius of the Kobe docks into black, smoldering ruins right before their eyes.

That was when their own POW hospital facility had been hit as well. "It wasn't safe to be outside the buildings…Flying pieces of metal, burning timbers, and bits of shrapnel were everywhere in the air, blown about by a high velocity wind created, I suppose, by the terrific currents of intermittent hot and cold air forming over the burning city," wrote Smith in his 1991 book, *Prisoner of the Emperor: An American POW in World War II.*

With the hospital unit located about three miles from the waterfront area, "in a completely residential area at the base of the mountains, slightly elevated from the rest of the city," he and his POW colleagues at first thought they would be safe from the holocaust below. But then came the flying debris. Then, as he sought shelter inside a building, "a blinding flash, a few seconds of semiblack-out, and the superstructure of plaster, timbers, walls, and overhead completely covered me and continued to shower down, wedging me in."

Smith managed to fight his way free, then helped others around him. Three POW-patients had been killed outright, while about thirty staff members and thirty additional patients were severely burned. And the danger was not yet past. With the bombs still falling two hours after the first B-29s had appeared overhead, "our only concern was to escape to the nearby mountain before we would be cut off by the flames surrounding us on all sides."

Their panic-stricken guards paying little attention, Smith and his fellow medical POWs carried their wards—"our sick"—through "narrow, burning, back streets, praying to be granted a few minutes' grace before being trapped by the raging fires."

As the POW doctors made their way up the mountain slopes, "we paused here and there to give what attention we could to the pitifully burned civilians along the way." Some were actually dying "while receiving first aid." Others kept coming for help, "although I am confident they realized we were in some way related to this calamity now engulfing them."

Eventually the bombing came to a halt. "We returned late that evening to find complete destruction of our hospital and equipment. We stood among smoking embers to view without obstruction the miles upon miles of leveled rubbish that, just a few hours before, had been the homes and industry of nearly a million people."

Next day, the POWs still able to walk were told to begin a trek to an abandoned camp at Kawasaki about ten miles away. Their designated path took them past groups of local citizens stoically digging under the rubble of their former homes for cherished personal items—or the burned remains of relatives or friends. Many of the victims had been trapped in air raid shelters under or between Kobe's "highly inflammable little homes."

These were "pitiful, distressed groups, whose intense suffering showed so plainly in their bewildered faces and their silently bowed hands as they gave expression to their grief with remarkable control."

No signs, as Smith passed by, of anger or desire for revenge...he saw no such emotions appear on their faces as "we slowly went on our way among them, we who were representatives of an enemy who yesterday had brought so much death and destruction to their homes, not one expression of hatred as we walked through the cluttered streets." And yet, even "the most conservative among them must have regarded [the attack] as a wanton and cruel attack."

That had been the case in June, and now, in late August, Smith and his two companions arrived at the Kobe rail station about 5 p.m., fully primed to arrange their passage by rail to Tokyo without further ado.

Somewhat to their surprise, they had to persuade the ticket agent that they really would be allowed to enter the newly established Tokyo military zone. An English-speaking onlooker, a Japanese, helped out by explaining things more clearly, then told the three Americans their train would leave at nine o'clock that night and arrive in Tokyo at 2:15 the next afternoon.

So far, so good. Soon, though, the Americans realized they were the only foreigners waiting for the train. Everybody else on the platform, in fact, were fully uniformed Japanese soldiers, hundreds of them, "each carrying a pack, in some cases larger than themselves."

When the train arrived, the uniformed crowd made a rush for both doors and windows—"Each one fought his way madly to get aboard with his pack of bedding and nondescript gear." The Americans, too, went aboard—were swept forward and "literally shoved through a window along with this mob of soldiers eager to get home."

As the train chuffed its way out of the Kobe railyards, Smith and his companions found themselves surrounded on every side by the soldiers. "After the turmoil subsided," wrote Smith, "we began to survey the situation around us: a trainload of returning soldiers who had accepted defeat at their emperor's request, bewildered, but until recently a very formidable adversary; a whole trainload of soldiers traveling with three former enemy naval officers crowded within their midst. We had to concede it wasn't an environment conducive to our personal welfare."

Surely not, but they made the best of it, chatting away for several hours while the troops on every side also talked among themselves. All conversation suddenly came to a standstill, however, when a Japanese soldier sitting across from Smith suddenly said, in clear English, "You are POWs?"

Startled, the Americans said they were doctors, "American Navy doctors."

"But you are POWs?" he persisted.

They, in turn, insisted they were doctors rather than prisoners of war, not entirely true under the Geneva Conventions, but close.

"Then you have been, let us say, detained by the Japanese military?"

Well, yes, the Americans allowed, "We had been so detained, first in the Philippines, then in Kobe, Japan."

"Ah yes," he then said. "Are you not then still to be considered under control of the military?"

Oh, no, they hastened to assure him, they had been granted liberty by a Japanese colonel in charge, and moreover, the soldier's own Japanese military hierarchy had given MacArthur assurances for the safety of American POWs still in Japanese hands…"and now we were on an errand of mercy into Tokyo to contact our advance forces, who would arrive there tomorrow, seeking through them immediate transfer of our seriously sick POW patients who would soon die if not evacuated."

That seemed to satisfy their interrogator, who now warned them in more friendly fashion of an approaching typhoon that would delay MacArthur's arrival by two days.

None too happy with the typhoon news, the POW trio arrived safely in Tokyo the next afternoon, a Sunday (all the soldiers having disembarked at various points along the way). They set out on foot through that also-ruined city in search of the Imperial Hotel, designed before the war by Frank Lloyd Wright. They soon noticed a wary attitude among the few civilians they encountered—"It was…apparent, from the surprised and equally grave expressions on the faces of the civilians we passed, that they were not at all convinced our presence on their deserted streets was by proper authority."

After a time, two soldiers in a military truck took the wandering Americans to the hotel, still fairly intact…and in operation. Trouble was, its usable rooms all had been reserved for a Japanese Foreign Office staff designated to meet with MacArthur's staff. A Japanese desk clerk put them together with a Foreign Office functionary who "found it hard to believe" they had made their trip to Tokyo in safety. "Didn't people throw stones at you, stare at you, attempt to molest you?" he asked. "We are daily confining hundreds of avowed fanatics who would gladly have taken your lives in one last gesture of revenge."

But…there they were, safe and sound for the moment. Hungry, in need of bath and beds too. And quite willing to toss around the name of General MacArthur, whom they would see on their errand of mercy. Plus, the war was over, wasn't it?

Nonplused for the moment, the Japanese gave in—they provided the three POWs a hotel suite for the next three days, plus guards, "with all meals served in our rooms or on a balcony overlooking the rest of the city."

On Tuesday, they watched the arrival of the lead Allied staff from that same balcony, "the big transport planes landing in the vicinity of Atsuji Airport."

In the end, though, they were denied access to their newly landed Allied compatriots. After a pleasant evening with the Swiss consul, neutral but representing American interests, they were sent back to Kobe "and the slower processes of liberation." But why couldn't they stay and see MacArthur, they asked.

"Possibly," explained their Foreign Office contact, "was it your intention to inform him [MacArthur] of your interpretation of prisoner atrocities perpetrated during the war, thereby attempting to influence him in some manner that would impose more severe penalties upon the Japanese people?"

And so, there it was. The Japanese were afraid of POWs telling POW horror stories before MacArthur laid out his final surrender terms.

"We realized our backs were against the wall, any further discussion pointless…" wrote Smith. So, he and his two companions returned to Kobe, reluctant but well aware their final and official freedom would come in a matter of days. In the meantime, they had informed the Swiss consul of the medical needs at Kobe; they knew, everybody knew, the atrocity stories would come out; the chief war criminals, those still living, would be hunted down and put on trial.

They also knew they had experienced a crazy, "most hilarious" few days as apparently the first Americans, "liberated and free in almost every sense of the word, to enter into Tokyo on their own after the cessation of hostilities."

Exciting as his brief Tokyo sojourn had been, however, Stanley Smith's most thrilling experience of the war came still later—when he returned home to

American soil and was reunited with his wife, Ila, and son, Duane...who, by no mere chance, edited his father's 1991 book.

★★★

Based upon Prisoner of the Emperor: An American POW in World War II *by Stanley W. Smith; Duane A. Smith, editor (University Press of Colorado, 1991).*

Postscript

ANOTHER DENTIST STORY, AND AGAIN in Tokyo, but this time in postwar Tokyo under American occupation...where plugging through a Japanese snowstorm by jeep one night in early 1947 were two U.S. Navy dentists bent upon a curious mission.

Sugamo Prison in Tokyo's Ichigaya district was their destination.

Hideki Tojo, the notorious war minister, onetime prime minister of Japan and now accused war criminal, was their patient.

They were desperate to see him, even though he was not planning on seeing them. He in fact was bedded down for the night in his cell. After all, it was nearly 11 P.M.

When they arrived, a friendly guard agreed to awake Tojo in his prison cell and "borrow" his false teeth.

Their business was not so much with Tojo himself, but with his teeth...the upper plate, specifically, that one of the two, navy dentist E. J. "Jack" Mallory, had created for the notorious Tojo.

Unbeknownst to Tojo, the inner side of his denture was inscribed with a series of dots and dashes—international code spelling out the words

REMEMBER
PEARL
HARBOR

At first no one but Mallory and fellow dentist George Foster knew about this dental coup, this branding of Japan's most vicious warlord...no one but them and, yeah, maybe a couple buddies or so, as well.

It made for a good story. Sure did. So good, in fact, that someone eventually

wrote home about it. And someone there, back in the States, told someone else…
and before you know it, the story was on the radio, it got on the news service
wires, it went around the world in a twinkling, relatively. It wound up back in
Tokyo, where Mallory and Foster wound up themselves…on the CO's carpet.

Mallory told the story in the Washington-based *Stars and Stripes* in early 1996.
As he related the facts, his buddy George provided dental treatment for the various
war criminals detained at Sugamo Prison. Friend Jack, the dental prosthetics officer
at 361st Station Hospital in Tokyo, was called in when it appeared necessary to
"extract" Tojo's remaining upper teeth. He then would need an upper plate.

Hideki Tojo at war crimes trial in Tokyo, January 6, 1946. (U.S Army)

Mallory offered a full upper and lower, since Tojo's seven lower teeth
weren't in great shape, either. "He pondered my words for a moment and then
replied via his interpreter, 'Oh, these will last me six months, and after that my
teeth I won't be needing anymore.'"

No doubt he was thinking of his likely execution as a war criminal. "He
spoke with a distant look on his face but in such a way that all in the room,
Americans and Japanese, broke into a chuckle,…followed momentarily by a
wide smile from *TojoSan* himself."

Far from the ferocious, raging bully—"Tojo the Razor"—that was Tojo's wartime image in the West, Mallory found the postwar Tojo to be "rather a tired, grandfatherly older man."

But that didn't stop Mallory from considering embedding the words "Remember Pearl Harbor" on the inside of Tojo's denture, instead of the usual military dental practice of embedding a slip of paper in the clear plastic with the owner's name, rank, and serial number. Friends at the hospital urged Mallory to go ahead, *do it.*

But "even at that young age," Mallory wrote years later, "I had enough brains to know that this would be a mistake from (1) a professional ethics point of view and (2) a poor choice as far as military ethics were concerned.

"So I refrained from the impulse."

Well, not quite. That's where the coded phrase entered the picture…that is, entered the denture, more properly speaking. As a "compromise."

But now, with the story out and the news wires buzzing, Mallory and friend Foster had been well roasted by their CO and told to get themselves out to that prison and grind out those telltale dots and dashes, forthwith.

As they sped through the night, through the Tokyo snowstorm, in a commandeered jeep, Mallory wrote, "We felt like a couple of international operatives."

At the prison, all went smoothly. "Down in the dental office I quickly used a grinding stone and removed all traces of the offensive dots and dashes."

The friendly guard then returned the smoothed denture to its owner in his cell. "I'm sure he wondered until his final days what that was all about," wrote Mallory.

Mallory and Foster now could truthfully say Tojo's denture did not carry any untoward inscription whatsoever.

Later, Mallory was able to visit the courtroom where Tojo and other war criminals were being tried before an international tribunal.

"At some point his eyes came to rest on me in puzzlement. Then, after what seemed a lengthy scrutiny, he broke into a big smile. Pointing a finger to his smiling teeth, he bowed toward me in a moment of recognition and gratitude.

"That was the last time I saw Tojo."

About eighteen months later, in fact, Tojo and several other convicted war criminals were executed for their horrendous crimes against humanity. Later still, Mallory happened to see a newspaper photograph showing Tojo's wife kneeling before a shrine.

"The only identifiable objects in the photo were his trademark round horn-rimmed glasses and the 'Remember Pearl Harbor' denture that Tojo wouldn't 'be needing anymore.'"

★★★

Based upon "What Everybody But Tojo Knew About the General's New Teeth," by E. J. "Jack" Mallory, Stars and Stripes: The National Tribune (Washington, D. C., February 11, 1996).

Eleanor Roosevelt: Woman for the Ages

By Ingrid Smyer

"I WAS AN EXCEPTIONALLY TIMID CHILD, afraid of the dark, afraid of mice, afraid of practically everything. Painfully, step by step, I learned to stare down each of my fears, conquer it, attain the hard-earned courage to go on to the next. Only then was I really free."

These are the words of Eleanor Roosevelt, the seemingly fearless wife of U.S. President and WWII leader Franklin Delano Roosevelt. Though a controversial figure, both loved and hated by her own countrymen, she became one of the most important women of the 20th century.

It might seem unlikely that a young girl, born into an aristocratic, socially prominent and politically connected family of bluebloods in late-Victorian New York, would ever have any reason to be fearful or feel the need to overcome anything, but in her book, *You Learn by Living*, she recounts the many difficulties of her life.

Her own ancestors, the Dutch who settled New York before the English, were among those who signed the Declaration of Independence and administered the oath of office to George Washington. Her grandparents on her mother's side were Valentine and Mary Hall, prominent social leaders who maintained a townhouse on fashionable East Thirty-Seventh Street in Manhattan and spent summer months at their estate, Tivoli, on the Hudson.

It was often said that Roosevelts only marry Roosevelts, but Eleanor's father, Elliott Roosevelt (brother of future President Theodore "Teddy" Roosevelt), broke this mold by marrying Anna Hall, known for her looks and grace. Both the Hall and Roosevelt women were notable for their captivating beauty—it was unknown for a Hall girl not to be the belle of the ball at every party.

Elliott, only 16 months younger than his brother Teddy, once admitted "that he lacked the foolish grit of Theodore's," according to biographer J. William T. Youngs, in *Eleanor Roosevelt: A Personal and Public Life*. It was Teddy who tried to live up to their father, also a Theodore, who had been known as a kind of patron saint in New York for his work with public charities, such as the Newsboys Club (later the Children's Aid Society). By almost any comparison, Elliott lived in the shadow of both his father and his brother.

Elliott made up for what he felt was his lack of success in business and other endeavors by riding to the hounds, playing polo, and drinking.

Every fall after the polo ponies were stabled for the winter, the social season began, and soon Elliot and Anna were making a name for themselves. During the 1880s, New York society was dominated by Mrs. William Astor as a supreme arbiter who determined who was in and who was out. Her elegant parties set the standards. Though Anna and Elliott Roosevelt could not afford to entertain on a matching grand scale, their charm and aristocratic lineage compensated—they were among the most popular young couples in New York society. When one news magazine assigned a reporter to interview high-society women, known as the "swells," Anna was one of the elegant ladies featured as "a leader in the exclusive circles she adorns."

Meanwhile, during the muggy summer of 1884, New Yorkers were all atwitter about the activity on Bedloe's Island, where Italian workmen were raising a huge stone platform in preparation for the promised statue from France. The metal figure representing liberty was ceremonially presented on July 4 to representatives of the United States in Paris. The actual statue itself would soon be shipped from France—in many pieces—to New York Harbor. That same year, on October 11, Anna Hall Roosevelt delivered a baby girl, promptly named Anna Eleanor.

This was an era of momentous changes for a nation and people that were still recovering from the turmoil of the Civil War that had ended only two decades prior. As biographer Youngs also points out, "There were no automobiles and few telephones or electric lights, and New York was a city of five-story buildings lit by gas." But the city, and indeed all America, would change rapidly in the early years of Eleanor's life, just as her personal life would.

Anna soon realized her little daughter was no beauty herself, and even as a child Eleanor sensed her mother's disapproval. What else to think when she was always surrounded by such a beautiful mother and pretty young aunts? Indeed, one relative told Eleanor in searing words no child would ever forget, "You are the ugly duckling of the family."

In addition, her mother often called her "Granny," because she considered

Eleanor so old fashioned, serious, and ill at ease. This dissatisfaction worsened after her two younger brothers, Hall and Elliot (called Ellie), were born, and her mother preferred them to her.

The one bright spot in little Eleanor's world was her father, who called her by the pet name Nell. Eleanor adored him and was devastated when he was sent away to Abingdon, Virginia, because of his severe drinking problem. It was hoped that the rural countryside of Virginia would help him to recover, and while he was gone he wrote her almost every day. She cherished these letters from her father and carried them with her throughout the rest of her life.

One such letter, quoted in *The Eleanor Roosevelt Story* by Archibald Macleish, was especially touching and memorable:

> *My darling little Nell…Because father is not with you is not because he doesn't love you. For I love you tenderly and dearly, and maybe soon I'll come back well and strong and we will have such a good time together, like we used to have.*

But this happy ending never came, and soon other hardships followed on the heels of this disappointment. In December of 1892, Eleanor's mother Anna, still a young woman, died quickly after contracting diphtheria. The following May both little brothers came down with scarlet fever, from which Hall recovered but three-year-old Ellie did not. Eleanor's father seemingly recovered from alcoholism for a brief time, but ended up spiraling back into his self-destructive behavior after suffering financial reversals in the panic of 1893. While living in New York with a former mistress, Elliot fell into a coma in August 1894 and died.

Eleanor, sent to Grandmother Hall's to avoid contagion, had to deal with the terrible loss of both parents and a sibling while in a home that was foreign to her. Eleanor later said that she had a deep sense of obligation bred in her and she felt very responsible for her younger brother Hall. More pointedly, a cousin and bridesmaid of Eleanor's, Corinne Robinson Cole, once observed, "Her horrible sense of obligation, and deep and isolating sense of loneliness—of life in a dream—made life difficult for Eleanor."

Eleanor and her brother Hall were now living permanently with Grandmother Hall on East Thirty-Seventh Street and, in the summers, at Tivoli on the Hudson. Eleanor, according to Macleish, remembered the Manhattan house as "the darkest, most desolate house I have ever seen. And Tivoli, too, was grim and lonely."

Eleanor also described her blueblood family's world as one that her grandmother was convinced would last, always the same, on and on. "It was never suggested to me that the world was going to be different."

Cousin Corinne, for her part, depicted their shared world of privilege as a "lovely world to be young in—to go dancing in—to do all the things that seemed simpler and surer and pleasanter than they ever could have been, we thought, in any other time or place." In contrast, the same Cousin Corinne also once said: "Eleanor belonged to that world of course, and she knew its customs. But though she 'belonged' she was never a part of it: her sadness and loneliness set her apart."

In her early teens Eleanor was like most teenagers, only much more ill at ease, sensitive to her inner thoughts, and worried about her looks. To make matters worse, one uncle who lived with them at this time also was a hopeless alcoholic and made Grandmother Hall tense because she never knew what he would do next. As a result, Mrs. Hall refused to have guests in the house and Eleanor wasn't able to have any friendships with peers or acquaintances with any adults other than her uncles and aunts.

Yet, despite all the adversity in her personal life, young Eleanor was able to take her experiences, sorrows, and upheavals and use them to develop an inner strength that would endure for a lifetime through all her many moments of loneliness and sadness.

Eleanor later decided that her grandmother undoubtedly was doing what she thought was best, but when an aunt discovered that young Eleanor still couldn't read she was horrified. Up to this point, the only education Eleanor had received was informal French lessons from a French nurse "who was bad for my character but good for my language." To make up for her ward's lack of real schooling, her grandmother began sending her to a fashionable little class conducted by "a pompous old gentleman named Mr. Rosa (apparently, Frederick Roser)."

Eleanor's Aunt "Bye" (Anna Roosevelt Cowles) suggested to Grandmother Hall that she send the teenager to a French school removed to Allenswood, England, during the Franco-Prussian War and directed by Mademoiselle Marie Souvestre. Aunt Bye, from Elliott's side of the family, had attended the school and had only good things to report about it. With this decision, a window to the world began to open for the young Eleanor.

Eleanor was trying to find her own place in that world and at the same time wanted to be a part of her small community of friends and relatives. Aunt Edith Carow, Uncle Teddy Roosevelt's wife, while on a visit to the family, noticed that Eleanor was still an awkward child, but said, "Poor soul, she is very plain... but the ugly duckling may turn out to be a swan."

Only time would tell how prophetic Edith might be, and in 1899 young

Eleanor was off to England. When she arrived at Allenswood, she was happy to find a new home that suited her better than any place had before. At Tivoli and in Manhattan, she had had to deal with a sulky aunt, a drunken uncle, a governess's cruelty, her grandmother's preoccupations, and her schoolmates' coolness. But here was a school designed to encourage every girl and to draw out shy youngsters like Eleanor. In addition, her French schoolmistress was a woman of high standards, and that suited the new American girl just fine. Mlle. Marie Souvestre opened Eleanor up to new ideas that would never have been tolerated in the tea parlors back home in America.

For instance, during this time the Boer War was going on in South Africa, with the English fighting the Dutch Boers, whom Mlle. Marie Souvestre sided with. She, of course, allowed those students who supported the British to celebrate their victories, but in the quiet of her study, where she invited only her favorite students, the French schoolmistress discussed the issues and explained her reasons for differing with the British viewpoint. Eleanor was both amazed and pleased to be presented with such new ideas and issues and was happy to be included in Mlle. Marie Souvestre's inner circle.

Mlle. Souvestre invited Eleanor to travel with her and they traversed the continent, having one adventure after another. Constantly learning more and more about how to be a tourist, Eleanor was always in awe of Mlle. Souvestre's willingness to try new things and ways. Eleanor vowed she would never again be "a rigid little person."

After three years of breathing such unrestricted fresh air, Eleanor now returned to America as a butterfly with her wings spread wide. She was excited at the prospect of seeing her family, but she had her regrets as well, and she reiterated her vow to not be rigid when she returned to the narrow confines of home.

Letters flew back and forth across the Atlantic as Mlle. Souvestre encouraged her favorite student to take up public service as a serious endeavor and not to let New York's "social dissipations," evenings out, flirtations, and like frivolities interfere with her good character. Despite her star pupil's good intentions, however, it was time for Eleanor to make her social debut.

Predictably, Eleanor's Assembly Ball was, for her, "utter agony." Her heartbreaking admission, noted by biographer Youngs: "I knew I was the first girl in my mother's family who was not a belle, and though I did not acknowledge it to any of them at the time, I was deeply ashamed."

Eleanor already felt the call to social service when by chance she met a handsome and popular young man on a train during the summer of 1902, after her return from England. On this particular day, she was traveling to Tivoli while young Franklin Roosevelt, a Delano on his mother's side of the family, was traveling with his mother Sara to their country estate at Hyde Park. Sara Roosevelt was a striking woman with patrician manners. She was dressed in black, for she was in mourning for her husband, who had died two years before. As a distant cousin, Eleanor's father Elliott had been the young man's godfather and the two young people had met occasionally over the years at parties.

Sara Roosevelt was studiously polite in addressing the young Eleanor, but Franklin was obviously thrilled to meet her again. During the next few months they frequently met at debutante parties, at first by chance, but soon they were conspiring to meet on purpose. Rather quickly, too, they were planning more important things.

One Sunday the two young cousins were visiting Eleanor's brother Hall at Groton, the same preparatory school Franklin had attended. After the church service Franklin suggested that he take Eleanor on a tour of the campus, since he was so familiar with it. It was autumn and the panoply of trees above them were radiant as Franklin looked into Eleanor's deep blue eyes and asked her to marry him. She quickly said yes.

Later, though, she began to have her doubts—after all, her mother had been so disappointed in marriage. Would she have the same fortune or would she be content at last, and have a family of her own? In the end, she decided he was hers to love; she hoped that they would be lovers and partners for life.

But there were hurdles to jump first. When his mother, Sara, heard of their plans, she insisted that they were too young to marry and hurriedly whisked Franklin off on a cruise to the West Indies. But Franklin's love survived and was fully intact when he returned. Soon Eleanor, with her charming ways, was able to win Sara over to their wedding plans though the two women subsequently maintained a sometimes rocky relationship that eventually grew and deepened over time.

Eleanor and Franklin were married in the Ludlow House at 8 East Seventy-Fifth Street, in a ceremony officiated by the Reverend Endicott Peabody. The wedding took place on March 17, 1905, with Uncle Ted—now President Theodore Roosevelt—in attendance to give the bride away. True to form, Teddy was the center of attention—the bride and groom found themselves alone, as all those in the wedding party had followed the president into the library, where refreshments were being served, and that was fine with them.

The couple honeymooned with a grand tour of Europe starting in London, where they were mistaken for the Theodore Roosevelts and given the royal suite at Brown's Hotel. Then they moved on to Paris, with a motor trip around France, before moving on to Italy. When Franklin refused to visit yet another church, they went on to Venice, and Cortina, where Franklin impulsively went mountain-hiking with a young woman they had met over a card game the night before. Eleanor was terribly miffed over this, but her new husband didn't realize it, since she didn't say how hurt she was. This unhappy moment gave the new bride pause enough to realize for the first time how different they were in temperament.

The newlyweds returned to live in a town house just a few blocks from mother-in-law Sara, who not only had rented it for them, but had also furnished the home and staffed it with servants. Ironically, the young bride who had escaped earlier familial confines to savor the freedoms of Mlle. Souvestre's tutelage now again would become all too dominated by her overpowering mother-in-law.

For the next ten years of her life Eleanor became the perfect wife and daughter-in-law and produced one baby after another. On May 2, 1906, Eleanor gave birth to her first child, a girl named Anna, who was quickly followed by five boys in a row. Her second child, James, was born just a year and a half after Anna. Only fourteen months later she gave birth to a second son, Franklin, Jr., who came down with the flu when he was only eight months old and died. Though his death broke Eleanor's heart, she had little time to mourn as ten months after losing little Franklin, a new Roosevelt was born, named Elliott after Eleanor's father. Two more boys would be born over the next few years: John and a second Franklin, Jr.

Meanwhile, in 1910 Franklin ran for public office even though his boss at the prestigious law firm where he worked said it would jeopardize his brilliant legal career. His mother, Sara, was also against Franklin entering a career that would throw him in the company of the non-elite masses. But Eleanor was very supportive of her husband.

Eleanor was right to be encouraging because soon the neophyte won a seat in the New York state senate. During his campaign Franklin had traveled from one end of the state to the other and gained significant experience for his future as a politician. Eleanor, too, was becoming involved in politics but surprisingly only supported women's suffrage because her husband did. As husband and wife they made a good support team in launching his political career, and Eleanor only encouraged him to attend political events without her in the occasional instances when he associated with people she disliked.

In June of 1912, Eleanor and Franklin attended the Democratic National Convention in Baltimore and she had high expectations for what she thought a political meeting should be. Instead, it was quite an eye-opening experience for her to see the delegates have heated discussions on the floor of the hall and to hear of the raucous arguments in the back rooms. In fact, Eleanor was so appalled that she left before the convention was over. Franklin stayed and led the New York Democrats in support of Woodrow Wilson, who then won the presidential nomination over House Speaker Champ Clark.

Wilson rewarded Franklin by appointing him Assistant Secretary of the Navy, which had always been his dream. Theodore Roosevelt had held the position only a few years before and had used it as a springboard to the presidency and now Franklin hoped to follow in the path of his cousin.

When the young Roosevelts moved to Washington, Franklin was thrilled to find that his desk was the same one that Teddy had used on his way to the presidency.

Eleanor, for her part, followed the examples of other politician's wives and spent her afternoons making calls, first to the wives of Supreme Court justices, then down the line. She especially sought out the wives of the New York delegation, confident that her calls would be of benefit to her husband.

If she were looking for something more substantial to do with her time than merely visiting other wives in Washington, however, her opportunity to do so was about to manifest itself most unexpectedly.

Most Americans hoped they could stay out of the horrifying war going on in Europe in 1914, but once war was declared by the United States in 1917, Americans rolled up their sleeves in fervent patriotism. Many men went abroad, and as a result many women began to find new responsibilities in their lives. One woman who got especially caught up in the spirit of the war was the wife of the Assistant Secretary of the Navy, Eleanor Roosevelt. She, like so many other women, sensed this was a great event historically and wanted to contribute. She reorganized her children, her servants, and her entire household into a wartime footing. She did such an outstanding job that her efficient system was selected as a model for large households by the Federal Food Administration.

When her brother Hall enlisted in the army, their Grandmother Hall was upset. The old woman asked Eleanor why Hall hadn't simply hired someone to take his place, as was a custom of some gentlemen during the Civil War? In her answer, Eleanor no longer passively answered her grandmother with a dutiful reply to her liking, but instead said, "A gentleman is no different from any other kind of citizen in the United States." And further: "It would be a disgrace to pay anyone to risk his life for you."

Thus, once-docile bride and young mother, though sometimes still dominated by her overbearing mother-in-law, was now taking control of her own life in ways that echoed the teachings of Mlle. Souvestre.

For the moment, even Sara was impressed at how Eleanor organized her household. Eleanor also finally decided to learn to drive—she had given up the idea in her mid-twenties when she suffered a slight accident in attempting to learn the art of the auto. She also worked in a canteen and helped to organize a knitting program that created socks for the Doughboys overseas, all the while feeling she was involved in the vital forces that were shaping history.

Even with all of these activities, the busy Eleanor felt she was not doing enough for the war effort. She wanted to be of real help, to go where the fighting was, but when she was offered a chance to go abroad with the Red Cross, she had say no; it simply wasn't realistic for the wife of a high government official—a mother of five to boot—to go anywhere near the front lines. Franklin, however, as Assistant Secretary of the Navy, had every reason to go, and in 1918 he went overseas on the destroyer *Dyer*. The trip was a thrill for the sailing buff; he was even driven to the front lines and to try firing a cannon.

Though Eleanor was enjoying her new self-assertiveness and quickly expanding responsibilities, a much bigger challenge lay just ahead.

Franklin returned from France in September, so ill with pneumonia that he was transported to his mother's house in New York City, to avoid exposing the children. Eleanor also went, in order to serve as a wifely helper and nursemaid. One day while she was unpacking his suitcase she made a painful discovery: a packet of love letters addressed to him in a familiar handwriting. Only then did Eleanor know the reality of what she had secretly suspected for some months. Her husband had fallen in love with another woman. And this was not just any woman, but her very good friend and social secretary, Lucy Page Mercer, who was a tall and beautiful woman with an adorable smile. Eleanor was completely stunned. How could he have betrayed her like that?

And her friend, how could she betray her too? Later, much later, recalled historian Doris Kearns Goodwin in *No Ordinary Time*, Eleanor acknowledged the terrible impact of that one moment in her life, saying, "The bottom dropped out of my own particular world and I faced myself, my surroundings, my world, honestly for the first time."

Though Eleanor offered Franklin a divorce, he realized that that was not what he really wanted, especially since Lucy, as a Catholic, could not marry a divorced man. Then, too, his mother Sara threatened to disinherit him if he left his marriage and Franklin's long-time political adviser, Louis Howe, warned him that his political career could not withstand the scandal of divorce. In the end, an agreement was reached between Eleanor and Franklin: she would stay, but he must never again see Lucy Mercer. For all outward appearances, Eleanor and Franklin went on with their lives, but there would be many more changes over time in what biographer Blanche Wiesen Cook has called "one of America's unique and abiding partnerships."

In 1920, now as vice presidential nominee on the Democratic ticket, Franklin took a campaign train across America to gather support for the party. No matter how the election went, he felt this would be a great opportunity to extend his political contacts, achieve national exposure, and gain added political experience.

Eleanor came along, too, and was very impressed with what she saw across this vast country. Louis Howe, Franklin's trusted political advisor and friend, was among those on the train. Eleanor had once considered Howe to be a strange man, but on the train they were often alone and she came to know him as an interesting political ally and a good friend. From the days when Franklin served in the state senate in Albany, Howe had recognized Eleanor's political talents. Now finding Eleanor receptive to his friendship, the former newspaperman began earnestly coaching her in the art of politics.

After the November election, when Republican Warren Harding was elected to the presidency, however, Democrat Roosevelt (FDR) was out of public life for the first time in a decade. When he and Eleanor moved back to Manhattan, Franklin again began to practice law. Eleanor, however, did not move back into her previous domestic roles and society activities (she had learned too much during her Washington days and on the campaign trail to simply regress into a housewife role) so she joined, and enthusiastically worked for, the newly formed League of Women Voters. Despite her personal wounds, Eleanor moved ahead with newly gained self-confidence and took the first step towards her own political evolution.

In the summer of 1921, the Roosevelts were off to their summer home on the rocky Canadian shore at Campobello. Franklin, still a vital young man at almost forty years old, engaged in all kinds of physical activity. One afternoon he helped put out a brush fire and went swimming in the cold waters of the Bay of Fundy, but lacked his usual stamina and quickly returned home to go to bed early. The next morning he could not move his legs—he was paralyzed. A doctor was sent for, and after his examination, told the family that the paralysis was indeed polio.

Totally helpless, Franklin was carried on a stretcher from the house to a motorboat for the two-mile journey to Eastport, then placed in a private railway car to New York and finally, moved into a hospital bed. He managed a cheerful face for the children's anxious eyes and with a brave wave he called out to them, "I'll be seeing you chicks soon."

For the next five years Franklin used all of his energy, both physically and mentally, to try to regain mobility. At first, both his arms and legs were paralyzed, but miraculously his arms regained mobility quickly.

Sara had moved next door again, and seeing her son suffering, she wanted to mother him, take him home to Hyde Park to live with her, and help him become the country gentleman she always thought he would be. But Eleanor stood her ground and said no. Gone were the days when Eleanor submissively said, "Yes, Mama," to every suggestion of her mother-in-law.

Eleanor saw a much more important job for herself. Her husband needed her and she was eager to help. Eleanor knew he could still have a useful life, and believed that in spite of everything he could offer leadership to his country. With the help of his family and friends, he could try to regain the use of his legs while remaining active in politics and law, and her new friend Louie Howe fully agreed.

But down in her most secret thoughts and dreams, Eleanor wanted more than to simply see her husband reenter the world of political power. She may not have realized at first but her husband's political aspirations would put her in a position to help others and make a difference to all those who suffered loss and pain as she had. The once lonely little girl still wanted to come into her own and this change for her husband could also help Eleanor reach her full potential.

Before either Eleanor or Franklin could begin to work toward their goals, the limits of his disability had to be handled. For the Roosevelt children, seeing their father struggle to regain his mobility was frightening. Still a relatively young man, Franklin had been their mentor in all kinds of activities, but now he was weaker than the youngest of them. They had to watch helplessly as their father first learned to roll himself into a wheel chair and to walk (more or less) with crutches, but soon he progressed to standing alone with the support of heavy iron braces and could even occasionally walk with a cane. Though these moments were rare, Franklin was sometimes able to use his strong hip muscles to move one leg in front of the other.

More than anything Franklin needed companionship, which Eleanor tried to give him, but it was Marguerite "Missy" LeHand who really became indispensable. Missy was a tall, good-looking woman who had come a long way from her blue-collar childhood in Somerville, Massachusetts. She had moved to New York, gone to secretarial school, and then worked on Roosevelt's vice-presidential campaign. Eleanor noticed the woman's skills and efficiency and asked her to come to Hyde Park after the election to help Franklin with his enormous piles of correspondence.

Missy not only understood her secretarial chores; she studied her boss, carefully read the letters he dictated, and came to know how he wanted certain kinds of correspondence answered. In later years after FDR's political career took off, Missy moved with him to the governor's office in Albany, New York, and then to the White House. Even in the beginning of her employment, only a year after Franklin was struck down with polio, Missy began to take on many of the household chores and duties, which allowed Eleanor to serve as a stand-in for her husband at many political meetings.

While serving as general helpmate, political stand-in, wife, and sometimes both mother and father figures to her children, Eleanor still found time to become closer with her husband. When Franklin balked at his strenuous exercise routine, she became "an old master sergeant," one doctor remembered at the time. She not only became the force that kept Franklin at his difficult and painful workouts, but also the spirit that urged him on and supported him in so many other endeavors as well.

While Franklin was busy strengthening his muscles, Eleanor was busy building up her own political muscle. Howe had helped her overcome some of her weaknesses in public speaking, and soon she would make it clear that she was more than a dilettante pouring tea at meetings. In fact, Eleanor began to take on responsibilities that were quite substantial.

First, she joined the Women's Division of the Democratic State Committee, and when the ladies needed an editor for their monthly newsletter, she jumped at the opportunity. But later, while traveling throughout New York State for the Democrats, she never forgot her interest in the organizations that were devoted to social reform. Eleanor began to realize that though she was born a member of the wealthy and privileged class, she actually belonged to a disadvantaged class: the female sex. In society and the home men were creating boundaries that women silently obeyed, but she believed this relationship drastically hindered women from playing an active role in both business and politics.

As early as the 1920s, Eleanor felt that if women were going to participate in these serious enterprises, they must prepare—and preparing to assume public office meant that they needed to learn and gain experience. To do so, in 1924 she insisted that women should be allowed to choose female delegates to attend the Democratic National Convention. Though most men were horrified at the idea of women in politics, with persistent campaigning the state of New York was represented that August by several women, thanks in large part to Eleanor.

More and more Eleanor found that the philosophy of the Democratic Party was in line with her liberal views and not just a platform she supported because of her husband. She also discovered a new community of friends in unmarried women who were active in politics. She likely would not have met these women in her rigid social set, but they quickly became the most interesting and important people in her life. Among them, Elizabeth Read, Eleanor's mentor in the League of Women Voters, was an accomplished lawyer and student of international law. Elizabeth shared an apartment with Esther Lapp, who was also an active League member and new friend. Eleanor also met friends Nancy Cook and Marion Dickerman at the New York State Democratic Committee, and each had a lot of experience fighting for women's suffrage and the abolition of child labor.

With her growing independence, Eleanor began to want a home of her own. She loved the beauty of the countryside at Hyde Park but it never felt like her home—she never felt comfortable bringing her new friends over for her mother-in-law Sara to entertain—and the Manhattan town house next door to Sara's was not really Eleanor's own either.

Franklin had bought a houseboat for his winters in Florida, but Eleanor hated the inactivity of sitting on a boat in the sunlight and wouldn't consider it as an option to live in. Perhaps the real reason for her dislike of the houseboat was that when the tropical moon and stars came out, according to biographer Youngs, she felt the dark waters were "eerie and menacing." Then, too, when Franklin famously invested in a rundown resort in Georgia called Warm Springs, Eleanor tried to like it but found the ambiance of the South alien to her. Well aware that her great-grandmother, Mrs. Theodore Roosevelt Sr., was a product of Georgia's slave-owning Bullock family, Eleanor was appalled at the mistreatment of blacks in the Deep South that was still going on. Only adding to her disdain, she thought the constantly romanticized moss hanging from the region's big oak trees was downright ugly and found the slow drawl of the Southern accent to be most unattractive.

Franklin had his circle of people who enjoyed fishing and soaking up the sun with him on the houseboat, and though he was sometimes insensitive to his wife's needs, he did realize that she needed to be surrounded by her own friends. He saw that she was unhappy and knew that her friends provided a companionship that he could not, and so he encouraged her to build a place of her own on the estate at Hyde Park.

They found a site near Val-Kill Brook, and began building a small structure, designed by Franklin himself and based on the old Dutch houses that were once found along the Hudson River valley. They named it Val-Kill Cottage and, at last, Eleanor had a place all her own. Finally, she was able to have friends like Nan and Marion Dickerman come to a place in Hyde Park where they'd be welcome, comfortable, and have a place to live when they visited.

It was at Val-Kill Cottage that Eleanor and her friends discussed politics and came up with new ideas to improve society. The three believed that small industries could be established in rural areas and they brought this idea to fruition by establishing a small factory that turned out fine reproductions of early American furniture. Nan and Marion, both former teachers, also suggested that Eleanor start up a new school. When they bought Todhunter School in New York City, Eleanor became a part owner and also joined the faculty, soon to develop into an outstanding teacher of history, drama, and English.

With so many accomplishments now under her belt, Eleanor was ready to focus even more intently on improving her family. She really wanted her two younger sons, James and Franklin, to experience the outdoors in the same way they would have if their father hadn't been disabled by polio. So, along with Nan and Marion, Eleanor took her younger sons on an extended camping trip that first went through parts of Canada and New England and then concluded in Campobello.

During this time, the relationship between Eleanor and Franklin hung in a precarious balance with each needing more than the other could give. They maintained their partnership by having their own circles of friends and interests and were able to hold on to their respect for one another by sharing certain goals.

In the 1920s, Franklin Roosevelt had made the difficult return to politics, which many credit to Eleanor's support. In any case, while giving a nomination speech for New York Governor Al Smith at the 1924 Democratic National Convention, FDR called his good friend and political ally the "Happy Warrior." But the real warrior at the convention was FDR who, despite an uneasy balance on his crutches, won the crowd over with his radiating confidence and received a resounding ovation.

Four years later, in 1928, Al Smith ran for president as the party nominee and lost, but Franklin, who was running for governor of New York, would finally win.

It had not been easy, but all the hard work by both husband and wife had paid off—or, to borrow a phrase from Macleish, they had achieved a political partnership that put "the future in their hands."

Eleanor was pleased that she had become her husband's political sounding board, but though she gave an outward impression of calm devotion, inwardly she was often stunned by the tough demands of politics.

If she sometimes felt overwhelmed by the process, Eleanor still remained the dutiful partner to her political husband. She had seen him lose the use of his legs, go through years of pain, and submit to rigid exercise programs and therapies without much physical improvement, but now he had bounced back in the world of politics that he adored. While she respected his achievement, which she herself had supported, Eleanor sometimes felt as though she was not yet fully included in his world of politics. But often without even trying, she found that she stood out even when alongside her husband, and she was determined to become involved.

In any case, by the time FDR ran for President in 1932 as the Democratic Party nominee, Eleanor was able to put the old insecurities aside and face the daily challenges with courage, even aplomb.

During the campaign, the Associated Press appointed journalist Lorena Hickok, who had covered Franklin since 1928, to cover the candidate's wife. "Hick," as she came to be called, was described by biographer Youngs in blunt terms: "a short, fat woman with a pugnacious temperament and a face that belonged with a cigar."

As Hick followed the candidate's wife, she was impressed with Eleanor's consideration to her and the other reporters. As they traveled on the campaign trail their friendship grew and their conversations became much more personal. They found they both had suffered unhappy childhoods and lost their mothers early, and Hick described her struggle to make her way in journalism. Later, on her forty-fourth birthday, Eleanor revealed a new side of her philosophy to Hick when she said, "It's good to be middle-aged. Things don't matter so much." As Youngs also reported, Eleanor added, "You don't take it so hard when things happen to you that you don't like."

But great things were happening for the Roosevelt family, and on March 4, 1933, Franklin Delano Roosevelt, with braces locked around his legs, stood on the podium to take the oath of office. Proud and tall, with his son James at his side, he addressed the Depression-era nation with confident, reassuring words: "Let me assert my firm belief that the only thing we have to fear is fear itself."

In the beginning of his presidency, the United States was in the depths of the Great Depression with about one in every four workers having lost their jobs. Mortgages were being foreclosed, homes were lost, and millions of Americans feared what would happen next. A new era was about to begin under President Roosevelt, who called his reform program the *New Deal*.

The nation also gained a new First Lady during these difficult times. The morning after FDR's election, Secret Service men surrounded the Sixty-Fifth Street house in New York where Eleanor was about to have breakfast with Louis Howe and her granddaughter Sisty. Eleanor lingered for a brief meeting with reporters before departing with Sisty. At the school she reassured her adoring students by saying, "I'm just the same as I was yesterday."

According to Youngs, shortly after this incident she and Hick were on a train together when she confessed that the term "First Lady" didn't really suit her. As if saddened by this, she wistfully looked out at the passing landscape and added, "There is just going to be plain, ordinary Mrs. Roosevelt."

To the contrary, she of course became one of the most famous and humanitarian First Ladies in all American history. As First Lady she was FDR's helpmate and chief political partner through the Depression, through his unprecedented four presidential elections, and through most of World War II. But outside of her husband's career, the First Lady wrote a daily, widely syndicated newspaper column, *My Day*, actively fought to advance civil rights and other social reforms, visited troops in the field during the war, and after the war served as a delegate to the United Nations and as chair of its Commission on Human Rights.

During the war, deeply troubled by its terrible human toll, this extraordinary woman often carried with her a prayer that said: "Dear Lord, lest I continue in my complacent ways, help me to remember that somewhere someone died for me today and help me to remember to ask am I worth dying for."

Sadly there would be one more unhappy betrayal for Eleanor to deal with—when FDR suddenly died of a stroke while visiting his beloved Warm Springs, Georgia, in April 1945, it was Lucy Mercer (now the widow Rutherfurd) by his side, and not Eleanor. She never let this last betrayal or the pain of her husband's death slow her down, and instead she kept on with almost all of her many activities and causes. Eleanor Roosevelt continued the newspaper column, lectured widely, wrote ten books, served on the NAACP's board of directors, helped found the Americans for Democratic Action, and served as chair of the Presidential Commission on the Status of Women, all until her death in 1962 at the age of seventy-eight.

Among her WWII activities, a sometimes dangerous, weeks-long trip to the embattled Pacific Theater of the war was a highlight. But she also used her White House platform to urge equal pay for women, to advocate a real combat role for all-black units such as the famed Tuskegee Airmen and to urge a more relaxed U.S. policy on admitting refugees, especially those fleeing Nazi persecution in Europe. The tireless Eleanor even maintained a "pen pal" correspondence with individual servicemen.

World War II: A Detailed Chronology

Events before Pearl Harbor

September, 1931, Japan begins hostilities in China with the occupation of Manchuria. *January 30, 1933*, Hitler becomes Chancellor of Germany. *March 7, 1936*, Germany occupies the Rhineland, violating the Treaty of Versailles. *October–November, 1936*, treaties linking Nazi Germany with Mussolini's fascist Italy; also with Japan (Anti-Comintern Pact). *July 7, 1937*, Marco Polo Bridge incident near Peking triggers real war between Japan and China.

March 13, 1938, Hitler's *Anschluss* binds his native Austria to Nazi Germany, where he is head of state. Fall of 1938, Munich Pact undermining Czech sovereignty; Hitler's takeover of the Czech Sudetenland. *March 15–16, 1939*, Nazi Germany marches into Prague, declares Czechoslovakia a protectorate. *August 23, 1939*, Nazi-Soviet Non-Aggression Pact signed. *August 24, 1939*, Great Britain mobilizes. *August 25, 1939*, British-Polish mutual assistance treaty.

September 1, 1939, Nazi Germany invades Poland. *September 3, 1939*, Britain, France, Australia and New Zealand declare war on Nazi Germany, with South Africa and Canada following suit over the next six days. *September 17, 1939*, the Soviet Union marches into eastern Poland, already succumbing to the German onslaught. *September 28, 1939*, Poland surrenders, is divided between Nazi Germany and the Soviet Union.

October 14, 1939, German U-boat sinks British battleship *Royal Oak* at Royal Navy facility Scapa Flow. *November 30, 1939*, USSR initiates Winter War with Finland. *December 17, 1939*, scuttling of the German pocket battleship *Graf Spee* off Montevideo, Uruguay.

April 9, 1940, Germany invades Norway and Denmark. *May 10, 1940*, Germany invades France and the Low Countries, while Churchill takes Chamberlain's place as British Prime Minister. *May 26–June 4 1940*, evacuation of more than 350,000 British and French troops from Dunkirk. *June 9–10, 1940*, Norway ends its open resistance as Allied forces evacuate. *June 17, 1940*, France will negotiate armistice with Nazi Germany, and it will be signed June 22. France's collaborationist Vichy government is established. *July 1. July 10–mid-November, 1940*, Battle of Britain, with 1,818 German aircraft lost, to Britain's 995, a materiel and moral defeat committing Nazi Germany to a difficult, extended war instead of a quick victory. *August 3–6, 1940*, USSR swallows up Baltic states—Estonia, Latvia, Lithuania.

August 27, 1940, United States returns to the military draft. *September 3, 1940*, United States gives Britain 50 destroyers in return for use of bases on British territory. *September 23, 1940*, Japanese attack French Indochina, now known as Vietnam. *September 25, 1940*, United States limits oil supplies for Japan. *September 27, 1940*, Germany, Italy, Japan adopt Tripartite Pact. *November 3, 1940*, FDR elected to third term as U.S. President.

November 14, 1940, German bombing of Coventry, England. *December 18, 1940*, Hitler tells his High Command to begin planning invasion of Soviet Union but on *January 10, 1941*, renews the Nazi–Soviet Pact anyway. *February 12, 1941*, Erwin Rommel takes his forces into Libya. *March 11, 1941*, approval of the U.S. Lend-Lease Act. *April 6–7, 1941*, German bombing of Belgrade kills 20,000. *April 18, 1941*, Yugoslavia surrenders to invading Germans. *April 21, 1941*, surrender of Greek army; *April 27*, surrender of Athens, followed by British evacuation of Greece *April 30–May 1*.

May 19, 1941, Ho Chi Minh forms the Viet Minh as anti-Japanese guerrilla force in Indochina. *May 24, 1941*, German pocket battleship *Bismarck* sinks British battleship *Hood* in the North Atlantic, but on *May 27*, British air and naval forces converge to sink the *Bismarck*. *May 28, 1941*, British begin evacuation of Crete.

June 22, 1941, Nazi Germany invades the Soviet Union, which now will be an ally of Britain and the United States in the war against the fascist powers of Europe. *August 9, 1941*, FDR and Churchill meet, announce their Atlantic Charter. *September 9, 1941*, first of 900 days in Siege of Leningrad; Germans also advancing on Kiev and the Crimea following seizure of Smolensk; their drive will continue until December before stalling outside Moscow in wintry weather.

Pearl Harbor and After

December 7, 1941, surprise Japanese attack on U.S. Pacific Fleet at Pearl Harbor with heavy American casualties, ship and aircraft losses resulting. *December 8, 1941*, America and Great Britain declare war on Japan. *December 11, 1941*, Germany and Italy declare war on the United States. *December 8–December 31, 1941*, Japanese invade Thailand and Malaya; the Gilbert Islands; Guam; the Philippines; northern Borneo; Sumatra. *December 10, 1941*, Japanese aircraft sink the British battleship *Prince of Wales* and battle cruiser *Repulse* in the South

China Sea. *December 16, 1941*, Germans thrown back by Soviet counter-offensive out of Moscow. *December 24, 1941*, Wake Island falls to the Japanese. *December 25, 1941*, Hong Kong succumbs as well.

January 14, 1942, in Washington, visiting Churchill and FDR organize military plans in Arcadia Conference. *January 16, 1942*, Japanese open Burma campaign. *January 20, 1942*, Wannssee Conference of German agency chiefs advancing plans for the liquidation of European Jews. *January 26, 1942*, Japanese move into the Solomon Islands group. *February 15, 1942*, British lose their Singapore base to Japanese. *February 27, 1942*, Japanese victorious in Battle of Java Sea. *March, 1942*, Japanese overrun Java, capture Rangoon, land in New Guinea, complete seizure of Singapore, but lose ships to American air attack at Salamaua on *March 10*.

March 28, 1942, British mount a costly raid on German drydock facility at Saint-Nazaire, France. *April 9, 1942*, surrender of U.S. and Filipino forces on Bataan Peninsula. *May 4–8, 1942*, American carrier-based aircraft stun Japanese in Battle of Coral Sea. *May 8, 1942*, Americans holding out at Corregidor finally surrender. *May 12, 1942*, mass gassing of Jews begins at Auschwitz.

June 3–7, 1942, Japanese lose four carriers to America's one in the Battle of Midway, considered turning point of the naval war in the Pacific. *July 2–4, 1942*, Rommel setback at first El Alamein. *July 4, 1942*, first U.S. air raids against Germany proper. *August 7, 1942*, U. S. Marines land on Guadalcanal, start to a six-month-long battle in the air, at sea, and on the island itself, finally ending in American victory. First, though, U.S. cruisers pummeled in Battle of Savo Island, *August 8–9*. *August 19, 1942*, British, Canadians, and a few U.S. Rangers in costly raid against German-held Dieppe, France.

September 6, 1942, opening rounds in the epic Battle of Stalingrad. *September 12, 1942*, Japanese drive on Port Moresby, New Guinea, halted. *October 23–November 4, 1942*, British General Bernard Montgomery begins victorious drive at El Alamein. *November 7–8, 1942*, Americans and British invade North Africa, first major joint offensive against Germans. *December 2, 1942*, in Chicago, first atomic chain reaction achieved.

January 14–24, 1943, FDR and Churchill in Casablanca Conference decide Germany and Japan ultimately must bow to the Allies in unconditional surrender. *February 2, 1943*, another turning point of the war: following Hitler's order against breakout attempt, Germans surrender to Soviets at Stalingrad. In the Solomons, Japanese abandon fight at Guadalcanal, *February 9, 1943*. *February 28, 1943*, Norwegian Resistance sabotages heavy water facility essential for German atomic weapon research. *March 20, 1943*, British Eighth Army advancing on Tunisia; link–up with American First Army in Tunisia to follow on *April 7. April 19–May 16, 1943*, ill–fated Warsaw ghetto uprising. *May 6–13*, Axis forces in Tunisia defeated. *July 10, 1943*, Anglo-American landing on Sicily, which falls *August 17. July 24–25, 1943*, Mussolini deposed in Italy.

September 8, 1943, surrender of Italian army under new Badoglio govern-ment, followed next day, *September 9*, by Anglo-American invasion of Italy at Salerno, followed in turn on *September 10* by German occupation of northern Italy and Rome. *September 14, 1943*, Americans and Australians drive Japanese out of Salamaua, New Guinea, followed two days later by capture of nearby Lae. *October 13, 1943*, former Axis partner Italy officially at war with Nazi Germany. *November 22–26, 1943*, Cairo meeting for FDR, Churchill, and China's Chiang Kai-shek, followed *November 28–December 1* by Teheran Conference—FDR, Churchill, and Stalin. Meanwhile, U.S. forces recapture Gilbert Islands of the Pacific in *November*.

January 22, 1944, Anglo-American landing at Anzio on west coast of Italy. *January 24, 1944*, Dwight D. Eisenhower named supreme commander of Allied forces in Europe. *January 31*, Americans land in the Marshall Islands (Kwajalein-Eniwetok) of the Pacific. *February 14, 1944*, Siege of Leningrad finally ended. *February 20, 1944*, Norwegian Resistance sinks ferryboat car-rying heavy water for German use. *March 4, 1944*, first U.S. daytime bomber raid on Berlin. All of *March, 1944*, Soviets advancing on wide front as Germans occupy ally Hungary. *March 25, 1944*, American landing at Hollandia, New Guinea—MacArthur's island–hopping Pacific campaign beginning to roll.

June 6, 1944, Normandy landings by vast Allied host with Americans in the lead, an event obscuring Fifth Army's seizure of Rome two days before. *June 27, 1944*, Cherbourg falls to Americans. On *July 18, 1944*, so does St. Lo, and now, with British capture of Caen *July 9* as well, begins Allied race across Europe to borders of Nazi Germany, Americans led by George S. Patton's armor-laden Third Army. *July 20, 1944*, failed assassination attempt against Hitler. In the Pacific, American forces land on Guam *July 21, 1944. August 25, 1944*, Paris falls to Allies.

September 25, 1944, increasingly desperate Hitler orders all German men 16 to 60 into Volksturm home defense army. Red Army moving into Eastern Europe and consolidating gains in Baltic states, *October, 1944. October 20, 1944*, Tito's forces seize Belgrade. *October 20, 1944*, MacArthur's return to the Philippines with U.S. landings on Leyte, followed by epic naval Battle of Leyte Gulf, *October 24–26*, a major Japanese defeat. *November 7, 1944*, FDR's fourth election as U.S. President. *November 12, 1944*, German pocket battleship

Tirpitz finally sunk by British bombers in Tromso Fjord, Norway. *November 13, 1944*, Red Army across the Danube.

December 16, 1944, Battle of the Bulge opens with broad German armored and infantry advance from the Ardennes. *December 23*, weather finally clears enough to allow Allied air strikes against advancing German columns. *December 26, 1944*, Red Army lays siege to Budapest. At same time, German "bulge" begins to recede as Bastogne is relieved by Patton's Fourth Armored Division. Germans in full retreat by *mid-January, 1945*. *January 27, 1945*, Auschwitz liberated by Red Army. *February 4, 1945*, Americans return to Manila as FDR, Churchill, and Stalin begin conference at Yalta in the recently liberated Crimea. *February 1945*, the Allied ring closing on heart of Germany as the U.S. First Army crosses Rhine and Red Army moves across Oder. *February 13, 1945*, Budapest falls to Soviets. *February 19, 1945*, U.S. Marines land on Iwo Jima.

March 7, 1945, Americans seize Rhine River bridge at Remagen. *April 1, 1945*, Americans land on Okinawa. Also in early April, German divisions in the Ruhr surrounded, on last legs. Soviets still advancing from the east, final Allied offensives in northern Italy and the Netherlands. *April 12, 1945*, death of FDR. *April 16, 1945*, final Battle of Berlin begins. *April 25*, San Francisco conference to write United Nations charter. *April 26, 1945*, American and Soviet forces meet at Torgau on the Elbe River. *April 29, 1945*, Germans in Italy surrender.

May 1, 1945, death of Hitler previous day, by suicide, is announced. *May 2, 1945*, Berlin falls to Red Army. *May 3, 1945*, Anglo-Indians regain Rangoon; Japanese finished in all of Burma. *May 7–8, 1945*, Nazi Germany's unconditional surrender. *June 26, 1945*, United Nations Charter signed. *July 16, 1945*, first atomic bomb detonated in New Mexico. *July 17–August 2, 1945*, FDR successor Harry S. Truman, Stalin, Churchill, Clement Attlee in Potsdam (Germany) Conference. Ultimatum demanding surrender issued to Japan (ignored).

August 6, 1945, Hiroshima, Japan, obliterated in first wartime use of atomic bomb. After no response from Japan, second atomic bomb dropped on Nagasaki *August 9*. Meanwhile, Soviet Union declares war on Japan *August 8*. *August 14, 1945*, Japan surrenders, formal announcement next day, *August 15*. World War II is over!

INDEX

ABOUT THE AUTHORS

C. BRIAN KELLY, A PRIZE-WINNING JOUR-
NALIST, IS A FORMER COLUMNIST FOR *Military
History* magazine and its first editor. He
also is a lecturer in newswriting at the
University of Virginia. As a reporter for
The Washington Star, he was named 1976
Conservation Communicator of the Year
by the National Wildlife Federation; he was
also cited for his political reporting by the
American Political Science Association and
for local reporting by the Washington-Baltimore Newspaper Guild.

Ingrid Smyer, his wife and co-author, also boasts a background in journalism, along with service on community historical boards. She is a member of
the Charlottesville (Va.) Historical Resources Committee and former member
of the board for the Lewis and Clark Exploratory Center of Virginia in
Charlottesville, Virginia.